The Economic Consequences of the War

T0300542

The 'German Question' dominated much of modern European history. In 1945, Germany was defeated and conquered, yet World War II did not destroy the foundations of her economic power. Dr Tamás Vonyó revisits Germany's remarkable post-war revival, tracing its roots not to liberal economic reforms and the Marshall Plan, but to the legacies of the war that endowed Germany with an enhanced industrial base and an enlarged labour force. He also shows that Germany's liberal market economy was in reality an economy of regulated markets, controlled prices, and extensive state intervention. Using quantitative analysis and drawing on a rich historiography that has remained, in large part, unknown outside of Germany, this book reassesses the role of economic policy and the importance of wartime legacies to explain the German growth miracle after 1945 and the sharply contrasting experiences of East and West Germany.

Tamás Vonyó is Assistant Professor of Economic History at Università Commerciale Luigi Bocconi, Milan. He has written extensively on economic growth in post-war Europe and Germany's economic development during World War II.

Cambridge Studies in Economic History

Editorial Board
Paul Johnson
University of Western Australia

Sheilagh Ogilvie
University of Cambridge

Avner Offer
All Souls College, Oxford

Gianni Toniolo
Universita di Roma 'Tor Vergata'

Gavin Wright
Stanford University

Cambridge Studies in Economic History comprises stimulating and accessible economic history which actively builds bridges to other disciplines. Books in the series will illuminate why the issues they address are important and interesting, place their findings in a comparative context, and relate their research to wider debates and controversies. The series will combine innovative and exciting new research by younger researchers with new approaches to major issues by senior scholars. It will publish distinguished work regardless of chronological period or geographical location.

A complete list of titles in the series can be found at: www.cambridge .org/economichistory

The Economic Consequences of the War

West Germany's Growth Miracle after 1945

Tamás Vonyó

Bocconi University

CAMBRIDGE
UNIVERSITY PRESS

University Printing House, Cambridge CB2 8BS, United Kingdom

One Liberty Plaza, 20th Floor, New York, NY 10006, USA

477 Williamstown Road, Port Melbourne, VIC 3207, Australia

314-321, 3rd Floor, Plot 3, Splendor Forum, Jasola District Centre, New Delhi - 110025, India

79 Anson Road, #06-04/06, Singapore 079906

Cambridge University Press is part of the University of Cambridge.

It furthers the University's mission by disseminating knowledge in the pursuit of
education, learning and research at the highest international levels of excellence.

www.cambridge.org
Information on this title: www.cambridge.org/9781107568716
DOI: 10.1017/9781316414927

© Tamás Vonyó 2018

This publication is in copyright. Subject to statutory exception
and to the provisions of relevant collective licensing agreements,
no reproduction of any part may take place without the written
permission of Cambridge University Press.

First published 2018
First paperback edition 2020

A catalogue record for this publication is available from the British Library

Library of Congress Cataloging in Publication data
Names: Vonyó, Tamás, 1979– author.
Title: The economic consequences of the War : West Germany's
growth miracle after 1945 / Tamás Vonyó.
Description: Cambridge, United Kingdom; New York, NY: Cambridge
University Press, 2018. | Series: Cambridge studies in economic history |
Includes bibliographical references and index.
Identifiers: LCCN 2017046242 | ISBN 9781107128439 (hardback)
Subjects: LCSH: Economic development – Germany (West) |
Germany (West) – Economic conditions. | Germany (West) –
Economic policy. | Germany – History – 1945–
Classification: LCC HC286.5.V65 2018 | DDC 338.943–dc23
LC record available at https://lccn.loc.gov/2017046242

ISBN 978-1-107-12843-9 Hardback
ISBN 978-1-107-56871-6 Paperback

Cambridge University Press has no responsibility for the persistence or
accuracy of URLs for external or third-party internet websites referred to in
this publication, and does not guarantee that any content on such websites is,
or will remain, accurate or appropriate.

To my father, *Édesapámnak*

Contents

Figures

Tables

Preface

Werner Abelshauser opened his seminal monograph on the history of the West German economy since the end of World War II with the statement that 'the history of the Federal Republic of Germany is above all its economic history' (Abelshauser 1983, 8). This interpretation is reflected in both the national and international historiography of the period. The economic revival of the nascent German state during the 1950s from its devastation a decade earlier has been considered its most remarkable achievement. The earliest contributions Germany made to the rebuilding of Europe and to European integration were fundamentally economic. However, this argument can be easily turned around, for the resurgence of the German economy from the desolate state caused by defeat, destruction, and dislocation was shaped by historical legacies, the long shadows of the war and the conditions it had left behind. As Joel Mokyr (1990) wrote, 'In economics, history is destiny'.

The Economic Consequences of the War revisits a major debate in German historiography and the economic history of modern Europe. It reveals the wartime origins of the post-war economic success that stunned contemporaries in Germany and captivated so many economists and historians. It is a comprehensive study of the quantitative evidence on both the domestic and external determinants of industrial development in West Germany in the quarter century that followed the most decimating war in modern history. That the German growth miracle, the *Wirtschaftswunder*, was a reconstruction phenomenon is not a novel proposition. It was pioneered by the Hungarian economist Ferenc Jánossy (1969) and brought to the attention of economic historians by Matthias Manz (1985) and Werner Abelshauser (1975, 1983). My aim has been to add quantitative substance to this literature and to synthesise the findings of a rich scholarship that has remained, in large part, unknown to international and non-specialist audiences. The study of detailed regional and industry statistics will demonstrate to the reader that one cannot explain the dynamics of post-war economies without understanding the role of economic geography and production structure, which have been neglected in the historiography. By filling in these gaps, my work supports an interpretation of the reconstruction theory that is more compatible with the historical evidence, and which also places the role that economic policy played in the *Wirtschaftswunder* into a new context.

After 1945, Germany was no longer the primary source of military threat in Europe but soon re-emerged as the leading industrial power on the continent. Since the economic foundations of German power are commonly believed to be rooted in a uniquely German approach to economic management, which many continue to see as the product of the post-war consensus, a renewed look at this era is highly topical in times when Germany is once more looked up to as the leader of Europe and the beacon of stability on a continent in crisis. In such a light, this monograph shall be of interest to a wider public, even though it focuses on a specific episode of post-war history and even though the aim of the enquiry was to provide an in-depth introspection into the dynamics of post-war economic growth.

The Economic Consequences of the War has been my long-term project and is the outcome of a decade of research. It builds on two dissertations that I wrote in the course of my graduate and doctoral studies. Both have received acclaim; they were awarded the Feinstein Prize for the best graduate dissertation in economic and social history at the University of Oxford in 2008 and the dissertation prize of the International Economic History Association in 2012 respectively. Part of the material presented and discussed in the chapters has been used in research papers published in peer-reviewed international journals, including three articles in the *European Review of Economic History* between 2008 and 2014 and a contribution to the German economic history yearbook, the *Jahrbuch für Wirtschaftsgeschichte*, in 2014. The findings of these analytical investigations are integrated into Chapters 2 and 3, but the book is much more than the reprint of my thesis or the collection of my articles. It is the synthesis of the research I have conducted for many years and describes, in great detail, the contribution of this research to the vast literature that has emerged on the topic.

The monograph is the work of not just a scholar but also a pupil of economic history. Therefore, an exhaustive list of acknowledgements and expressions of due gratitude would be almost as voluminous as the book itself. Most certainly, it could not have been written without the benefit of my former supervisor, Oliver Grant, to whom I am indebted for his astute guidance, his informed comments, and his unwavering personal support. I must thank my Oxford professors, especially Avner Offer, Jane Humphries, and Knick Harley, for they were a constant source of inspiration and my guides into the art of economic history. Mark Spoerer provided vital support during my first lengthy fieldwork in Berlin in 2008, which was financed by a Scatchered European Scholarship from Oxford. Matthias Beer hosted me in Tübingen twice and helped me understand the complexities of post-war displacement in Germany. My examiners, Nicholas Dimsdale and Albrecht Ritschl, offered invaluable advice, worth a great deal throughout my postdoctoral career. Albrecht has become one of my best colleagues and collaborators in the profession. Material from our joint work is included in this monograph, in the final section of Chapter 3. Herman de Jong, who gave me my first job and supervised my postdoctoral research at Groningen University, and other distinguished colleagues of the Groningen Growth and Development Centre helped me expand my skills in quantitative analytical methods, in the fields of both productivity analysis and growth accounting. My research on the theme of this book has been presented at conferences of the Economic History Association, the Economic History Society, the European Historical Economics Society, and the European Social Science History Conference, as well as on congresses of the International Economic History Association, and at numerous research seminars. I must express my most sincere gratitude to all of my colleagues who have shown interest in my work and made constructive comments on how to enhance the fruits of my efforts.

The monograph itself could not have been completed without the help of others. My editor at Cambridge University Press, Michael Watson, provided professional guidance throughout the process. The series editors and the external reviewer helped me improve the manuscript. Their scholarly input is very much part of this book. The chapters that I wrote last were completed in Berlin and London, where invitations from Nikolaus Wolf and Albrecht Ritschl gave me access to libraries and archival resources that I still had to consult. Jaap Sleifer and Jonas Scherner kindly let me use the data they had compiled in their earlier work at the Bundesarchiv in Berlin-Lichterfelde. Tobias Vogelsang has offered to let me read and cite his yet unpublished dissertation. Throughout my work, I have been assisted by the endowments and financial support of Bocconi University and the Dondena Centre for Research on Social Dynamics and Public Policy. Lastly, and most importantly, I must thank my father, to whom I dedicate this book. Born on the very day when World War II ended in my native Hungary and growing up in the misery that characterised post-war life throughout Europe, he became a professor of history and a passionate educator. Without his love and support, I would not be half the man or the scholar that I am today.

Abbreviations

ASE	Amt für Stahl und Eisen (Verwaltung für Wirtschaft des Vereinigten Wirtschaftsgebiets)
Außenhandel	*Der Außenhandel der Bundesrepublik Deutschland*
BArch	Bundesarchiv
BDI	Bundesverband der Deutschen Industrie
BdL	Bank deutscher Länder
BW	Baden-Württemberg
CAP	Common Agricultural Policy
COCOM	Coordinating Committee for East–West Trade
DGB	Deutscher Gewerkschaftsbund
DIW	Deutsches Institut für Wirtschaftsforschung
DM	Deutsche Mark
DQP	Differentiated Quality Product
ECA	European Cooperation Act
ECSC	European Coal and Steel Community
EEC	European Economic Community
EFTA	European Free Trade Agreement
EPA	European Payments Agreement
EPU	European Payments Union
ERP	European Recovery Program
EStG	Einkommensteuergesetz
FDI	Foreign Direct Investment
FSE	Fachstelle Stahl und Eisen der Verwaltung für Wirtschaft des Vereinigten Wirtschaftsgebiets
GARIOA	Government and Relief in Occupied Areas
GATT	General Agreement in Tariffs and Trade
GDR	German Democratic Republic
IARA	Inter-Allied Reparation Agency
IndBRD	*Die Industrie der Bundesrepublik Deutschland*
JEIA	Joint Export–Import Agency
KfW	Kreditanstalt für Wiederaufbau

Kultusminister-konferenz	Ständige Konferenz der Kultusminister der Länder in der Bundesrepublik Deutschland
Länderrat	Länderrat des Amerikanischen Besatzungsgebiets
MCC	Ministerial Collecting Center
NRW	North Rhine-Westphalia
OEEC	Organisation for European Economic Cooperation
OEED	Overall Economic Effects Division (OMGUS)
OMGUS	Office of Military Government for Germany (US)
POW	Prisoner of war
Reichsamt	Reichsamt für Wehrwirtschaftliche Planung
RM	Reichsmark
RP	Rhineland-Palatinate
Sachverständigenrat	Sachverständigenrat für Begutachtung der gesamtwirtschaftlichen Entwicklung
SchH	Schleswig-Holstein
SME	Social Market Economy
StatBRD	*Statistik der Bundesrepublik Deutschland*
StatDR	*Statistik des Deutschen Reichs*
TFP	Total Factor Productivity
UNRRA	United Nations Relief and Rehabilitation Administration
USSBS	United States Strategic Bombing Survey
Wissenschaftlicher Beirat	Wissenschaftlicher Beirat beim Bundesministerium für Wirtschaft

Introduction

This monograph revisits a major topic in the economic history of modern Germany. The quarter century that followed World War II has been enshrined in collective memory as perhaps the most remarkable era of macroeconomic stability and social progress in the Western world (Milward 1992). In striking contrast with the period that Churchill (1948) famously labelled the Second Thirty Years War, this 'golden age of economic growth' (Crafts 1995) was marked by an amalgamation of rapid technological advancement, widening prosperity, and sound governance. Among that of all the Western industrialised nations, the economic performance of West Germany during these decades was arguably the most impressive, especially against the backdrop of military defeat in 1945 and the disintegration in the years that followed. Astonished contemporaries thought of witnessing an 'economic miracle', and the notion of the *Wirtschaftswunder* found resonance in subsequent academic research at home and abroad. World War II inflicted an unprecedented scale of material damage upon the defeated, demoralised, and in large part displaced population of the Third Reich. The devastating impact of strategic bombing has been documented in both German and international historiography (see Mirzejewski 1988; Eichholz 1999; Friedrich 2002; and Tooze 2006). On the day of the unconditional surrender of all German land, sea, and air forces, not a single bridge spanned the Rhine, and industrial production had come to a standstill with the destruction of the transport system. Demolished buildings and roads clogged the urban landscape and scenes of human misery were impossible to avoid. Not surprisingly, contemporary observers were astounded by the rapidity with which the German economy propelled itself forward, akin to a phoenix rising from ashes.

The earliest accounts of the *Wirtschaftswunder* were in accord that the West German revival began in 1948 and that it was engineered by the combination of radical economic reforms and Western economic aid. The 'structural break hypothesis', as this institutional view has been referred to in German historiography, attributed an instrumental role to the Social Market Economy in the success of post-war reconstruction. Firmly in line with the 'Freiburg school' of liberal economics that dominated the political philosophy, even if not always the policy praxis, of post-war West German governments, this interpretation posited that the institutional framework of the Federal Republic was fundamentally different from that of Imperial Germany, Weimar, and the Third Reich, for it had been built on the ruins of a vanquished and devastated country.[1] Wallich (1955) presented the seminal critique of this traditional view by identifying favourable supply-side conditions and the reintegration of the Bonn Republic into the international economic order as 'the mainsprings of the German revival'. However, the notion of Ground Zero (*Stunde Null*) was still very much present in the subsequent writings of Hoffmann (1965) and Roskamp (1965). They believed, alongside many others, that the German growth miracle was driven by extraordinary levels of investment that replaced the outdated and largely destroyed productive arsenal of German industry, and thus they suggested an important catalysing role for economic policy.

A new wave stormed into the German historiography of the post-war era after 1966, when Jánossy (1969) proposed an inspiring theory to explain the economic miracles that the world had witnessed since 1945. In a nutshell, the 'reconstruction thesis', as the work of the prominent Hungarian economist has been referred to in the international literature, proposed that war-shattered economies would automatically recover to their long-run productive potential following the cessation of hostilities and the removal of the most immediate impediments to normal market activity. Wartime destruction and distortions in the efficient allocation of productive forces promised high returns on future investment, prompting accelerated capital accumulation in the reconstruction phase. Once the economy had returned to its long-run growth path, the rate of economic growth would abate abruptly and dramatically. The potential for further growth in productivity would depend solely on improvements in labour qualifications and technical knowledge.

The Jánossy thesis was published at a critical juncture during the first economic recession Germany had endured since the first years after the war, which signalled the end of the reconstruction period, but the role of reconstruction dynamics in post-war growth is, in fact, a much older notion. John Stuart Mill had already talked about a *vix mediatrix naturae* that lifted nations out of their devastation and restored them to their normal conditions (cited in Abelshauser 2004, 282). Modern

---

[1] For a general summary of this literature, see Klump (1985), 23–5 and Borchardt (1991), 99–103.

economists, including Milton Friedman, remarked on this phenomenon, claiming that the wartime dislocation of economies can give rise to extraordinarily high growth rates in the post-war period (Friedman quoted in Klein 1961, 291). Jánossy formalised this concept and applied it specifically to explain the growth miracles of his age. Abelshauser (1975, 1983), Manz (1985), and Borchardt (1991) introduced his pioneering work into the German literature. After two world wars and two severe interwar slumps, they argued, an 'accumulated developmental deficit made it possible, as long as it had not been fully absorbed, to achieve significantly higher growth rates of per capita national product than prior to the onset of [the above] crises' (Abelshauser 1983, 92). In turn, as the growth potential inherent in post-war reconstruction had been exhausted by the early 1960s, the ensuing slowdown of the West German economy was interpreted as the necessary outcome of re-convergence to an established growth path. This interpretation left little room for the political and economic reforms after 1948 as the propellers of the *Wirtschaftswunder*. Instead it introduced an economic dimension to the emerging revisionism in German historiography, exhibited most notably in the works of Fischer (1969, 1979) and Wehler (1973, 1975), that placed growing emphasis on historical continuities in the development of German society over the discontinuities brought by the major calamities of the early twentieth century.

The international scholarship on post-war growth also recognised the relevance of the Jánossy model (see Carlin 1996 and Crafts and Toniolo 1996, among others). Cliometric studies have confirmed the presence of a powerful reconstruction dynamic in Western industrialised nations during the 1950s (Dumke 1990; Wolf 1995; Temin 2002; Eichengreen and Ritschl 2009). My contributions to this literature have shown that the relative growth performance of member states of the Organisation for Economic Co-operation and Development (OECD) reflected, above all, the scale of post-war dislocation until the late 1960s (Vonyó 2008) and that the falling behind of Eastern European economies in the early post-war era was, in large part, due to significantly stronger reconstruction dynamics in the West (Vonyó 2017). My econometric analysis has confirmed that the reconstruction thesis has particularly strong predictive power for the West German growth record. The reconstruction effect was more persistent than it seemed to have been on the basis of earlier studies. The absorption of this unique growth potential, in turn, caused the sharp slowdown of the fastest-growing Western economies in the early 1970s. Nations shattered by war, Germany included, maintained their war-induced potential for high productivity growth even after their industrial and public infrastructure had been rebuilt and the bottlenecks to efficient factor allocation resulting from wartime destruction had been eliminated.

One of the key contributions of these cross-country investigations has been to integrate the Jánossy model into the broader literature on the drivers of post-war growth. The sheer vastness of this scholarship makes a comprehensive overview impossible and arguably superfluous. It is still in order here to delineate the most prominent interpretations, for they provide the context in which the West German growth miracle has to be understood. For three decades, the dominant view has seen post-war growth as the product of high investment in physical and human capital and cross-country convergence in productivity (Abramovitz 1986; Maddison 1991; Wolff 1991; Nelson and Wright 1992; Crafts 1995). This interpretation was derived from the neo-classical theory of economic growth that was itself the product of the post-war era (Solow 1956; Cass 1965). The seminal contributions in economics on cross-country convergence (Baumol 1986; Dowrick and Nguyen 1989; Barro 1991; Barro and Sala-i-Martin 1992; 1995; Mankiw, Romer, and Weil 1992) have all been conducted using harmonised cross-country data from this period.

Economic historians adopted the concept of conditional convergence mainly from Abramovitz (1986, 1994), who argued that catching up through successful technology adoption was conditional on the presence of adequate 'social capabilities for growth' and 'technological congruence' between converging economies. Both relate to the capacity of societies to accumulate a sufficient stock of physical and human capital and to use these endowments efficiently in the production process. European nations and Japan, it was argued, reached this developmental stage by the early post-war period, from whence they began to close the vast transatlantic productivity gap that had emerged since the nineteenth century. Subsequent empirical work has supported this view. The canonical article of Hall and Jones (1999) argued that the 'social infrastructure' of different countries determined the rate of accumulation in both physical and human capital as well as technological efficiency, and these factors, in turn, accounted for the striking variance in levels of labour productivity across countries. Economic historians (Crafts 1995; Broadberry 1996; Toniolo 1998) have shown that convergence in income and productivity between Western industrialised nations was much stronger during the post-war golden age than in any period before or since.

Comparative growth accounts (Maddison 1991, 1996; Crafts 1995; Van Ark 1996; O'Mahony 1999; Bosworth and Collins 2003; Crafts and Toniolo 2010) have confirmed that robust economic growth in post-war Europe was driven by both capital deepening, meaning the intensified use of production tools per unit of labour, and by advancements in productivity. O'Mahony (1996) showed that convergence in labour productivity between the United States, north-western Europe, and Japan from the 1950s to the late 1970s reflected convergence in both capital-labour ratios and joint factor productivity. Structural modernisation has long been viewed as an important source of catch-up growth in addition to capital accumulation. Denison (1967) was the first to show quantitatively that the growth miracles of several European countries were strongly associated with the reallocation of labour from agriculture to manufacturing and market services (see also Feinstein 1999). Kaldor (1966) argued that modern growth was driven by industrial expansion and thus the relative growth potential of different economies depended on their capacity to boost industrial employment. Temin (2002) showed that relative growth performance in Western Europe during the post-war golden age reflected substantial differences across countries in the share of agricultural employment at the start of the period. Broadberry (1997b), among others, stressed the role of the same factor in explaining the striking growth differential between West Germany and the United Kingdom.

In large part because of the influence of the reconstruction thesis, the theory of conditional convergence has featured much less prominently in German historiography. The main exception is the work of Lindlar (1997), who argued that the West German growth miracle should be understood within an international context and as the consequence of technological catch-up rather than post-war reconstruction. What neither cross-country investigations nor the literature on the *Wirtschaftswunder* explored in detail are the actual dynamics of reconstruction growth and the exact nature of wartime destruction and post-war dislocation. Focussing on the aggregate growth effect ignores perhaps the most critical contribution of the Jánossy thesis, in which reconstruction is understood as an inherently structural process that entails the reorganisation of production and the reallocation of production factors in post-war economies. Beyond the destruction of physical assets, the war caused serious distortions in the allocation of both capital and labour across industries and regions. This phenomenon, which Jánossy termed 'structural incongruence', represented a unique source of growth. Subsequent investment and organisational efforts aimed at restoring the structural balance, in other words reducing the disproportion and misallocation of the complementary factors of production, were bound to generate high growth. This more nuanced interpretation of the Jánossy model concurs with the revisionist historiography of the West German growth miracle, which argued that the war had merely dislocated the German economy; it had not destroyed its foundations.

Even though, economically, the notion of Ground Zero has been considered out of date in the prism of this literature, it has survived, at least in a subtler version. Hockers (1986) formulated the concept of a foundational crisis (*Gründungskrise*) to emphasise the severity of the political and socioeconomic challenges that the early post-war years had imposed on Germany and that its subsequent growth miracle so remarkably cleared from collective consciousness. In this conceptualisation, the reconstruction process is to be evaluated against these inauspicious starting conditions. This view demands the incorporation of political decisions about the legal and economic constitution as well as the social infrastructure of post-war Germany into any comprehensive study on the revival of the West German economy. Historical accounts emphasising the role of the post-war economic reforms retained some ground in the literature not least thanks to the new institutional theories that offered an alternative explanation for the uniqueness of the golden age in the history of advanced Western democracies.

In a hugely polemical thesis, Olson (1982) postulated that stable democracies were eventually doomed to face a slowdown of economic growth because the undisturbed accumulation of 'distributional coalitions' would gradually undermine the efficient functioning of markets through the misallocation of resources and the incomes generated by their application. Olson located the origins of post-war supergrowth in the defeated powers of Germany, Japan, and Italy precisely in these very dynamics. He argued that the demolition of distributional coalitions, both trade unions and corporatist industrial organisations, by the authoritarian or totalitarian regimes between the wars, and under Allied occupation after 1945, allowed free markets to function more efficiently than in many stable democracies hampered by bad institutional legacies. Even when special interest groups re-emerged after 1950, they were more encompassing and less distortive to market mechanisms than their predecessors had been until the 1920s. Murrell (1983) developed an Olsonian view of post-war Germany postulating that the institutional inertia associated with the corporatist organisation of German industry were effectively swept away between 1933 to1948 and that, therefore, the institutions of the West German economy in the 1950s should be regarded as new.

Eichengreen (1996, 2007) offered a more elaborate and more widely accepted explanation for the persistence of high growth rates in post-war Europe. To the extent that economic growth emerges from the shifting of resources from present-day consumption to investment in future gains, economic development is conditioned by the social contract between employees and employers on how to redistribute profits between labour and capital. In dynamic game theory, the social contract is undermined by what economists call the time inconsistency of optimal plans. Workers have no incentive to support wage moderation if they are not certain that firms reinvest their profits, and firms have no incentive to reinvest profits if they are not sure that unions will accept wage moderation in return. Eichengreen saw the institutional reforms of the early post-war era and, in particular, the enhanced role of governments in industrial relations as novel contract-enforcement mechanisms binding social partners to their commitments. This, together with international trade liberalisation and the avoidance of competitive devaluations thanks to the international monetary regime conceived at Bretton Woods, was instrumental in sustaining an equilibrium characterised by high investment, high productivity, and wage moderation in most Western economies during the golden age and that facilitated convergence between them. Eichengreen and Iversen (1999) provided empirical support for this view. This interpretation has placed the Social Market Economy into an international perspective. As Spoerer (2007) has recently argued, if West German catch-up after the war was a miracle, then it was a European rather than a German miracle, at least one shared by the Western economies that introduced some form of coordinated capitalism.

Economic historians, for the most part, have been critical of these new institutional interpretations. The year 1945 did not represent a *tabula rasa* in the evolution of political, social, and economic institutions (Maier 1981; Reich 1990). Trade unions and industrial organisations managed to regroup very shortly after the war and, in reality, did not become significantly more encompassing than they had been in the interwar period (Booth, Melling, and Dartmann 1997). The development of institutions in the former belligerent nations showed more signs of continuity than discontinuity, and the differences one can observe in the characteristics of distributional coalitions across countries cannot account for the large variance in growth rates among Western economies in the 1950s and 1960s (Paqué 1994; Ritschl 2005). Recent research has shown that even in Scandinavia wages, in fact, increased faster than productivity during the golden age, and that the result of wage bargaining depended on power relations and trade union ideology rather than on government regulation (Bengtsson 2015). There is equally scarce evidence to support the existence of a broadly based social consensus in post-war Germany. The presence of surplus labour rather than institutional reforms was the prime reason for wage moderation and accelerated capital accumulation in the reconstruction phase (see especially Paqué 1995). This view concurs with the theory of Kindleberger (1967), in which labour-supply flexibility arising from underemployment in agriculture, rising labour participation, or immigration limited real-wage growth and thereby made investment more profitable in post-war economies. Investment in new technology, in turn, enhanced labour productivity, which further raised the profitability of investment.

Just as John Maynard Keynes in *The Economic Consequences of the Peace* forecasted that the troubles of interwar Europe would be the outcome of the Carthaginian peace settlement of 1919, *The Economic Consequences of the War* postulates that the origins of post-war growth in Europe, and West Germany in particular, are to be searched in the calamities of the 1940s and the economic conditions they had left behind. My aim has been to add quantitative substance to the existing literature of the *Wirtschaftswunder* with a detailed account of industrial development, both its internal and external determinants, in wartime and post-war Germany. The thorough analysis of contemporary statistical material and the vast secondary literature that, in large part, has remained unknown to the international audience, revisits the origins of the West German growth miracle in five major chapters.

Chapter 1 gives an overview of the early years of post-war recovery in West Germany between 1945 and 1948, which set the stage for the growth miracle that followed. I open with an audit on the impact of the war on productive capacity and the labour force. As the title of the grand memoir from Meinecke (1946) suggested, the outcome of six years of carnage and twelve years of totalitarianism was nothing short of catastrophic. The earliest accounts painted a gloomy picture about the long shadow of the war. They estimated that much of the pre-war capacity of West German industry had been destroyed and, on this basis, accentuated fears of 'deindustrialisation' (Niederschlag 1947; Eisendraht 1950). Such claims were soon proved erroneous, when the reports of the United States Strategic Bombing Survey were published and made available to researchers. Subsequent analyses of this material revealed that the productive assets of the German economy had survived the war with remarkably little damage, and that the industrial capital stock had even increased substantially, despite wartime destruction, as a result of colossal investments in new equipment during the late 1930s and early 1940s. Moreover, in spite of the initial intentions to the contrary, the dismantling of machinery under the post-war reparations regime was surprisingly modest in scale.

Post-war West Germany was also endowed with a plentiful supply of labour. Even with the enormous wartime casualties, especially among men of working age, there was robust population growth between 1939 and 1950. This was the joint consequence of the expulsion of ethnic Germans from East and Central Europe, in accord with the Potsdam Agreement, and the exodus of refugees from the part of post-war Germany under Soviet occupation. However, a deeper introspection into the literature and the examination of census data offers a differentiated picture. Both the age and gender composition of West German society were severely distorted, and millions of returning soldiers were often physically or mentally incapacitated for work. The miserable urban living conditions and poor public health of the late 1940s further limited the ability of industrial firms to draw on these labour reserves.

The final section of the chapter reviews the literature and contemporary sources on the economic institutions of Allied occupation and how they inhibited post-war recovery in West Germany. The two most important features were the lack of a stable currency, on the one hand, that made rigid price controls and widespread rationing necessary and severe restrictions on foreign trade on the other, which resulted in recurrent shortages of input materials in several industries. Together, they had created a shortage economy, in which firms were guided by the principle of resource hunger rather than profit maximisation, and where conventional trade practices were replaced by barter. As money wages were practically worthless, industrial employers could provide little incentive for their workers, and absenteeism was rampant. These conditions, the literature has proposed, prevailed until the currency and market reforms of July 1948 and the lifting of import restrictions in 1949 restored business confidence; rationalised the use of production inputs; and, with the help of Western aid, eliminated most of the remaining production bottlenecks.

Chapter 2 challenges this consensus and demonstrates that the impact of post-war dislocation on West German industry was much more persistent than previously argued. The economy remained dislocated until the early 1950s, even though the raw material shortages and institutional chaos of the immediate post-war years had already been overcome. The chief limiting factor of industrial expansion was the regional misallocation of labour that resulted from the wartime destruction of the urban housing stock. On paper, German industry had ample endowments in factors of production at the start of its post-war recovery. Still, production levels were well below their pre-war peak even by 1950. Available capacities in urban industry, which had been considerably enhanced during the war, remained underutilised, even though demand for manufactures was booming at both domestic and international markets. By contrast, mass unemployment raged over the countryside, which had seen its productive assets diminished after 1939, when the resources of the rural economy were systematically diverted for the purposes of war production.

As the influx of expellees and refugees from the East swelled the population of rural and small-town Germany, urban labour scarcity coexisted with rural unemployment and capital shortage. Under normal economic conditions, factor markets would have cleared, but the urban housing deficit was far too large to surmount without extensive state intervention, which was not feasible before the establishment of a sovereign West German government and the restoration of functioning capital markets. These conditions, in turn, created the potential for a growth miracle in the 1950s. The temporarily displaced labour reserves of the country were gradually absorbed as the urban housing stock was rebuilt in a gigantic national housing program between 1949 and 1957. At the same time, the rural economy with its surplus labour could build up capital rapidly in an era of high rates of investment and wage moderation. Reconstruction growth in the early 1950s was driven by the improved allocation of productive forces, induced by relative scarcities in the complementary factors of production: labour and capital. The analysis of detailed regional statistics reveals the geographic dimension of the West German growth miracle that the literature had previously overlooked. It contributes to the growing body of quantitative work on historical economic geography, particularly to a recent line of research on the lasting impact of war-induced shocks on local economies (Fishback and Cullen 2013; Brakman, Garretsen, and Schramm 2004).

Geography was only one dimension of post-war dislocation in the German economy; production structure was another. Chapter 3 presents an in-depth account of industrial development in West Germany from the late 1930s to the late 1960s. Methodologically, I follow the standard growth accounting approach, originally developed by Solow (1957) and commonly used by economists to isolate the contributions of factor accumulation and productivity advancements to economic growth (see Crafts 2009). Drawing from contemporary statistical data, I construct index numbers for net industrial production, labour input expressed in annual hours worked, and the stock of physical capital in thirty-two branches of mining and manufacturing. With this dataset I compute labour productivity at the industry level, and use these estimates to determine Total Factor Productivity, the residual in growth-accounting formulae that measures the overall efficiency with which the factors of production are used. Finally, I apply simple decomposition techniques to demonstrate the contribution of individual industries and structural change to aggregate labour-productivity growth.

Between 1938 and 1948, industrial production declined sharply, with an even bigger fall in labour productivity and with the largest contraction recorded in the most closely war-related industries. The period of reconstruction reversed this trend, but the recovery after 1948 had a paradoxical outcome. While output grew by more than one-half between 1938 and 1955, labour productivity scarcely surpassed pre-war levels until the end of this period. Total Factor Productivity in mining and manufacturing did not increase at all. Reconstruction growth was driven predominantly by enhanced labour input, not productivity improvements. The resulting fifteen-year backlog in productivity growth moved Germany far away from the technologically most efficient frontier. Industrial expansion slowed down considerably after 1955, but productivity growth accelerated. This acceleration was achieved by improvements in the quality of factor inputs and the adaptation of more capital-intensive modes of production from the late 1950s onward.

This is how West German industry was able to maintain remarkably high rates of productivity growth throughout the post-war golden age, despite a gradual moderation in the pace of economic expansion. That the post-war productivity gap took so long to close reflected, in part, the persistence of dislocation demonstrated in Chapter 2. Besides regional labour scarcity resulting from the urban housing shortage, the speed of recovery was limited by structural disproportions in industrial production caused by the division of Germany. This economic legacy of the post-war settlement has been overlooked in the literature, at least in the West German context. Surplus capacity in coal mining and steel-based capital goods stood in contrast with excess demand for engineering and consumer products, many of the major suppliers of which had been located in East Germany before 1945. The relative growth performance of different industries after 1948 can be explained by these inherited structural disproportions, once we control for the post-war reconstruction effect. During the *Wirtschaftswunder*, industrial recovery could tap into surplus capacity in some sectors and increased domestic market potential in others.

German historiography provides ample material to explain the paradox between high rates of output growth and relatively more modest technological progress in the early post-war years. The opportunity to expand within existing capacity and the pent-up demand of a war-torn population for manufactures that had already been marketed before 1939 thwarted technological progress and product innovation. Moreover, strong population growth and the ensuing expansion of the labour force across the war disguised serious human-capital deprivation, which resulted in the diminution of effective working skills. The quantitative evidence backs up this claim, and shows how the expansion of technical education after 1950 reversed this trend. Detailed labour statistics reveal a remarkable increase in skilled-labour endowments in the early 1950s that allowed West German industry to retain highly skill-intensive modes of production and thus continue to specialise on high-value-added quality products. Manufacturing enhanced its weight in total employment without the need to compete with other sectors of the economy for scarce labour. An historically unprecedented rate of industrialisation, in turn, allowed West Germany to maintain high rates of economic growth until the end of the golden age.

These quantitative findings have important implications for the periodisation of post-war growth in Germany. Both traditional and revisionist accounts distinguished between the 1950s and the 1960s as phases of extraordinary and normal growth respectively. Both saw the early 1960s as the dawning of a new era in the history of the West German economy and society. Both geopolitical and domestic events underscored this view. The building of the Berlin Wall in 1961 and the Cuban missile crisis in 1962 signalled the permanence of international divisions and within them the division of Germany itself. A year later, the death of Theodor Heuss, the first president of the Federal Republic, and the changing of the guard between chancellors Konrad Adenauer and Ludwig Erhard symbolised, for many, the passing of the founding fathers. Economic growth also appeared to slow down and the grave economic challenges of the post-war years seemed to be images of a gloomy past. In his inaugural address to the Bundestag on 16 October 1963, Erhard himself acknowledged that the era of the *Wirtschaftswunder* had come to an end (see Weimer 1998, 154–62).

Careful analysis of the statistical evidence reveals that, in fact, the 1960s were still very much part of the post-war period of extraordinary growth, and that the German economy returned to the normal growth path only in the 1970s. The pace of economic growth fell considerably from the late 1950s, but this was mostly the reflection of first stagnating and then declining labour input and slowdown in structural change. By contrast, productivity per unit of labour continued to increase at remarkably high rates until the end of the golden age, while labour productivity growth within industry even accelerated between the 1950s and the 1960s.[2] If the growth accounts of German industry for this period reveal any fundamental changes in the nature of growth dynamics, then they occurred between the early phase of post-war reconstruction that lasted

---

[2] Indexes of industrial labour productivity are reported in Chapter 3. Data on GDP per man hour worked can be obtained from *The Conference Board Total Economy Database* (www.conferenceboard.org/data/economydatabase/).

until the mid-1950s and a longer phase of belated industrial modernisation that followed.

Chapter 4 shifts focus from the internal dynamics of Germany's post-war revival to its external determinants. It is widely agreed that trade expansion was instrumental in the growth miracles of post-war Europe (Lámfalussy 1963; Boltho 1982; Eichengreen 2007). Perhaps nowhere did this catalysing role seem more evident than in West Germany, where exports grew twice and three times as fast as industrial output and national income respectively. Hence, many since Wallich (1955) have interpreted the *Wirtschaftswunder* as the product of an even more staggering export miracle. Contrary to this dominant view, after the early phase of post-war reconstruction, the growth of West German industry can no longer be characterised as export led based on the statistical evidence. In order to investigate the competing hypotheses that the literature has to offer to explain the German export boom, particularly the presence of path dependency in the evolution of Germany's external trade, I reconstructed the regional composition and the commodity structure of German and West German exports from the interwar period to the late 1960s.

During the war, Nazi Germany reorganised intra-European trade in order to boost her war production and to maintain her war effort. The confidential foreign trade statistics suggest that the German economy became more eastward oriented with the eastward expansion of the Third Reich and the eastbound drive of its armies. Germany had to increase her exports to her allies constantly to keep them in the war and to secure the essential raw-material supplies they could provide. Hitler's *Drang nach Osten* was the major force of trade diversion within wartime Europe. This finding confirms traditional accounts, but it is in contrast with a recent revisionist view, which argued for a continued westward orientation (most notably in Ritschl 2001). The legacy of 'Fortress Europe' was short lived. The growth of West German exports in the phase of post-war reconstruction also reflected a reconstruction dynamic, which, by and large, restored the trade patterns of the interwar period. The post-war settlement and the institutions of the new international order did not reshape Germany's external trade fundamentally during the 1950s, except in relation to Eastern Europe. The geography and the commodity structure of West German exports began to deviate from historical patterns only after the launching of the European Economic Community. Trade statistics do not support claims of path dependency between forced trade integration during World War II and voluntary market integration in Western Europe after 1958, at least not from a German perspective.

Industry statistics demonstrate that in the reconstruction period up to 1955, the growth of both industrial output and productivity was strongly export led. However, once the commodity structure of West German exports began to part with long-established comparative advantages, due to trade diversion caused by the customs union of the Common Market, the strong positive correlation between the growth of export intensity and industrial expansion broke down. After 1955, industrial development in West Germany was no longer driven by exports, in part because a dramatic shift towards expansionary fiscal policy and rapid real-wage growth from the late 1950s made the domestic market more attractive for German manufacturers.

A serious attempt at unravelling the mysteries of the *Wirtschaftswunder* must include the critical analysis of the role that economic policy played in the process. This is the theme of Chapter 5. In turn, the more in-depth understanding of the dynamics of post-war dislocation and reconstruction compared to what has been possible prompts us to revisit our views on the relative significance of government in the German economy after 1948. A renewed look into post-war economic policy in West German is seriously overdue, as old myths on the topic continue to persist in international historiography and, at the level of public discourse, even in Germany itself. This is due to the fact that the otherwise vast and often incredibly detailed literature of recent decades has remained, in large part, unknown to the international and non-specialist audiences.

Contemporaries led by Ludwig Erhard (1957), the celebrated father of the *Wirtschaftswunder*, located the origins of the West German growth miracle in the currency reform of July 1948 and the introduction of a liberal economic system based on flexible prices and wages, stronger competition, and a general restraint from government intervention. Eulogies of the Social Market Economy have retained some weight in the recent literature, not least thanks to their accordance with the Olsonian interpretation of post-war recovery. However, the relevance of such arguments has been diminished in the modern historiography, which has painted a picture of a still strongly corporatist post-war economy that showed more continuity rather than discontinuity from the institutions of the German Reich. The liberalisation of markets was incomplete: prices for primary inputs and staple foodstuffs remained fixed, wage controls and rationing were retained for years to come, capital markets disintegrated, and there was substantial red tape over the financial sector at large. The quantitative evidence also suggests that recovery had begun well before the currency reform and that it was not transformed into sustained growth until the early 1950s, as the most detrimental war-induced bottlenecks to efficient resource allocation persisted much longer than 1948.

The other mythical notion in the earliest accounts of the *Wirtschafts-wunder* was the catalysing role attributed to Western economic aid. The Marshall Plan is to the present day widely considered a major success story in the history of the twentieth century. The dominant view in post-war historiography saw it as the product of American magnanimity that saved the war-shattered nation from poverty and communism, and propelled the German economy towards sustained growth. Revisionist accounts since the 1980s have shown these interpretations to be hugely exaggerative. In sheer numbers, the Federal Republic was rather the step-child of the Marshall Plan. Foreign aid never accounted for more than a modicum of national income, and its relative importance had declined, not increased, after 1948. Investments financed by the counterpart funds between 1949 and 1952 accounted for one-tenth of net capital formation in the West German economy.

The more recent literature shifted focus from the overall impact of Marshall Aid to its instrumental role in the elimination of input–output bottlenecks and in the restoration of intra-European trade. The former was said to be accomplished by the allocation of the counterpart funds to critical investments in coal mining, steel, and electrical power; the latter through the establishment of the European Payments Union. However convincing these arguments might have been, they do not stand up against the quantitative evidence on industrial development. Chapter 3 will show that West Germany possessed substantial surplus capacity in heavy industry and the energy sector, and thus their alleged bottleneck status was a sheer myth. Chapter 4 will argue that the West German export boom was driven by the restoration of pre-existing trade patterns until the mid-1950s and not by the new multilateral arrangements.

The last two sections of Chapter 5 focus on fiscal and monetary policy during the 1950s and 1960s. Traditional schools of German history attributed a role of critical importance to the independent Bundesbank and its predecessor the Bank deutscher Länder, which managed to sustain price stability in an era of rapid economic growth. In these interpretations, the true miracle of the *Wirtschaftswunder* was the conservation of remarkably low rates of inflation by international comparison. This tribute to the federal bank of issue is exaggerative and, in most aspects, erroneous. During the early 1950s, West German monetary policy was, in fact, rather expansionary. The money supply grew almost twice as fast as national income and the volume of bank credit increased even more spectacularly. Industrial recovery went alongside low inflation and cheap money, which boosted aggregate demand. The prevention of run-away inflation was the achievement of fiscal, not monetary policy. Under finance minister Fritz Schäffer, the massive surpluses of the federal budget were deposited in the central bank for the purpose of eventual rearmament. By withdrawing money from circulation, fiscal policy prevented the expansion of liquidity and successfully contained imported inflation despite increasing net capital inflows. This gave monetary policy significant room to manoeuvre, not having to embark on restrictive measures to curb economic growth.

This pattern changed in the late 1950s, when domestic and international developments drastically altered the conditions under which the central bank was to fulfil its obligations. Soaring exports generated large cumulative surpluses in the balance of trade, and through that rising gold and foreign-exchange reserves. Remilitarisation from 1955, increased social expenditures after 1957, and the coal crisis of 1958 enhanced government expenditure to an extent that swiftly eliminated budget surpluses and depleted the accrued central-bank deposits. As fiscal policy turned expansionary, and the inflow of foreign exchange seemed relentless, the volume of money in circulation began to grow at a dangerous pace. To prevent inflation, the Bundesbank was forced to switch course and implement restrictive measures.

Fiscal policy not only turned increasingly expansionary throughout the post-war period; it was also much more interventionist than what the principles of the Social Market Economy would have predicted. For the most part, government intervention provided limited support for growth. Public investment and subsidies favoured predominantly declining sectors and industries that, in reality, had excess rather than insufficient capacity due to the structural disproportions created by the division of Germany. By contrast, until the mid-1960s, the Federal Republic invested very modestly in education and scientific research by international comparison and, as a result, lagged behind in industrial innovation and in frontier technologies. The most significant contribution of public policy to the West German growth miracle was the leading role that the state assumed in rebuilding the urban housing stock and in resettling the displaced populations trapped in rural areas after World War II into the industrial heartlands of the country. Without the national housing programs and the state-sponsored resettlement of refugees, this miracle may have never materialised.

Displacement and forced migration defined the post-war crisis in Germany more than anything else. They were the principal source of mass unemployment, they exacerbated the shortage of housing, and enhanced the need for foreign aid in order to avert starvation in the years of foreign military occupation. The necessity to rebuild the existence of the millions of refugees and reintegrate them into West German society dominated the agenda of the first post-war governments, as they sought to avoid the explosion of social conflict in the overpopulated rural communities and through that the reinvigoration of political extremism. Following this logic, the internal resettlements, urban reconstruction, and industrial restructuring associated with the process may have made Germany subsequently into the more open, more tolerant, and economically more dynamic society that the Western world has marvelled ever since. Parallels with the migrant crises that Europe faces today could not be more striking. Despite their ethnicity, German expellees often endured as much hostility from the indigenous population of their new homeland as they did before their exodus from Central and Eastern Europe. Their integration was managed amidst vicious disagreements between regional polities and the federal government. Finally, German experts in the early post-war years were just as concerned as they are today that restoration of the livelihoods of the millions of refugees in Germany was being thwarted by the unwillingness of European leaders to accept that the forced resettlements were a European and not just a German problem (see Granicky and Müller 1950, 4).

This monograph was written with the aim of making important contributions to a major debate in German economic history. It will enrich the reservoir of historical data on industrial development, regional economies, and external trade. It will, I hope, invoke renewed attention towards the economic impact of strategic bombing, which on the basis of my research appears more complex and persistent than it has been conventionally believed. Perhaps most crucially, the analysis of detailed regional and industry statistics will demonstrate to the reader that one cannot understand the dynamics of post-war dislocation and reconstruction growth without taking into account economic geography and production structure, which have been largely neglected in the historiography of the *Wirtschaftswunder*. By filling these gaps, my investigation supports an interpretation of the reconstruction thesis that is more compatible with the historical evidence, and that also places the role of economic policy in the German miracle into a new context.

Jánossy and the economic historians who have benefited from his pioneering work rightly argued that rapid growth following the post-war slump originated from a unique potential intrinsic to reconstruction. However, World War II and its aftermath not only caused a sudden collapse of output; they dislocated the German economy in more ways than one through the displacement of labour, the distortion of industrial structure, the diminution of effective working skills, and the disruption of external trade. In post-war Germany, these dislocating forces operated for much longer than traditionally argued and the economy required extensive state intervention to eventually overcome them. Finally, post-war Germany was more than just the Federal Republic, and thus we cannot overlook the conditions east of the Elbe and of the Iron Curtain, if we wish to understand the origins of the West German growth miracle.

Just as in the golden age, the German economy once again fascinates contemporaries, as the bulwark of stability in a world of calamity and caprice. As several European economies have been faltering and even the European project appears to be tumbling under the pressures of financial distress, illegal migration, and Brexit, Germany stays atop the global competitiveness rankings, and her fiscal foundations are rock solid. While politicians across Europe have been debating how to tackle soaring youth unemployment and political radicalism, Germany appeared to be the beacon of tolerance and solidarity, and her companies have pleaded with the government to allow migrants from war-torn regions swift access to the German job market to alleviate the pressing labour shortage in manufacturing. At the same time, the recent successes of the anti-immigrant AFD party in the federal elections of September 2017 reminded us that Germany's long association with these progressive values cannot be taken for granted and requires reassertion. Since the structural and institutional characteristics of the German economy are believed to be rooted in a uniquely German model to economic management, a *Modell Deutschland*, that many continue to see as the product of the post-war consensus, a renewed look at this era is highly topical.[3]

---

[3] Hertfelder (2007) offers a general discussion on the concept, its origins, and its interpretations over recent history.

1   The Audit of Defeat: Initial Conditions

As the guns went silent and the smoke evaporated in May 1945, the German landscape left little doubt among contemporaries that the country had hit Ground Zero. Almost 6 million German citizens had lost their lives in the worst of all wars; 12 million were held captive in Allied prisoner-of-war camps. Innumerable souls had perished at the hands of the Nazi terror or had found refuge abroad. After the Allies had dropped more than 2 million tons of bombs over German territory, the population that survived the carnage lived among ruins (Kramer 1991, 14). Even at the start of 1946, industrial production attained scarcely one-fifth of the pre-war level.[1] Total war had resulted in total collapse, and those who waged it were well aware of the damage they had caused. When Soviet and American soldiers shook hands at the river Elbe, they could see nothing but rubble around them. The architect of the Nazi war machine, Albert Speer, confessed in a letter to Hitler on 15 March 1945 that defeat was inevitable and forecasted the breakdown of war production within six to eight weeks.[2] In the same month, propaganda minister Joseph Goebbels scribbled these words into his diary:

> The air war still celebrates its wildest orgies. We are utterly defenceless against it. The Reich is gradually turning into a total desert … The situation becomes day by day more unbearable and we possess no means to defend us against this development.[3]

In the first post-war years, foreign observers from Isaac Deutscher to former US president Herbert Hoover reported of conditions unimaginable to the human senses that surpassed even the boldest military objectives of yesteryear.[4] The earliest scholarly accounts offered no

---

[1] OMGUS, *Industry,* No. 12, 1.
[2] *Memorandum von Rüstungs- und Bewaffnungsminister, Albert Speer an dem Führer, 15 März 1945.* In Ruhl (1982), Document No. 22, 73–6.
[3] My own translation from the German text cited in Krause (1997), 37.
[4] See the letter from Deutscher, 'Bavarian roads', in *The Economist,* 23 June 1945, reprinted in Kramer (1991), Document No. 11, 229. On the report of Hoover as special envoy of President Truman, see Vogelgsang (2016), 199–200.

less gloomy prophecies about the lasting economic impact of wartime destruction. They reckoned that the restoration of the transport infrastructure alone would take years, the rebuilding of the devastated cities and towns perhaps decades.[5] They were convinced that the occupying powers would dismantle large parts of an already decimated arsenal of industrial machinery and thus would effectively deindustrialise Germany. The defeated, disillusioned, and demoralised population had little hope for better days. Evacuated from their cities and towns during the war, their families annihilated or driven apart, their homes and businesses destroyed, their savings now all but worthless, they could hardly cherish dreams of prosperity. Initially, the presence of millions of refugees and internally displaced persons aggravated the situation further. Hunger, cold homes, and depression competed against one another in an evil race to create more misery.

For a while, it appeared that peace would turn the conditions created by war for the worse. As Figure 1.1 demonstrates, Germany lost a quarter of her territory within the 1937 borders. Almost two-thirds of the industrial production of the former Reich had concentrated in the west of the country, but the secession of the vast agricultural hinterland in the east deprived the German economy of its breadbasket, while the re-annexation of Alsace-Lorraine and the temporary control of the Saarland by France put the adequate supply of coal and iron for German industry in peril. The division of what remained Germany after the Potsdam Conference in July and August 1945 into four autonomously administered occupation zones and the carving up of Berlin into different sectors made the coordination of emergency measures and reconstruction attempts, if such were undertaken at all, nearly impossible. As long as the future of the country remained undecided, the internal borders made economic cooperation and trade across regions equally difficult (Spoerer and Streb 2013, 209–10).

Contemporary accounts of a crippled economy proved misguided. Historians gradually came to realise that the heritage that World War II and the post-war settlement bequeathed upon the western part of Germany was rather magnanimous. The fundamentals of the economic miracle that astonished those living at the time were laid in the 1940s. On the eve of its remarkable revival, the West German economy was endowed with more plentiful and modern productive assets than ever

---

[5] An OMGUS report in June 1947 forecasted that only repairing the dwellings damaged by war in the areas under its control would take approximately thirty years, but restoring the supply of housing to pre-war standards, accounting for the need to replace or renovate worn-down facilities and to expand the housing stock to accommodate an increased population, would require between forty and sixty years (OMGUS, *Industry*, No. 24, 28).

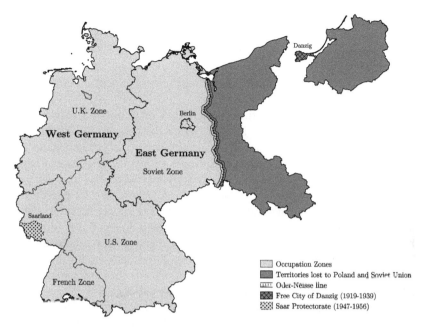

Figure 1.1 The territorial losses and division of Germany after World War II.
Source: Construction based on GIS shape files used for Figure 1 in Braun and Mahmoud (2014), 73. The authors have kindly shared their shape files.

before. The living conditions of the early post-war years hindered reconstruction, for certain and in more ways than one, but the war left behind ample supplies of labour, substantially greater than the pre-war working population. The consensus that has emerged from more recent historiography claims that economic recovery was held back by infrastructural bottlenecks and the restrictive institutions of occupied Germany that Carlin (1989) described as a system of 'vegetative control'. To unleash the expansive forces of the German economy required no more than the removal of these obstructions. As Abelshauser argued, 'West Germany was poor yet not underdeveloped. Given the political commitment to reconstruction, the resurgence of the West German economy was foreseeable, once the efforts sufficed to eliminate the institutional and infrastructural chaos' (Abelshauser 1983, 32). This chapter begins with an audit of the impact that the war and the peace had on the productive capital of German industry. It then describes their consequences for the size of the German population and the living conditions it endured during the occupation years. The final section reviews the literature and contemporary sources on the factors that delayed the revival of markets and stifled the revitalisation of industry.

1.1   Production Capacity

To reveal the impact of wartime destruction on industrial capacity in Germany was a chief concern already before the cessation of hostilities, when the United States Strategic Bombing Survey (USSBS) began one of the most monumental statistical crusades in history. It operated with more than 1,000 military and civilian staff from London and several regional headquarters in Germany (MacIsaac 1976, 68). Its personnel were often found in harm's way when striving to uncover and salvage the German government records that were dispersed across the country in the final phase of the war. The field teams often arrived at target locations before the advancing Allied army divisions. Their perhaps most adventurous and arguably most significant mission was an undercover raid into the Soviet sector of Berlin in July 1945 to abduct Rolf Wagenführ, the former chief economist and statistician of the German armaments ministry and undoubtedly the most knowledgeable expert on the Nazi war economy (MacIsaac 1976, 90–4).

The data collection was completed after the war at the Statistical Office for German Industries that the Office of Military Government for Germany (OMGUS) had created in Bad Nauheim in June 1945. Built on remnants of German ministerial divisions that had established contact with US authorities already in March, two months before VE-Day, Bad Nauheim was endowed with remarkable resources. Beyond the expertise of the former German government officials and the statistical material they had rescued from Berlin, the experts of the bombing survey had access to the Ministerial Collecting Center, the chief statistical facility of OMGUS in the vicinity of Kassel. The centre managed to get hold of all that was left of the Imperial Statistical Office staff in West Germany and amass the vast stock of records on which our knowledge of the German economy at war and under Allied occupation has been largely constructed even to this day. The Collecting Center was a real monster: its 300 buildings scattered over three villages, five camps, and a former munitions factory. It housed more than 1,000 tons of documents and an equal number of former German government personnel as well as 70,000 tons of film and scientific apparatus (Vogelgsang 2016, 165–71).

Of the 208 USSBS reports on the European war, the most important for economic historians are those prepared by, or with the assistance of, the Overall Economic Effects Division (OEED), made up of no lesser scholars than J. Kenneth Galbraith (director), Burton Klein, Paul Baran, Nicholas Kaldor, and Edward Denison, among others. The *Over-all Report* (USSBS 1945) summarised the detailed division reports of USSBS cataloguing the effects of the bombing campaign on each of the major industries, military and public infrastructure, civilian defences, and civilian morale.[6] The final report of OEED, entitled *The Effects of Strategic Bombing on the German War Economy* (USSBS–OEED 1945), presented an extensive analysis of the development of industrial production as well as capital and labour reserves during the war and evaluated the impact of the air attacks on both armaments production and the supply of civilian goods. It owed much to the statistical work of Wagenführ and reflected his view on the trajectory of German armaments production.

The overall report reveals the paradox in the legacy of the air war. On the one hand, 'it brought home to the German people the full impact of modern war with all its horror and suffering' (USSBS 1945, 107). On the other, the magnitude of destruction in industrial plant and machinery directly caused by the air attacks was surprisingly small. Most industries were never prime targets, as production sites were too numerous, geographically dispersed, and often not identifiable from the air. Hitting strategic assets in the transportation system and the residential areas of major industrial cities proved to be a more effective means of reducing Germany's war potential. 'The Allies did not attempt to destroy the German economy as a whole. The bombing offensive sought rather to stop it from operating by damaging key points' (USSBS 1945, 37).

The reports demonstrated equally well the existence of ample capacities in both steel production and machine tools on the eve of the war. As a result, the German economy was never short of capital goods before the breakdown of the transport system. Even in the armaments industry, capacity reserves remained substantial throughout the war, thanks to the fact that more than 70 per cent of machine-tool production was sold to the armed forces or to munitions manufacturers.[7] In one of the first scholarly publications based on the statistical work carried out by USSBS, Kaldor (1946) emphasised that most of the primary metals and metal processing industries in Germany had operated with single work shifts during the war. The bombing survey estimated that the inventory of machine tools in Germany had grown from around 1.3 million to

---

[6] Before publication of the *Over-all Report*, OMGUS prepared a brief non-technical version, the *Summary Report*, which was aimed at senior politicians and the American press.
[7] See USSBS–OEED, 1945, Table 21, 49.

2.1 million pieces between 1938 and 1943.[8] These findings were 'in striking contrast with the experience of the United States and Great Britain, where machine tools were kept working 24 hours a day seven days a week', and where the machinery industry was pushed to the limits of its capacity (USSBS–OEED 1945, 8).

Much to the surprise of contemporaries, the reports also found German armaments production to be little affected by the bombing campaign, at least directly. Total munitions output was reduced by no more than 5 per cent until 1943 (USSBS–OEED 1945, 148). Even thereafter the main economic impact of aerial bombardment was the diversion of the labour force from production to rubble removal and repair work. It was the destruction of the railway network combined with concentrated attacks on key waterway targets in the second half of 1944 that brought the German economy to its knees (see Levin 1992, 163–9). By 14 October, coal transports from the Ruhr on the Rhine to the south ceased and the cargo capacity of the *Reichsbahn* had declined dramatically. Even though hard-coal production in the Ruhr fell from 10.4 million tons in August 1944 to 4.8 million tons in February 1945, stockpiles of both coal and coke in the mining district increased fivefold over the same period (USSBS 1945, 61–4). Based on a meticulous study of USSBS reports and archival records, Mierzejewski (1988) demonstrated how the production system of the German war economy had been built on the railways. As a consequence, the destruction of key railway hubs could effectively dismantle the input–output network of the war economy (Mierzejewski 1988, 162–76).

By contrast, productive capital in most industries suffered remarkably little damage. From the data reported by the bombing survey, post-war economists estimated that merely 17.4 per cent of the capital stock of West German industry was destroyed as a direct consequence of aerial bombardment and ground fighting. Even less, only 6.5 per cent, of industrial machinery and equipment was substantially damaged (Abelshauser 2004, 68). Even such strategic industries as steel, electrical power, and the electric supply system did not become primary targets for enemy forces. The most important exceptions, where strategic bombing proved to have notable impact, were the manufacturing of synthetic materials, electrical equipment, and especially military aircraft and naval hardware (USSBS–OEED 1945, 8–9). On 30 March 1945, Hitler issued one of his most diabolical orders that called for the demolition of all non-movable industrial assets in Germany prior to the arrival of Allied troops. The *Nero-Befehl* could have inflicted much larger damage on German

[8] Ibid., Table 18, 44.

productive capacity than what the Allied bombers managed, but, with the support of factory owners and often by arming the workers, armaments minister Albert Speer successfully sabotaged the implementation of this suicidal creature of a most monstrous mind (Müller 1993, 373–5). Following the disintegration of the war economy, industrial firms could divert resources from production to reconstruction work and essential repairs, while they built up large inventories of precious input materials. The enormous profits they had earned during the war also allowed them to retain their skilled workforce even at depressed levels of output.[9]

In the aftermath of World War II, capital accumulation in German industry was affected most strongly by reparations and, as part of that, the dismantling or transfer of plant and machinery. The Potsdam Protocols obliged Germany to pay reparations in the value of 20 billion dollars, half of which would serve as compensation for material damage in the Soviet Union (Maier 1991, 20). According to the agreement, each occupying power would exert its reparations claims from its own zone of occupation, but the USSR was to receive an additional 10 per cent of the equipment dismantled in the three Western zones and a further 15 per cent in exchange for deliveries of food and other agreed commodities from the Soviet occupation zone of the corresponding value.[10] The *Plan for Reparations and the Level of Post-war German Economy* (hereafter first level of industry plan) issued by the Allied Control Authority on 26 March 1946 limited industrial production until 1949 to about 50 to 55 per cent of the 1938 output level. It prohibited the manufacturing of armaments, synthetic oil, rubber and ammonia, primary aluminium and many other non-ferrous metals, ball bearings, heavy tractors and other types of heavy machinery, radioactive material, and radio transmitting equipment. Production in chemicals, primary metals, and the engineering industries was restricted to fractions of the pre-war levels. Capacities deemed unessential for attaining the output ceilings were to be dismantled.[11]

Initially, American occupation policy was shaped by national security concerns and particularly by the objective of reducing Germany's war potential. The blueprint for achieving this was the Morgenthau Plan, named after the Secretary of the Treasury who submitted a proposal that sought to convert Germany into a dominantly agrarian economy through the physical destruction of productive capacity, especially in industries critical to waging war. Directive JCS 1067 of the Joint Chiefs of Staff still reflected these objectives and instructed the military government

---

[9] OMGUS, *Industry*, No. 12, 5.
[10] OMGUS, *Three years of reparations*, 1.
[11] 'The Plan for Reparations and the Level of Post-war German Economy in Accordance with the Berlin Protocol', reprinted in OMGUS, *Reparations*, No. 48, Annex B, 21–5.

to demilitarise the German economy (Settel 1947, 14–15). The first level of industry plan earmarked about 1,800 manufacturing plants in West Germany for dismantling. The second, revised plan adopted by the British and US military governments on 29 August 1947 listed only 859 establishments, in addition to the list of 176 plants presented by the French authorities, thereby effectively exempting more than 700 plants from dismantling. On 13 April 1949, the three military governors of the Western occupation zones announced that their respective governments had authorised the partial or complete removal of an additional 159 factories or factory parts from the reparations schedules.[12] As the occupation forces failed to fulfil even these modest quotas, only a fraction of industrial machinery that had survived the war was actually dismantled. Estimates put the value of all assets affected by reparations and restitution at approximately 4 per cent of the gross capital stock of West German industry in 1950 prices (Plumpe 1999, 43; Spoerer and Streb 2013, 214). Arguably, occupation policies exerted a more negative influence on capital formation indirectly, as manufacturing firms had no incentive to invest in new machinery or even to carry out essential repairs in plants that were expected to close down. It has been estimated that this 'fear factor' reduced the industrial capital stock by almost 3 per cent between April 1945 and June 1948 and made the available machinery, on average, older and more poorly maintained (Abelshauser 1983, 22).

Geopolitics may have been the main driver behind the seemingly radical shift in US policy towards occupied Germany, but actions on the ground had already been at odds with the goals of the Carthaginian peace shortly after the war and certainly well before the announcement of President Truman's containment strategy and the Marshall Plan. Concerned by the catastrophic economic situation in the country as well as the deteriorating relationship among the occupying powers, Deputy Military Governor General Lucius Clay, an adamant adversary of the Morgenthau Plan, ordered the halt of all reparations deliveries to the French and Soviet occupation zones as early as 4 May 1946. This order came barely a month after the first transports had just left Bremerhaven for the USSR (Settel 1947, 15). On 6 September of the same year, in his famous address in the Stuttgart opera house, Foreign Secretary James Byrnes promised effective American assistance in the rebuilding of the country (Weimer 1998, 25–6). The notion that the economic recovery and security of Western Europe had depended on rebuilding German industry was common sense in the US administration during the war. The policy of a hard stance favoured by Roosevelt and Morgenthau had

[12] OMGUS, *Reparations*, No. 48, 4.

its strongest opponents in the War Department and the US Army that gradually gained the upper hand in the administration of OMGUS by late 1946 (Gimbel 1968).[13]

Vogelgsang (2016) gives a vivid illustration of this discrepancy between spirit and action through the case of IG Farben, one of the most emblematic enterprises of Nazi Germany. It had grown into the largest chemical corporation in the world, was a key supplier of the German war machinery, the exclusive supplier of Zyklon B, and one of the main profiteers from slave labour. As such, it was destined to become the prime object of destruction, de-concentration, and de-Nazification. However, history defied these odds.

From 1946 onwards Germany's industry in general and IG Farben in particular were increasingly less perceived as a threat to world peace. IG Farben was in the centre of attention again on 5 June 1947, when 24 executives were charged in the Nuremberg trials. Records on Farben ... were destroyed before the process. Prosecutor Josiah E. DuBois was discredited as Jewish, i.e. partial, and a 'follower of the Communist creed'. The trial ended very favourably for the defendants and for IG Farben. They were found to have no collective responsibility for the war or war crimes and only some individuals were sentenced for crimes like participation in looting. The maximum sentence was eight years and some managers continued their career at IG Farben after their time in prison ... When the chemicals giant was finally dismantled from February 1947 onwards, the outcome were not the dozens of small companies once envisioned, but three large corporations and a few smaller ones. The best-known successor companies of IG Farben are BASF, Bayer, Hoechst and Agfa (Vogelgsang 2016, 189–90).

Whereas American occupation policy in Germany reflected a change of hearts between 1945 and 1947, the British government never fully supported plans of crushing the German economy. However, in the immediate aftermath of the war, there were powerful advocates within both industry and the Board of Trade for punitive measures aimed at restricting production capacity in industries in which British manufacturers had key competitors among German firms. Transport vehicles offer a prime example. The first level of industry plan established annual quotas of only 20,000 cars and 21,000 trucks for the British zone, to be supplied exclusively by the Ford factory in Cologne. The Volkswagen plant in Wolfsburg was, therefore, listed as surplus to requirements and was scheduled for reparations. Its death sentence was quickly repelled. The revised level of industry plan adopted since January 1947 for the jointly administered British and American occupation zones (hereafter Bizonal Area) raised

---

[13] The actions of the occupation authorities diverged from the directives of Washington bureaus in similar ways in Japan under the command of General Douglas Macarthur, especially from 1947 (see Nishida 2007, 415–18).

the output ceiling for car producers from 40,000 to 160,000 and with that stroke of a pen exempted the German automobile industry from dismantling (Tolliday 1995, 290–6). The revised plan also increased substantially the production limits and the required capacity for iron and steel, steel constructions, and machine tools.[14] Although the prohibitive regulations pertaining to war-related industries remained in place, the plan stipulated that no factory in these industries would be available for reparations until the satisfactory conclusion of inter-Allied disputes over the future status of Germany, which appeared increasingly unlikely.[15]

Stalin was unmoved by the growing restraint that the Western Allies exercised in their reparations activity and Soviet leaders remained adamant on their demands for Germany to pay a price commensurate to the suffering that the Soviet people had endured as a consequence of Nazi aggression. This price had to be paid, in increasing part, by the Soviet occupation zone alone. The impact thereof on East German industrial capacity has played a prominent part in historical narratives, and finds support in some, even though by no means all, quantitative accounts. One estimate valued the productive assets dismantled between 1945 and 1953 at 50 billion marks, which would have been tenfold the losses that the several times larger West German economy incurred. Within the metal processing industries as well as chemicals, reparations are claimed to have reduced productive capacity by between one-third and one-half (Buchheim 1991, 57). In their testimony to the Bundestag after German reunification, Baar, Karlsch, and Matschke (1995) provided a dramatic account of the crippling effect that dismantling had exerted on the East German economy. They claimed that 30 per cent of the industrial capital stock that had survived the war was subsequently transferred to the USSR and Poland as reparations. Earlier estimates were often more optimistic (see Zank 1987 and Matschke 1988). The most recent revisions suggest that there was sharp reduction in the size of East German manufacturing capacity during the immediate post-war years in comparison with West Germany. Between 1936 and 1944, the stock of industrial fixed capital in the later German Democratic Republic (GDR) increased by more than 40 per cent, but by 1948 it fell back to scarcely four-fifths of the pre-war level (Ritschl and Vonyó 2014, 169). It is difficult to refute that, even if other factors were at play, it was above all Germany's division along the demarcation lines of the Cold War that saved West German industry from this crippling reparations burden.

---

[14] OMGUS, *Economic data on Potsdam Germany*, 37.
[15] Section IV in 'Revised Plan for Level of Industry: US–UK Zones of Germany', reprinted in OMGUS, *Reparations*, No. 48, Annex C, 32–3.

Even though the USSBS reports and the modest rate of dismantling in the Western occupation zones were known to contemporaries, they still misjudged the impact of the war on capital accumulation. The earliest accounts published in post-war West Germany estimated that by 1947 the industrial capital stock had been reduced to less than two-thirds of the 1936 or 1939 levels.[16] Not only were these gross overstatements of the extent of material damage caused by wartime destruction; they also overlooked the staggering expansion of industrial capacities during the late 1930s and the first war years. Contemporary views on the war economy were drawn from the conviction that Nazi Germany had not prepared for a long war. The overall report of USSBS itself stressed that the limits of productive capacity in the engineering industries were not seriously stretched before 1942 and that the machine-tool stock of man-ufacturers had expanded as a consequence of hoarding (USSBS 1945, 31–3). The *Blitzkrieg* hypothesis remained influential in the post-war literature, among others in the works of Klein (1959), Fischer (1968), and Milward (1965, 1975). Recent scholarship, however, has shown that from the launching of the Four Year Plan in 1936, and even more following the outbreak of the war, production capacity increased sub-stantially both in the armaments industry and within heavy industry in general (Budrass, Scherner, and Streb 2010; Scherner 2010, 2013). In the course of the armaments boom, the growth of machine-tool produc-tion was remarkable. By 1944, the machinery stock of German industry had doubled relative to that in 1929. This accumulation of machine tools was not due to the disproportionate retention of old machinery, as once believed, but to new acquisitions, many of them high-volume production equipment. The growth of industrial output during the war was strongly capital intensive; it was not in first order the outcome of productivity miracles (Ristuccia and Tooze 2013, 963–5).

In the 1950s, the German Institute of Economic Research (DIW) undertook the task of quantifying capital formation in the West German economy. It was made clear immediately that the colossal invest-ments of the early 1940s had substantially increased industrial capac-ity (Wagenführ 1954, 57–9). It was estimated that the gross value of industrial fixed capital had grown by 75 per cent between 1936 and 1943 and, despite wartime destruction, post-war dismantling, and dis-investment, was still considerably larger in 1948 than it had been before the war (Krengel 1958, 94). Measured in constant prices, annual gross investment in West German industry doubled between 1936 and 1939,

---

[16] See among others Niederschlag (1947), 41, Seume (1947), 143, and Eisendrath (1950), 126.

and then grew by an additional 20 per cent until 1942 (Baumbart and Krengel 1970, 75). Recently published evidence from revised investment statistics suggests an even higher rate of wartime capital accumulation (Scherner 2010, 438).

Structural shifts magnified these aggregate effects. From the late 1930s, investments in the Nazi economy focussed on machinery rather than buildings and on heavy industry at the expense of consumer goods. Annual gross investment in the producer goods industries in 1939 was two and a half times larger than it had been in 1928 (Petzina 1975, 80). Most investment went into metallurgy, chemicals, machine tools, transport vehicles, and electrical and precision engineering (Eichholz 1999, 343–4). The vigorous wartime expansion of productive capacity improved the technological standards of industrial machinery as well. The investment drive of the armaments boom had made manufacturing equipment, on average, younger and more modern. These vintage effects were notable even if firms continued to invest in established technologies alongside the innovations of recent years (Ristuccia and Tooze 2013, 965). The astonishing growth of industrial capacity in the late 1930s and early 1940s outweighed, by far, the diminutive impact of wartime hostilities and post-war dismantling in qualitative as much as in quantitative terms. Claims made at the time, which had accentuated fears of 'deindustrialisation' in Germany after 1945, were shown to be erroneous. West German industry was not only well-endowed with physical capital on the eve of its post-war growth miracle; it was much better endowed than it had ever been before World War II.

This overall assessment does not imply that the war did not have serious negative consequences on industrial development at the local level. Indeed, whereas West German industry as a whole had emerged from the defeat and disintegration of the German Reich with a productive base it could have never aspired to obtain in peacetime, the fortunes of several leading manufacturing firms were doomed. Precision attacks in the final year of the war destroyed much of the synthetic material and petroleum industries (USSBS 1945, 81–90) that, consequently, had to rebuild during the reconstruction years. The machinery of the electro-technical and shipbuilding industries was substantially, and that of aircraft manufacturing almost completely, dismantled (Baumgart and Krengel 1970, 48–9). The automobile industry had considerably larger production capacities after 1945 than before the war, but the experience of the main car producers was not uniform. Opel had dominated the German automobile market until 1939, but could not retain its leading position in the post-war era. It suffered greater damage than either Ford or Volkswagen, its factories in Brandenburg were overtaken by the Soviet occupying forces, and parts of the Rüsselheim plant that had survived the war were dismantled by the US authorities, to be transferred to the USSR as reparations. By contrast, both the Ford works in Cologne and Volkswagen in Wolfsburg, after having suffered only small war scares, enjoyed more favourable treatment under British occupation. Their dispersed equipment was quickly retrieved and their production lines reassembled with the help of the occupying troops. Having retained essentially all their equipment, most of them recently installed, they were now destined to carve out much larger shares from the German and European car markets than they had commanded before the war (Tolliday 1995, 301–3).

1.2   Population and Living Conditions

The West German economy was endowed not only with enlarged industrial capacity after the end of the war but also with plentiful supplies of labour. War casualties were enormous for sure. No fewer than 4 million from the western part of the country had perished by 1945. Additional millions died in Soviet captivity or returned home severely wounded and mentally damaged. The adult male population that had traditionally formed the core of the industrial workforce suffered particularly severe losses. Yet, remarkably, the West German population – fewer than 40 million in June 1939 – grew to almost 48 million by the end of 1950. Even the male population had become larger, albeit very moderately (Steinberg 1991, 155–7). Despite the increased share of the economically inactive, the labour force expanded by more than 12 per cent in the same period (Ambrosius 1996, 47–8).

This paradoxical pattern was the product of the post-war settlement, perhaps the most important consequence thereof for the economic future of Germany. In accordance with Article XIII of the Potsdam Agreement, approximately 15 million ethnic Germans were uprooted from their historical settlements in East and Central Europe until 1951, as a means of collective punishment for the Nazi war crimes. One million were deported to the Soviet Union, with another 700,000 forcefully resettled from the European to the Asian territories of the USSR, and 13.3 million expelled to post-war Germany and Austria. Two million were killed or went missing during the years of these deportations (Reichling 1986, 29–30). The earliest comprehensive account estimated that 20 per cent of the German population in the affected areas had perished during and after the war. It put the number of post-war casualties at 2.3 million, but this figure included all the ethnic Germans never to return from Soviet deportations, regardless of whether they had survived these calamitous years or not (Statistisches Bundesamt 1958, 37–47).

Quantifying the mass population movements invoked by the war and its aftermath is a monumental task and one finds it challenging not to get lost in the numbers, not least because of the inconsistencies between the different sources.[17] When the guns went silent in May 1945, 16.9 million ethnic Germans were de jure residents of East and Central European states west of the interwar Soviet borders, including the former Reich provinces east of the rivers Oder and Neisse. Of these, only 15 million lived in the same area in 1945 as they had in 1939. The remaining 1.9 million had migrated into the region voluntarily or by administrative resettlement during the war. Deportations to the USSR began in January 1945 as the Red Army advanced into German territory and reached their peak in March. Some 300,000 of the forcefully deported eventually returned from the Soviet Union, but many of them were subsequently expelled to Austria or Germany (Reichling 1986, 26–8). Most of the 9.5 million expellees from the eastern provinces of Prussia fled without official warning before the advancing Soviet troops. By the end of the war, about 5 million had already lived in what would become Potsdam Germany (Bundesministerium für Vertriebene 1954, 23E). Central European countries, recently liberated from Nazi occupation, began expelling ethnic Germans in their earnest even before the meetings of the Potsdam Conference commenced. In November 1945, the Allied Control Authority estimated the number of Germans de facto still living in the former eastern provinces at only 3.5 million (Steinert 1995, 558–60).

The evacuations from large cities in the region began in 1943. The naval strongholds Stettin and Königsberg, regularly pounded by the British and the Soviet air forces, had lost more than a third of their prewar population by the end of 1944. Even though the first Russian troops crossed the Memel into Germany in June 1944, the more densely populated eastern provinces were overrun only during the first months of 1945 (Bundesministerium für Vertriebene 1954, 9E–23E). Perhaps the most epic episode of the exodus that followed took place in the last war winter. In one of the very few exercises of humanity by the German armed forces, the *Kriegsmarine*, helped by an enormous merchant fleet, carried out the largest transport mission in naval history, one that dwarfed even the D-day landings. More than 1,000 vessels shipped 2 million Germans

---

[17] For the most comprehensive academic accounts, see Reichling (1986) and Steinberg (1991), 103–42. The population statistics of the German settlement areas affected by the deportations were first reported in Statistisches Bundesamt (1958).

from Baltic ports to western harbours between January and May 1945. Often travelling through frosty waters and under frequent attack from the Allied air forces, surface war ships, and submarines, they managed to bring more than 98 per cent of all those on board to safety. The vast majority of the desperate they had saved were civilians, many of them severely wounded; only 240,000 were soldiers and naval staff (Steinberg 1991, 131–2).

The population census of October 1946 registered 9.8 million expellees in the four occupation zones of Germany, including Berlin (Kornrumpf 1950a, 37). Until September 1950, their number had grown to 12.2 million: almost 7.9 million in the Federal Republic, 148,000 in West Berlin, and about 4.1 million in East Germany.[18] More than half of the expellees had lived in the eastern provinces of Prussia before the war, almost a quarter in Czechoslovakia, and 5 per cent in interwar Poland (Statistisches Bundesamt 1958, 38, 45–6). In addition, 1.56 million refugees with a permanent pre-war residence on the territory of the Soviet occupation zone and East Berlin had migrated to the West between 1944 and 1950.[19] In order not to spell confusion, we must clarify the distinction that official terminology has made between the two population groups. Immigrants of German ethnicity who in 1939 had lived outside of Germany or in the eastern provinces of the Reich are referred to as expellees; those who resettled from post-war East Germany are classified as refugees.[20]

The demographic impact of war-induced migration is recognisable not only in the size but also in the structure of the population. For one, the share of men and women of working age was substantially higher among the expellees and the refugees than in the indigenous population.[21] One in two refugees was twenty-five years of age or younger, and very few were elderly. Their favourable age structure made them an invaluable reservoir of labour during the following decades (Heidemeyer 1994, 48). Immigration was also responsible for the moderate growth of the male population, and thanks to that also growth of the industrial labour force, in West Germany between 1939 and 1950. In September 1950, within the total population, 62.8 per cent of the economically active were men. Among the expellees and the refugees, the corresponding shares were 64.6 per cent and 67.3 per cent respectively (Ambrosius 1996, 50). From

---

[18] StatBRD, Vol. 35.9 (1956), 68–72; Reichling (1989), 14.
[19] StatBRD, Vol. 114 (1955), 13.
[20] Children born into expellee or refugee families in post-war Germany had the same status as their father, children born out of wedlock that of their mother (see StatBRD, Vol. 34, 15–17).
[21] StatBRD, Vol. 35.9 (1956), 28–30.

an economic point of view, perhaps the key characteristic of the expellees and refugees was their exceptional occupational mobility. Between 1939 and 1950, 48 per cent of them changed occupation or their specific job within the same occupation, while the respective ratio in the rest of the population was only 34 per cent.[22]

Table 1.1 demonstrates the impact of mass migration on population growth in West Germany during the 1940s: it was large overall, but far from uniform across the country. Bremen and Hamburg both had fewer residents in 1950 than at the start of the war. By contrast, the population of agrarian states, most notably Bavaria, Lower Saxony, and Schleswig-Holstein, increased dramatically. Clearly, population growth after 1945 was driven by the influx of expellees and refugees. The West German population increased by almost 8.4 million between May 1939 and September 1950. This total comes 1 million short of the number of expellees and refugees living in the Federal Republic at the end of the period, which confirms that, in the absence of mass immigration, the population of the country would have declined during the 1940s. As the French government did not agree to the implementation of Article XIII of the Potsdam Agreement, the French occupation zone did not accept either expellees or refugees between May 1945 and the unification of the three Western zones in April 1949 (Granicky and Müller 1950, 4–5). Consequently, the population share of immigrants in the southwest of Germany was very modest at first, but increased sharply by 1950.

Chapter 2 will expose the economic geography of post-war dislocation in detail. At this point, it is sufficient to highlight that the livelihoods of the German population after 1945 were devastated by both mass migration and the urban housing shortage that resulted from the destruction of residential buildings during the war. The joint consequence of both factors was that despite the influx of millions into West Germany the urban population of the country suffered the most severe setback it had seen since the Thirty Years' War (Bauer 1947, 28–9). The number of residents in the largest cities fell considerably between 1939 and 1946, as Figure 1.2 demonstrates. By contrast, overpopulated villages and small towns reported astronomical rates of unemployment for many years to come. As I will explain in Chapter 2, the urban housing deficit was too large to surmount without extensive state intervention, which necessitated the creation of a sovereign West German government. In the late 1940s, the dire housing conditions were a constant source of human misery and social conflict, and an impediment to economic reconstruction.

---

[22] StatBRD, Vol. 211 (1958), 33–34, 70. See also Kornrumpf (1950b), 95–6.

Table 1.1 *Expellees and refugees in the West German population after World War II*

	Total population (thousands)		Share in total population (%)		
	1950	1939	Expellees		Refugees 1950
			1946	1950	
British occupation zone					
Hamburg	1,606	1,712	4.6	7.2	4.2
Lower Saxony	6,797	4,539	23.8	27.2	5.4
North Rhine Westphalia	13,196	11,934	6.1	10.1	2.9
Schleswig-Holstein	2,595	1,589	32.7	33.0	5.2
US occupation zone					
Bavaria	9,184	7,084	20.1	21.1	2.5
Bremen	559	563	5.4	8.6	3.8
Hesse	4,324	3,479	13.8	16.7	3.8
Württemberg-Baden	3,909	3,218	14.8	16.6	2.4
French occupation zone					
Baden	1,339	1,230	2.0	7.4	2.1
Rhineland-Palatinate	3,005	2,960	1.3	5.1	1.5
Württemberg-Hohenzollern	1,184	1,030	3.2	9.6	1.8
Federal Republic	47,696	39,338	13.9	16.5	3.3

Source: Braun and Mahmoud (2014), 77. Author's calculations. For a more detailed decomposition of the resident population by country and region of origin, see StatBRD, Vol. 35.3 (1953), 6–27.

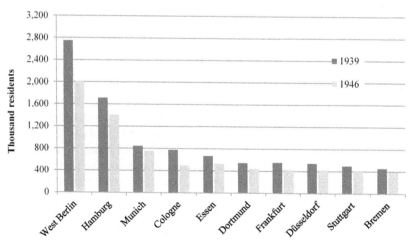

Figure 1.2 The population of the largest West German cities in 1939 and 1946.
Source: StatBRD, Vol. 35.9 (1956), 99–109.

The war had turned Germany into a land of refugees, for immigration from the East was preceded by the mass evacuation of urban dwellers during the Allied bombing campaign. By the end of the war, close to 9 million residents of German cities had taken refuge in the countryside. One-third of them were unable to return until 1947. One million residents had abandoned Berlin alone. Almost the same number had been evacuated from Cologne and smaller towns in its vicinity by January 1945. The corresponding figures for Essen, Düsseldorf, and Hamburg each surpassed 300,000. Almost half of all the evacuees at the end of the war had fled from Berlin, Hamburg, and the Rhine-Ruhr agglomeration (Krause 1997, 175–8, 186). Expellees, East German refugees, and the internally displaced all competed for the scarce resources that the local population had to share with them, housing more than anything else. Administrative assignments and mandatory housing provisions were common practices across the country and remained in place until the early 1950s (Steinert 1995, 562–3). The increasingly hostile sentiments of the different population groups towards one another are richly documented in the historiography. The millions displaced by war, whom Kleßmann (1982) described as the post-war 'collapse-society', invoked social conflict in the communities that had to accommodate them. The presence of unwelcomed 'newcomers' in the villages and small towns of Germany in the 1940s, adhering to different customs and norms and speaking different dialects, undermined the hitherto organically evolved cohesion of the countryside (Erker 1988). That the impact of these tragic transformations shook the traditional life, morality, and Weltanschauung of rural society to its foundations after 1945 was already noted in the most canonical monograph on the German crisis (Meinecke 1946).

Many were anxious to escape this alien and intolerant environment, but returning to the cities was made difficult by several obstacles: poor living conditions in the still destroyed urban landscape, the policy of the occupation authorities to retain sufficient manpower on the farms, or simply the lack of finances required for the return journey (Krause 1997, 13). The end of the war did not bring an end to the evacuations either. Hundreds of thousands were relocated in both 1945 and 1946 from cities to the country, many of them more than once. The Allies requisitioned a vast number of buildings for military and administrative purposes and as living quarters for their staff. Other dwellings were 'made free' for essential reconstruction workers, or for former political prisoners and other victims of persecution during the Nazi era, in line with Law No. 18 enacted by the Allied Control Authority on 8 March 1946.[23] Public

---

[23] OMGUS, *Manpower, trade unions and working conditions*, No. 20, 12–13.

health authorities, fearing the outbreak of epidemics, evacuated those who had found shelter in bunkers and cellars. On similar grounds, the occupying forces often prevented evacuees from returning to their cities. In the summer of 1945, the British closed down the main bridge over the Elbe to Hamburg, forcing tens of thousands to camp outside the city for months. On 11 August 1945, OMGUS decreed that those who had returned to Stuttgart without authorisation from the mayor would not receive ration tickets for basic provisions (Krause 1997, 190–1, 201). Hundreds of thousands thus remained evacuated in rural counties until the end of the 1940s, especially children, women, and the elderly. The livelihoods of the most desperate were even more dire. The housing census of September 1950 registered almost 1 million residents still in refugee camps that the occupation authorities had intended only to function as temporary facilities. An additional 1.3 million lived in emergency shelters outside the camps, including ships, abandoned factories, or railway buildings.[24]

Although the historiography of the early post-war era has focussed on the conditions of ethnic German refugees, the presence of displaced persons brought to Germany during the war as prisoners of war (POW) and as foreign workers was an equally pressing concern. Thanks to the efforts of the United Nations Relief and Rehabilitation Administration (UNRRA), most were repatriated to their home countries until early 1946 (Jahn 1950, 101–2), but at the start of 1947 almost 1 million still lived in West Germany. One reason for their prolonged presence was that the British military government continued to employ foreign miners in the Ruhr to maintain coal production, but many forced labourers or POWs from Eastern Europe refused to return home for fear of political persecution. In April 1950, the refugee camps of the Federal Republic still sheltered 200,000 foreigners (Granicky and Müller 1950, 5).

The catastrophic living conditions and the unwelcome presence of refugees and expellees not only invoked social conflict and public distress; the inadequate housing supply was an impediment to economic recovery, too. With the millions displaced by war trapped in rural communities, urban industry could not find sufficient labour to lift production. Much of the working time and energy of the existing urban workforce was diverted to rubble removal and reconstruction efforts, often in the context of administrative work assignments under the command of the occupation authorities (Kramer 1991, 71). Given the congestion of living space and the desolate state of the public heath infrastructure, it is not surprising that the war-shattered cities of Germany were ravaged

[24] StatBRD, Vol. 41 (1955), 12–13.

by mass epidemics. According to the report of the British military government on 20 August 1946, the spread of diphtheria, tuberculosis, and typhoid had reached alarming proportions (cited in Weimer 1998, 13). Conditions in the Soviet zone were even more appalling. In 1947, the number of deaths from tuberculosis per 10,000 inhabitants in East Germany was three times, in 1949 still twice, as high as it had been in 1938 in Germany as a whole (Schwarzer 1995, 127).

The manifestations of poverty and desperation were plentiful, but in the collective memory of the post-war generation, the late 1940s were associated with hunger above all else. Daily food rations were officially limited to 1,550 kilocalories that corresponded to one-half of per capita food consumption in Germany in 1936. Children, pregnant women, essential workers doing heavy manual labour, and patients with certain medical conditions were to receive complementary rations, but the actual provisions depended on harvest results and the willingness of the occupying powers to supplement the inadequate domestic production with expensive food imports. Despite the efforts that the Allied military governments had made from the start of the occupation to support agriculture, food shortages were increasingly acute owing to the continuing influx of refugees into the Western zones.[25] Foodstuffs of high nutritional value were particularly scarce. Bread and potatoes made up more than 80 per cent of the calorific content of the basic rations in the Bizonal Area over the course of 1947, meat and fish accounting for 5 per cent, and fats for only 4 per cent.[26] The supply of animal fat and protein was drastically reduced by the mass slaughter of hogs and poultry in the most critical months of 1945, further aggravated by the restrictions of the occupation authorities on the use of grains as fodder. In addition, farmers were particularly reluctant to deliver animal products at official prices, and thus black markets became the key suppliers of eggs, meat, and dairy.[27]

The nutritional situation became most alarming during the winter of 1946–7, when the monthly average day rations fell below 1,300 kilocalories in both the French and Soviet occupation zones. Although basic rations in Berlin were more generous than in the rest of the country, the food supply was typically tighter in urban than in rural counties. In the early months of each year until 1948, rations fell to 1,000 kilocalories in large cities and often to as little as 800 kilocalories in the Ruhr (Schwarzer 1995, 126). According to an official survey, in June 1947, scarcely more than a fifth of urban dwellers in the American zone

[25] OMGUS, *Food and agriculture*, No. 9, 2–3.
[26] Ibid., No. 32, 13–15.
[27] Ibid., No. 20, 2–3, 8–9.

found the availability of food sufficient, as opposed to almost two-thirds among those living in the countryside (cited in Bignon 2009, 4). Despite improved organisation and increased transport capacity, the food supply remained insufficient and erratic until the later months of 1948. Imports from the Soviet zone that the Western Allies had counted on were not forthcoming. East German agricultural output collapsed after the war and its recovery was retarded by both the lack of chemical fertilisers and the vastly reduced stock of farm machinery.[28]

Malnutrition had dire consequences for public health. Surveys conducted in April 1946 in cities under US occupation found that adults were significantly below the reference weights for their age groups.[29] Over the course of 1946, different cohorts of adults living in the American zone lost, on average, between 1.8 and 6.3 pounds in bodyweight, elderly men being the most affected.[30] During the following winter, authorities in Hamburg recorded more than 20,000 deaths due to hunger and frostbite (Schwarzer 1995, 127). In West Berlin, in the first quarter of 1947, the annual death rate exceeded the birth rate by 28.5 to 10.7 per 1,000 inhabitants and nearly doubled the national average.[31] The most desperate took illegal means of acquiring food and other basic supplies, especially after Cardinal Frings, the archbishop of Cologne, had promised salvation to those committing theft out of necessity in his emblematic 1946 New Year mass (Schröter 2000, 360). To avert a humanitarian catastrophe, the British and American authorities spent 1.5 billion dollars on food imports in the first three years of the occupation. This nearly equalled the total value of the Marshall Plan deliveries that the Western occupation zones subsequently received (Giersch, Paqué, and Schmieding 1992, 22). The need to supplement domestic food supplies in Germany forced the British government to maintain rationing at home for several years longer than it would otherwise have been necessary (Leaman 1988, 27).

Hunger spurred public discontent, culminating in the general strike of 3 February 1948 that brought 3 million to the streets. People did not work assiduously even when not out on strike. Industrial labourers spent typically four or five of their six weekly workdays in the factories. The rest of their time was devoted to foraging for food and other necessities for the survival of their families (Nicholls 1994, 128). In the largest cities, worker absenteeism was rampant. Every morning, urban dwellers packed

---

[28] Ibid., No. 2, 8.
[29] OMGUS, *Public health and medical affairs*, No. 10, 18.
[30] Ibid., No. 22, 1.
[31] Ibid., 11.

the trains and rushed to the countryside in quest of farmers willing to sell them food that would supplement their inadequate rations. Actual hours worked across twenty-five industries surveyed in the American zone averaged around forty per week both in September 1946 and in the same month of 1947, well short of the forty-eight-hour official work-week. Since the workers of bottleneck industries, especially coal miners, were given generous extra rations, many other less preferred sectors of the economy suffered from critical labour shortages, in spite of the over-all expansion of the labour force. Iron and steel, building materials, and the construction industry faced the most severe scarcity of manpower, partly because of their almost exclusive reliance on male labour, partly due to their concentration in large cities with inadequate housing.[32]

As often the case in the historiography written by men, the living con-ditions of women and children have long been an undeservedly over-looked aspect of the post-war humanitarian crisis. Not only were the consequences of the war and its aftermath particularly harsh on families; these consequences were often the most persistent. Roughly one-fourth of all children in post-war West Germany grew up without a father. In most cases, the fathers either died or went missing during the war, but the proportion of births out of wedlock also increased dramatically.[33] The share of incomplete families was highest in the cities and among the evacuees, expellees, and refugees. Families that could reunite after the war were not necessarily more fortunate, for they often had to wel-come home physically incapacitated or mentally damaged fathers and husbands. Many among the millions of men brutalised by the oppres-sions of war brought terror into their homes, making the lives of innu-merable women and children unbearable even through the years of economic prosperity that soon followed (Willenbacher 1988). Countless more lived in split families, in which the male breadwinners had to spend their workdays in faraway cities that could offer them jobs but no accom-modation for their dependants (Granicky and Müller 1950, 4).

Without doubt, the darkest memories haunted those who had seen hell on earth during the first months of 1945 in the eastern parts of the country overrun by the Red Army. Sheer vengeance and the blood-thirsty propaganda campaign spearheaded by the influential writer Ilja Ehrenburg invoked unbounded brutality in Soviet soldiers. Their offi-cers often explicitly ordered them to exercise revenge on the German

[32] OMGUS, *Manpower, trade unions and working conditions*, No. 32, 4 and 22. According to a confidential report of the Bizonal Economic Authority, throughout 1947, nearly 20 per cent of work hours were lost in the iron and steel industry of the British zone (ASE, *Statistical annual report 1947*, 50).
[33] See StatBRD, Vol. 35.9 (1956), 51–2.

population falling under their control. Hundreds of thousands of women, from young girls to their grandmothers, were savagely raped, often publically and often more than once, brutally tortured, and even murdered. Thousands died from sexually transmitted diseases or after illegal abortions of unwanted pregnancies carried out in primitive conditions. Many committed suicide, unable to carry on with the humiliation and the social stigma it implied. The Federal Ministry for the Expellees later estimated that, including the summary executions, between 75,000 and 100,000 civilians had perished from the Red Army rank and file running amok in the eastern provinces of the Reich in the first half of 1945 (Bundesministerium für Vertriebene 1954, 60E–65E). Those who survived their flight or deportation to West Germany were tormented by their experience for years to come and often until the end of their lives.

1.3   The Economics of Allied Occupation

In the immediate post-war years, the resurgence of industrial production in West Germany was not held back either by capacity shortages or by the supply of labour. It was retarded instead by infrastructural bottlenecks and institutional rigidities. The devastation of the transport and communications networks by the air war was the chief culprit in the sudden collapse of German industrial output from the second half of 1944. One-third of the 1.6 million tons of bombs that the Allies dropped over Germany during 1944 and the early months of 1945 hit the transport system and an additional 124,000 tons fell on seaports in the north.[34] The bombers destroyed most bridges. In the largest cities, water, electricity, and gas supplies had all but completely shut down by the end of the war; most radio transmitters were severely damaged. At the same time, the strategy pursued in the final phase of the bombing campaign enabled the occupying forces to remove the most critical bottlenecks with relatively little effort after the war. Their attacks had concentrated on damaging key points in the transport network and the energy-supply system, while most roads, railways, pipelines, cables, and transmitters, as well as most power stations, were left undamaged (USSBS 1945, 59–64, 82–4).

Traffic on the Rhine in the US occupation zone was reopened already at the end of August 1945.[35] Telegraph and telephone lines across the whole country were repaired until February 1946 (Settel 1947, 25–6).

---

[34] The calculations based on USSBS records were reported in Abelshauser (2004), 70.
[35] OMGUS, *Transport*, No. 2, 1.

42   The Audit of Defeat: Initial Conditions

All internal waterways had been cleared of rubble by April 1946 and
until the summer, the British and US military governments managed
to restore all railways and bridges in their occupation zones.[36] That
insufficient capacity in rail transport still remained the greatest impediment to industrial recovery for another year was due to the fact that the
rolling stock of the *Reichsbahn* was drastically reduced from its pre-war
level. By May 1945, 31 per cent of the transport wagons and 39 per
cent of the locomotives had been put out of use by war damage and
the neglect of repairs.[37] Restitutions and reparations aggravated these
losses. After industrial production in the British and American zones
had approached 40 per cent of the 1936 level during the fourth quarter
of 1946, the following winter brought the economy to its knees again.[38]
In record low temperatures, the frost blocked all the major internal
waterways on 20 December 1946. This meant that both passenger and
cargo transport had to move exclusively on the railways, which also
struggled to cope with the harsh conditions.[39] The outcome thereof
proved the worst in the northwest and along the Rhine, as coal could
not leave the pitheads in the Ruhr. The lack of fuel forced temporary
shutdowns in several industries, while the lack of heating coal, combined with the difficulty of transporting food to the cities, was largely
to blame for the urban health crisis described in the previous section
(Abelshauser 1983, 42).

The result was the sharp decline of industrial production in the British
and American zones between the last quarter of 1946 and the first quarter of 1947, as shown in figure 1.3. The occupying forces considered the
supply of coal to be the most important bottleneck of economic recovery
in the Western zones besides the food shortage.[40] Even though the number of miners employed in the Ruhr was 38 per cent higher in 1947 than
what it had been in 1936, coal production was still substantially below
the pre-war level due to poor productivity. The volume of coal extracted
per man-shift averaged 1.6 tons in 1936; ten years later it was scarcely
more than half thereof. The machinery of the coalmines was out of date
and their capacity was reduced by the neglect of repairs during the war.
The influx of unskilled labour mobilised by the British authorities from
the countryside damaged the morale that had already been diminished
by the extensive use of forced labour before 1945 as well as the dismal
living conditions and the politically motivated purge of the management
ranks thereafter (Roseman 1989, 100–1). However, the breakdown of

[36] OMGUS, *Industry*, No. 12, 2–3.
[37] OMGUS, *Transport*, No. 14, 26–7.
[38] OMGUS, *Industry*, No. 24, 10.
[39] OMGUS, *Transport*, No. 26, 2.
[40] See OMGUS, *Economic data on Potsdam Germany*, 37–8.

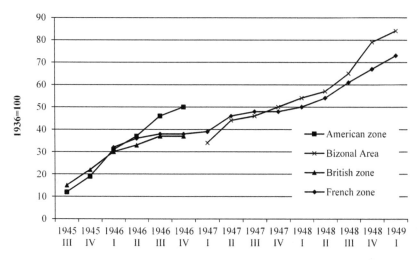

Figure 1.3 Indexes of net industrial production in the western occupation zones.
Source: Abelshauser (1983), Table 6, 34.

economic recovery during the winter of 1946 was not rooted in insufficient coal production. On the contrary, during the recession, between October 1946 and March 1947, coal extraction in the Ruhr increased by 24 per cent to 235,000 tons per day.[41] At the same time, stockpiles in the mining district jumped from 318,000 tons to 1.2 million tons. Not the lack of fuel but the lack of sufficient transport capacity thwarted the early revival of West German industry (Abelshauser 1983, 36).

Learning from the catastrophe of the winter crisis, the Allied military governments made the railways their top priority in the following year. Using the blueprint of the Speer ministry during the war, concentrated planning developed capacities in parallel in all industries that were essential for the production of railway equipment. By November 1947, the number of working locomotives was brought back to pre-war standards, and thus the Ruhr coalmines could run down their inventories almost fully until February 1948 (Abelshauser 1983, 43). Unlike that of coal mining and transport infrastructure, the reconstruction of the iron and steel industry was not among the initial objectives of the occupying powers. Metallurgical capacity was to be reduced in order to limit Germany's ability to wage war (Settel 1947, 8). In reality, the administrative restrictions made little practical impact. Until late 1948, steel

[41] OMGUS, *Industry*, No. 24, 14.

output never even came close to the 5.8 million ton annual quota set for the British zone in 1946, let alone the upward revised ceiling of 10.7 million tons for the Bizonal Area in 1947.[42] Instead, the recovery of the steel industry was held back by chronic shortages of raw materials, both iron ore and steel alloys. Before the war, two-thirds of the iron ore processed in Germany had been imported from Sweden. With stringent foreign-exchange controls in force, the occupation authorities prohibited all ore imports until 1948. As West German steel producers had to shift to lower quality domestic iron deposits, their production became more fuel intensive (Kramer 1991, 101–2). Since coal supplies were insufficient until late 1947, output in primary metals and steel products, including machinery, remained the lowest relative to available capacity among all industries in the Anglo-American zones.[43]

The division of Germany itself obstructed the rebuilding of the German economy. The unrestricted domestic transfer of goods and services was replaced after 1945 by complicated transactions akin to trade deals between nations. As relations among the former Allied powers deteriorated trade between the eastern and western parts of the country became difficult to revive. Although the disruptions in inter-zone trade were relatively less harmful for West German industry than for its counterpart east of the Elbe, as Chapter 3 will demonstrate, the input–output bottlenecks that it had created limited the growth of industrial production until the early 1950s. If there had not been enough obstacles to economic recovery, the Allied occupation imposed even more serious restrictions on external trade, which all but collapsed after 1945. While the industrial output of the Bizonal Area reached 40 per cent of the 1936 level in third quarter of 1947, industrial exports were still negligible. In 1947, West German exports totalled 315 million dollars, approximately 5 per cent of German exports in 1936 (Lindlar 1997, 233). Thirty years later, three work hours would have sufficed to generate the corresponding value of sales abroad (Weimer 1998, 22–3). The post-war settlement with Germany made the swift restoration of West German exports impossible. The country was deprived of its merchant fleet; the foreign assets of German companies as well as German patents, trademarks, and overseas investments worth billions of dollars were expropriated by the Allied powers. Later chapters discuss the role of exports and industrial restructuring in the resurgence of West German industry. In

[42] See OMGUS, *Economic data on Potsdam Germany*, 39.
[43] OMGUS, *Industry*, No. 12, 1, 8; Ibid., No. 24, 20.

the late 1940s, imports, particularly imports of food and industrial raw materials, were the more crucial limiting factor of economic recovery.

Even though this was not the stated objective of the occupying powers, they effectively sabotaged West German trade with the outside world until 1949. Under the occupation statuses, international trade was the monopoly of the Joint Export–Import Agency (JEIA) in the Bizonal Area and of the *Office du Commerce Extérieur* in the French zone. Their centralised bureaucracies prevented the restoration of pre-existing trade links between German companies and their partners abroad (Braun 1990, 156). The regulatory framework of West German foreign trade during the occupation that the Allied Control Authority determined in September 1945 imposed three damaging constraints on the West German economy (Buchheim 1990, 1).

1. The volume of imports was limited to the requirements of maintaining consumption at subsistence level in each of the occupation zones.
2. Importers of German goods abroad could purchase West German exports only in US dollars or other currencies accepted by the Allied Control Authority.
3. The export revenue generated in each occupation zone was used, in principle, to finance its own imports. Trade surpluses could be redistributed between the different zones only with the special permission of the Allied Control Authority.

Although these regulations were designed to be temporary, they remained in force practically until 1949 as the Western Allies were unable to come to an agreement with the Soviet Union over the economic future of Germany. The main objective of the 'dollar clause' was to allow West German producers and consumers to access the cheapest sources of imports using the hard currency earned from exports. Since most Western European currencies were significantly overvalued against the US dollar, imports from continental markets were not competitive. However, the dollar clause also limited the demand for West German exports in neighbouring countries, as they were equally short of hard currency reserves. This led to the dramatic, albeit temporary, distortion of pre-existing trade patterns. Before the war, 10 per cent of German industrial exports consisted of raw materials, 13 per cent of intermediary products, and 77 per cent of finished goods. The corresponding shares in 1947 were 64, 25, and 11 per cent respectively (Buchheim 1990, 24–5).

Besides the rigid regulatory regime, the other major force behind this transformation were the efforts of the Inter-Allied Reparation Agency

(IARA), established by the Paris Agreement on Reparations in January 1946, to extract forced exports of coal, coke, and primary metals from West Germany at below world market prices.[44] Between May 1945 and September 1947, Ruhr coal was exported at 10.5 dollars per ton, while international prices fluctuated between 25 and 30 dollars. The losses thus incurred by German exporters until the end of 1947 were estimated at 200 million dollars. One author labelled the forced exports of fuels and electrical energy 'reparations in disguise', as they became an integral, even if not official, component of the post-war reparations regime (Abelshauser 1983, 30–2). Without sufficient export revenue, West Germany could not pay for the food imports required to feed her starving population and the raw materials necessary to kick-start industrial production. Two-thirds of West German imports between 1945 and 1948 were paid for by the occupying authorities, hence effectively by British and American taxpayers (Kramer 1991, 109–10), even though developing a German economy that could be sustained without substantial foreign assistance was a key objective of the JEIA (Spaudling 1997, 300).

Limited access to imports was not the only major institutional obstacle to economic recovery. The misallocation of resources was equally prevalent within the country and even at the regional level as markets had become restricted and dysfunctional. Economists were concerned that after the war, the supply of industrial firms with raw materials and intermediate inputs would run into serious bottlenecks. In reality, manufacturers had begun to stockpile vast input and fuel reserves from the early months of 1945.[45] By the end of 1947, input inventories were often large enough to secure production for an entire year and would have allowed for much higher levels of output in most industries than anything achieved prior to the currency reform in June 1948 (Buchheim 1990, 55–6). What limited the growth of industrial production and the effective use of productive capacity was not the scarcity but the misallocation of available resources. West Germany under Allied occupation was essentially a shortage economy. Kornai (1980) described such an economy with excessive inventories of inputs and finished goods vital for firms to be able to respond to bottlenecks periodically arising from insufficient marketing. The accumulation of inventories, in turn, limits the volume of raw materials and intermediary products sold on the market, which creates new or aggravates already existing production bottlenecks, motivating firms to stockpile even larger inventories.

---

[44] On the history of the IARA and of the reparations claims filed by its member states, see Buxbaum (2013).
[45] OMGUS, *Industry*, No. 12, 5, 37.

Most of the existing studies found the root causes for the dysfunction of input markets in post-war Germany in the war years and, in particular, in the monetary conditions that war financing had left behind (see Spoerer and Streb 2013, 210–11). In the Nazi economy, monetary policy was subordinated to military objectives and the need to expand armaments production. Its sole purpose was to secure the liquidity required for the financing of the war effort. As defence expenditure had increased by a factor of 23 and government spending in total quadrupled between 1933 and 1939, increased taxation alone could not keep the budget in balance (Ambrosius 2000, 338–40). As in the case of other major military powers, the swelling deficit was financed predominantly through borrowing (see Boelcke 1975). From 1938, the expansion of government debt hugely outstripped the growth of national income and even the growth of military spending. Between 1939 and 1943, total expenditure on the armed forces increased by 160 per cent, while the cost of debt service grew nearly ninefold. According to official budgetary statistics, public borrowing covered more than half of military spending during the war (Hansmeyer and Caesar 1976, 401). Savings banks (*Sparkassen*) were the most important sources of credit. By 1944, their deposits had grown to 123 billion marks, while the external debt of the Third Reich amounted to 119 billion marks (Boelcke 1993, 98–114).

The international literature attributed great importance to the exploitation of occupied lands in German war financing (see among others Ránki 1993; Eichholtz 1997; and Overy 1994, 1997). Recent scholarship has shown the expansion of domestic public debt to be more significant (Spoerer and Streb 2013, 204–6), even though Germany managed to fund more than one-third of its war effort with the resources of occupied countries, including the value obtained from the employment of their labour (Klemann and Kudryashov 2012, 367). The third principal source of public finance, especially in the final phase of the war, was the printing press. Between 1932 and 1945, money in circulation increased from less than 6 billion to 73 billion marks, and most of this growth took place after 1938, as Figure 1.4 demonstrates. Over the same period, the nominal value of bank deposits grew eightfold. The value of coins and banknotes per head of the population was almost ten times larger in 1945 than what it had been before the Nazis came to power (Boelcke 1993, 113). The money supply increased further with the 12 billion marks worth of new banknotes issued by the Allies during the first ten months of the occupation. The velocity of money was relatively high owing to the pent-up demand for consumer goods and unwillingness of cash earners to keep their savings in marks (Leaman 1988, 27–8). As long as real output was only a fraction of pre-war levels, the astronomic

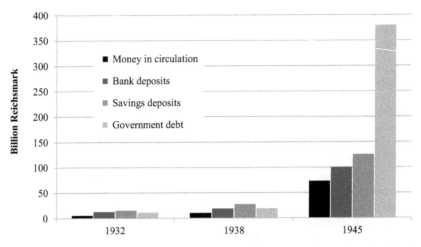

Figure 1.4 The growth of money supply and sovereign debt in Nazi Germany.
Source: Abelshauser (1983), Table 7, 46.

expansion of liquidity represented the danger of hyperinflation. To avoid the repeat of 1923, the Allies kept inflationary pressures under check by retaining the wartime system of price and wage controls. However, in the presence of surplus liquidity, money had lost most of its primary functions. Investors had no incentive to store their wealth in the banks and firms were increasingly unwilling to sell their products at official prices (Buchheim 1990, 394).

Effectively two economies operated side-by-side with one another. Within the official economy, the limited number of transactions took place on the basis of bureaucratically determined quotas and rations at artificial prices. The excess demand for consumer goods brought to life the other economy of grey and black markets with more or less free-market prices (Kramer 1991, 125). The discrepancy between official and real market prices was astounding and led to absurdly distorted terms of trade in the economy. Whereas the monthly average day rations of basic foodstuffs and other necessities were valued at less than 10 marks, consumers had to pay 40 marks for one cigarette and often as much as 3,000 marks for a radio on the black market (Weimer 1998, 31). The extent of excess liquidity is reflected in the fact that black market exchanges accounted for only 10 per cent of domestic trade but represented about 80 per cent of consumer spending (Owen Smith 1994, 16). Monthly reports of the US military governor reveal that illegal exchanges of foodstuffs accounted for 20 per cent of all trades. Six months later, this ratio increased to 50 per cent for certain goods (cited in Bignon 2009, 5). As money was worthless, on illegal markets, American cigarettes and food rations became the most valuable mediums of exchange (Spoerer and Streb 2013, 211).

Black markets were widespread already in the early post-war months. In the US occupation zone, farmers refused to deliver food to the rationing system, even when armed soldiers accompanied the German officers.[46] The withholding of food from the official markets was the prime motive for urban dwellers to go foraging for food in the countryside. Illegal markets also emerged in large cities and near the train station of almost every town. Farmers were not only unwilling to accept official prices; most of them also insisted on being paid in kind. Thus workers or traders from the city travelled to the countryside with some valuables in hand and searched for farmers willing to buy these items. The need to find suitable partners meant that this type of trade incurred very high transaction costs. Even if buyers had access to information about local sellers, search costs were still substantial in the absence of money. Thus cigarettes gradually emerged as commodity money, universally accepted in post-war Germany as a means of payment. The use of cigarettes as money had become so widespread that in May 1947 the US Army prohibited the free import of tobacco by its members and appealed to the general public for co-operation (Bignon 2009, 9–17).

Official prices reflected real market values only for new products, whose prices were fixed after 1945. The presence of both pre-war and post-war prices for different types of manufactures severely distorted the structure of industrial production. While basic industries had little incentive to increase output, firms selling consumer articles that were seen as luxury items in these harsh times and that were rationed throughout the war were remarkably dynamic. Glass products, chinaware, and entertainment instruments recorded the fastest employment growth of all industries in the American zone between 1946 and 1948.[47] While the consumption of these luxuries absorbed a substantial part of national income, the insufficient supply of raw materials and intermediate inputs created bottlenecks in several industries, in building materials and construction above all else, delaying urban reconstruction and thus holding back economic recovery.[48]

Illegal transactions were equally present on producer markets. Despite regulations prohibiting barter trade between companies in place, compensation deals became increasingly widespread and by early 1948 accounted

---

[46] The problem was already highlighted in the first confidential reports of the US Military Governor (OMGUS, *Food and Agriculture*, No. 2, 6).
[47] OMGUS, *Manpower, trade unions and working conditions*, No. 32,   30.
[48] OMGUS, *Industry*, No. 24, 28–9.

for more than half of all transactions between industrial enterprises. This is another typical means by which firms operate in the shortage economy. Bartering with other companies allows them to supplement their own inventories of input materials. For this purpose, however, firms also had to keep large stocks of their own products that could serve as inputs for others. Furthermore, inventories of finished goods, especially processed foods and other consumer necessities, were vital to create incentives for workers by supplementing their money wages with provisions in kind. In 1948, industrial enterprises spent one-sixth of their revenue on such provisions (Kramer 1991, 125). To manage their compensation deals, large firms had to establish complex barter networks, which was enormously time consuming and increased transaction costs (Buchheim 1989, 395).

In the prevailing monetary environment, the banking system could not fulfil its functions of allocating capital and disseminating information. In the absence of effective financial intermediation, new temporary institutions were required to manage financial transactions between firms, which increased transaction costs further, but could not allocate savings as efficiently as well functioning banks do (Klump 1989, 409–14). The lack of real market prices and the collapse of the banking system also increased information asymmetries and thus undermined the rational expectations of investors. With few incentives to invest and without the institutions capable of concentrating savings, bottleneck industries could not expand their capacities, nor could they carry out substantial repairs on rundown and damaged equipment. Investment decisions did not depend on profit expectations and access to credit. Instead, they were determined by the ability of enterprises to acquire scarce raw materials and intermediate inputs. The rationing system gave priority to bottleneck industries and exporting firms, and their ability to retain their premiums hinged on them meeting their output and export targets. As their production could run into input shortages at any time, maintaining inventories was particularly important for firms in these high-priority industries.

According to Buchheim, it was the inconsistency between existing institutions and the policies of the military governments more than the direct consequences of the war that crippled the West German economy after 1945. The rationing of consumer goods and industrial inputs as well as fixed prices and wages were incompatible with the adherence to the market economy. Firms had no real incentives to increase production beyond levels necessary to secure key raw materials, especially imports, and to retain their skilled workforce. Instead of producing for the market, they turned to compensation deals that required excessive inventories and increased transaction costs (Buchheim 1991, 61–2). However, historians also recognised the influence that expectations about future economic reforms made on the behaviour of private firms in the early post-war years. Businesses were well aware of the intentions of Allied governments to reform the monetary system, which were strongly supported by German experts. The main obstacle for the currency reform they envisaged was that the Soviet government opposed the extension of the reform to the whole of Germany, which the US administration continued to prefer until early 1948 (Roeper and Weimer 1997, 20–1). The expectation that an effective financial system would soon emerge was perhaps the main motive for West German enterprises to survive by maintaining production and to retain their equipment, their core workforce, and their supplier network. The objective of preserving productive capacities far larger than what were put into effective use in the years after 1945 contributed significantly to the modest growth that the capital goods industries achieved already before the economic reforms of June 1948 (Buchheim 1990, 56–8).

At the same time, these expectations also held back production, especially production for the market, in the first half of 1948, as firms went into overdrive to acquire as much input materials as possible on the cheap before their prices would rise and to delay selling their own products until the introduction of the new currency. Under the conditions that prevailed in post-war Germany, such behaviour from firms was perfectly rational. Unlike in the Soviet occupation zone, the Western military governments did not guarantee the survival of firms with the exception of strategic enterprises that were often publicly owned, which meant that businesses had to remain liquid and profitable after the currency reform. Excessive inventories served this very purpose. On the one hand, they enabled firms to secure sufficient liquidity by bringing products to the market in large volumes once they were paid in a currency that had real value. On the other, they made the supply side of the economy more flexible, so that producers would not run into bottlenecks immediately after the reintroduction of free markets. All in all, the bureaucratic allocation of scarce resources, the flourishing of illegal markets, and the coexistence of excess liquidity with administratively fixed prices generated high transaction costs, low productivity, poor capacity utilisation, and abnormally high inventory–output ratios in an economy in which the inadequate supply of raw materials and intermediary inputs prevented faster recovery in the first place. The elimination of production bottlenecks and institutional inconsistencies were thus vital for the revival of West German industry. Both were soon accomplished with the economic reforms and new forms of international cooperation initiated in 1948, but they will be the subjects of later chapters.

2   The Economic Geography of Post-War Dislocation

Chapter 1 gave an illustrative account of the economic conditions that prevailed in West Germany after World War II and that defined the constraints of the post-war recovery. The bulk of the historiography shares the conviction that the German economy, industry in particular, was endowed with plentiful reserves of labour and physical capital. Hence its resurrection was claimed to be conditional on the elimination of the transport bottlenecks, shortages of input materials, and institutional restrictions that obstructed effective market allocation. These impediments to economic revival did not seem to persist beyond the late 1940s. However, industrial output was still significantly below its pre-war peak, despite the greatly enhanced production capacities. In this chapter, I challenge the consensus view by emphasising that capacity utilisation within industry remained limited throughout the early 1950s. This was due to the geographic misallocation of complementary factor endowments, namely capital and labour, which had, in turn, resulted from the wartime destruction of urban housing and from insufficient reconstruction efforts in the late 1940s. The implication of the evidence presented henceforth is that the economic impact of war-induced dislocation persisted much longer than conventionally believed.

The historical evidence has shown that the industrial sector benefited from a powerful wartime boost to capital accumulation. By contrast, the economy as a whole underwent a very different transition. The gross value of fixed capital was 7 per cent smaller in 1950 than it had been before the war. Even though this contraction was due entirely to the destruction of residential housing and public infrastructure, the stock of machinery and equipment likewise did not increase between 1938 and 1950 (Gehrig 1961, cited in Eichengreen and Ritschl 2009, 197). Industry and transportation expanded at the expense of other sectors of the economy. Figure 2.1 reveals that residential construction and public building activity were squeezed out in the early 1940s by the hunger for investment in war-related production. From February 1940, the government prohibited all new civilian construction except for the workers' lodgings

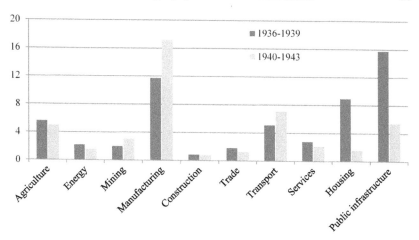

Figure 2.1 Gross fixed investment in the West German economy, 1936–1943 (billion 1954 DM).
Source: Kirner (1968), 100–2.

required by munitions manufacturers (Hafner 1994, 63). Agriculture and services had already been allocated insufficient resources under the Four Year Plan between 1936 and 1940, but subsequently their position deteriorated further. The accumulation of physical capital during the war was concentrated in the urban-industrial sector, while the endowments for the rural economy became substantially smaller.

The opposite geographical pattern confronts us in labour allocation. For the economy as a whole, the expansion of the labour force outpaced the growth of the capital stock. This observation has led German economists, both at the time and since, to argue that the relative shortage of capital limited economic growth in West Germany during the early 1950s (Krengel 1962, 40–1; Paqué 1987, 11–17). The jump in the national unemployment rate from 5 per cent in July 1948 to 14 per cent in February 1950 seemed to confirm this view (Carlin 1989, 58–9). However, we can interpret mass unemployment as a symptom of capital shortage and of a corresponding labour surplus, only if capacity utilisation remained at normal levels. Within mining and manufacturing, such levels did not prevail. The utilisation rate in West German industry averaged 55.6 per cent in the second half of 1948, 66.8 per cent in 1949, and 79 per cent in 1950 (Krengel 1960, 81). The only remaining physical constraint on capacity utilisation that persisted into the early 1950s was an urban labour shortage, as evidenced by the regional dispersion of unemployment rates. Figure 2.2 reports a very strong relationship between the rate

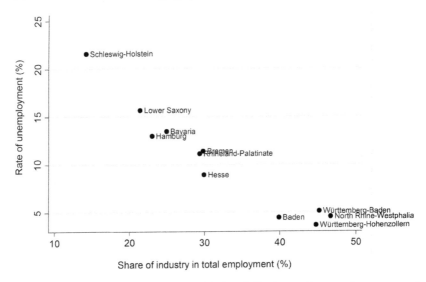

Figure 2.2 Regional levels of industrialisation and unemployment as of
30 December 1950.

Sources: Data on unemployment from Bundesministerium für Arbeit
(1951), 6; on total employment from Bundesministerium für Arbeit
(1955), 10–11; on industrial employment from IndBRD(1951), Part 1,
Vol. 1, (December), 5.

of unemployment and the share of industry in total employment across
the West German federal states in December 1950.

Highly industrialised North Rhine-Westphalia and the three states
that were later unified as Baden-Württemberg all reported unemployment below 5 per cent. By contrast, 21.6 and 15.6 per cent of the labour
force was out of work in predominantly agrarian Schleswig-Holstein
and Lower Saxony respectively. A simple regression of the unemployment rate on the share of industry in total employment generates coefficients of –0.5 for the explanatory variable and 26 for the intercept. These
results predict that in a region where half of all employees were active
in mining and manufacturing only 1 per cent of the labour force would
have been left without work. This statistical evidence suggests that the
supply of labour was inflexible in the Ruhr and other major industrial
agglomerations. The most dynamic industries may have faced a critical
labour shortage. The existence of surplus capacity and labour scarcity
in urban manufacturing in parallel with mass unemployment in the
countryside confirms the presence of geographic dislocation in the West
German economy. This phenomenon persisted for many years, long after

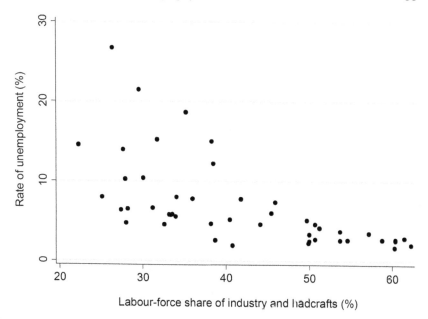

Figure 2.3 The rate of unemployment and industrialisation in large cities as of 13 September 1950.
Source: Eicher (1952), 61–6.

the raw-material shortages and transport bottlenecks had been overcome and the Allied control restrictions had been lifted.

We can obtain even more direct evidence for this argument from employment statistics collected for large cities specifically. In December 1950, the registered unemployed accounted for 3.9 per cent of the total urban population, including West Berlin. The corresponding number was much higher in the former imperial capital and in the main northern seaports of Bremen, Hamburg, Kiel, and Lübeck. By contrast, the population share of the unemployed was less than half, often less than one-third, of the national average in the most prominent industrial cities in the Ruhr, including Bochum, Duisburg, Düsseldorf, Essen, and Gelsenkirchen, and in the southwest, such as in Stuttgart, Mannheim, and Ludwigshafen (Becker 1951, 71, 81). The scatter diagram in Figure 2.3 demonstrates full employment in the most highly industrialised cities with a population of more than 100,000.[1] By contrast, large

---

[1] Both the rate of unemployment and the rate of industrialisation are defined slightly differently in the sources from which the data for Figures 2.2 and 2.3 were obtained; hence the moderate inconsistency in the exact levels of both indicators.

cities with a primarily commercial profile reported notably higher rates of unemployment and, in addition, much larger variation in joblessness. The old Hansa cities that had long specialised in shipbuilding and overseas trade, and thus suffered from the administrative restrictions of production still in place in 1950, all recorded much higher unemployment rates than inland regional trade centres such as Munich, Frankfurt, and Nuremberg.

The urban housing shortage was the last remaining obstacle to the optimal allocation of labour in the industrial sector. It was the legacy of the wartime devastation of residential buildings. Consequently, even though the West German population expanded dramatically during the 1940s, the number of citizens who lived in the largest cities fell considerably. By contrast, villages and small towns were overpopulated and reported high rates of unemployment. Labour scarcity in industrial cities coexisted with rural capital shortage. In a well-functioning economy, factor markets would have cleared such imbalances, but the urban housing deficit was far too great to surmount without extensive state intervention, and that could be put in place only after the establishment of a sovereign West German government. From another perspective, these conditions also laid the foundations for the growth miracle of the 1950s, for this revival was propelled by improved regional factor allocation, not by capital accumulation per se. In this way, wartime dislocation made a lasting impact on the development of the West German economy.

2.1   The Urban Housing Shortage and Its Consequences

There is an extensive literature on the miserable housing conditions of the early post-war years. On 17 May 1939, cities and towns with more than 20,000 inhabitants in the western part of Germany and West Berlin had almost 6 million dwellings. Data from the 1946 population census published by the Deutscher Städtetag demonstrate that more than 40 per cent of this housing stock was destroyed during the war. As shown in Table 2.1, large cities suffered proportionately the biggest losses. In sheer numbers, the greatest damage was recorded in Berlin, Hamburg, and Cologne, where together almost 1 million dwellings were destroyed (Kästner 1949, 369). Close to half of this destruction concentrated in the Rhine-Ruhr agglomeration, which had accounted for 37 per cent of urban housing before the war (Steinberg 1991, 51–4). Seventy per cent of homes in Cologne were demolished; several other cities in North Rhine-Westphalia recorded similar losses. A handful of towns had almost completely vanished from the face of Earth. The war left 95.6 per cent of

Table 2.1 *The wartime destruction of urban housing in West Germany*

In cities with a population of	Inhabitants	Housing stock	Dwellings destroyed	In % of 1939 housing stock
	17 May 1939			
More than 100,000	10,844,310	3,265,951	1,481,267	45.4
50,000–99,999	2,170,244	621,329	175,074	28.2
20,000–49,999	1,456,243	399,164	65,989	16.5
Free cities [a]	5,025,286	1,666,843	693,489	41.6
All cities [b]	19,496,086	5,953,287	2,240,264	40.6

[a] Bremen with Bremerhaven, Hamburg, and West Berlin.
[b] Including West Berlin.
Source: Calculation based on data from Kästner (1949), 374–9.

the pre-war housing stock in Paderborn and 99.2 per cent in Düren in ruins (Kästner 1949, 380–91).

In severely damaged buildings, most of the furniture and household appliances were also destroyed (Steinberg 1991, 51–4). Land-tax returns provide an additional indicator of the magnitude of urban housing destruction. Returns, adjusted for changes in the tax rate, declined by 38 per cent between 1938 and 1946. Large cities recorded, on average, an almost 45 per cent contraction. In some of the pivotal economic centres of the country, including Cologne and Frankfurt, the respective figures were higher than 55 per cent. Middle-sized cities, Würzburg and Darmstadt among others, recorded even higher rates (Kästner 1949, 371–2). Although my quantitative work has focussed on the destruction of urban housing in West Germany, the consequences of strategic bombing were equally harsh east of the Elbe. Berlin, throughout the war, was the highest priority target of the Allied air forces alongside Hamburg. Other major eastern cities were hit during the last months of the war, when the precision and destructive power of aerial bombardment were the highest. Of the approximately 80 million pieces of the most commonly used firebombs produced in Britain, 650,000 were dropped on Dresden over a single night in February 1945 (Friedrich 2002, 27).

The post-war housing shortage further aggravated the deficit from the late 1930s, when building capacity had concentrated on projects deemed necessary for war preparations. The years of hostility that followed brought civilian construction to a virtual standstill. As a result of sluggish building activity and wartime destruction, the number of urban dwellings in West Germany fell 4.3 million short of the estimated housing requirements in mid-1945. In the years that followed, reconstruction activity could not keep pace with growing demand, due to shortages in building materials and skilled labour (Hafner 1994, 99–100). Even by the end of 1949, construction firms operated at less than half of their capacity. The construction index reached its 1936 level, which by itself did not represent the highest standard, only towards the end of 1949.[2] The staggering volume of debris that still clogged the urban landscape also obstructed the building effort. By December 1949 most small towns and many medium-sized cities had completed the task of removing all the rubble left amid the buildings and other infrastructure demolished during the war. By contrast, according to the Deutscher Städtetag, the removal rate was only 11 per cent in Hamburg; 12 per cent in Essen; and less than 20 per cent in Cologne, Düsseldorf, Frankfurt, and Nuremberg (Gabriel 1950, 435–6). Furthermore, reconstruction work was held up by the main outcome of the urban housing shortage: the urban labour scarcity. Small towns and rural communities could mobilise idle workers to remove rubble; many of the largest cities could not. Consequently, cities with more than 100,000 inhabitants recovered only 82.4 per cent of their pre-war population by September 1950 (Steinberg 1991, 161–6).

According to official figures, until the end of 1949, almost 1 million dwellings had been restored or newly erected.[3] In the meantime, however, 2.3 million additional flats were needed to accommodate the inflow of expellees and refugees from East Germany, and the new households established after 1945 demanded 1.2 million more. Furthermore, a vast number of buildings had suffered minor damage during the war, and their renovation, albeit not urgent, was inevitably going to divert resources away from new construction. Different estimates, including or excluding West Berlin, put the total housing shortage in West Germany in 1950 between 4.2 million and 5.9 million dwellings (Arndt 1955, 11; Schulz 1994, 39–40). Given that the stock of regular housing in September 1950 totalled 9.4 million dwellings (10.1 million including West Berlin), the deficit amounted to at least one-third of the required facilities.[4]

Accommodation was not only in short supply but often of inferior quality as well, as the housing stock had become older. According to the 1950 housing census, two-thirds of the 5.25 million residential buildings in West Germany were built before 1918 and another 29 per cent during the interwar period; only 6 per cent were constructed during the 1940s.[5] Available housing was more crowded than ever, not least due to the mandatory accommodation (*Einquartierung*) of evacuees and, later,

[2] Federal Ministry for the Marshall Plan (1953), 72.
[3] StatBRD, Vol. 39 (1955), 12.
[4] StatBRD, Vol. 40 (1955), 7.
[5] Ibid., Vol. 39 (1955), 11.

of expellees. Between 1927 and 1950, the number of residents per 100 rooms increased from 98 to 117.[6] In September 1950, emergency housing still made up one-fifth of all the residential buildings in Hamburg and West Berlin.[7] These accommodated, on average, 179 people in 100 rooms. Since available urban housing did not suffice even for the indigenous West German population, the millions of expellees and refugees arriving in the country found shelter initially in villages and small towns. Many did not find accommodation of any sort. Even as late as January 1953, more than 300,000 people lived in refugee camps.[8]

Without access to an urban residence, it was difficult to find jobs, as the major cities with surplus industrial capacity were often too far for the rural unemployed to reach by daily commuting. Most expellees were settled in the predominantly agrarian states of Schleswig-Holstein, Lower Saxony, and Bavaria and, consequently, were strongly under-represented in heavily industrialised North Rhine-Westphalia, as well as in Hamburg and Bremen. As explained in Chapter 1, regions that were under French occupation until 1949 – the Rhineland-Palatinate, South Baden, Württemberg-Hohenzollern, and Lindau – did not share the demographic expansion that characterised the rest of the country. The regional settlement pattern of German expellees severely limited their otherwise exceptional occupational mobility. They were thus particularly affected by mass unemployment that emerged precisely because labour and capital were geographically misallocated. In December 1950, the national unemployment rate among expellees (16.1 per cent) was nearly twice as high as for the rest of the population (9.2 per cent), and this ratio remained stable until the mid-1950s.[9]

Urban labour scarcity coexisted with rural unemployment and, therefore, industrial establishments in different parts of the country faced fundamentally different labour-supply conditions. Coal extraction in the Ruhr basin could be maintained, at first, only by the continuing employment of former forced labourers at exceptionally generous wages (Steiner 1995, 566). Once foreign miners returned home and the demand for coal skyrocketed following the outbreak of the Korean War, Transylvanian expellees originally deported to Austria were brought to the region as migrant workers under the so-called 'Coal Action' in 1953. There was no alternative, despite the still substantial unemployment in the country, given the absence of suitable accommodation in

[6] StatBRD, Vol. 41 (1955), 7.
[7] Ibid., Vol. 39 (1955), 8.
[8] Ibid., Vol. 114 (1955), 9–10, 65.
[9] Calculations based on data from Bundesministerium für Arbeit (1951), 5–6, and StatBRD, Vol. 114 (1955), 4–19, 82.

nearby cities that could have offered permanent residence for families (Beer 2000, 225). Total employment in the primary metals and metal processing industries in West Germany was virtually the same in 1950 as it had been in 1939. However, the aggregate figures disguised a 21 per cent decline in large factories and a corresponding 31 per cent increase in small and medium-sized establishments, many of which were based in rural towns.[10] The growth of urban industry suffered a severe setback, despite robust labour-force growth at the national level.

Regional labour scarcity was not the only constraint on capacity utilisation in West German industry. Input shortages and transport bottlenecks were undoubtedly present during the early post-war years, but they had been largely overcome by 1950. Contemporary views positing that German manufacturers still faced shortages of energy and intermediate inputs after 1950 cannot be substantiated.[11] Whereas the occupation authorities prioritised the rebuilding of the transport and energy-supply networks after 1945, they did not encourage the revival of industrial production to the same extent. Manufacturing output was still below the 1938 level in 1950; by then electrical power generation had already surpassed its pre-war peak by 50 per cent. Although coal mining had still not fully recovered, it was traditionally export oriented. Almost 30 per cent of the allegedly insufficient hard coal extracted in 1950 was sold abroad. In subsequent years, coal production grew at much more modest rates than manufacturing; still, the remarkable resurrection of West German industry was not held back by coal shortages. Similarly, the metal processing industries received adequate supplies of steel and light metals; otherwise, they could not have grown nearly twice as fast as the metallurgical sector, as will be shown in Chapter 3.

Furthermore, as I explain in the rest of this chapter, employment contraction in urban industry before 1950 was more than offset by the expansion of rural industry and handcraft manufacturers. It is not credible to claim that shortfalls in input materials limited the utilisation of existing capacities only in urban areas but not in the countryside. Large firms in cities most probably had easier access to imported inputs than scattered rural workshops did. By the early 1950s, the war-induced urban housing shortage was the only remaining physical constraint that prevented West German industry from fully exploiting its productive

---

[10] Calculations based on data from StatBRD, Vol. 47.1 (1956), 98–9.

[11] In January 1952, the Bundestag passed the Investment Aid Act (*Investitionshilfegesetz*) that obliged manufacturers of consumer goods to support new investment in coal mining, electrical power generation, water supplies, iron and steel, and the German Federal Railway in the order of 1 billion DM (Abelshauser 2004, 165–6). See the further discussion in Chapter 5.

potential. It was also the only factor that could explain the persistence of a dual labour market, characterised by labour scarcity in the urban and by labour surplus in the rural economy, particularly given that demand for manufactures was booming in both domestic and external markets and that West German firms continued to pay relatively modest wages by international comparison.

2.2 Data on Regional Economic Development

The present chapter investigates the geographical dislocation of productive forces in West German industry, based on a regional dataset that accounts for the resident population, employment in industry and handcrafts, the number of expellees, the stock of normal housing, and the gross output of local economies. I compiled data at the county (*Kreis*) level, using official sources from the census years of 1939, 1950, and 1961 and from 1956, when national surveys were carried out on all the socioeconomic indicators relevant for this chapter. In the 1950s, the Federal Republic consisted of 9 federal states, excluding West Berlin, 36 administrative districts (*Regierungsbezirk* or *Verwaltungsbezirk*), and 558 counties. Of the latter, 140 were independent cities and 418 rural counties.[12] The three smallest states, Bremen, Hamburg, and Schleswig-Holstein, formed one administrative district each, while the remaining states were composed of several districts. The disaggregated evidence presented in Tables 2.2 and 2.3 is reported at the state or district level, but the aggregate figures for the urban and rural economy in Tables 2.4 and 2.5 have been computed from the county-level data.

The German system of local governance enables us to compare the development of urban and predominantly rural areas. This approach is critical if we wish to determine to what extent the wartime destruction of housing created fundamentally different conditions in the urban and the rural economy and what role geography played in post-war recovery. Since the only previous quantitative investigation into the topic focussed exclusively on large cities, it overlooked these important differences (Brakman, Garretsen, and Schramm 2004). In order to achieve intertemporal consistency and to guarantee that the dataset is split along the urban-rural divide, I re-incorporated the 24 small country towns in Bavaria, which acquired independent status after 1945 into their former rural counties. This adjustment was essential to make the data

---

[12] This system of regional governance was achieved after Baden, Württemberg-Baden, and Württemberg-Hohenzollern were unified under the new federal state of Baden-Württemberg on 25 April 1952 and Lindau was incorporated into Bavaria.

comparable with pre-war statistics. The analysis treats West Berlin as a
separate unit that, during the 1950s, was not formally under the jurisdiction of the Federal Republic, and its post-war development reflected special circumstances. These revisions result in a dataset of 115 urban and
418 rural counties. Salzgitter and Wolfsburg, two cities that did not com-
prise independent urban counties before 1950, are included as urban
counties for the 1950s, but are treated as part of the surrounding rural
counties for the period 1939–50.

Population data at the county level are reported in the statistical
yearbooks. The 1956 yearbook also reports the share of expellees in the
total population.[13] For 1950, the number of expellees in each county
can be obtained from the published records of the population census, together with territorially consistent population figures for 1939
and 1946, adjusted for the minor changes in local district boundaries enacted until 1950.[14] From 1961, the annual population surveys
ceased to distinguish the expellees from the rest of the population at the
county level. The number of expellees published in the records of the
1961 population census is inconsistent with the corresponding figures
for 1950 and 1956 because it accounts only for citizens with identifi-
cation cards issued for expellees.[15] Thus, the share of expellees in the
resident population in 1961 can best be computed using population
data for December 1960.[16]

The stock of normal housing is reported in the censuses of September
1950 and June 1961 and in the federal housing survey of September
1956.[17] Unfortunately, no published census data are available on residential housing prior to 1950. Post-war surveys provide evidence for 1939
and 1945, but only for cities with a pre-war population of at least 20,000
(Kästner 1949, 374–9). This implies that we can measure the growth
of the housing stock during the 1940s directly for only urban counties.
Thankfully, the 1950 census recorded for each county the percentage of
the housing stock that had suffered substantial wartime damage, and this
measure provides a valid proxy for the scale of destruction.[18]

Employment data are reported in the industry statistics for the post-
war years.[19] German statisticians distinguish industrial plants from handcraft workshops with a crude method. Establishments that pursued some

[13] *Statistisches Jahrbuch* 1956, 34–9.
[14] StatBRD, Vol. 35.9 (1956), 99–109.
[15] Fachserie A, VZ 1961, Vol. 6 (1967), 66–79.
[16] Fachserie A/1 (1962), 32–42.
[17] StatBRD, Vol. 38.2 (1955), 34–56; Fachserie E (1961), 6–24; StatBRD, Vol. 201.1 (1957), 110–30.
[18] StatBRD, Vol. 38.2 (1955), 58–81.
[19] IndBRD, Series 4, No. 16 (1957), 4–24; Fachserie D/4 (1964), 4–201.

form of industrial activity with at least ten employees fall into the former category. Those with nine employees at most belong into the latter. This practice can yield excessive rates of employment growth for rural counties dominated by small firms. If a handcraft workshop with eight employees hired two additional workers, it turned into an industrial factory in the eyes of the record keepers, and hence employment in industry proper expanded by ten rather than by two in their statistics. Therefore, aggregate data for industry and handcrafts are more appropriate to use, especially because the only available source for 1939 does not report employment for the two types of establishments separately.[20] For 1950 and the following years, these aggregates can be established from the regional volumes of the 1950 and 1961 non-agricultural workplace censuses and from the published records of the 1956 handcraft census, combined with the aforementioned sources on industrial employment.[21] In order to compare pre-war and post-war regional data, 1939 levels are adjusted for the amendments in district boundaries that came into effect after 1945, using population figures for 1939 according to both 1939 and 1950 boundaries.[22] I also took account of differences in employment structure between the affected counties, as reported in the 1950 workplace census.[23]

No previous study ever reported comparable employment data at such level of disaggregation for the interwar and post-war periods. The results of my calculations are summarised for administrative districts in Table 2.2. Although industrial employment increased marginally between 1939 and 1950, it could not keep pace with population growth. Geographically, both variables developed in tandem across the war and the years of Allied occupation. This relationship weakened during the early 1950s, when industrial employment continued to expand even in regions that saw their population decline, although the economically most dynamic urban centres undoubtedly recorded the highest rates of population growth. In comparison, the late 1950s present geographically more balanced patterns of demographic and economic expansion.

A measure of local economic output, or a viable proxy thereof, is essential to account for regional variations in the impact of war-induced dislocation. Official sources do not report production below the state or provincial level. The best available proxy for gross output in counties is total turnover from the annual turnover-tax statistics that were published

[20] StatDR, Vol. 568.8–14 (1942–4).
[21] StatBRD, Vol. 46.1–7. (1953); StatBRD, Vol. 203.2. (1958); Fachserie C (1965).
[22] StatDR, Vol. 550. (1941); StatBRD, Vol. 35.9 (1956), 99–109.
[23] StatBRD, Vol. 46.1–7 (1953).

Table 2.2 *Population and industrial employment in West Germany and West Berlin (thousands)*

Administrative districts	Resident population				Employment in industry and handcrafts			
	1939	1950	1956	1961	1939	1950	1956	1961
Schleswig-Holstein	1,589	2,595	2,271	2,329	191	203	236	248
Hamburg	1,712	1,606	1,793	1,841	281	229	357	320
Bremen	563	559	649	712	117	87	122	129
Hannover	1,018	1,385	1,408	1,462	179	173	220	254
Hildesheim	625	1,018	952	947	100	125	147	157
Lüneburg	548	992	933	959	66	82	106	124
Stade	393	654	586	584	27	38	39	42
Osnabrück	516	681	686	715	68	82	99	106
Aurich	296	385	361	371	18	21	24	25
Braunschweig	567	872	851	859	90	115	138	153
Oldenburg	578	811	764	779	49	64	84	94
Düsseldorf	4,180	4,302	5,035	5,420	1,003	967	1,186	1,287
Cologne	1,596	1,669	1,940	2,154	277	277	352	441
Aachen	763	774	878	945	139	136	166	180
Münster	1,602	1,910	2,138	2,275	298	361	432	424
Detmold	1,114	1,500	1,556	1,617	233	257	318	335
Arnsberg	2,680	3,042	3,443	3,618	608	654	817	811
Darmstadt	1,050	1,340	1,446	1,569	191	206	243	302
Kassel	972	1,261	1,245	1,265	130	144	164	191
Wiesbaden	1,457	1,723	1,913	2,028	260	276	351	400
Koblenz	854	900	984	1,019	107	111	130	138
Trier	451	429	460	462	32	30	34	35
Montabaur	217	240	246	257	27	28	32	34
Rhine-Hesse	393	385	431	452	53	44	52	61
Palatinate	1,045	1,051	1,204	1,249	180	163	208	228
North Württemberg	1,942	2,435	2,789	3,070	441	507	708	797
North Baden	1,275	1,473	1,598	1,714	262	266	345	391
South Baden	1,230	1,339	1,531	1,642	209	213	260	302
South Württemberg	1,029	1,184	1,315	1,413	233	226	292	326
Upper Bavaria	1,935	2,456	2,581	2,793	274	315	384	445
Lower Bavaria	786	1,081	975	965	70	98	100	124
Upper Palatinate	686	897	874	895	81	101	114	131
Upper Franconia	808	1,116	1,080	1,090	171	203	222	243
Middle Franconia	1,077	1,284	1,323	1,387	220	218	276	301
Lower Franconia	844	1,038	1,048	1,097	127	125	153	179
Suabia	947	1,312	1,310	1,367	153	180	224	247
Federal Republic	**39,338**	**47,696**	**50,595**	**53,316**	**6,945**	**7,338**	**9,142**	**9,959**
West Berlin	2,750	2,147	2,204	2,189	436	244	343	427

Note: West Berlin was officially not under the jurisdiction of the Federal Republic.
Sources: See beginning of Section 2.2.

from 1950 onward. This source is useful as it lists actual turnover disaggregated across the main sectors of the economy.[24] Although such detailed figures do not exist for 1939, the 1938 tax records report revenue from the turnover tax in financial districts (*Finanzamtbezirk*), which, with a few exceptions, corresponded with the boundaries of local governance.[25] Necessary adjustments were made based on employment data and employment structure, as reported in the 1939 workplace census.

I computed total turnover for 1938 from total tax revenue and the average tax rates that I estimated for urban and rural counties separately within each federal state. This has been the most challenging and complicated task in constructing a complex dataset on local economies. Appendix 1 explains the exact procedure. Table 2.3 reports the results for administrative districts. I did not include an estimate for West Berlin in 1938 because, owing to the special status of the former capital under federal tax legislation, the pre-war and post-war figures reported in the official records are not comparable. The regional pattern is strikingly similar to the one we can observe for population growth and housing construction. Between 1938 and 1950, total turnover declined in Hamburg and Bremen, in the most heavily industrialised districts of North Rhine-Westphalia and in the French occupation zone, except in South Württemberg-Hohenzollern. Although the contraction was not substantial in most cases, we must remember that it had occurred despite five years of vigorous industrial expansion between 1938 and 1943. During the first half of the 1950s, precisely the same regions recorded the highest growth rates. Economic expansion was particularly robust in West Berlin; in the districts of Düsseldorf, Cologne, and Arnsberg; in the Rhineland-Palatinate; but also in heavily industrialised North Württemberg and North Baden, as well as Upper Bavaria. After 1956, we can observe a considerably more balanced regional pattern of economic growth.

Before we turn our attention to the geography of wartime dislocation and post-war reconstruction, it is important to discuss the substance of the turnover data in detail, with particular emphasis on their validity as a proxy for local output. The statistics represent turnover as defined by federal legislation. Imports of raw materials and intermediary products destined for further processing within Germany were excluded from this definition. The implication is that total turnover accounts for domestic production, which is precisely what we aim at measuring. Exports received exemption only for deliveries that did not follow direct sales,

---

[24] StatBRD, Vol. 112 (1955), 186–207; StatBRD, Vol. 212 (1958), 74–93; Fachserie L/7 (1963), 80–9.
[25] StatDR, Einzelshriften, No. 39 (1941), 310–24.

Table 2.3 *Total turnover in West Germany and West Berlin in million 1950 DM*

Administrative districts	1938	1950	1956	1961
Schleswig-Holstein	7,119	8,304	11,033	13,455
Hamburg	23,229	22,399	35,093	42,834
Bremen	7,317	6,733	9,690	10,641
Hannover	6,124	7,358	11,398	14,052
Hildesheim	2,789	3,568	4,734	5,681
Lüneburg	2,502	3,052	4,740	7,257
Stade	1,326	1,640	2,097	2,599
Osnabrück	2,046	2,732	3,975	4,905
Aurich	895	936	1,385	1,955
Braunschweig	3,988	3,507	5,331	6,903
Oldenburg	2,145	2,390	3,327	4,323
Düsseldorf	42,482	38,512	72,521	84,698
Cologne	11,914	10,638	19,788	24,314
Aachen	4,013	3,637	5,618	6,692
Münster	5,947	7,588	11,771	13,708
Detmold	6,079	6,377	10,374	13,513
Arnsberg	15,077	14,533	29,088	32,992
Darmstadt	4,426	4,495	7,850	11,128
Kassel	4,261	3,828	5,873	7,590
Wiesbaden	13,818	14,084	20,582	26,265
Koblenz	2,941	2,741	4,786	6,114
Trier	1,268	1,062	1,508	1,930
Montabaur	601	534	913	1,197
Rhine-Hesse	2,713	1,739	2,810	3,241
Palatinate	4,697	4,160	7,138	8,622
North Württemberg	12,831	14,075	24,359	33,640
North Baden	7,155	7,747	13,690	17,182
South Baden	5,505	5,102	8,515	11,342
South Württemberg	4,211	4,637	7,457	9,980
Upper Bavaria	10,644	10,993	18,179	26,512
Lower Bavaria	1,692	2,347	2,951	3,800
Upper Palatinate	1,997	2,209	3,134	3,845
Upper Franconia	3,273	4,133	5,611	6,837
Middle Franconia	5,949	6,017	10,343	11,701
Lower Franconia	3,066	3,002	4,892	6,388
Suabia	4,193	5,067	7,323	9,478
Federal Republic	**240,366**	**241,876**	**399,875**	**497,590**
West Berlin	—	8,403	16,269	18,772

Note: West Berlin was officially not under the jurisdiction of the Federal Republic.
Sources: See the previous page. For the detailed explanation of all the computations see Appendix 1.

such as the transfer of goods within a given firm to build up inventories abroad. Services that were not provided by enterprises and/or were not paid for were also excluded. Personal services were liable for income tax, not for turnover tax. Public utilities provided by state authorities for free and the services to the occupation forces were also exempt. In handcrafts and retail trade, production preserved for personal consumption was taxed, but investments were not.[26]

The statistics do not offer perfectly complete coverage of total turn-over even in the categories that fell under the relevant legislation. Annual turnovers under 1,000 DM in most sectors, under 2,000 DM in agriculture, and under 4,000 DM in wholesale trade were not recorded. These numbers, however, are relatively small for West German enterprises in the 1950s, especially in wholesale trade, and can only represent family farms or the smallest workshops. With the exemption of real-estate contracts, some forms of rent were also unrecorded in the statistics. In the transport sector, the turnover of communal tramlines and small urban transport companies was not reported, but that of the much more significant Federal Railways and the postal services was. Individual entrepreneurs in the liberal arts, or private brokers, who generated a turnover of less than 6,000 DM a year, were also granted exemption. However, these regulations had either no or no significant impact on the main sectors of the economy. The few exceptions were public utilities, shipbuilding, tax-free turnover generated in the free seaports or abroad, workshops in the clothing industry, private service providers with small turnovers, and small farms.[27]

Prior to the war, transportation with motor vehicles was freed from the duty to pay turnover tax, after the freight tax had been introduced in October 1936.[28] However, motorisation was still in its infancy in the 1930s and, therefore, this exemption did not significantly affect reported turnover. Between 1950 and 1961, federal legislation on the turnover tax was amended eleven times. Tax rates were raised proportionally in June 1951, but the coverage of the statistics remained unchanged. In February 1956, wholesale trade in dairy products was exempted, followed by direct sales in agriculture in April of the same year.[29] The latter had a significant impact on reported turnover levels in some rural counties from 1956 onwards, most typically in Bavaria, which may distort our view on the growth of economic activity in these regions. A string of amendments in 1961 granted exemption to all wholesale trade in foodstuffs and minerals

[26] StatBRD, Vol. 112 (1955), 10–12.
[27] Ibid., p. 12.
[28] StatDR, Einzelschriften, No. 39 (1941), 18.
[29] StatBRD, Vol. 212 (1958), 6.

as well as deliveries of dairy products at all levels of commerce. The case of foodstuffs in wholesale trade is not likely to have altered the regional distribution of taxed turnover, but the preferential treatment of minerals had much to account for the apparent decline of total turnover in mining districts, especially the Ruhr.[30] These changes, however, had no effect on reported turnover within industry and handcrafts, which I use as a proxy for regional output in the 1950s in the last section of this chapter. Total turnover is used to account for regional economic growth only between 1938 and 1950, as the pre-war data are not disaggregated by sector of origin.

Turnover is not a perfect proxy for regional output. It is expressed in values, and thus the estimated growth rates may differ as a result of divergence in the prices, not the volumes, of goods and services. Since I used only one price index, namely the GNP deflator, to adjust for all price changes, regional growth rates may disguise structural differences. Even in the computation of growth rates for turnover in industry and handcrafts, the composite producer price index leaves differences in price movements across branches of industry unaccounted for. To express industrial turnover in 1950 DM, I used the official producer price index for industry as a deflator (Statistisches Bundesamt 1973, 134–5).

Finally, it must be noted that companies were obliged to pay turnover tax in the counties where their office headquarters resided. In a few cases, these did not correspond to the actual production sites. Firms in agglomeration areas could move their headquarters from one city to another, if those had suffered wartime damage on a markedly different scale. Erlangen represents a special case: a small town largely unscathed by the horrors of war but located in the immediate vicinity of Nuremberg, a major commercial hub burnt to ashes by the Allied bombers. Hence, the little-known Bavarian town (where the celebrated father of the *Wirtschaftswunder*, Ludwig Erhard, began his career) recorded astronomical growth rates in total and particularly industrial turnover, both prior to and after 1950. By contrast, it had to endure severe contraction after 1956, once the housing stock of Nuremberg had been rebuilt (Keyser 1971, 187–97).

Overall, albeit not a direct measure of production, turnover provides a valid and the best available proxy for regional output. The data are highly disaggregated, largely consistent over time, and clearly defined in federal legislation. Potential shortcomings can be precisely determined, and are either not very significant or not relevant to the scope of this study. For a handful of counties, substantial biases may well occur, but they represent

---

[30] Fachserie L/7 (1963), 4–5.

special cases and hence can and shall be treated as outliers. Without an
adequate proxy for local output, we cannot explore the economic geography of wartime destruction and post-war reconstruction, which is the
main task of this chapter. The comparability of turnover figures for 1938
and 1950 is especially valuable for future research on the development of
the West German economy across World War II.

2.3   The Economic Impact of Wartime Destruction

Table 2.4 reports aggregate data for the urban and rural counties separately. Almost half of the urban housing stock suffered substantial wartime damage, which affected less than 14 per cent of rural dwellings.
As a result, the population of large and medium-sized cities declined by
2.4 million between 1939 and 1946, while rural counties had to accommodate 6.7 million additional residents. The link between the two indicators is the share of expellees in the total population, which was exactly
twice as high in rural counties as in the urban areas. Whereas both industrial employment and total turnover diminished by more than 8 per cent
in urban counties, the rural economy recorded quite remarkable growth
rates. These figures suggest that, in the late 1940s, the geography of
industrial expansion and economic growth was linked to demographic
shifts and, through that, to regional labour scarcity.

In order to confirm the wartime destruction of urban housing as the
leading cause of regional labour shortage, it is essential to explain the
vast regional differences in the scale of housing damage in the west of
Germany. This takes us directly to the strategic motives of the Allied
bombing campaign. Until early 1942, the Royal Air Force (RAF) targeted specific industrial sites critical for the German war effort: oil
refineries, aluminium plants, and factories manufacturing military aircraft. This strategy proved ineffective as long as German defences made
daytime precision raids dangerous, if not impossible. As I have already
noted in Chapter 1, the USSBS reports gave no indication that war production until 1943 would have been higher in the absence of strategic
bombing. The Area Bombing Directive, issued in March 1942, made
city centres the focus of the air offensive. The essence of the new strategy, first proposed to Churchill by the physicist Frederick Lindemann,
was that destroying the urban infrastructure would depress the morale
of the German population and the displacement of workers would distort industrial activity, even if production sites were not severely affected
(Gruchmann 1991, 158).

Following the Casablanca Conference in January 1943, the RAF
was joined in the pursuit of area bombing by the US Eighth Air Force.

Table 2.4 *The development of urban and rural counties in West Germany, 1939–1950*

		1939	1946	1950
Urban counties	Population (thousand)	16,751	14,356	16,628
	Industrial employment (thousand)	3,663		3,372
	Share of expellees (%)			10.1
	Housing stock (thousand)	4,997	2,921	3,668
	Total turnover (billion 1950 DM)	162.2		150.2
Rural counties	Population (thousand)	22,646	29,321	31,069
	Industrial employment (thousand)	3,284		3,966
	Share of expellees (%)			20.0
	Housing stock (thousand)			5,772
	Total turnover (billion 1950 DM)	75.8		90.5

Note: Share of expellees calculated from population data and the number of expellees.
Sources: See text in Section 2.2.

Thanks to their combined efforts, in which the Americans carried out mainly daytime attacks against specific targets in the same areas where the British bombed overnight, almost every major West German city suffered considerable damage and more than half a million Germans lost their lives (Levine 1992, 192–3). Relative economic importance was not the decisive motive for target selection. Under Sir Arthur Harris as head of Bomber Command, the offensive focussed on condensed town centres, where incendiary bombs proved the most effective, while the majority of industrial plants was located in the outskirts of cities (for a first-hand account, see Harris 1947).

The introduction of area bombing changed the nature of the air war completely. In 1940–1, the success of an attack depended on the skills of the pilot. The crew of a Lancaster knew two words about targeting: hit and missed. Two years later, they were guided by detailed pre-prepared maps, on which experts had coloured the sectors that contained the most inflammable material. The result of a campaign was now decided in the laboratories, where researchers studied aerial maps and calculated the ideal combination of explosive material that the bombers had to carry. This altered the topography of destruction. While precision bombing affected large buildings, like factories or power stations, old town centres now became the prime targets, as their building density and wooden constructions made them highly inflammable. Interestingly, precision and area bombing were technologically interconnected. The firebombs that allowed the Allies to successfully destroy German (and later Japanese) cities were developed initially to improve the effectiveness of precision bombing. Since the heavy bombers had to fly at high altitude to be protected from ground artillery, they could not see their targets during the night. Therefore, smaller aircraft flew in first and dropped small firebombs to illuminate the destination for the main fleet behind them (Friedrich 2002, 23–5). The first victim of the Area Bombing Directive was Lübeck, attacked on 28 March 1942. On 31 May followed the first raid involving more than 1,000 aircraft that unloaded 1,500 tons of bombs over Cologne. The joint campaign of the British and US air forces between 24 July and 3 August 1943, codenamed 'Operation Gomorrah', flattened the residential areas of Hamburg. After a week of constant bombardment, only one-fifth of the city's dwellings remained unaffected (Krause 1997, 26–9).

The essence of the Allied bombing strategy was summed up in the motto of Bomber Command: 'Strike Hard, Strike Sure'. The objective was to maximise damage with minimal risk. This could be achieved by attacking urban centres easily identifiable from the air that did not require deep penetration into German airspace, at least as long as the Luftwaffe was capable of mounting resistance and daytime flights remained dangerous. The attack against Berlin in August 1943 cost the RAF 8 per cent of the crew. In the same month, the American squadrons that raided Regensburg and Schweinfurt in southern Bavaria lost a third of their aircraft as they flew across the whole country (Friedrich 2002, 45). The casualties of Bomber Command throughout the air war were enormous: 55,000 dead or missing, almost 10,000 taken prisoner, and nearly the same number wounded on the planes that returned (Levine 1992, 189). At the same time, targeting was notoriously inaccurate. The four-month campaign between March and July 1943 that devastated most city centers of the Ruhr area barely caused hardship for the major munitions manufacturers (Gruchmann 1991, 159). In May, the Allies dropped about 300,000 firebombs aimed at Wuppertal. More than 10 per cent of the bombers missed the city completely and hit neighbouring Solingen and Remscheid instead. The rest managed to unload their bombs within a 5-kilometre radius from the target zone (Friedrich 2002, 20).

In my previous work (Vonyó 2012), I tested the impact of different determinants of target selection econometrically. The analytical results confirmed that geographical characteristics influenced the scale of bombing damage in urban counties, but differences in the rate of industrialisation did not. The most decisive factor was proximity to Britain. On average, air raids inflicted 8.3 percentage points less damage on residential housing in cities that were located 100 kilometres further away from the English shores. Targets along the northern coastline and major rivers, which were consequently more visible from the air, suffered heavier losses than other urban counties. Population size was the least influential determinant; it proved significant only for the very largest cities. Cologne was hit 150 times during the war, and Munich also suffered far greater destruction than smaller towns in southern Bavaria (Vonyó 2012, 106–7).

The first map in Figure 2.4 demonstrates clearly that geography was the predominant factor behind wartime destruction. Besides Berlin, the share of damaged housing was highest on the western bank of the Rhine, a dominantly agrarian region that saw its historic towns, such as Aachen and Trier, flattened. In these districts, fierce ground fighting aggravated the impact of aerial bombardment as the Allies pushed forward following the Battle of the Bulge in early 1945. The two maps also indicate that the regional distribution of war damage strongly influenced the subsequent settlement of expellees. The level of housing destruction was exceptionally high in Hamburg, Bremen, West Berlin, and along the Rhine, where the share of expellees in the resident population in 1950 was correspondingly low. Regions that initially had to accommodate the bulk of the expellees in the north and the southeast of the country suffered relatively minor damage in residential housing. Regions under French occupation in the Rhineland-Palatinate and southern Baden-Württemberg represented the only exceptions from this general pattern.

These findings support previous empirical work that documented the decisive impact of strategic bombing on population growth in large German cities (Brakman et al. 2004, pp. 204–6). The most important reason behind this correlation is that the legacy of wartime destruction was not even significantly mitigated, let alone offset, either by wartime building activity or by the reconstruction efforts of the late 1940s. Since new construction was insufficient even to make possible the return of former urban dwellers evacuated during the bombing campaign, the expellees could not settle into large and medium cities, at first. Therefore, the labour force in these counties had become substantially smaller relative to 1939, even if the productive assets of urban industry had survived the war largely unscathed, and even though, by the late 1940s, the transport infrastructure of the country had been completely rebuilt.

In theory, one could put forward an alternative explanation. If there was statistically significant correlation across regions between housing destruction and the decline in the stock of industrial fixed capital, then population movements after the war would reflect the relative scarcity of jobs due to insufficient production capacity. This argument, however,

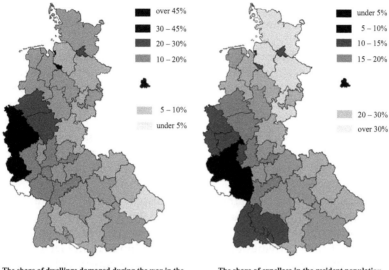

over 45%

30 – 45%

20 – 30%

10 – 20%

5 – 10%

under 5%

under 5%

5 – 10%

10 – 15%

15 – 20%

20 – 30%

over 30%

The share of dwellings damaged during the war in the
housing stock on 13.9.1950

The share of expellees in the resident population
on 13.9.1950

Figure 2.4 Regional variation in housing damage and the settlement of expellees.

Sources: See text in Section 2.2.

Note: The maps represent the administrative districts of the Federal Republic and West Berlin.

rests on two assumptions that are untenable in the case of the German war economy: (1) that cities which suffered disproportionately from aerial bombardment also recorded disproportionate losses in industrial assets, and (2) that the scale of wartime destruction determined the overall rate of capital accumulation in industry and handcrafts between 1939 and 1950.

We cannot directly test the validity of these assumptions in the absence of disaggregated regional data on industrial fixed capital, but very strong arguments can be made against them. First, the scale of destruction in residential and industrial infrastructure was quite simply incomparable, precisely because of the strategy that Bomber Command pursued from 1942 onwards. Only a minute fraction of the 1.7 million tons of bombs that the Allies dropped on Germany in 1944 and early 1945 hit industrial plants outside aircraft manufacturing and synthetic-fuel generation (Abelshauser 2004, 70). Second, attacks aimed at specific production sites were notoriously ineffective. Factories were located far from the city centres, they were better protected than residential buildings, their structures were less vulnerable to incendiary bombs, minor damages were quickly repaired, and machinery was often moved under the surface or temporarily dispersed into strategically safer areas. Between December 1941 and February 1942, Bomber Command directed forty-three night raids against Essen with the aim of destroying the Krupp Works. Subsequently, during March and April, 1,500 bombers were flown over the city. Ninety per cent of the bombs exploded outside Essen. Krupp had one fire and saw two bombs dropping on an adjacent railway installation. That was all the damage to its industrial assets. In the few residential buildings actually hit in the area, 63 civilians lost their lives and the only building completely destroyed was the one housing prison labour (Friedrich 2002, 38).

Much has been written on the strategic dispersal of production during the war (see Zilbert 1981 and Eichholtz 1999 among others). Even though the available evidence does not allow us to measure precisely the impact of such activities on industrial development in Germany as a whole, firm histories offer ample examples to demonstrate its importance for local economies. Volkswagen is perhaps the best-documented case study. Traditional accounts shared the notion that the firm had to rise 'like a phoenix from ashes' to eventually become one of the leading industrial corporations of post-war Germany (see, e.g., Sloniger 1980). More recent studies revealed that the *Volkswagenwerk* survived the war with remarkably little damage. A thorough analysis of USSBS records (Reich 1990) has shown that the more than 2,000 tons of bombs dropped on the factories in July and August 1944 destroyed only 8 per cent of the installed machinery, a small setback after half a decade of staggering expansion. Besides the ineffectiveness of the air raids, equipment was saved by their temporary relocation to northern Bohemia. After the end of the war, the British Army dispatched a mission to reclaim the assets from Czechoslovakia, before the Soviet forces could establish their control over the area (cited in Tolliday 1995, 286–7).

Another noted example is the city of Ingolstadt in Upper Bavaria. Given its strategically safe location, it was already among the most rapidly industrialising towns in Germany during the late 1930s. Having specialised in the production of military vehicles, it also enjoyed continued expansion in industrial employment during the war. Even though several bombing raids in the first months of 1945 destroyed large parts of its housing stock, the production capacity of its leading industries was much larger after the war than what is had been a decade earlier. Not surprisingly, Ingolstadt became one of the leading centres of car manufacturing in post-war Germany (Keyser 1971, 271–9, 317–25).

The third, and perhaps most important, reason to argue that regional variation in the destruction of industrial assets could not determine the geography of subsequent employment growth is that, on average, wartime destruction was far outweighed by the colossal investments of the early 1940s. As noted in Chapter 1, these investments were heavily concentrated in chemicals, primary metals, and the engineering sector. Consequently, industries that suffered the most war-related damage had often recorded the highest rates of net capital formation between 1939 and 1950. By contrast, rural workshops producing consumer goods were deprived of resources, despite their strategically favourable location. Finally, the dismantling of industrial assets after the war acted as another offsetting mechanism in the regional distribution of capital losses: machinery dismantled for reparation needs, by definition, had survived the war unharmed.

All in all, the wartime destruction of industrial fixed capital had only a minor impact on changes in stock between 1939 and 1950, contrary to the case of housing. Since the geography of capital accumulation in German industry was shaped by several influential factors that often acted to cancel out one another, the most realistic assumption we can make about the correlation between relative bombing damage in residential housing and capital formation in industry is that (1) it was random and that (2) its impact on the regional variation of employment growth was, therefore, insignificant.

The figures reported in Table 2.4 confirm that the growth potential of local economies depended on their scope for employment expansion. Output in urban industry remained well below its pre-war peak in the presence of labour scarcity. This contraction was more than offset by the growth of the rural economy. However, as rural industry substituted labour for capital to meet the increasing demand for manufactures in the face of insufficient urban production, the war-induced reallocation of industrial employment made a devastating impact on labour productivity in the West German economy. Data on total turnover alone do not allow us to measure these productivity effects accurately. Turnover is an indicator of gross output, not value added, and thus depends greatly on economic structure, namely on the relative weight of sectors at different stages of the value chain in the production process.

Geographic shifts in population constituted the main source of regional variations in employment expansion and economic growth. Even though the aggregate statistics reported in Table 2.4 strongly support this argument, there are several special cases, which demonstrate different dynamics. They can be considered outliers, but they also illustrate the complexities of war-induced dislocation in the German economy after 1945. Lübeck was the first victim of the Area Bombing Directive in March 1942, but only a small fraction of its housing stock was actually destroyed. Located on the border of the Soviet occupation zone, it became a major destination for refugees who had begun to flee the eastern provinces already in late 1944. However, it recorded considerable decline in industrial employment as the restrictions imposed on shipbuilding by the occupying powers remained in force until 1951. These restrictions were also detrimental for employment growth in Kiel, whose population had almost recovered to pre-war levels, despite heavy bombing damage, thanks to the influx of expellees into Schleswig-Holstein. The experience of Wilhelmshaven, once home to the German high-sea fleet, followed the opposite path. As housing was destroyed on a grand scale and the navy was dismantled, the population of the city declined sharply. Still, after the fleet had been disbanded and the dockyards detonated in Operation Bailiff in early 1950, the industrial workforce increased thanks to the reallocation of labour from naval services into manufacturing (Keyser 1952, 144–52, 379–83).

Finally, it must not be neglected that despite the decisive role of regional labour scarcity, in specific cases, economic recovery was indeed hampered by the destruction of productive capacity, or by persistent bottlenecks resulting from chronic shortages of input materials. Even though West German industry as a whole suffered relatively little wartime damage and post-war dismantling was modest, several important industrial sites were severely hit by aerial bombardment, or by post-war reparations. The factories of the chemical giant Bayer in Leverkusen as well as several large steel mills and power plants in the Ruhr area are prime examples for the former (Tooze 2006, 650). The shipbuilding cities on the northern coastline and, even more so, the main sites of aircraft production, such as Friedrichshafen in South Württemberg-Hohenzollern, were paralysed in the occupation years by the stringent output restrictions or production bans, while a vast share of their machinery and other equipment was dismantled.

2.4   The Economics of Urban Reconstruction

Between 1950 and 1961, in West Germany, more than 5 million dwellings were constructed or underwent serious renovation (Statistisches Bundesampt 2000, 49). Social housing accounted for almost 3 million, approximately 55 per cent of the total (Krummacher 1988, 452). Simultaneously, urban flats became more spacious and comfortable, so that the housing conditions of the working class improved considerably

(Schulz 1994, 336). Until 1957, almost half of all building activity in the country focussed on housing, which was heavily subsidised by the state. In the same period, a quarter of gross fixed investment was spent in the housing sector, one-third of which was covered by public funds (Sachverständigenrat 1965, 200; Weimer 1998, 90, 144–5). The preeminent role that social housing played in the economic policy of the first West German governments will be discussed in Chapter 5. In the present context, it suffices to point out that housing construction on an historically unprecedented scale initiated a period of rapid re-urbanisation. Thanks to the high natural birth rate and the continuing influx of East German refugees, the population of West Germany grew by 2.9 million, or 6 per cent, between 1950 and 1956, but the rate of urbanisation still increased from 39 per cent to nearly 43 per cent. The urban population expanded by more than 3 million and, as a result, recovered to the prewar level (Steinberg 1991, 167–9).

Besides rapid population growth and urban reconstruction, state-sponsored voluntary resettlement programmes stimulated re-urbanisation. The expellees, who had suffered disproportionately from displacement after the war, benefited the most from the improved allocation of labour after 1950. A federal government decree issued on 29 November 1949 announced the resettlement of 300,000 expellees from Schleswig-Holstein, Lower Saxony, and Bavaria into other regions of the country, to be followed by a string of similar legislation.[31] Between 1949 and 1953, a total of 621,000 expellees were resettled under this legal framework.[32] Their number reached 957,000 by the end of the 1950s. In addition, 1.7 million expellees and refugees resettled to another federal state by their own means (Steinert 1995, 570). The prime destinations were the industrial heartlands of North Rhine-Westphalia, where the number of expellees doubled from 1.3 million in 1950 to 2.6 million in 1961, and the regions formerly under French occupation: the Rhineland-Palatinate and the south of Baden-Württemberg. Although the expellees demonstrated extraordinary regional mobility, resettlement was not their exclusive predicament. In total, 9 million German citizens migrated to another federal state between 1950 and 1959 (Hafner 1994, 171).

A widely shared thesis in German historiography granted a critical role to expellees in the industrial expansion of the 1950s (for a full exposition, see Ambrosium 1996). Abelshauser (2004) argued that it was their sheer presence and outstanding occupational as well as regional mobility that allowed West German industry to grow unhindered by the need to

---

[31] Federal Ministry for the Marshall Plan (1951), 134.
[32] StatBRD, Vol. 114 (1955), 35.

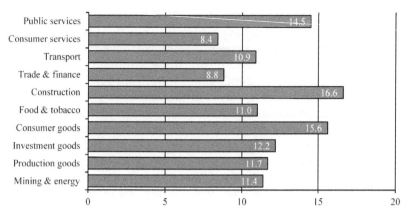

Figure 2.5 The share of expellees in non-agricultural employment on 13 September1950 (%).
Sources: Calculations based on data from StatBRD,Vol. 47.1 (1956), 20–1.

compete for scarce labour with other sectors of the economy. According to a micro-census conducted in the mid-1950s, the share of industry and handcrafts in the occupational structure of expellees increased from 28 per cent at the time of their flight or deportation from East and Central Europe to one-half by late 1954.[33] Although the latter proportion was indeed higher than the national average, it is difficult to interpret as an indication that the expansion of industrial employment in the early 1950s was driven by the resettlement of expellees. First, the share of industrial and construction workers among all employed expellees had already been above 50 per cent in September 1950, when the resettlement programmes had barely begun to make an impact.[34] Second, as Figure 2.5 demonstrates, expellees were strongly overrepresented among the seasonally employed construction workers and in light manufacturing, which embraced numerous small workshops. Consequently, their respective share in large-scale industry remained relatively modest. Finally, since all the expellees active in the non-agricultural branches of the economy totalled fewer than 1.9 million in September 1950, they could not have been primarily responsible for the overall employment growth in West German industry, which amounted to 1.7 million between 1950 and 1955 (Statistisches Bundesamt 1973, 44).

The contribution of expellees to industrial development became fundamentally different in the late 1950s. By then, the booming economy

[33] StatBRD,Vol. 211 (1958), 51.
[34] StatBRD,Vol. 114 (1955), 86.

had largely absorbed the indigenous West German labour reserves. Although the urban population continued to increase faster than the number of rural dwellers, between 1956 and 1961, the regional pattern of demographic expansion had become significantly more balanced than what it had been earlier. Small towns and the rural outskirts of agglomeration areas, in particular, recorded exceptionally high growth (Steinberg 1991, 178). This, to a large extent, was made possible by the marked improvements in suburban and intercity commuting, which were the fruits of heavy expenditure on public transport and the vast increase in the number of private automobiles. According to the 1961 occupational census, every fourth employee in the country travelled daily or weekly to another town or city for work. In the course of the 1950s, their number had doubled and surpassed the 6-million mark (Südbeck 1993, 186). The greatly improved urban housing conditions and commuting facilities eased infrastructural constraints on the growth of urban industrial employment. In addition, owing to the large number of middle-sized establishments operating in the fast-growing engineering industries, these factors also resulted in a more balanced geographical distribution of industrial expansion.

Table 2.5 reports aggregate statistics on the development of the urban and rural economies during the 1950s. In the first half of the decade, only large and medium-sized cities witnessed significant population growth, as the urban housing stock increased by almost 50 per cent. The fact that, even in the absence of any notable change in population size, almost 1.7 million dwellings were added to the existing endowments in rural counties points to an important aspect of post-war reconstruction. Although rural and small-town Germany suffered relatively minor damage in residential housing during the war, it did not remain unaffected. With the avalanche of expellees and refugees unable to find shelter in the devastated urban centres and with the evacuation of millions of former urban dwellers, rural Germany became dangerously overcrowded in the late 1940s. Consequently, the regional resettlements after 1950 were driven not only by a pull but also by a push factor, namely that the capacity of rural counties to accommodate newcomers had been seriously over-stretched.

From the aggregate data reported in Table 2.5, we can also derive that 46 per cent of the urban population growth between 1950 and 1956 was due to the resettlement of expellees. It fuelled employment expansion, which in turn generated exceptionally high growth rates of industrial output. Following a contraction during the 1940s, total turnover in large and medium-sized cities grew by 74 per cent. Simultaneously, rural counties, which had grown substantially after the war, recorded more modest growth rates in the first half of the 1950s. Although employment

Table 2.5 *The development of urban and rural counties in West Germany, 1950–1961*

		1950	1956	1961
Urban counties	Population	16,653	19,303	20,472
	Employment in industry and handcrafts	3,387	4,408	4,699
	Employment in industry	2,336	3,484	3,853
	Share of expellees (%)	10.0	14.7	17.1
	Housing stock	3,675	5,238	6,169
	Total turnover	150.8	262.2	319.2
	Turnover in industry	57.5	116.3	168.5
	Turnover in handcrafts	10.8	13.3	22.9
Rural counties	Population	31,044	31,291	32,847
	Employment in industry and handcrafts	3,952	4,726	5,240
	Employment in industry	2,285	3,468	4,015
	Share of expellees (%)	20.1	19.2	19.3
	Housing stock	5,765	7,481	8,829
	Total turnover	89.9	138.0	177.9
	Turnover in industry	34.5	64.6	92.1
	Turnover in handcrafts	12.9	17.9	33.4

Note: Population, employment, and housing stock are expressed in thousands, turnover in billion 1950 DM.
Sources: See text in Section 2.2.

growth was driven by urban reconstruction, production capacity in rural industry had to expand to meet the rising demand for manufactures in both domestic and foreign markets. Not surprisingly, industrial production continued to increase rapidly in the rural economy as well.

As shown in Figure 2.6, the industrialisation of rural Germany was facilitated largely by the reallocation of small-scale production away from large cities, which in turn even managed to increase their dominance in large-scale industry between 1950 and 1956. Reconstruction growth was driven by factor reallocation, which proceeded in both directions, according to relative scarcities in the complementary factors of production. Labour migrating from the countryside fuelled the expansion of urban industry, leading to better exploitation of previously underutilised capacities. At the same time, investment in new plant and equipment was channelled, in large part, into rural counties endowed with surplus labour. In the second half of the 1950s, regional economic development in West Germany became considerably more balanced. Industrial employment and turnover continued to increase, but growth rates were

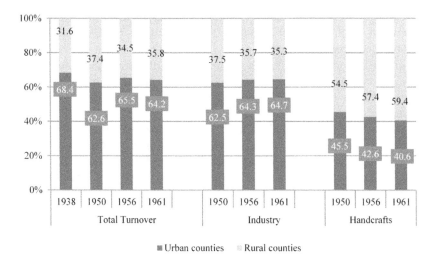

Figure 2.6 The share of urban and rural counties in total and industrial turnover.
Sources: See text in Section 2.2.

significantly more modest than they had been until 1955, and the difference between urban and rural counties became less striking. Therefore, their respective shares in total and industrial turnover did not change substantially.

These findings reveal an important outcome of the *Wirtschaftswunder*. The glory days of industrial growth in West Germany brought with them the relative decline of handcrafts. The number of employees in small workshops fell by almost 20 per cent in the country as a whole and by more than one quarter in the rural economy. Apart from Hamburg, there was not a single administrative district in the country to witness employment growth in handcraft manufacturers. The process of urban reconstruction could not keep pace with the increased demand for labour in West German industry. Hence, employment growth in large and medium-scale manufacturing was, to a notable extent, facilitated by labour reallocation from smaller workshops into larger factories, or by the growth of handcraft workshops into small industry plants.

In addition, as small-scale industry was relocated from urban centres into small towns in their vicinity, handcrafts in rural counties were also forced to cut back employment, in the absence of population growth. At the same time, with gradually improved access to capital came the modernisation and concentration of production in both urban and rural workshops. Despite the sharp decline in employment, total turnover in handcraft manufacturers increased by 32 per cent between 1950 and 1956, measured in constant prices; and the bulk of this growth was achieved in rural counties. The regional data illustrate that the industrialisation of the German countryside was not the outcome of wartime dispersal activity, as often argued before, but the consequence of the economic miracle itself.

Analogous to the preceding decade, the recovery of the urban economy after 1950 also demonstrated notable regional differences. Even though the dynamics described above were predominant, a few important outliers merit discussion. Emden and Salzgitter in Lower Saxony achieved exceptional rates of employment growth even with a virtually stagnant population in the early 1950s. An industrial city and Germany's westernmost seaport, Emden was hit hard by aerial bombardment during the war. When the construction of maritime vessels was allowed to resume, employment at the dockyards increased rapidly, absorbing the labour surplus of the surrounding countryside that had been flooded with expellees after 1945. Thanks to its rich iron-ore deposits, Salzgitter harboured one of the flagships of the Nazi war economy, the Hermann Göring Works. Despite repeated air raids over the city, the mines, and the iron works, even the residential areas remained largely unaffected by bombing damage. Therefore, production increased sharply once the demand for iron and steel had begun to surge during the Korea Boom (Keyser 1952, 123–6, 320–2). Leverkusen and Ludwigshafen were home to two of the world's largest chemical corporations, Bayer and BASF respectively. Both emerged from the infamous IG Farben and, consequently, suffered very substantial destruction during the war. However, both enjoyed no less extraordinary expansion after 1950, due in particular to soaring export sales. Since both cities were located in agglomeration areas, their lucrative job markets attracted employees from the comparatively much larger neighbouring counties of Cologne and Mannheim like magnets (Keyser 1956, 292–6; Keyser 1964, 245–5).

Wolfsburg, a middle-sized town in Lower Saxony, arguably best illustrates the economics of urban reconstruction in post-war Germany. Its resident population grew by 80 per cent while employment in industry increased by 135 per cent between 1950 and 1956. Wolfsburg, a newly established city, was dominated by Volkswagen, which employed practically all able-bodied men in town and the surrounding rural county. Its flagship product, the 'Beetle', conquered the world markets and enjoyed rapidly increasing domestic sales. In the eyes of many contemporaries, its success story symbolised not only the meteoric rise of the German automobile industry, but also the West German economic miracle itself (see Wellhöner 1996).

The analysis presented in this chapter confirms that post-war recovery in urban industry was limited by labour scarcity, which in turn resulted from the urban housing shortage that emerged after the Allied bombers had demolished the cities of Germany. The temporary displacement of workers fuelled the remarkable expansion of the rural economy during the 1940s, where capital was the more crucial bottleneck. The major puzzle that remains to be solved is why factor markets could not clear, or at least substantially mitigate, these vast regional imbalances, which persisted even after the establishment of the federal government and the successful reintegration of West Germany into the international economic order.

As for the lack of capital mobility, the explanation is straightforward. The disintegration of capital markets and the commanding heights of the financial sector at large was an essential component of Allied policy to dismantle the monopolistic structures of the German economy. As I will demonstrate in Chapter 5, anti-trust competition policy did not remain very aggressive for too long, but during the early post-war years it undeniably had important consequences. The three large universal banks, Deutsche, Dresdner, and Commerzbank, were broken up into quasi-independent regional subsidiaries, and later into three independent regional banks each (Bank deutscher Länder 1955, 293). This intervention made the concentration of assets required for major industrial projects extremely difficult and the transfer of private savings across federal states almost impossible (Pohl 1983, 232–40). In the early 1950s, market capitalisation accounted for only one-tenth of gross fixed investment in industry (Bornemann and Linnhoff 1958, 18–21). Therefore, short-term borrowing remained the most important source of financing alongside retained earnings, with a 40 per cent share in 1950 (Baumgart, Krengel, and Moritz 1960, 84–5).

On labour markets, institutional constraints aggravated the impact of the initially insurmountable housing shortage. German industry was highly unionised. Contrary to Olsonian arguments concerning the destruction of distributional coalitions under the Nazi regime and Allied occupation, the major trade unions were re-established by 1949 and their decisive role in industrial relations was codified in the corporatist Co-Determination Act of 1951 (Eichengreen and Ritschl 2009, 211–12). According to reports of the US military governor, the revival of the labour movement was undertaken by former union officials of the

Weimar period immediately after the end of the war.[35] Given the prevalence of large industry-level unions, wage settlements were negotiated annually in each major industry group. Agreed targets for skilled and unskilled labour were practically binding in firm-level wage bargaining. Although these periodic settlements were made for each federal state separately, it was difficult to enforce substantial adjustments in regional wage differentials within specific industries in response to relative scarcities in the factors of production.

The Federal Statistical Office conducted two large surveys into the structure of industrial wages during the 1950s: one in November 1951, when the impact of post-war dislocation was still present, and another in October 1957, after the urban housing stock had been rebuilt and the economy had returned to full employment. These sources are useful particularly because they report wage data disaggregated according to branch of industry, federal state, skill level, and gender. Average wages in each category are specified both per hour and per week, based on which we can compute the length of the average workweek.[36] We can then compare working wages in 1957 by region with the wage levels that would have been attained if wages in each state had risen in line with the national average increment from 1951 to 1957. The gaps between actual and fitted values measure to what extent wages were adjusted in response to regional labour scarcity.

Figure 2.7 suggests that regional wage differentials remained relatively stable over a period that saw the urban housing stock rebuilt and millions resettled within the country. This finding confirms that labour markets did not clear primarily through prices in the early 1950s, but industrial employers did exploit their limited room for manoeuvre under the stringent regulative framework. In Hamburg and Bremen, where residential areas were still partially in ruins, the average hourly wage of male workers was relatively high. By contrast, mass unemployment depressed wages in Schleswig-Holstein, Lower Saxony, and Bavaria.

Without sufficient wage flexibility, industrial firms operating under tight labour-supply conditions created incentives for their workers to work longer hours. Work time was reduced in every federal state in 1956 after trade unions had achieved a three-hour cut in the official workweek. However, as shown in Figure 2.8, heavily industrialised North Rhine-Westphalia and the states that were partially or completely under French occupation during the late 1940s, Baden-Württemberg and the Rhineland-Palatinate, witnessed the sharpest decline in weekly hours for

---

[35] OMGUS, *Manpower, trade unions and working conditions*, No. 20, 3–4.
[36] StatBRD, Vol. 90. (1954); StatBRD, Vol. 246.1 (1960).

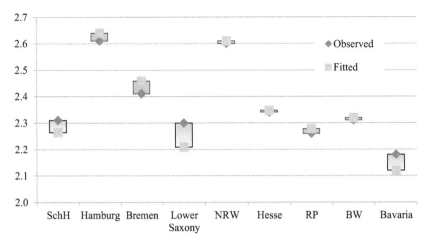

Figure 2.7 Average hourly wages for male workers in West German industry in 1957 (DM).

Notes: Fitted values were computed by multiplying 1951 wage levels by the average increase in wages in West German industry as a whole between 1951 and 1957.

Sources: StatBRD, Vol. 90. (1954); StatBRD, Vol. 246.1 (1960).

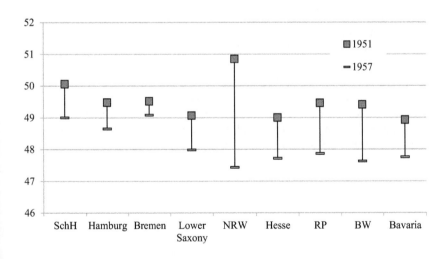

Figure 2.8 Average weekly working hours for male workers in West German industry.

Sources: StatBRD, Vol. 90. (1954); StatBRD, Vol. 246.1 (1960).

male workers. If we accept that 1957 values simply reflect regional differences in employment structure, then the gaps in the length of the standard workweek between the two years account for the fact that firms located in these regions had to adjust labour input upward by demanding extra hours from their workers in 1951. This evidence provides further support for the main punchline of this chapter that the recovery of urban industry, particularly in the Rhine-Ruhr agglomeration, was limited by regional labour scarcity. As long as the urban housing stock was not rebuilt, labour could not be reallocated in numbers sufficient to fully utilise existing industrial production capacity. Higher levels of utilisation could be achieved only by longer working hours, instead of expanding employment. Once urban reconstruction had been completed, the utilisation rate stabilised at a high level and fluctuated only with the business cycle.

In a comparative framework, it is worth pointing out that the relatively much more devastating consequences of the post-war settlement for East Germany were aggravated by the fact that the war-induced misallocation of labour and capital was present just as much as in the western part of the country. In 1946, the housing stock fell an estimated 1.9 million dwellings short of requirements, even excluding East Berlin that was laid to ruins by the Allied bombers and Soviet heavy artillery (Steinert 1995, 562). Although urban reconstruction was initially faster under Soviet occupation than in the West, by 1950, cities with more than 100,000 inhabitants managed to recover only 85.2 per cent of their pre-war population. The corresponding figure for West Germany was 82.4 per cent (Steinberg 1991, 162). As a result, the share of large cities in the total population dropped from 26.7 per cent in 1939 to 20.7 per cent in 1950. The urban housing shortage was just as much a constraint on capacity utilisation in East as in West German industry. Thus we cannot argue that the comparatively much heavier reparations burden of the East German economy was partially offset by relatively more severe war-induced infrastructural bottlenecks in the West.

3   Growth Accounts for West German Industry

It was demonstrated in Chapter 2 that the recovery of West German industry after the early post-war years was limited by the regional misallocation of productive forces. Labour scarcity in urban industry coexisted with a notable labour surplus and hence shortage of physical capital in small and medium-scale manufacturing that often settled into more remote rural areas. This finding has an important implication for the post-war growth miracle. Whereas economists at the time and many economic historians since agreed that capital accumulation propelled industrial expansion after 1950, persistent dislocation suggests a more complex explanation. As long as infrastructural bottlenecks to the effective utilisation of productive capacity were not eliminated, the scope for employment expansion, not the rate of net capital formation, limited the growth of urban industry. To trace this argument further we need to gain deeper insight into the development of factor endowments and the growth dynamics of West German industry both during the war and in the reconstruction phase, which is the purpose of this chapter.

The debate over the drivers of reconstruction growth has important implications for how we interpret the West German growth miracle of the 1950s and early 1960s. The bulk of German historiography treated these remarkable years as part of a period that Abelshauser (1987) coined 'the long fifties'. This view reflects contemporary accounts on the economic development of the Federal Republic, which saw the mild recession of 1966–7 not simply as a cyclical interruption of the growth process but as the end of the post-war era. Leading Keynesian economists of the time, above all the Council of Economic Experts (Sachverständigenrat), argued that this downturn was the product of the strongly pro-cyclical fiscal policy pursued by the government of Ludwig Erhard prior to and after the general elections of 1965 and of the restrictive measures that the Bundesbank implemented in the course of 1966 (Sachverständigenrat 1968, paragraphs 230–2). According to this interpretation, market forces alone were no longer capable of sustaining high rates of economic growth and, therefore, expansionary state intervention was necessary at times of cyclical downturns to avoid further recessions.

In a very influential but equally unorthodox account, Ernest Mandel (1969) offered a Marxist explanation for the recession, which, for him, signalled the crisis of an economy that reached a mature stage of capitalism. He argued that capacity utilisation in West German industry had already declined over the ten years leading up to 1966. Record investment levels led to the over-accumulation of capital and hence to a sharp reduction in the returns on investment. Decreasing returns, in turn, entailed a gradual increase in the fixed costs of production, which was inevitably going to squeeze out profits once market demand became sluggish. According to Mandel, this is precisely what happened in the capital goods industries during the mid-1960s, when the growth in surplus capacity urged firms to cut back on investment in new machinery and equipment. The crisis that evolved in heavy industry in the course of 1966 forced employment cuts, and the declining purchasing power of former wage earners depressed domestic demand for consumer goods as well.

Inspired by the reconstruction thesis, Abelshauser (2004) also came to accept that the mid-1960s marked an historic milestone: the end of an extended post-war reconstruction period. Once the West German economy had recovered to its long-run productive potential, the slowdown in the rate of growth that followed was inevitable and, thus, cannot be seen as the product of the macroeconomic policy failures emphasised by economists at the time. What all contemporary observers and many economic historians hitherto have agreed on is that West German economic growth was investment-driven until the mid-1960s, after which further expansion required technological innovation as well as structural and organisational reforms.

However, the evidence reported in Chapter 2 suggests that West German industry was still far from exhausting the productive potential inherent in existing capacities in 1950. Therefore, the early 1950s seem to tell a markedly different growth story from the one characteristic of subsequent years. The quantitative accounts that this chapter will present highlight two fundamental aspects of industrial expansion during the post-war golden age: (1) that a distinction between the early and late 1950s is much more useful than a similar borderline between the 1950s and the 1960s, and (2) that there was no structural break in the growth process during the 1960s. In other words, the 1966–7 recession did not make a lasting impact on the growth potential of West German industry. The transition from exceptional to normal growth rates did not occur before the early 1970s.

The most accurate periodisation of economic growth in the post-war era separates the reconstruction years leading up to 1955 from the subsequent decade and a half. During the former, idle labour reserves and productive assets were reintegrated into the production process. After this initial phase of post-war recovery, further expansion depended more strongly on improved productive efficiency gained through technological modernisation. The period of extensive growth was followed by the phase of intensive growth, both shaped by fundamentally different factor dynamics. Thus, the growth accounts presented in this chapter investigate industrial development in three sub-periods: 1938–48, 1949–55, and 1956–70. The year 1938 serves as the most suitable pre-war benchmark, the last full calendar year preceding the outbreak of hostilities. 1970 represents the last business-cycle peak before the 1973–4 worldwide recession that brought the golden age to an end. It also marks the apogee of German industrialisation, when the combined share of mining and manufacturing in total employment and national income began its sharp and steady decline.

3.1   Industrial Output and Factor Inputs

The investigation opens with a detailed quantitative account using official data to determine levels of industrial value added and both capital and labour input in five major sectors and thirty-two branches of mining and manufacturing for several benchmark years reflecting the aforementioned periodisation. One industry, namely aircraft manufacturing, is excluded from this account. The production of new aircraft was prohibited in West Germany until the 1955 accession to NATO, and thus the industry was virtually non-existent during the reconstruction years. All figures reported on the following pages refer to post-war West German territory and are adjusted for any changes in the official data regarding the status of the Saarland and West Berlin. German industry statistics traditionally exclude construction and the public utilities, which are thus not discussed here. Data on industrial output and capital stock are deflated in order to arrive at constant price estimates.

Table 3.1 reports index numbers for net industrial production. The most prominent feature of the late 1940s was the historic nadir in output levels not seen since the late nineteenth century. Between 1938 and 1948, industrial value added in constant prices declined by more than one-half. The metallurgical and metal processing industries suffered the sharpest contraction. Output also plummeted in the fuel industry, china and earthenware, entertainment instruments, paper products, leather and footwear, and tobacco manufactures. The extraction of crude oil and

Table 3.1 *Index of net industrial production (1950 = 100)*

	1938	1948	1955	1960	1965	1970
Mining	*117.4*	*76.0*	*127.7*	*131.7*	*135.2*	*130.9*
Coal mining	120.8	78.0	119.7	116.3	113.4	95.0
Metallic ores	104.5	65.2	134.7	182.6	121.5	96.2
Salt mining	98.2	61.0	163.5	184.6	229.9	256.9
Crude oil and gas	49.4	58.7	271.2	469.4	757.6	1,286.4
Production goods	*112.9*	*53.0*	*175.6*	*253.9*	*348.3*	*496.7*
Fuel industry	84.1	22.9	235.9	516.2	1,039.4	1,545.1
Iron and steel	142.3	48.6	178.2	230.5	251.8	314.4
Non-ferrous metals	119.3	47.1	187.7	269.0	320.2	413.3
Construction materials	108.5	53.4	171.4	228.0	311.9	360.3
Chemical industry	97.6	53.7	174.8	283.4	450.3	763.6
Rubber and asbestos	114.3	68.7	199.1	278.0	368.1	498.3
Timber industry	105.4	69.6	124.2	159.4	185.0	228.6
Paper and pulp	107.3	47.4	154.4	203.6	239.9	322.3
Investment goods	*117.3*	*50.2*	*216.0*	*322.8*	*423.5*	*570.8*
Steel constructions	224.5	56.5	173.7	209.3	257.2	277.4
Machine tools	127.3	45.5	206.2	277.5	342.8	418.2
Transport vehicles	92.1	33.5	264.4	486.1	691.7	1,011.1
Shipbuilding	237.3	50.7	369.2	412.7	415.8	515.0
Electrical engineering	65.7	54.5	243.6	431.4	613.2	929.9
Optical and precision engineering	103.0	44.8	210.0	282.0	352.9	460.6
Fabricated metal products	121.9	66.3	192.1	272.7	348.0	455.0
Consumer goods	*99.6*	*46.1*	*167.4*	*234.6*	*304.2*	*385.7*
China and earthenware	132.8	56.3	188.3	223.0	263.5	293.7
Glass industry	68.0	55.0	167.7	264.4	362.6	479.3
Entertainment instruments	207.5	63.4	277.4	386.3	516.7	595.3
Woodworking	103.9	57.1	169.3	235.4	312.7	425.4
Paper and board	112.1	39.7	156.2	237.0	325.7	421.5
Printing and publishing	95.9	42.2	157.3	230.1	302.1	404.4
Plastic products	67.0	46.0	353.6	1,257.1	2,689.3	5,258.9
Leather industry	148.6	57.7	152.2	175.3	192.3	186.8
Footwear industry	138.0	54.3	140.8	182.9	203.8	192.8
Textile industry	93.6	41.9	153.9	205.0	238.7	284.1
Clothing industry	64.7	45.0	199.4	270.1	360.8	394.4
Food and tobacco	*104.0*	*56.8*	*157.7*	*220.9*	*285.3*	*339.6*
Food and beverages	90.0	65.8	159.6	224.2	289.5	344.6
Tobacco manufactures	134.2	37.6	154.0	208.3	278.1	333.6
Total industry	**109.7**	**53.4**	**176.3**	**248.2**	**324.0**	**426.7**

Source: Statistisches Bundesamt (1973), 50-53; IndBRD, Series 4, No. 8 (1956), 17. Sub-industries aggregated using 1950 value-added weights (ibid., 9).

natural gas, which was still in its infancy in the 1930s, was the sole industry that managed to increase production. By contrast, the reconstruction
period after 1948 saw the fastest growth ever recorded in German history across most industries. By 1950, industrial value added was already
close to its pre-war peak. In 1955, it was more than 60 per cent larger
than what it had been in 1938. In the first years of post-war recovery,
the consumer goods industries led the race; production and investment
goods were responsible for most of the continued expansion after 1950.
Between 1938 and 1955, the fastest growing industries were crude oil
and natural gas, fuels, transport vehicles, electrical engineering, and
plastic products. They were all closely connected to Germany's belated
motorisation, which was the dominant force of technological change and
productivity growth in the post-war era.

Despite all the populist propaganda to the contrary, Nazi economic
policy had shown a very poor record in motorisation during the late
1930s. This resulted partially from the concentration of investment in
the more traditional branches of heavy industry, and partially from the
limited purchasing power of the middle class, which, in turn, depressed
domestic demand for consumer durables (Südbeck 1993, 171–2). The
catch-up potential in the post-war years was consequently enormous.
Between 1949 and 1960, the number of passenger cars in West Germany
climbed from half a million to 4.2 million and the stock of trucks also
doubled (Henning 1993, 221–2).

While road transport remained underdeveloped in Germany relative
to that of other leading industrial nations, the production of transport
vehicles made tremendous progress under the Nazi dictatorship, especially during the war. While the German land forces were much less
mechanised than their British and US counterparts, the manufacturing
of military aircraft grew at a staggering pace in the early 1940s. This
spectacular growth was made possible not only by the expansion of productive capacity. Even more critical were the adoption and development
of new technologies and the remarkable improvements in productivity
achieved through rationalisation. Supplier networks became thicker and
geographically more extended, often into occupied foreign lands in Nazi-
dominated Europe. The aircrafts industry became a giant web of highly
specialised firms that reaped huge gains from scale economies and learning by doing (Budrass, Scherner, and Streb 2010). As aircraft production was shut down after the war and remained prohibited until 1955,
the car industry became the beneficiary of this wartime legacy. In order
to stay in business and avoid their assets being dismantled by the Allies,
former aerospace manufacturers and their suppliers had to change their
industry profile quickly, transplanting the production regime they had

developed in the war economy into the engineering of motor vehicles for civilian and commercial use (Scherner and Streb 2010).

Apart from the industries that directly benefited from this motorisation drive, the highest growth rates were recorded in chemicals and investment goods, where Germany had long-established comparative advantages. The expansion in steel-based engineering products during the reconstruction years represented the rebounding from the immediate post-war contraction. Hence growth rates slowed down after 1955, especially in shipbuilding, where German firms began to suffer from low-cost Japanese competition. By contrast, electrical engineering maintained remarkable growth rates throughout the post-war golden age. The success of this industry was also increasingly tied to car manufacturing and to the consumer revolution that began to gain momentum in the late 1950s, reflected in the rapidly increasing demand for electrical household appliances (Wildt 1993, 280).

The rest of West German industry, including iron and steel, construction materials, most consumer goods, as well as food and tobacco, achieved slower than average growth. Industrial expansion during the post-war era concentrated in production and investment goods at the expense of light manufacturing, food processing, and even more mining. However, as Figure 3.1 reveals, the patterns of structural change before and after 1955 were quite different. The engineering industries were the locomotives of reconstruction growth, while subsequent years were marked more by the increasing share of production goods. The only trend that proved persistent over the whole period was the sharp relative decline of mining. This resulted from the switch between domestically produced coal and imported but domestically processed hydrocarbons in fuel consumption and from the increased application of synthetic materials in the production of consumer goods. The share of crude oil and petroleum in total energy consumption jumped from less than 10 per cent in 1950 to above 50 per cent by 1970. Thus, both the extraction and the processing of hydrocarbons belonged to the most dynamically expanding industries throughout the post-war period.[1]

The construction of a comprehensive dataset on labour and capital inputs with levels territorially and methodologically consistent over time was a complicated task. The appendices provide the detailed technical exposition. Appendix 2 reports capital-stock estimates at the industry level for the pre-1950 period, broken down into structures and equipment, fully consistent with the existing time-series evidence for the post-war era that had been constructed by the German Institute for Economic

---

[1] Calculations based on data from Sachverständigenrat (1991), 426.

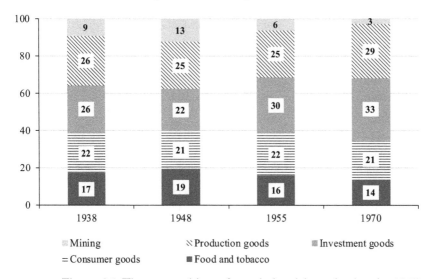

Figure 3.1 The composition of net industrial production in 1950 prices (%).

Sources: Shares of industry groups in total value-added derived from the index numbers reported in Table 3.1 and levels for 1950 reported in IndBRD, Series 4, No. 8 (1956), 9.

Research (DIW). Appendix 3 presents comparable levels of employment drawn from various sources and explains the procedure used to compute total hours worked by industry for the years prior to 1950. In the main text of this chapter, I spare the reader from having to digest all the technicalities of the underlying data work and focus instead on the main results.

Table 3.2 reports index numbers for gross capital stock, calculated from the existing post-war data and the estimates shown in Appendix 2. The sources do not allow us to separate tobacco manufactures from food and beverages, as we can do for industrial production and labour input. As previous research discussed in Chapter 1 has demonstrated, the capital stock of West German industry increased during the war and continued to expand rapidly in the reconstruction period. In the 1940s, accumulation was fastest in mining and production goods. After 1948, the engineering sector and consumer goods were leading the pack. At the industry level, the fastest growth occurred in timber and woodworking, the paper industry, china and earthenware, and the clothing industry. Nazi economic policy in the late 1930s did not give priority to the production of consumer goods. Therefore, it was necessary to expand

Table 3.2 *Index of gross industrial capital stock (1950 = 100)*

	1938	1948	1955	1960	1965	1970
Mining	81.4	97.4	131.0	*169.2*	*183.2*	*167.0*
Coal mining	80.6	97.9	129.7	165.6	173.8	148.9
Metallic ores	74.2	91.0	146.4	208.4	240.1	224.2
Salt mining	99.4	97.2	122.0	145.6	171.1	193.1
Crude oil and gas	75.2	93.4	153.9	233.8	310.2	374.9
Production goods	*77.5*	*99.3*	*130.1*	*187.0*	*267.9*	*350.3*
Fuel industry	73.9	99.6	119.7	192.2	285.5	399.1
Iron and steel	82.1	101.0	148.8	225.3	324.8	375.8
Non-ferrous metals	81.1	102.3	112.6	142.8	181.7	233.7
Construction materials	86.6	93.9	154.3	252.3	440.6	580.3
Chemical industry	72.9	101.7	115.0	153.8	209.9	294.0
Rubber and asbestos	69.2	91.6	131.4	183.1	275.0	398.6
Timber industry	71.3	64.1	176.4	262.4	359.3	455.2
Paper and pulp	95.5	91.0	172.5	256.4	353.8	471.8
Investment goods	*79.3*	*94.9*	*153.5*	*251.6*	*397.3*	*542.3*
Steel constructions	72.7	92.7	165.0	260.8	385.0	471.9
Machine tools	84.4	95.4	150.1	226.4	334.4	445.4
Transport vehicles	76.3	97.7	151.8	276.9	508.6	731.7
Shipbuilding	68.0	101.2	122.2	166.7	191.3	216.2
Electrical engineering	73.1	90.1	164.7	282.6	447.5	618.0
Optical and precision engineering	80.5	98.3	141.4	236.3	347.3	462.4
Fabricated metal products	88.6	93.1	165.5	284.6	458.1	633.2
Consumer goods	*99.1*	*86.2*	*151.0*	*235.5*	*343.3*	*455.6*
China and earthenware	90.8	84.3	181.5	290.9	396.2	481.3
Glass industry	93.2	87.9	155.3	252.0	438.1	635.7
Entertainment instruments	133.3	98.5	117.2	168.1	289.7	452.9
Woodworking	78.9	70.5	165.0	253.7	377.5	512.9
Paper and board	86.2	79.8	191.8	391.8	707.0	1,124.3
Printing and publishing	118.0	90.2	159.5	273.9	406.3	535.2
Plastic products	68.9	85.9	198.0	501.5	1,180.9	2,240.7
Leather industry	94.8	87.0	118.6	150.1	190.7	206.0
Footwear industry	89.2	88.9	152.3	219.4	275.1	315.4
Textile industry	101.3	88.4	136.8	193.8	255.6	312.2
Clothing industry	95.0	78.4	229.2	419.0	616.9	772.1
Food and tobacco	*97.5*	*87.0*	*139.9*	*199.4*	*277.3*	*358.5*
Total industry	**83.4**	**95.1**	**138.9**	**205.2**	**292.2**	**374.9**

Sources and methods: Index for 1970 calculated from Krengel et al. (1973), 36–8. For all
other years, see Appendix 2.

existing capacities considerably in order to satisfy the hitherto restrained
demand after the currency reform in the second half of 1948.

The index numbers reported for industrial value added and gross
capital stock for the period up to 1955 suggest huge fluctuations in the

efficiency with which capital was employed. This reflects the nature of war-induced dislocation and post-war reconstruction described in the previous chapter. Following the reconstruction phase, output growth depended on the further expansion of productive capacity. The rate of capital accumulation remained very high until the end of the golden age, both in engineering and consumer goods. As I will discuss later, both sectors were characterised by rapid growth in capital intensity during the 1960s, when firms adopted mass production technologies.

Table 3.3 reports index numbers for annual labour hours. Adjusting labour input for changes in the average work time was especially important for 1948, when actual weekly work hours fell about 20 per cent short of the corresponding figures for both 1938 and 1950. Employment data alone would have suggested stagnation in labour input between 1938 and 1948, and only a minimal increase during the late 1940s. After the appropriate adjustments, the patterns of labour expansion and output growth correspond well, even though both the contraction until 1948 and the recovery thereafter appear much more modest in work hours than in value added. As employment was maintained at higher levels than production in the late 1940s, it also recovered more quickly to the pre-war peak.

Labour input in mining increased substantially between 1938 and 1948, but subsequent employment growth was most dynamic in engineering and consumer goods. In the reconstruction period, the growth of output was driven primarily by labour expansion, as suggested in Chapter 2. Branches of heavy industry that operated large-scale establishments with surplus capacity could increase production with little investment in new plant and equipment. The capital stock expanded faster in industries in which the share of small and medium-sized establishments that often settled in rural areas with flexible labour supply was more notable: investment and consumer goods.

After West German industry had achieved full capacity utilisation during the 1955 boom, even though capital accumulation accelerated in the late 1950s, employment growth slowed down considerably. Between 1955 and 1960, the number of industrial workers and employees still increased by more than a million, but this was completely neutralised by the shortening of the average workweek from 48.8 to 45.6 hours (Schudlich 1987, 158; see also Görzig 1972, 49–50). As a result, labour input measured in annual hours worked by the manual workforce did not increase significantly. The economy returned to full employment in 1959 and the inflow of East German refugees, whose number had averaged more than 200,000 annually, terminated as the Berlin Wall was erected in August 1961. West German industry ran out of the domestic labour reserves that it could exploit. Employment growth in

Table 3.3 *Index of annual labour hours (1950 = 100)*

	1938	1948	1955	1960	1965	1970
Mining	*74.7*	*89.01*	*105.3*	*81.3*	*58.4*	*34.9*
Coal mining	73.0	90.05	101.2	79.5	58.0	34.5
Metallic ores	103.9	76.94	105.0	75.4	33.5	19.1
Salt mining	64.6	88.74	137.7	113.1	93.6	61.7
Crude oil and gas	42.0	77.37	133.7	97.7	64.0	39.2
Production goods	*100.2*	*68.52*	*127.6*	*128.8*	*122.7*	*115.0*
Fuel industry	113.9	77.72	107.9	118.4	97.1	85.3
Iron and steel	138.7	66.33	136.1	136.8	125.3	112.9
Non-ferrous metals	99.8	60.72	142.5	144.9	139.6	141.1
Construction materials	99.6	68.82	129.9	119.5	114.8	96.6
Chemical industry	70.1	69.99	118.3	130.4	134.6	136.6
Rubber and asbestos	78.4	74.71	153.1	175.5	181.5	197.3
Timber industry	80.0	85.25	100.0	84.9	74.1	62.7
Paper and pulp	78.3	51.63	121.9	121.1	105.0	97.3
Investment goods	*87.6*	*68.91*	*158.6*	*179.7*	*180.3*	*190.1*
Steel constructions	64.8	80.48	128.7	131.6	131.6	117.6
Machine tools	76.0	67.76	156.6	174.5	173.2	183.1
Transport vehicles	68.1	62.71	144.1	178.9	211.1	246.2
Shipbuilding	169.9	64.91	207.4	187.4	141.3	131.9
Electrical engineering	58.8	74.75	178.7	234.5	236.8	255.8
Optical and precision engineering	96.2	74.30	174.5	170.9	150.3	155.1
Fabricated metal products	134.1	64.11	152.7	161.0	152.3	151.9
Consumer goods	*85.9*	*60.75*	*132.5*	*126.4*	*115.8*	*109.3*
China and earthenware	86.9	70.75	161.0	137.1	115.7	102.0
Glass industry	58.4	61.76	165.9	178.0	160.0	156.8
Entertainment instruments	74.5	75.29	205.6	179.6	166.9	150.6
Woodworking	81.5	77.86	128.4	119.6	106.4	104.6
Paper and board	107.1	46.72	154.3	176.2	177.1	180.7
Printing and publishing	70.1	50.48	136.4	149.5	154.2	157.5
Plastic products	48.8	62.38	197.5	342.5	440.7	589.2
Leather industry	104.7	84.24	128.6	109.8	94.3	69.2
Footwear industry	97.6	75.93	124.8	118.1	99.5	86.9
Textile industry	86.5	49.94	113.3	97.5	78.2	68.4
Clothing industry	95.1	67.96	152.2	148.9	150.9	135.1
Food and tobacco	*98.3*	*68.22*	*124.7*	*124.7*	*116.9*	*110.0*
Food and beverages	82.4	73.24	130.1	137.7	135.5	129.8
Tobacco manufactures	167.7	48.35	102.4	71.5	41.7	30.6
Total industry	**91.8**	**70.03**	**135.1**	**136.9**	**129.2**	**125.2**

Sources and methods: See Appendix 3.

commercial services and especially in the government sector during
the 1960s at the expense of all other spheres of economic activity made
labour-supply conditions even tighter for manufacturers. For the first
and only time in its peacetime history, Germany entered a period of

severe and sustained labour shortage that lasted until 1972. In twelve out of fourteen years after 1958, the rate of unemployment remained below 1.5 per cent; in nine of these years, it did not even reach 1 per cent. During the cyclical peaks of 1965 and 1970, the ratio of vacancies to registered unemployment in the country averaged between four and five (Paqué 1988, 2–3).

After 1961, West German manufacturers could maintain employment only by attracting migrant labour from abroad. The federal government had already signed an agreement with Italy in 1955 allowing German firms to recruit workers south of the Alps. Further treaties followed in the 1960s with Spain, Greece, Turkey, Portugal, and finally Yugoslavia. There were already 279,000 migrant workers in West Germany in 1960. Their number surpassed 1 million in 1964 and reached 2 million in the early 1970s (Weimer 1998, 170). Between 1960 and 1970, the share of foreign workers in the economy climbed from 1.5 per cent to 9.1 per cent (Schmidt 1995, 113), with four out of every five migrants finding jobs in manufacturing (Paqué 1988, 6–7). However, since the trade unions succeeded in further shortening of the workweek, effective labour input declined throughout the 1960s. This was the main force that pushed employers to adopt more capital-intensive modes of production, especially in industries where craft methods utilising skilled labour were traditionally more predominant (Radkau 1993, 130–1).

3.2   Industrial Labour Productivity

From the figures reported in Tables 3.1 and 3.3, we can construct index numbers for labour productivity at the industry level. Table 3.4 demonstrates that industrial value adder per worker hour fell sharply between 1938 and 1948, but increased rapidly thereafter. This follows the trajectory of output growth, but with a major difference. Whereas production grew by more than 60 per cent between the outbreak of World War II and 1955, labour productivity was scarcely 10 per cent above its pre-war peak in the mid-1950s. Given the constraints on industrial efficiency that the Nazi regime had created through direct intervention in both labour allocation and the redistribution of profits, and given the improvement of domestic market institutions and international trade liberalisation after 1948, this is an astonishingly poor result.

In mining, rubber and asbestos, the paper industry, steel constructions, machine tools, and several consumer goods industries, labour productivity had not recovered to the pre-war level even by 1955, despite robust output growth. The sharp fall in productivity that we can observe in steel constructions and entertainment products reflects, in part, shifts in the

Table 3.4 *Index of industrial labour productivity (1950 = 100)*

	1938	1948	1955	1960	1965	1970
Mining	*157.2*	*85.4*	*121.2*	*162.1*	*231.3*	*374.7*
Coal mining	165.5	86.6	118.3	146.3	195.4	275.1
Metallic ores	100.6	84.7	128.3	242.4	362.6	502.8
Salt mining	152.1	68.7	118.7	163.1	245.7	416.6
Crude oil and gas	117.7	75.9	202.9	480.4	1,183.4	3,278.5
Production goods	*112.6*	*77.4*	*137.6*	*197.2*	*283.9*	*431.9*
Fuel industry	73.8	29.5	218.7	435.9	1070.4	1812.1
Iron and steel	102.6	73.2	130.9	168.5	200.9	278.5
Non-ferrous metals	119.5	77.6	131.7	185.7	229.4	292.9
Construction materials	108.9	77.6	132.0	190.8	271.6	373.2
Chemical industry	139.2	76.7	147.8	217.4	334.7	559.2
Rubber and asbestos	145.8	92.0	130.1	158.4	202.9	252.5
Timber industry	131.7	81.6	124.2	187.7	249.7	364.4
Paper and pulp	137.0	91.8	126.6	168.1	228.5	331.1
Investment goods	*133.9*	*72.9*	*136.2*	*179.7*	*234.8*	*300.3*
Steel constructions	346.6	70.2	135.0	159.0	195.4	235.9
Machine tools	167.5	67.2	131.7	159.0	197.9	228.4
Transport vehicles	135.3	53.4	183.6	271.7	327.6	410.7
Shipbuilding	139.7	78.1	178.1	220.3	294.2	390.5
Electrical engineering	111.7	72.9	136.3	183.9	259.0	363.5
Optical and precision engineering	107.1	60.3	120.4	165.0	234.7	296.9
Fabricated metal products	90.9	103.5	125.8	169.4	228.5	299.4
Consumer goods	*116.0*	*75.9*	*126.4*	*185.7*	*262.6*	*352.7*
China and earthenware	152.8	79.6	117.0	162.6	227.7	287.9
Glass industry	116.5	89.0	101.1	148.5	226.6	305.6
Entertainment instruments	278.5	84.2	134.9	215.1	309.5	395.3
Woodworking	127.5	73.3	131.9	196.8	294.0	406.7
Paper and board	104.7	85.0	101.2	134.5	183.9	233.3
Printing and publishing	136.8	83.6	115.3	153.9	195.9	256.8
Plastic products	137.2	73.7	179.0	367.0	610.2	892.6
Leather industry	141.9	68.5	118.4	159.6	204.0	270.0
Footwear industry	141.4	71.5	112.8	154.9	204.7	221.8
Textile industry	108.2	83.9	135.8	210.2	305.2	415.7
Clothing industry	68.0	66.2	131.0	181.4	239.0	292.0
Food and tobacco	*105.8*	*83.3*	*126.5*	*177.2*	*244.1*	*308.8*
Food and beverages	109.2	89.8	122.6	162.8	213.7	265.4
Tobacco manufactures	80.0	77.8	150.4	291.2	666.3	1,091.7
Total industry	**119.5**	**76.3**	**130.5**	**181.3**	**250.7**	**340.9**

Sources: Industrial value-added from Table 3.1; labour hours from Table 3.3.

product mix after 1945. To some extent, these resulted from the shutdown of the armaments factories, which were highly mechanised and adopted mass production methods to meet the demands of total war.[2] In coal and salt mining, or in the leather and footwear industries, it is more difficult to attribute worsening productivity to changing product composition over time. By contrast, productivity growth between 1938 and 1955 was exceptionally high in the extraction of crude oil and natural gas, the fuel industry, transport vehicles, the clothing industry, and tobacco manufactures. A brief glance at the index numbers on capital stock and labour input is sufficient to recognise that the initial productivity surge in these industries was primarily the consequence of increased mechanisation.

Whereas the rate of output expansion declined sharply after 1955, labour-productivity growth did not slow down until the end of the postwar golden age. By 1970, value added per worker hour was almost three and a half times as large as it had been twenty years earlier. Productivity increased especially fast in production goods, but mining and most consumer goods industries also performed better than the engineering sector. In crude oil and natural gas, fuels, plastic products, and tobacco manufactures, the rates of productivity growth, already outstanding during the reconstruction years, increased further after 1955. In the mining sector and the tobacco industry, labour productivity soared despite sluggish output growth, particularly in the 1960s. In these industries, the substitution of capital for skilled labour drove the productivity surge from the late 1950s onward, whereas continued labour expansion fuelled by the influx of migrant workers limited productivity growth in investment goods.

Such variation across industries in the growth of value-added per worker hour begs the question to what extent structural change can explain aggregate labour-productivity growth in West German industry. Decomposition techniques are frequently used in disaggregated growth accounts to exploit the richness of data for a better understanding of the aggregate growth process. The specification I apply follows the framework suggested by Jorgenson, Gollop, and Fraumeni (1987) and adopted in Timmer et al. (2010, 153–4). It defines the growth of aggregate nominal value added (Y) over period t as the weighted growth of industry-specific value added (Z) in all industries j, where weights represent the period-average shares of each industry in Y.

$$\Delta \ln Y_t = \sum_j \bar{v}^Y_{Z,jt} \Delta \ln Z_{jt} \qquad (3.1)$$

---

[2] Before 1945, the production of artillery was counted under steel constructions, and the manufacturing of small firearms under entertainment products that included sport and hunting weapons in the German industry classification.

Labour-productivity growth in industry j is computed as the growth of value added divided by the increase in labour hours (L) over period t.

$$\Delta \ln z_t = \Delta \ln Z_{jt} - \Delta \ln L_{jt} \qquad (3.2)$$

Using this formula, aggregate labour-productivity growth can be decomposed into a set of industry contributions and a residual that measures the effect of labour reallocation across industries.

$$\Delta \ln Y_t / L_t = \sum_j \Delta \ln z_{jt} \bar{v}^Y_{Z,jt} + \left(\sum_j \Delta \ln L_{jt} \bar{v}^Y_{Z,jt} - \Delta \ln L \right)$$
$$= \sum_j \Delta \ln z_{jt} \bar{v}^Y_{Z,jt} + R_t \qquad (3.3)$$

The term R_t is positive whenever industries with above-average levels of labour productivity increase their weight in total labour input, or when industries with modest productivity levels see their employment shares decline. The decomposition results are reported in Table 3.5. In all the three sub-periods, aggregate labour-productivity growth was the result of industry contributions. The overall impact of structural shifts was insignificant and, if anything, moderated the rate of decline in industrial output per worker hour until 1948 as well as the productivity surge after 1955.

To demonstrate specifically which industries were driving productivity growth in West German industry, Figure 3.2 presents the industry-weighted contributions on a horizontal bar chart, separately for each of the three sub-periods. The diagram demonstrates that the sharp fall in aggregate labour productivity between 1938 and 1948 came primarily from the most important war industries: coal mining, iron and steel, chemicals (explosives), steel constructions (artillery), machine tools (tanks), and transport vehicles. Productivity in coal mining fell both during and immediately after the war because production was maintained through the increased application of unskilled, previously forced, and often poorly integrated foreign labour, as explained in Chapters 1 and 2. The primary metals and metal processing industries suffered disproportionately after the war from the dismantling of machinery, de-Nazification in management boards, and the output ceilings imposed by the occupation authorities.

Table 3.5 *Decomposing labour-productivity growth in West German industry (log %)*

	1938–1948	1949–1955	1956–1970
Aggregate labour productivity	−44.9	53.7	96.0
Industry contributions	−46.5	53.4	97.8
Labour reallocation	1.6	0.3	−1.8

Sources and methods: For industrial value added see references for Table 3.1; for labour input see Appendix 3. Methods are explained in Equations 3.1 to 3.3 and the text.

Productivity growth in the reconstruction phase was more evenly spread, but once again, the metallurgical industries, chemicals, and investment goods made very substantial contributions. Textiles, food and beverages, and tobacco manufactures carved out large shares from industrial production in early post-war Germany and, therefore, were also important drivers of aggregate labour-productivity growth. After 1955, we can observe significant structural shifts. The chemical industry became the most powerful locomotive of the productivity surge in West Germany, but food and tobacco, together with the largest consumer goods industries, also made a bigger contribution than the engineering sector, despite the considerably larger and constantly expanding share of investment goods in industrial production.

3.3 Total Factor Productivity

This section distils the quantitative evidence on industrial production and factor inputs into standard growth accounts for West German industry. Growth accounting is an analytical tool applied by economists to isolate the contributions of factor accumulation and productivity improvements to economic growth. The exact procedure is determined by how national income is modelled in the economy. This depends on the production function, first proposed by Tinbergen (1942), that predicts the proportional relationships between the growth of output and factor inputs. Still the most commonly used form is the Cobb–Douglas production function used in the neoclassical growth model developed by Solow (1956, 1957).

$$Y_t = A_t \left(K_t \right)^{\alpha} \left(L_t \right)^{1-\alpha}$$

$$(3.4)$$

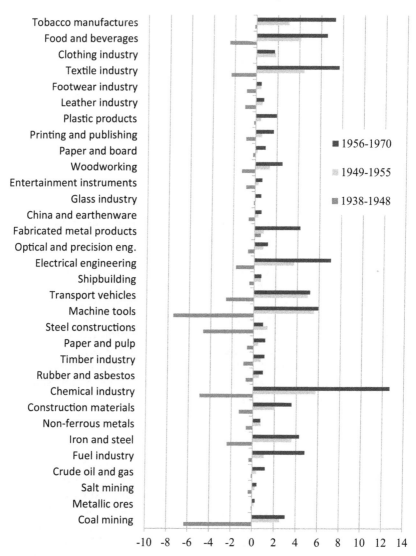

Figure 3.2 The industry origins of labour-productivity growth (%).
Sources and methods: See the notes for Table 3.5.

Value added (Y) at time t is the function of the available stock (K_t), the size of the labour input (L_t) and Total Factor Productivity (TFP, A_t), which reflects the level of technological advancement and the overall efficiency of factor use in the economy. The coefficients α and $1 - \alpha$ represent the elasticities of output with respect to capital and labour. In a dynamic framework, output growth can arise either from the expansion of factor inputs or from TFP growth, which represents technological progress and improvements in the efficiency with which factor inputs are used.

$$\Delta \ln Y = \alpha \Delta \ln K + (1 - \alpha) \Delta \ln L + \Delta \ln A \tag{3.5}$$

The terms α and $1 - \alpha$ stand for the respective shares of capital and labour in gross value added, while TFP growth is measured by the residual that remains after we subtract weighted input growth from the growth of value added. Equation (3.5) can be rewritten to express this residual as the proportion of labour-productivity growth that is unexplained by capital deepening, i.e. the increase of the capital-labour ratio. This formula is more appropriate if we wish to understand the dynamics of industrial development, in which capital intensity and technological progress are the main determinants.

$$\Delta \ln A = \Delta \ln (Y / L) - \alpha \left[\Delta \ln (K / L) \right] \tag{3.6}$$

Growth accounts for advanced economies most commonly use the value of one-third for α, which is a reasonable approximation of the share of capital in national income. Constant returns to scale, meaning that weighted input growth yields a proportional increase in output, constitute another important feature of the model. These assumptions cannot hold for industries that are highly capital intensive and cluster in order to increase efficiency through intensified specialisation and lower transaction costs between firms. Since we lack reliable data required to determine factor shares and returns to scale at the industry level, we can compute rates of TFP growth only for industry as a whole. However, disaggregate data are still useful because they can be applied to estimate both the overall scale effect and the factor shares with regression analysis. This approach confirms the constant-returns to scale assumption for the industrial sector as a whole and suggests an elasticity of output with respect to capital of approximately 0.4, which I apply in Tables 3.7 and 3.8.[3]

---

[3] Output elasticities with respect to labour and capital were estimated by a standard growth regression with industry fixed effects on a panel of all thirty-two industries and four subsequent five-year periods between 1950 and 1970. Using these factor shares, regressions of output growth on weighted input growth determine returns to scale. The coefficients do not differ enough between periods to substantially affect the estimates for the rate of TFP growth reported in Tables 3.7 and 3.8.

As I noted earlier, both the years of war-induced contraction and of post-war reconstruction witnessed large swings in capital utilisation. In the presence of substantial spare capacities, capital-stock levels do not accurately measure capital input. Using industry-specific estimates for the rate of capacity utilisation, constructed by the DIW, Table 3.6 reports index numbers for nominal and effective capital intensity, measured as gross capital stock per worker hour, for the five major sectors of mining and manufacturing. The adjusted figures suggest that capital deepening fuelled the growth of labour productivity after 1948, and particularly in the early 1950s. Unfortunately, we have no reliable data on capacity utilisation for the period prior to 1948. Assuming identical rates for 1938 and 1955 would imply that the effective capital-abour ratio in West German industry declined by about 20 per cent between 1938 and 1948, which would explain a considerable part of the productivity meltdown documented earlier.

The aggregate growth accounts are reported in Table 3.7. Industrial value added grew between 1938 and 1955 largely because of labour expansion. Since capital intensity had increased substantially over the same years, the growth of TFP was negligible. Within each of the first two sub-periods, TFP played a more prominent role. Even after adjusting for capacity utilisation, neither the sharp decline of labour productivity before 1948 nor the rapid recovery thereafter can be explained by capital deepening. This result confirms the findings of Eichengreen and Ritschl (2009) for the total economy. However, it must be emphasised that reconstruction growth in West German industry was not the outcome of a productivity miracle. More than half of the expansion in industrial value added between 1948 and 1955 came from increased labour input, and close to one-third of labour-productivity growth was due to increased capital intensity. In other words, factor accumulation explained two-thirds of output growth in the reconstruction phase.

Over the period 1938–55, TFP growth averaged 0.23 per cent annually, and even this result must be considered an upper bound estimate. It is highly unlikely that capacity utilisation before the war could attain the same level as during the 1955 boom. A lower utilisation rate for 1938 would imply a higher rate of capital accumulation, and thus a larger contribution of capital deepening to labour-productivity growth. This means that industrial efficiency in West Germany did not improve at all between the outbreak of World War II and the end of the post-war reconstruction years. Reconstruction growth merely restored the levels of industrial TFP that had already been achieved by the late 1930s. The resulting backlog in productivity growth, accumulated over a period when the

Table 3.6 *Index of capital intensity in West German industry* *(1950 = 100)*

	1938	1948	1955	1960	1965	1970
Nominal						
Mining	109.0	109.4	124.4	208.3	313.5	478.1
Production goods	77.3	145.0	102.0	145.2	218.3	304.6
Investment goods	90.6	137.8	96.8	140.0	220.3	285.3
Consumer goods	115.3	141.9	114.0	186.4	296.4	416.7
Food and tobacco	99.1	127.5	112.2	159.9	237.3	326.0
Total industry	90.8	135.8	102.8	149.9	226.1	299.6
Effective						
Mining		93.5	122.2	213.4	321.2	526.7
Production goods		94.4	126.9	179.9	251.9	364.6
Investment goods		94.1	144.9	198.9	294.7	426.2
Consumer goods		78.3	131.6	212.0	326.4	481.5
Food and tobacco		102.5	137.9	197.1	296.7	408.5
Total industry		91.4	130.8	180.9	250.4	356.7

Notes: Capital intensity is measured as gross capital stock per worker hour. Effective levels of capital intensity are computed by adjusting nominal levels for changes in the rate of capacity utilisation.
Sources: Capital stock from Table 3.2; labour hours from Table 3.3; rates of capacity utilisation from Krengel (1960), 81 and Baumgart (1972), 74.

Table 3.7 *Growth accounts for West German industry 1938–1970* *(log %)*

	1938–1948	1949–1955	1938–1955	1956–1970
Value-added	−72.0	119.4	47.4	88.4
Labour hours	−27.1	65.7	38.6	−7.6
Labour productivity	−44.9	53.7	8.8	96.0
Capital input	13.1	37.9	51.0	99.3
Effective capital input	−42.4	93.3	51.0	100.1
Effective capital intensity	−15.3	27.6	12.4	107.8
TFP	−38.8	42.7	3.9	52.9

Methods: Capital input is measured as gross capital stock adjusted for capacity utilisation, assuming identical utilisation rates for 1938 and 1950. For the method used to compute TFP growth, see Equations 3.5 and 3.6 and the supporting text.

Table 3.8 *Annualised growth accounts for West German industry, 1950–1970 (log %)*

	1951–1955	1956–1960	1961–1965	1966–1970
Value-added	11.3	6.8	5.3	5.5
Labour hours	6.0	0.3	−1.1	−0.6
Labour productivity	5.3	6.6	6.5	6.1
Capital input	6.6	7.8	7.1	5.0
Effective capital input	10.6	7.6	6.2	6.2
Effective capital intensity	4.6	7.4	7.3	6.9
TFP	3.5	3.6	3.5	3.4

Sources: Value-added and labour hours from Statistisches Bundesamt (1973), 48–53; gross capital stock from Baumgart and Krengel (1970), 82–3; rates of capacity utilisation from Krengel (1960), 81, and Baumgart (1972), 74.
Methods: See notes for Table 3.7.

Western world witnessed considerable technological progress, moved German industry far away from the frontier of the most efficient production possibilities. In turn, this implied a vast catch-up potential in labour productivity that could not be exhausted before the end of the golden age. After the displaced labour reserves were reintegrated into the urban-industrial economy, the further expansion of industrial output could come only from robust labour-productivity growth, which was driven approximately equally by capital deepening and by improvements in factor utilisation as well as the quality of factor inputs.

Table 3.8 reports the annualised growth accounts for the post-war period. These rates confirm that the mid-1950s separate two phases of industrial expansion that represent periods of extensive and intensive growth respectively. Output growth in West German industry slowed down markedly after 1955, but labour-productivity growth even accelerated and remained very fast until the end of the 1960s. Since the rate of capital accumulation did not diminish, capital intensity also increased more rapidly than during the reconstruction phase, even if we adjust for changes in capacity utilisation. However, capital deepening did not run into diminishing returns, which provides the strongest evidence for the fact that the potential for catch-up growth was still very large after the reconstruction phase. Given that each of the four five-year intervals after 1950 connects business-cycle peaks, the period-average growth rates reported in Table 3.8, and the conclusions about changing factor dynamics that we can derive from them, are not subject to any significant cyclical bias.

3.4   The Limits of Post-War Growth

The post-war resurgence of West German industry was driven by factor accumulation more than by productivity growth. To the extent and as long as output increased on the basis of existing capacities, growth was fuelled by labour expansion and did not require productivity-boosting technical advances. TFP growth could be achieved by the improved allocation of the complementary factors of production. As we saw in Chapter 2, the urban economy gradually absorbed the rural unemployed with the help of the state-sponsored housing and resettlement programs. In parallel, rural industry, endowed with surplus labour, built up capital rapidly in an era characterised by high investment and moderate wages. The requirements of urban industry, which was able to utilise initially idle capacities, did not crowd out rural investment.

The disaggregate data presented in this chapter confirm that the expansion of industry up to 1955 was driven by employment growth. Figure 3.3 demonstrates that West German industry derived a large part of its growth potential during the reconstruction years from spare capacities. Industries that had the most surplus capital in 1948 had suffered the sharpest contraction of employment previously, as a consequence of war-induced dislocation, but they also had the greatest potential for labour expansion and output growth in the reconstruction period that followed.

One additional factor behind the persistence of war-induced dislocation, namely the division of Germany, has been largely overlooked in the literature. Scholars have recognised its crippling impact on the East German economy, which had depended greatly on imported raw materials and intermediate inputs from the West, particularly coal and primary metals (Zank 1987; Matschke 1988; Sleifer 2006). However, because of the high degree of regional specialisation, structural disproportions were also substantial in West German industry after 1945. Surplus capacity in coal mining, iron and steel, and heavy equipment contrasted with excess demand for consumer products. Sleifer (2006) used the rich archival records of the 1936 industry census to determine levels of output, intermediate inputs, and employment at a highly disaggregated level in both East and West Germany, as well as in the eastern provinces that were ceded to Poland and the USSR after 1945. This information allows us to calculate the share of the three major parts of the former Reich in gross value-added across the thirty-two industries represented in the previous analysis.

Table 3.9 reveals that two-thirds of German industrial output was generated in the western part of the country before the outbreak of the war.

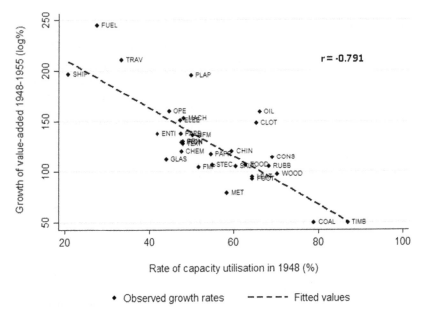

Figure 3.3 Growth potential derived from spare capacities in West German industry.
Note: r denotes the correlation coefficient between output growth and capacity utilisation.

We can observe an even higher degree of concentration in mining, primary metals, and most of the metal processing industries, as well as rubber and asbestos. Given that East German coal deposits were composed almost exclusively of brown coal and lignite, the western share in the extraction of higher quality hard coal was close to 90 per cent. By contrast, West German firms were relatively underrepresented in consumer goods, particularly in glass and plastic products, textiles and clothing, but also in transport vehicles. Whereas structural disproportions in the western part of the country appeared mostly in the form of excess capacity in raw materials and intermediate inputs, the paper industry serves as a counterexample. Western manufacturers were responsible for less than half of the paper and pulp production in Germany in 1936, but they processed more than 60 per cent of these materials.

To the extent that inter-zone trade in post-war Germany fell short of East–West transactions within the former Reich before and during World War II, and as long as external trade did not make up for this deficiency, industrial expansion reflected (at least in part) the need to eliminate structural disproportions. According to the official estimates shown in

Table 3.9 *The regional distribution of gross value-added in German industry in 1936*

	West Germany	East Germany	Eastern provinces
Mining	*70*	*19*	*11*
Coal mining	71	17	12
Metallic ores	78	14	8
Salt mining	44	56	0
Crude oil and gas	100	0	0
Production goods	*71*	*23*	*6*
Fuel industry	64	33	3
Iron and steel	87	10	3
Non-ferrous metals	69	31	0
Construction materials	64	22	14
Chemical industry	69	29	2
Rubber and asbestos	81	18	1
Timber industry	58	25	17
Paper and pulp	48	31	21
Investment goods	*70*	*28*	*2*
Steel constructions	84	8	8
Machine tools	67	30	3
Transport vehicles	59	40	1
Shipbuilding	94	3	3
Electrical engineering	74	25	1
Optical and precision engineering	66	33	1
Fabricated metal products	74	24	2
Consumer goods	*59*	*35*	*6*
China and earthenware	57	37	6
Glass industry	47	39	14
Entertainment instruments	76	24	0
Woodworking	64	28	8
Paper and board	61	34	5
Printing and publishing	65	31	4
Plastic products	56	39	5
Leather industry	73	24	3
Footwear industry	74	22	4
Textile industry	55	39	6
Clothing industry	46	45	9
Food and tobacco	*67*	*26*	*7*
Food and beverages	67	24	9
Tobacco manufactures	67	32	1
Total industry	**67**	**27**	**6**

Sources: The author thanks Jaap Sleifer for the data drawn from an electronic dataset that he compiled and partly published in Sleifer (2006). Sleifer computed industrial value-added from data on sales revenue in BArch R 3102/3309 and on the use of raw materials, fuels, and intermediary inputs in BArch R 3102/5922.

Table 3.10 *Domestic and international trade in industrial products in 1936*

	West Germany	East Germany	Berlin
% of industrial output sold			
a. In other parts of Germany	22	49	64
b. In the form of exports	18	15	12
% of industrial products bought			
a. From other parts of Germany	21	55	64
b. In the form of imports	12	6	9

Source: Gleitze (1956), 8, calculated from United Nations, *Economic Bulletin for Europe*, Vol. 3, 1949.

Table 3.10, one-fifth of the net output of West German industry in 1936 was sold in the eastern half of the Reich. A similar share of manufactures consumed in the West was produced east of the Elbe. The dependence on imports and on export markets was less critical. At low levels of output, West Germany could remain largely self-sufficient in industrial production until the late 1940s, but the impact of structural disproportions became evident during the reconstruction period. Quantitative evidence drawn from several sources can confirm that inter-zone trade in the postwar years was negligible by pre-war standards.[4]

Federau (1953) documented official trade between the Western occupation zones and the Soviet zone. It was relatively significant from 1947 to mid-1948 and its composition was shaped by pre-existing patterns of regional specialisation. Coal, coke, metallurgical products, machine tools, and basic chemicals from the West were exchanged for foodstuffs, lumber, brown-coal briquette, and paper and glass products from the East. After the Berlin Blockade had come to an end, inter-zone trade was restored by late 1949, reached a temporary summit in 1950, but then declined as Cold War tensions intensified again. At their peak in 1950, official West German exports to East Germany amounted to 328.5 million DM (Federau 1953, 402). In the same year, West German exports to all countries totalled 8.2 billion DM. Exports to Denmark alone were larger than exports to the GDR. The published records of the 1936 industry census report regional shares in export revenue at the industry level (Reichsamt 1939, 148–59). From this information, we can calculate that the West German share in total industrial exports was 65.8 per cent.

[4] For an official account of inter-zone interdependence, see OMGUS, *Economic data on Potsdam Germany*, 14–19, 29.

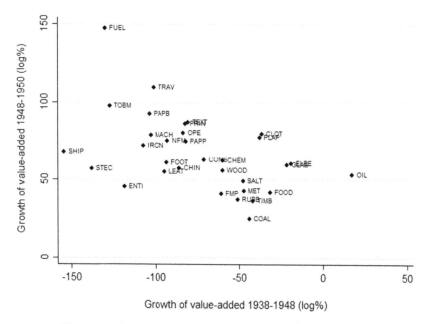

Figure 3.4 Reconstruction growth in West German industry.

Using the commodity series published in post-war trade statistics, we can compute the value of German industrial exports in 1936: 13.9 billion DM in 1950 prices. West German industrial exports in 1936 can, therefore, be estimated at 9.5 billion DM in 1950 prices. According to the figures reported in Table 3.10, the total value of West German industrial goods sold in the eastern part of Germany in 1936 then comes out to 11.6 billion DM. This figure surpasses the sum of official West German exports to the GDR in 1950 by an astonishing factor of 35.

This suggests that industrial recovery, to a large extent, depended on rebalancing the disproportionate production structure that the division of Germany had created. The quantitative evidence presented in this chapter confirms this indication in two ways. First, the western output share in 1936 can explain the growth of industrial value-added in the years of post-war recovery, controlling for the reconstruction effect. Figure 3.4 reveals a very strong negative relationship between growth rates of output in the periods prior to and after 1948 for all but a few industries. Most of these outliers exhibited growth dynamics different from what the reconstruction thesis would predict, precisely because of structural disproportions. Steel constructions and entertainment instruments suffered large output shocks between 1938 and 1948, but their high initial level of concentration in West Germany limited their growth potential thereafter. In the case of shipbuilding, this was complemented by output restrictions that remained in place with the occupation statutes until 1951. By contrast, electrical engineering, plastic products, and the clothing and the glass industries all achieved strong growth after 1948, despite a relatively modest decline of output during the 1940s. The western share in German industrial production in 1936 was the smallest in clothing, glass, and plastic products, which thus benefited from extended market potential following the division of Germany. The expansion of electrical engineering reflected the mass relocation of both large and medium-sized firms in the late 1940s from the Soviet occupation zone and Berlin mostly to southern Germany. This well-documented exodus was prompted both by fear from expropriation and severe shortages of intermediate inputs (Hefele 1998).

The only odd outlier in Figure 3.4 is crude oil and natural gas, which recorded exceptionally fast growth in value-added, even though it had concentrated exclusively in the western part of Germany in 1936. As noted earlier, the extraction of hydrocarbons was still in its infancy before the war, and in a country strongly dependent on fuel imports, its development in the post-war era was viewed as a strategic necessity. To exploit their market potential, industries previously underrepresented in West Germany had to expand their production capacity after 1948, and particularly in the 1950s, in order to satisfy booming consumer demand. Therefore, as shown in Figure 3.5, the growth of gross fixed capital between 1948 and 1955 was strongly determined by how much each industry had concentrated in West Germany before the war.

World War II dislocated the West German economy in more ways than one. As long as these effects lingered on, pre-war levels of industrial efficiency could not be surpassed. Millions of displaced workers had to be reintegrated into the urban economy, and new capacities had to be built up both in overpopulated rural areas and in industries that faced excess demand after the division of Germany. Consequently, industrial recovery was driven by the extended use of capital and labour, rather than productivity growth. In fact, the opportunity to expand on the basis of existing capacities and the need to meet the pent-up demand of a war-torn population for manufactures that had already been on the market before 1939 thwarted technological progress and product innovation, especially given the scarcity of skilled manpower. The resulting backlog in productivity growth created further scope for improvement in industrial efficiency through the adoption of new technologies from the late 1950s onward, when labour-supply constraints became tighter for the economy as a whole. Therefore, growth rates of industrial labour productivity and

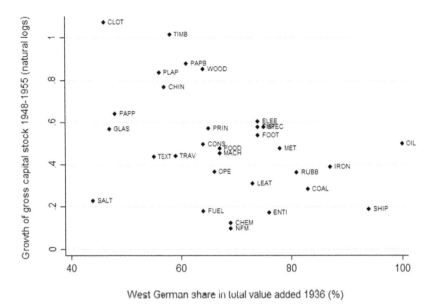

Figure 3.5 Rebalancing industrial capacities during the reconstruction phase.

TFP remained remarkably high by international standards until the end of the golden age.

German historiography provides ample evidence for the persistent impact of war-induced dislocation on productivity growth. First, as long as efficiency gains could be achieved through the improved allocation of productive forces and through the abolition of market restrictions and the state-sponsored monopolies that had characterised the Nazi era, industrial firms had little incentive to increase their costs by boosting research and development expenditure. Second, after a decade of hardship and destitution, German society had an insatiable thirst for traditional consumer goods, especially durables (Wildt 1993). In 1950, three out of four households had coal heating and only 7 per cent of them were equipped with an electrical stove. Even by 1958, only every fifth family owned a refrigerator, and there was substantial demand for simple household appliances as well as furniture and textile products (Weimer 1998, 116).

Urban reconstruction at home and the restocking of industrial plants in countries that Nazi Germany had plundered during the war meant that manufacturers of both production and investment goods could thrive in domestic as well as foreign markets by operating with the

technologies of the 1930s. In steel constructions, German firms continued to sell coal furnaces and steam-powered locomotives, while the dar-
ling of the automobile industry became the Volkswagen 'Beetle'. In key
industries, most notably machine tools, precision engineering, and fabri-
cated metal products, insufficient plant size prevented standardised mass
production (Radkau 1993). In the engineering sector, Germany had long
specialised in skilled-labour-intensive, high-value-added differentiated
quality products, and thus West German exporters continued to focus
on product rather than process innovation. Quality engineering goods
with the lucrative 'Made in Germany' label faced highly income elastic
demand, meaning that consumer demand increased faster than disposable income. Thus, engineering firms could maintain high profits without making significant real efficiency gains, which would have required
technological and managerial innovation (Ambrosius and Kable 1992;
Ambrosius 1993).

This does not mean that German industrialists were unaware of the
striking technological and organisational superiority of their American
counterparts after World War II. The increased presence of US companies on German soil and the tours organised for German businessmen
and engineers under the Marshall Plan made it easier to establish con-
tacts to and learn from the technology leaders. However, even in the
largest, traditionally export oriented, and globally present German firms,
the process of technology and know-how adoption was, at best, selective.
The most frequent obstacles were the lack of funds needed to purchase
expensive licences and machinery, organisational differences that made
mass production difficult to achieve, and, in some market segments, the
absence of visible American competitors (Hilger 2004).

Even the main showcase of industrial mass production in Germany
owed its success to the Nazi era rather than post-war innovation. Blessed
by the enormity of its production infrastructure, which had largely survived the war and escaped post-war dismantling, and its exceptionally
limited product range, Volkswagen was able to scale up its output rapidly after 1950. This enabled the firm to achieve spectacular productivity gains and to outcompete its rivals both within Germany and in
markets worldwide for cheap working-class cars. The number of vehicles that Volkswagen produced went from fewer than 20,000 in 1948 to
more than 100,000 in 1951, half a million in 1958, and approximately
1 million in 1961. Meanwhile exports jumped from 30,000 in 1950 to
almost half a million in 1960 (Tolliday 1995, 327). Not until 1957 did
Volkswagen began to face up to the need of making additional investment in new assembly capacity. As one of the pet projects of megaloma-
niac Nazi leaders, the original works were built for an annual capacity of

around 220,000 cars, which could be relatively easily stretched to almost 300,000 by 1956 with little auxiliary investment. This capacity was outrageously large given the likely demand of the late 1930s. Volkswagen had a competitive edge due to low production costs owed, in large part, to its uniquely narrow product range and extraordinary economies of scale. As early as 1952, its daily output of 550 cars was already the highest of any company in Europe. By 1957, the 40,000 cars that rolled out every month from its main plant could be matched only by monster assembly lines of Detroit (Tolliday 1995, 335–8).

Tolliday summed up the unique experience of the Wolfsburg auto giant in the brief extract that follows, which presents perhaps the most illustrative case for the wartime origins of West German industrial success. Volkswagen was originally an enterprise conceived, financed, and operated by the state, not by private capital, and served political and strategic more than economic needs. Still, its unconventional upbringing provided unique advantages that competitors could not aspire to rival.

It was inconceivable that any commercial enterprise would have invested on the scale or grandiose conception of the VW project either before or immediately after the war. In terms of conventional business calculation the project was absurd and infeasible. Yet it turned out to be a 'triumph of folly'. The plant survived the war, its debts were effectively wiped out, and it was able to achieve to the full its innate potential in the radically unforeseen environment of the post-war recovery. An economic institution conceived for political purposes turned out to be the crucial vehicle for economic recovery in the automobile sector. (Tolliday 1995, 347)

During the 1950s, broadly speaking, German industrialists made little effort to make use of American know-how, even though there were important exceptions. Siemens, to name one prominent example, actively cooperated with US partners in electrical power generation, semiconductors, and electronic data analysis. Caution was also exercised in adopting the diversified product portfolios of American corporations, as they were difficult to operate in an environment that emphasised product quality, customer service, and self-trained management. This made West German firms adhere to their core business, especially in established industries, such as car manufacturing or machine tools. In general, two factors differentiated German companies in their attitude towards technology adoption: how strong was the competition they faced from US firms and how modern the industry was. In frontier segments of the chemical and electro-technical industries, traditional markets were too small to meet growth targets, and it was impossible to expand without facing American competition. In established industries, however, growth could be achieved through the post-war recovery of the base markets for the core business products, while long-established partnerships secured an edge for German firms against their new competitors (Hilger 2004).

Finally, restoring pre-existing levels of industrial productivity in the early post-war period was made difficult by the worsening of labour qualifications. The tremendous wartime casualties reduced the share of men aged between twenty and thirty-five years in the total population from 12.1 per cent in 1939 to 7.4 per cent in 1946 (Kramer 1991, 11). Increased female participation in subsequent years could not sufficiently substitute for male employment, as manual work in industry was physically demanding and female employees had, on average, significantly lower levels of qualification than their male colleagues. In September 1950, the skilled-labour ratio of the manual workforce was 50 per cent for men but only 16.2 per cent for women.[5] Unlike in many other belligerent economies, most working-age women in Germany had little opportunity to acquire industrial working skills during the war years. If anything, the labour-market policies of the Nazi regime depressed the level of female employment in general (Milward 1977, 87).

Although the early 1940s witnessed large structural shifts in industrial employment, the reallocation of labour into heavy industry was achieved by the increased application of voluntary and forced foreign labour, which provided more than 3 million employees in 1944 for manufacturing and mining alone and 7 million for the total economy. Besides mining and agriculture, migrant and prison labour was employed primarily in the defence industries (Ambrosius 2000, 347). For several munitions manufacturers, foreigners made up more than 70 per cent of the workforce (Müller 1993, 368–9). As a consequence, the reallocation of indigenous workers between sectors remained very limited. Figure 3.6 demonstrates that the number of women working in German industry stagnated until 1942 and began to increase only in the phase of total war. The economy was also clearly running out of indigenous labour reserves at a dangerous pace as a result of conscription and civilian casualties. Thus the size of the industrial workforce could be maintained only by the sudden spurt in the employment of foreigners between 1942 and 1943, which raised the number of both male and female employees.

Abelshauser (1999) suggested that the introduction of compulsory apprenticeships before the war induced considerable improvements in industrial working skills, and potentially increased productivity in the post-war period. The new Imperial School Act (*Reichsschulgesetz*) came into effect in July 1938. It made it mandatory for all elementary school (*Volksschule*) graduates who did not subsequently enrol in secondary

[5] StatBRD, Vol. 45.2 (1952), 81.

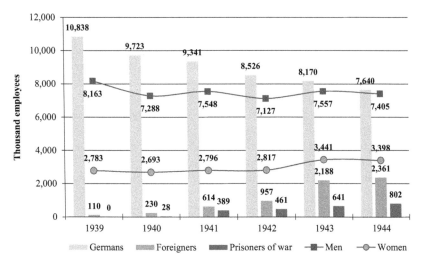

Figure 3.6 The composition of industrial employment in Germany during World War II.
Note: Foreign labour does not include prisoners of war. Figures refer to 1937 borders.
Source: OMGUS. 1946. *Statistical handbook*, Part I, B. 1a–f.

schools to complete three years of vocational training and offered one-year apprenticeships for girls on a voluntary basis (Tenorth 1993, 245). As compelling as it may seem, what Abelshauser proposed does not find support in the historical evidence. World War II administered a massive blow to human-capital accumulation in German industry. Vocational school teachers were conscripted into the armed forces, except in the most directly war-related occupations. In addition, the government preferred on-the-job training to formal apprenticeships, given the urgency of war production, and thus shut down most of the training workshops that had been established shortly before the war (Grüner 1989, 305). Enrolment in polytechnics diminished even faster after most students were either drafted or were forced to graduate before they could complete the normal training period, if they had specialised in fields critical for armaments production. Towards the end of the war, several polytechnics were completely closed down (Pätzold 1989, 284–5).

The most direct impact of wartime destruction on technical education was the demolition of schools and training facilities, as the overwhelming majority of these establishments were located in industrial cities, prime targets of aerial bombardment. The loss of educational facilities in urban areas also made a decisive impact on the geographic and, through that, sectoral composition of vocational training. Before the war, handcrafts had trained roughly as many apprentices as industry and commerce together, but this changed fundamentally by the late 1940s. Craft workshops were able to employ more apprentices because they were often settled in rural counties with adequate supply of labour and did not require a large pool of workers with standardised qualifications that would have necessitated formal training in industry-specific vocational schools. This, in turn, implies that the growth of urban industry in the early post-war era was constrained not only by regional labour shortage, but also by the scarcity of skilled labour in particular.

Not surprisingly, industry and commerce accounted for the bulk of the expansion in vocational training during the early 1950s. The number of apprentices in both sectors climbed from 379,000 in 1949 to 837,000 in 1956, whereas the increase in all other types of non-agricultural apprenticeships amounted to fewer than 100,000. Growth was particularly strong in large-scale manufacturing, where the number of training workshops rose by more than 50 per cent between 1952 and 1958, and where the share of apprentices in the manual workforce increased despite the high overall rate of employment expansion. However, the mid-1950s also represented a clear trend break in the structure of human-capital formation in West German industry. From an historic summit, the number of apprenticeships in all occupations began to decline. Between 1956 and 1960, enrolment in vocational schools dropped by 650,000, which meant a decline of almost 30 per cent (Hoffmann 1962, 62, 112–14).

This shift in trend can be explained by two factors: (1) the replacement of the large birth cohort of the late 1930s, when Nazi economic and social policy managed to push up the birth rate significantly, by the very small cohort born during the war; and (2) the declining popularity of skilled manual work in favour of white-collar professions, especially public service, which required upper-secondary or tertiary qualifications. In the period 1952–60, the share of juveniles between the ages of sixteen and nineteen enrolled in formal education rose by 5 percentage points. However, while enrolment in vocational schools (Berufsschule) declined by 3 percentage points, it increased by the same margin in technical high schools (Realschule) and grammar schools (Gymnasium) (Liefmann-Keil 1964, 429–31).

Within technical education, enrolment shifted away from the vocational schools to upper-secondary polytechnics (Fachschule), after the Association of German Engineers (VDI) reported critical shortages of engineers and technicians in West German industry. Various estimates put the deficit in the range of 30–35,000. The Conference of the Ministers of Culture representing the federal states agreed in the autumn of 1956 that available capacities had to expand by 50 per cent to close the gap within the following years. Between 1958 and 1968, total enrolment in engineering schools increased by 62 per cent. The evolution of technical education followed the development of the economy, as the number of product engineers trained in the investment goods industries expanded the most until the early 1960s. Agriculture became more important thereafter, due to the mechanisation drive in the farming sector. Enrolment in technical colleges began to decline only when the birth cohorts of the early 1940s reached adulthood, and especially with the rapid increase in university admissions after 1968 (Kultusministerkonferenz 1969, 1–4).

During the post-war era, vocational training was instrumental in shaping the qualification structure of the industrial workforce in the Federal Republic. For the first time, this chapter reports territorially consistent industry-level data on the number of skilled workers and their share in the manual workforce in the 1950s and 1960s. For 1964 and 1970, the figures were taken directly from official employment statistics.[6] The skilled-labour ratio of a given branch of industry is simply computed by dividing the number of skilled workers with the number of all manual workers, excluding apprentices who were in the process of completing their three-year vocational training at the time of investigation. Although such detailed statistics are not available for the 1950s, the Federal Statistical Office conducted two major surveys on the structure of industrial wages in November 1951 and in October 1957, which classified manual workers according to their industry of employment and skill level.[7] Since these surveys are less disaggregated than the standard industry statistics, the industry classification presented here is slightly different from the one used in the previous analysis. The relatively large samples probed in both surveys were intended to be representative of the skill composition of total employment within the individual industries. On this basis, I could compute the number of skilled workers in every branch of industry by multiplying the skilled-labour ratios determined from the surveys by the total number of manual workers reported in monthly industry statistics.[8]

Table 3.11 reveals that the skilled workforce of West German industry continued to grow rapidly even after urban reconstruction and the resettlement of displaced workers had been completed. This was the outcome of surging enrolment in vocational training in the early

---

[6] Bundesminiterium für Arbeit und Sozialordnung (1966), 48–51; idem (1971), 60–3.
[7] StatBRD, Vol. 90 (1954), 42–5; StatBRD, Vol. 246.1 (1960), 14.
[8] IndBRD, Part 1, Vol. 1.11 (November 1951), 8–10; IndBRD, Series 1, Vol. 7.10 (October 1957), 9–11. Since the November 1951 survey investigated all non-agricultural sectors of the economy, not only industry proper, in my computations, I account for manual workers only in establishments with at least ten employees, thus excluding handcraft workshops.

Table 3.11 *The number of skilled workers in West German industry*

	1951	1957	1964	1970
Mining	*316,060*	*347,479*	*296,438*	*152,959*
Hard coal	268,557	297,616	259,796	130,474
Brown coal and lignite	19,254	19,325	16,515	9,227
Metallic ores	17,067	15,678	6,716	3,483
Salt mining	7,141	8,766	8,506	6,903
Other mining	4,041	6,095	4,905	2,872
Production goods	*286,951*	*342,327*	*410,514*	*424,170*
Construction materials	48,485	67,795	73,177	73,399
Iron and steel	109,906	127,498	157,230	137,732
Non-ferrous metals	23,142	25,497	23,579	26,109
Chemical industry	59,807	69,208	101,877	119,462
Fuel industry	6,652	8,540	11,254	12,984
Rubber and asbestos	12,686	18,660	25,077	35,966
Timber industry	26,274	25,129	18,320	18,518
Investment goods	*670,900*	*912,810*	*1,084,906*	*1,155,108*
Steel constructions	65,478	85,938	108,067	103,142
Machine tools	243,086	325,781	392,532	426,855
Transport vehicles	100,184	141,855	175,192	206,322
Shipbuilding	32,790	53,439	48,429	45,691
Electrical engineering	88,946	138,227	194,420	209,336
Optical and precision engineering	34,253	40,765	37,518	38,311
Fabricated metal products	106,162	126,805	128,748	125,451
Consumer goods	*502,558*	*561,669*	*641,028*	*623,338*
Pottery and glass products	31,654	39,842	39,159	38,227
Woodworking	93,209	91,784	81,557	82,183
Entertainment instruments	14,973	18,862	15,337	14,834
Paper and printing industry	77,896	98,974	124,904	132,369
Plastic products	4,306	8,633	19,083	29,852
Leather and footwear	62,775	53,391	62,229	45,384
Textile industry	133,823	133,111	150,919	127,184
Clothing industry	83,922	117,071	147,840	153,305
Food and tobacco	*118,034*	*127,567*	*119,741*	*112,478*
Food processing	54,299	61,599	62,178	61,190
Beverages	25,120	35,946	46,870	46,291
Tobacco industry	38,615	30,023	10,693	4,997
All industries	**1,894,503**	**2,291,852**	**2,552,627**	**2,468,053**

Sources: See the text and notes on the previous page.

1950s. Proportionally, the rate of expansion between 1951 and 1957 was almost twice as high as from 1958 to 1964, but the skilled workforce grew by more than a quarter million in both periods. Until 1957, the numbers increased most rapidly in investment goods, particularly transport vehicles, shipbuilding, and electrical engineering. In the late

1950s and early 1960s, the growth of skilled manpower slowed down considerably in the engineering sector, while it maintained its pace in both production and consumer goods. Two factors can largely explain this shift in trend. Ferrous metals, chemicals, and the printing industry paid the highest wages for skilled workers in the mid-1950s, and the auspicious earning opportunities proved attractive for new apprentices (Markmann 1964, 453). The textile and clothing industries traditionally employed mostly female workers, and thus could enhance their skill endowments due to the increasing participation of girls in vocational training during the 1950s.

In West German industry as a whole, the skilled workforce began to shrink only in the late 1960s, and even then very moderately. Although enrolment in vocational schools diminished after 1957, the newly trained apprentices entering the industrial labour force continued to outnumber the skilled workers moving into retirement for a while longer. Between 1964 and 1970, the number of skilled workers grew further in the most dynamic industries, non-ferrous metals, chemicals, rubber and asbestos, machine tools, transport vehicles, and plastic products, despite the increasing capital intensity of production, which I demonstrated earlier. Table 3.12 points to the most important consequence of the expansion of vocational training during the reconstruction phase: the skilled-labour ratio of the industrial workforce remained remarkably stable on a very high level throughout the post-war golden age.

However, the overall trend disguised important differences across industries. The skilled-labour ratio increased sharply from an already high level in the mining sector. By contrast, it remained stable in both production and consumer goods, and declined considerably in investment goods as well as food and tobacco. The share of skilled labour in mining increased in the early 1960s because employment in total fell like a rock following the 1958 coal crises, and it took several years to reduce capacities in vocational training in accordance with changing labour demand. Mining companies initially preferred to economise on unskilled labour and to retain their skilled workforce, which dominated the powerful trade unions.

Employment contraction between 1964 and 1970 also increased the share of skilled labour in production goods, most prominently in construction materials, timber, and the fuel industry. Similar patterns prevailed in textiles as well as leather and footwear, where the workforce began to shrink already in the early 1960s, but the number of skilled workers continued to increase until 1964. By contrast, even the most substantial expansion of vocational training could not keep pace with the staggering employment growth in engineering, where the skilled-labour

Table 3.12 *The skilled-labour ratio of the industrial workforce (%)*

	1951	1957	1964	1970
Mining	58.2	62.3	71.2	60.6
Hard coal	61.1	65.9	76.2	62.5
Brown coal and lignite	43.3	42.5	42.5	41.0
Metallic ores	58.0	56.4	58.8	59.2
Salt mining	42.3	43.4	51.4	64.7
Other mining	32.8	47.2	60.4	62.1
Production goods	30.1	29.8	31.9	34.0
Construction materials	24.0	30.2	31.7	38.1
Iron and steel	34.6	31.5	34.5	33.1
Non-ferrous metals	33.9	30.7	26.7	27.6
Chemical industry	26.8	26.0	30.6	33.0
Fuel industry	42.5	41.6	47.6	62.2
Rubber and asbestos	26.0	25.2	26.4	32.6
Timber industry	33.8	33.4	30.3	35.7
Investment goods	52.8	49.4	43.4	41.6
Steel constructions	70.2	67.8	66.3	68.5
Machine tools	64.1	60.3	56.4	55.2
Transport vehicles	60.0	57.3	44.6	42.5
Shipbuilding	78.8	71.4	77.7	78.2
Electrical engineering	38.4	37.0	30.5	28.1
Optical and precision engineering	45.8	38.3	33.0	32.0
Fabricated metal products	37.6	33.4	29.5	28.3
Consumer goods	39.0	34.9	38.0	37.7
Pottery and glass products	30.2	28.1	26.7	26.8
Woodworking	60.3	49.8	45.8	45.9
Entertainment instruments	47.3	37.1	33.1	32.4
Paper and printing industry	41.6	40.0	39.4	39.5
Plastic products	20.6	20.3	21.3	22.8
Leather and footwear	51.6	35.3	43.7	38.2
Textile industry	26.8	24.6	33.4	32.0
Clothing industry	49.5	47.1	46.8	50.6
Food and tobacco	41.0	38.0	30.9	30.7
Food processing	30.5	29.3	24.9	24.8
Beverages	53.4	54.6	44.7	47.9
Tobacco industry	61.5	50.7	32.2	21.6
All industries	**43.6**	**41.7**	**40.6**	**39.2**

Sources: See the text and notes before Table 3.11.

ratio declined by more than 11 percentage points between 1951 and 1970. However, the reliance on craft-based production technology continued to require a highly qualified workforce in small and medium-scale engineering plants, which pushed up wages for skilled workers. As skilled-labour input became more expensive, large firms began to shift towards more capital-intensive modes of production, particularly in transport vehicles and electrical engineering, leading to an increase in the capital-labour ratio documented in the previous analysis.

Whereas labour-supply constraints forced factor substitution in investment goods, the declining skilled-labour ratio in food and tobacco reflected improved access to capital in industries, which had been deprived of resources during the Nazi era. Standardised mass production became dominant in the tobacco industry from the late 1950s onward. Investment in fixed capital was used to attain optimal factor shares in accordance with the best available production technologies, while vocational training was massively downscaled. Consequently, the share of skilled labour in the manual workforce plummeted no less than 40 percentage points between 1951 and 1970. Factor substitution in this particular industry was also prompted by the gradual shift in employment structure, away from labour-intensive cigar manufacturing to highly mechanised cigarette production.

The maintenance of a skilled workforce combined with induced factor substitution in some of the most dynamically expanding branches of manufacturing meant that West German industry was effective in adopting modern production techniques, leading to fast growth in TFP until the end of the golden age. An additional factor, namely immigration from East Germany, was often attributed an instrumental role in enhancing the supply of skilled labour during the 1950s, which in turn sustained wage moderation and enhanced the profitability of investment in fixed capital (Schmidt 1996). Ambrosius (1996) and Heidemeyer (1994) emphasised the exceptionally high rate of economic activity among GDR dissidents. Abelshauser (1983) drew attention to the selective nature of the otherwise mass exodus, as a vast army of highly qualified people crossed the border in hope of freedom and a better life: between 1952 and 1963, more than 20,000 engineers and technicians, approximately 4,500 medical doctors, and more than 1,000 university lecturers and professors. Emigration seemed a particularly attractive option for technical personnel. While the share of engineers in the total population was significantly higher in West than in East Germany during the late 1950s, the universities and polytechnics of the GDR actually trained more engineers relative to population size (Abelshauser 1983, 96–7).

Although we cannot precisely tell to what extent these refugees altered the qualification structure of the West German labour force, there is some quantitative evidence on their composition according to age, gender, and original occupation, as well as employment and educational attainment. From 1944 until 1961, almost 3.6 million people emigrated from East Germany to the Federal Republic and West Berlin, more than

2 million after 1950, while fewer than half a million crossed the border in the opposite direction. Many of these migrants were former expellees who were allowed to reunite with their families residing in the other German state. The number of actual refugees totalled 2.7 million.[9] In 1961, when the Berlin Wall effectively brought this exodus to an end, 6.4 per cent of the West German population reported to have lived in East German territory before the war (Steinert 1995, 570).

The year of the brutally repressed East Berlin Uprising, 1953, represented a pinnacle in the number of defections. After 1957, somewhat improved economic conditions in the GDR and the slowdown of employment expansion in West Germany made emigration slightly less attractive for East German citizens. In 1961, during the last months before the border between the eastern and western sectors of Berlin was finally sealed, the numbers increased sharply once more, and for the last time. The share of men among the refugees gradually declined during the 1950s, and after 1961 the clear majority were women, mostly pensioners who did not need to leave partners and children behind. Before the building of the Wall, more than three-quarters of the refugees were between the ages of fifteen and sixty-four. This compared very favourably with only 65 per cent for the rest of the population (Ambrosius 1996, 50).

Consequently, the share of those employed or actively seeking employment among the refugees was exceptionally high, averaging more than 60 per cent, while the corresponding rate for the West German population as a whole peaked at 48.8 per cent in 1957. As a result, the participation rate declined substantially during the 1960s, after mass immigration from the GDR had terminated (Sachverständigenrat 1991, 344). The role of East German refugees in the development of the West German labour force was also influenced by their modern occupational structure. Since illegal emigration from the GDR was dominated by urban dwellers, especially residents of Berlin, agricultural labourers were underrepresented. The share of those with occupations in industry, handcrafts, or construction increased over time, but stayed below the corresponding level in West Germany. Hence, service employees, and especially members of the medical profession, had a much larger share among the refugees than in the total economically active population.[10]

East German refugees differed in their qualifications also from other industrial employees. The share of engineers and technicians in the total labour force increased from 1.4 per cent in 1950 to 1.9 per cent in 1957, and surpassed 2 per cent in the early 1960s. The same figure

[9] Fachserie A/4 (1966), 18, 36.
[10] Ibid., 37.

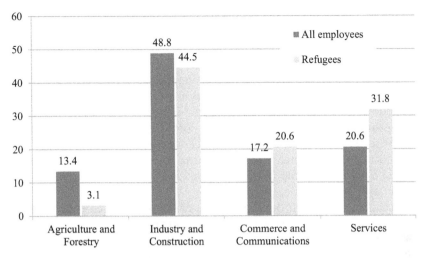

Figure 3.7 The employment structure of East German refugees in West Germany in 1961 (%).
Source: Calculations based on data from Fachserie A/4 (1966), 92–3.

for refugees rose sharply from a modest 0.3 per cent in 1953 to 2.6 per cent in 1961.[11] This implies that the integration of GDR citizens possessing higher technical qualifications into the West German labour force was indeed largely responsible for the increased employment of engineers and technicians in industrial production during the late 1950s and early 1960s, which was critical for the adoption of mass production.

As a result of occupational differences, the employment structure of the refugees at the end of their mass exodus from East Germany in 1961 also diverged from that of the entire labour force. Figure 3.7 shows that only 3 per cent found jobs in agriculture, which still accounted for more than 13 per cent of total employment in West Germany. Immigration from the GDR was not directly responsible for the growth of industrial employment either. Refugees were overrepresented in trade and transportation, and strongly overrepresented in services, especially in health care. However, the high share of refugees employed in the tertiary sector meant that industrial employment continued to expand longer than in most other Western countries. In other words, manufacturers did not need to compete with firms in other sectors of the economy for increasingly scarce labour.

[11] Ibid., p. 37; *Wirtschaft und Statistik*, Vol. 1961, 270–2 cited in Liefmann-Keil (1964), 428.

The quantitative evidence confirms that immigration from the GDR strengthened not so much the production as the research and development capabilities of the West German economy until the early 1960s, besides supporting the expansion of public services. Consequently, the educational system in West Germany retained its strong focus on intermediate qualifications acquired in the framework of vocational training, and allowed for only a slow and gradual increase of enrolment in full-time education at the upper-secondary and tertiary levels. This strategy guaranteed an adequate supply of skilled workers and technical staff for the most dynamic branches of West German industry, which thus continued to expand primarily in high-value-added engineering products and other capital goods.

As was the case with the dismantling of industrial machinery to meet reparations demands, historical developments that brought gains to West Germany implied mounting hardships east of the Elbe. Whereas the West German economy was endowed with surplus labour, its eastern counterpart suffered from an increasingly chronic shortage of skilled labour, and faced general labour scarcity from the late 1950s onward. Since the bulk of East German refugees who emigrated during the late 1940s were young adults, the natural birth rate in the GDR lagged behind the death rate until 1949. This also limited the potential for future population growth. The male population that provided the backbone of the industrial labour force even declined between 1939 and 1950. Since men had much higher qualification levels than women, there was a particularly acute shortage of skilled labour in industry and handcrafts that only became worse during the 1950s due to emigration (see Steinberg 1991, 39–40).

In addition, if structural disproportions created by the division of Germany limited post-war growth in West German industry, they were devastating for the East German economy. The two nascent German states followed very different paths of recovery. At low levels of output, the West remained largely self-sufficient in industrial production until the late 1940s, but the East suffered from crippling input–output bottlenecks immediately after the war. These were the consequences of the industrial structure that East Germany had inherited, dominated by higher order manufactures, mostly consumer goods. As I explained earlier, the production of the key primary and intermediate inputs had concentrated almost exclusively in the West before World War II. Wartime investments further aggravated these structural disproportions. By 1943, East German firms produced 37.8 per cent of the machine tools, 47.3 per cent of the aluminium, and nearly half of all petroleum manufactured in the territory of post-war Germany, but accounted for only

0.5 per cent of total output in coke, 1.6 per cent in raw iron, and 6.9 per cent in steel (Matschke 1988, 101). To the extent that primary metal imports from the Western occupation zones fell short of interwar and wartime trade volumes, they thwarted growth in the metal processing industries.

The shortage of coal was even more critical. East German coal deposits consisted almost exclusively of brown coal and lignite. Despite vast deposits of these lower-quality coals and despite the presence of a large petrochemical industry, domestic production could cover only half of the East German fuel demand. As opposed to the situation in West Germany, coal shortages in the East also worsened over time, especially when Western hard-coal transports were suspended in retaliation over the Berlin Blockade (Zank 1987, 19–20). Vital inputs were not only in short supply. They were also difficult to allocate with insufficient transport capacity, which has been considered the most paralyzing bottleneck of the East German economy and persisted long after it had been eliminated in the West. The Western literature has blamed Soviet dismantling policy that further reduced metallurgical capacities and socialist planning that prioritised material production over the transport sector in the early post-war years (Zank 1987; Karlsch 1993). In addition, East Germany produced very little railway material and rolling stock, and thus could have increased transport capacity, in the short run, only with equipment imported from the West (Ritschl and Vonyó 2014).

Building a domestic heavy industrial base in the GDR required large investments in new capacities. Without access to foreign capital, these investments could be financed only if consumption was depressed. In turn, this had negative consequences for labour incentives and public welfare, pushing East German citizens into emigration. With insufficient supplies of coal and intermediate inputs, the production capacity of the consumer and engineering industries remained underutilised until well into the 1950s (Zank 1987, 22). These unfavourable conditions, together with the fear from expropriation, prompted the aforementioned relocation of manufacturing firms from the Soviet zone to West Germany. Besides the direct impact on output, their exodus had important secondary outcomes for productivity growth in both parts of Germany. The substantial transfer of know-how permanently hurt East German competitiveness in several industries. Since most firms that relocated were small and medium-sized enterprises, their absence weakened supplier networks in East Germany and strengthened industrial clusters in the West. Finally, as small firms had traditionally trained the majority of industrial apprentices, their relocation had a differential impact on human capital formation in the two German states. The demise of the once flourishing handcraft industries in East Germany was not least the outcome of insufficient capacity to train apprentices (see Hefele 1998, 176–7).

It should, therefore, not come as a surprise that West Germany forged ahead in industrial labour productivity already before 1948, when the institutional development of the Eastern and Western occupation zones began to take radically different paths. By 1950, output per worker in East German industry had fallen below 70 per cent of the Western level. In industrial TFP, the East actually led the West in the first post-war years, but the Federal Republic reversed this gap by the beginning of the 1950s (Ritschl and Vonyó 2014, 172–3). In relative terms, this productivity divergence translated into increasingly inferior living standards in East Germany, which, in turn, provided the strongest incentive for emigration from the GDR during the 1950s. In the early years of post-war misery, provisions of basic necessities and public services were even slightly more generous in the Soviet zone; by 1950, living conditions for the working class in West Germany had become far better (Schwarzer 1995).

4   Made in Germany: The Post-War Export Boom

The previous chapters described in great detail the economic conditions that prevailed in post-war Germany and that became the foundations of the *Wirtschaftswunder*. I have demonstrated that wartime destruction and the dislocation of productive forces limited economic recovery until the mid-1950s, and thus West German industry still had vast scope for catch up in the global productivity race. This chapter shifts focus from the internal dynamics of post-war reconstruction to its external determinants. Persistent structural disproportions caused by the division of Germany after 1945 and the significance thereof for subsequent growth, discussed in Chapter 3, suggest important links between both sets of factors. In particular, to the extent that West German industry had surplus capacity in the production of primary materials and capital goods, one would expect that external trade was instrumental in her post-war revival. Industries, on the other hand, that faced excess demand at home with the breakdown of East–West trade within Germany could expand further by taking advantage of the export opportunities that their East German competitors had relinquished.

It is widely agreed that trade expansion was vital for the growth miracles of post-war Europe. Perhaps nowhere did this catalysing role seem more evident than in West Germany. Soon after its establishment, the Federal Republic was firmly integrated into the economy of post-war Europe and the Western world, and this became increasingly pronounced during the golden age. Throughout the 1950s, the ratio of exports to GDP more than doubled and by 1960 almost recovered to the highest level of export intensity that Germany had attained before World War I (Jäger 1988, 233). Between 1950 and 1958, industrial exports grew by 19.7 per cent annually, twice and three times as fast as industrial production and national income respectively (Delhaes-Guenther 2003, 17). After the temporary slowdown caused by the US recession of 1958, exports surged again in the 1960s at a still remarkable average rate of 10.6 per cent (Giersch, Paqué, and Schmieding 1992, 164). It is, therefore, not without justification that scholars often interpreted the West

German economic miracle as the consequence of an even more remarkable export miracle (see, among others, Wallich 1955 and Boltho 1982).
This view certainly accords with the impression foreign observers would
have made at the time. During the 1950s, the growth rate of manufacturing exports was twice as high as in Italy or the Netherlands, five times
as high as in France, and ten times as high as in the United Kingdom.
Between 1948 and 1958, the share of West German exports in world
trade increased sevenfold, before it reached its all-time peak at 11.7 per
cent in 1968 (Delhaes-Guenther 2003, 17).

The purpose of this chapter is to understand the dynamics of the
West German export boom and to connect them to the forces behind
the growth of industry in the post-war era. The discussion opens with
an outline of the main interpretations that the literature on the subject has offered. The sections that follow present detailed quantitative
evidence on both the geographical distribution and the commodity
structure of German exports, to account for trade diversion and path
dependency in the context of the war economy and in the post-war
period. I will show that, from the German perspective, trade statistics
do not support a direct link between forced economic integration during World War II and voluntary market integration in Western Europe
in the 1950s. In the reconstruction phase, the growth of West German
exports likewise followed a reconstruction dynamic that, by and large,
restored the trade patterns of the interwar period. The post-war settlement and the new institutions of the new international order did not
alter the composition of West Germany's external trade fundamentally, except for trade with Eastern Europe. The geography and the
commodity structure of West German exports began to deviate from
pre-existing patterns only after the European Economic Community
(EEC) had been established.

The final section of the chapter will use detailed industry statistics
on the growth of output and labour productivity as well as the share of
exports in total turnover to account for the role that export intensity
played in industrial expansion. The main conclusion to emerge from
this analysis is that, contrary to the dominant view in the literature, the
growth of West German industry cannot be characterised as export-
led after the early phase of post-war reconstruction. Once the commodity structure of industrial exports began to part with long-established comparative advantages, due to the trade diversion caused by
regional market integration in Europe, the until then very strong positive correlation between the growth of export intensity and industrial
expansion broke down. The restoration of external trade was, indeed,
essential for the revival of West German industry in the early 1950s,

but the export boom was not responsible for its continued growth and modernisation.

4.1   Alternative Explanations

The West German export miracle inspired three widely acknowledged interpretations. The first proposed that the new international institutions promoting trade liberalisation and market integration in post-war Europe made the conditions for export-led growth better than ever. The second argued that favourable domestic production costs and monetary protectionism enhanced the competitiveness of West German firms abroad. The third views the development of external trade as path dependent, and claims that both the commodity structure and the geography of West German exports reflected patterns, or followed trends, that had been established long before the post-war golden age. Some went even further by arguing that the continental division of labour was intensified within the framework of Nazi Germany's extended economic space, which laid the foundations for the main institutional pillars of European market integration in the 1950s.

Trade Liberalisation and European Integration

The presence of a responsible trade hegemon and the credible commitment to fixed exchange rates within the Bretton Woods system undoubtedly created favourable conditions for trade among Western industrialised nations. In the first half of the twentieth century, world trade in raw materials and manufactures grew at comparable rates. After the General Agreement in Tariffs and Trade (GATT) had come into effect, this trend changed fundamentally. Between the late 1940s and the late 1950s, industrial exports worldwide increased by 90 per cent, whereas primary exports grew by only 56 per cent. In 1960, intra-industry trade, i.e. trade in manufacturing goods between industrialised nations, already accounted for 27 per cent of world trade, and it was becoming more and more prominent (Rotschild 1964, 350–1).

This radical shift in the structure of international trade reflected, in large part, the steep decline of agricultural imports by advanced Western nations, which introduced restrictive trade policies with the aim of promoting domestic production and made remarkable improvements in farming productivity. In 1938, Western Europe was 74 per cent self-sufficient in staple foodstuffs. This rate increased to 81 per cent until 1956, even before the Common Agricultural Policy (CAP) of the EEC came into effect (Rotschild 1964, 355). Intra-industry trade became even more significant as Western trade with the Soviet bloc declined, which was particularly important for the Federal Republic. During the interwar period, one-sixth of German exports went into east and southeast Europe. Due to rising Cold War tensions, this share dropped to 5 per cent by 1949–50 (Neebe 1999, 118). The Coordinating Committee for East–West Trade (COCOM), formed by NATO in November 1949, prevented the restoration of these trade relations. The ever more comprehensive lists of 'strategic goods' that could not be exported to member states of the Warsaw Pact included more and more of Germany's core export products (Wörmann 1982, 16). As a consequence, the share of West German exports to Eastern Europe shrunk to 2 per cent by 1952. Although the embargoes were eased considerably during the 1960s, by that time, structural differences had made trade with the Soviet bloc unattractive for producers on the Western side of the Iron Curtain (Neebe 1989, 58–61).

The late 1940s saw little trade even among Western European nations. This historical anomaly was caused by the severe dollar shortage that constrained the capacity of the region to import the capital goods required for the maintenance and expansion of industrial production, which, in turn, were necessary to generate sufficient export revenue to pay for other imports. As Chapter 5 will explain, the founders of the Marshall Plan had exactly this problem in mind when they designed their strategy for mobilising German industry to provide for the reconstruction needs of Western Europe and for securing, at the same time, in the form of a revitalised West German economy, the market that could absorb the manufacturing exports of neighbouring nations (Berger and Ritschl 1995b).

The first institution responsible for implementing this strategy was the European Payments Agreement (EPA), signed by the member states of the Organisation for European Economic Cooperation (OEEC) on 16 October 1948. The EPA aimed at eliminating structural imbalances in intra-European trade by committing the countries with surplus exports, among them the Western zones of Germany, to export goods to deficit countries free of charge in the value of their drawing rights, which were financed by the Marshall Plan (see Section 5.2). According to Milward (1987), it was due to this arrangement that the Federal Republic could swiftly replace the United States as the major supplier of capital goods to Western Europe. Therefore, it was seen as the first step towards regional trade integration. Between 1948 and 1952, the American share in the machinery and vehicle imports of Austria, Denmark, France, Great Britain, Norway, Italy, and Switzerland declined from 39 per cent to 26 per cent, while the corresponding share of those of West Germany catapulted from 4 per cent to 24 per cent (Buchheim 1993, 80–81). In addition, since EPA drawing rights paid for, in large part, the German capital goods exported to neighbouring countries, France and the Netherlands in particular, the agreement was responsible for the permanent export surplus that West Germany achieved on these markets in the post-war era (Berger and Ritschl 1995b, 227–8).

Perhaps even more importantly, by eliminating the chronic imbalances in continental trade, Western Europe could commit firmly to trade liberalisation and currency convertibility. In November 1949, the council of the OEEC issued its first directive on the reduction of quantity controls. In the following year, the establishment of the European Payments Union (EPU) created a multilateral clearing system that, despite the still critical dollar shortage, enhanced the capacity of European countries to trade with one other. In addition, the EPU provided short-term credit to member states that experienced balance-of-payments difficulties (Buchheim 1990, 105–6). Consequently, trade within the OEEC increased from 10 billion to 23 billion dollars between 1950 and 1959, while imports from North America grew from 4 billion to only 6 billion dollars (Eichengreen 1995, 172). By 1954, trade among EPU members was virtually free of quantity controls, whereas trade liberalisation vis-à-vis the United States was still in its infancy (Dezséri 2000).

However, over time, the growing share of transactions between European countries in world trade and the mobilisation of their gold and foreign exchange reserves also promoted the expansion of overseas imports into Western Europe (Eichengreen 1995). The clearing system was a mechanism for trade creation rather than trade diversion, especially in the late 1950s, when the dollar shortage was no longer sufficiently severe to necessitate discriminatory measures. The European Coal and Steel Community (ECSC) was the first step towards more exclusive regional trade integration. It abolished the international control of the Ruhr and, with that, all restrictions still in place regarding private property and production levels in the German coal and metallurgical industries. Steel output in West Germany increased from 11.8 million to 21.3 million tons between 1950 and 1955, in the same period when it grew by only 14 per cent in France (Leaman 1988, 97). Still, from the German perspective, the ESCS was not paramount for the restoration of intra-European trade. Industrial exports soared towards almost all member states of the OEEC, regardless of whether they were one of the 'Six' or not. Additionally, in the rate of export growth, coal mining and primary metals lagged far behind manufacturing, over which the ECSC had no authority (Gillingham 1995).

Many agreed that 1958 marked an historic milestone in regional trade integration: the clearing system of the EPU was abolished with the return to full convertibility, and the EEC created an exclusive trading bloc from already well integrated continental markets. Barriers to trade in minerals and manufactures among the six member states were dismantled by 1960, the CAP was launched in 1962, and the customs union was completed in 1968, when commercial policy also moved to the supranational level. Protection from external competition was significant. During the 1960s, import duties for industrial goods declined significantly worldwide within the framework of GATT, but the average EEC tariff rate remained above the 1958 level until 1972. This diverted West German exports towards the 'Six' from the rival regional trading bloc, the European Free Trade Association (EFTA). The EEC proved particularly effective in promoting intra-industry trade. The share of manufactures in West German exports and imports with other members climbed from 62.3 per cent in 1960 to 75.8 per cent in 1972, while EFTA markets became less significant (Giersch et al. 1992, 167–72). However, despite the clear differences in the structure and objectives of the two institutions, similar to the EPU, the EEC has also been viewed as strongly trade-creating but, overall, not trade-diverting, at least from the German perspective. Between 1959 and 1972, West German exports to the other member states increased much faster than home demand, but the growth of exports to EFTA countries also kept pace with domestic sales (Lindlar and Holtfrerich 1997, 231).

There is broad consensus in the literature that West German exports grew rapidly because demand conditions in the core markets were extremely favourable for the industries in which German firms had long-established positions. Post-war reconstruction and industrial modernisation in Western Europe generated booming sales for investment goods, especially machinery, while the long years of sluggish consumption since the Great Depression increased the thirst for consumer durables, including electrical appliances and automobiles. In the golden age of economic growth, demand for these income elastic goods increased much faster than demand for textiles and food products. This entailed massive Terms-of-Trade gains for the major exporters of engineering goods, West Germany first among them, much more integrated into continental markets than the United Kingdom or the United States (Rotschild 1964; Ambrosius 1984). The West German Terms of Trade improved by 35 per cent between 1950 and 1958, and by another 15 per cent over the following twelve years (Glastetter, Högemann, and Marquardt 1991, 71–3). Declining raw-material prices alone cannot explain these gains. They came predominantly from an even greater improvement in the specific Terms of Trade for manufactures, which increased by 50 per cent during

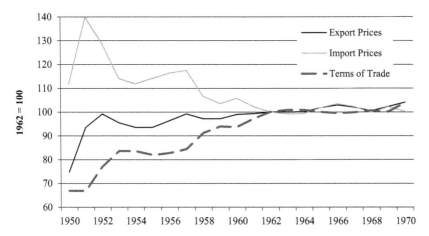

Figure 4.1 The development of export and import prices and the Terms of Trade.
Sources: Außenhandel, Part 1 (1961), 7; Fachserie G/1 (1971), 7.

the 1950s and by an additional 44 per cent between 1959 and 1972 (Giersch et al. 1992, 88; calculated from Henker 1976, 198–9).

However, the level of export prices relative to import prices did not develop as consistently and gradually throughout the post-war period as the foregoing arguments would suggest. Annual trade data reveal the true dynamics (see Figure 4.1). To begin with, there was relatively little movement in either import or export prices during the 1960s compared with the 1950s. Large gains in the Terms of Trade resulted from external shocks to import prices; average export prices hardly changed after the impact of the Korea Boom had vanished. During the boom itself, export and import prices increased rapidly but at similar rates, leaving their ratio largely unaffected. As the turbulence on commodity markets abated and input inventories were reduced, raw-material prices fell. This induced a much sharper decline in import prices than in export prices. Since hard coal was the only primary product that West Germany exported in large quantities, manufactures made up a considerably larger proportion of exports than of imports. Between 1953 and 1957, export and import prices moved in line, so that the Terms of Trade remained within a 1-percentage point band.

The recession of 1958 in the United States was the second major shock to hit international commodity markets. As Western economies scaled down production, demand for fuel and industrial inputs declined sharply, which once again brought down import prices and improved the Terms of Trade by 10 per cent. The 1960s saw the share of raw materials in West German imports diminish further and commodity prices became significantly less volatile. Thus the ratio of export to import prices was also much more stable than in the preceding decade. From 1961 to 1969, the Terms of Trade remained almost constant. The only improvements were connected to the revaluations of the Deutschmark against the dollar by 4.6 per cent in March 1961 and by 9.3 per cent in October 1969 (Roeper and Weimer 1997, 164–5). The fact that export prices continued to increase after each revaluation does not necessarily imply that West German exporters had, initially, offered very competitive prices. Exporting firms adjusted quantities rather than prices when the domestic market became more lucrative, as it will be explained later.

Data in current prices (see Figure 4.2) suggest that the staggering growth of exports during the 1950s was, above all, the consequence of the Korea Boom, when the value of exports increased by an astronomical 74 per cent within just one year. The impact of the 1958 American recession and the 1961 revaluation is also reflected in the figures. The export surplus appears to have grown during cyclical downturns, in 1953, 1958, 1963, and 1966–7. On the contrary, in the boom years of 1955, 1960, 1965, and 1969–70, imports increased faster than exports. This evidence seems to support the widely shared view that exports were a stabilising factor in industrial production. They supplemented domestic demand as long as the West German business cycle did not move together with the rest of Western Europe, that means as long as external demand turned buoyant whenever domestic demand was sluggish (Sachverständigenrat 1965, 11–12; Ambrosius 1984).

This pattern, however, reflected favourable price changes rather than trade volumes, at least during the 1950s. When trade data are expressed in constant prices (see Figure 4.3), the growth of the export surplus disappears almost completely in 1953, and in 1958 even appears to have declined. Domestic recovery was driven by external demand only during the Korea Boom and the recession of 1966–7. The growth of the West German export surplus can be attributed mainly to these two short episodes. Whereas the late 1950s saw little more than the conservation of the surplus that had emerged until 1952, strong domestic demand during the early 1960s shifted the balance of trade back to where it was in 1951. This finding, in turn, already suggests that industrial expansion may have been export-led only in the early 1950s and in the immediate aftermath of the recession of 1966–7, which was unique to West Germany. As I will explain in Chapter 5, fiscal policy was mainly responsible for the strengthening of domestic demand from the late 1950s onward.

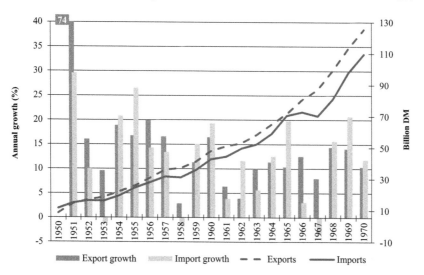

Figure 4.2 The growth of West German exports and imports in current prices.
Sources: See Figure 4.1. Author's calculations.

Figure 4.3 also reveals a key episode of trade expansion in post-war Germany. Imports stagnated in 1951, when the growth of industrial production and the export boom were both in overdrive. Contrary to what one may expect, the Korean War had a much larger impact on imports than on exports in West Germany. As the crisis in East Asia pushed up raw-material prices, industrial firms began to build up large inventories, fearing the return of the import bottlenecks that had crippled them during the late 1940s. Likewise troubled by their memories, consumers stormed the shops to purchase vast quantities of basic necessities. Many liquidated their last savings to get their hands on quintals of washing powder and pounds of spices (Weimer 1998, 91). Despite the skyrocketing surge of exports, the sharp deterioration of the Terms of Trade that this excess demand for imported primary commodities caused in late 1950 enlarged the deficit on the balance of trade (Temin 1997, 363). As the central bank did not possess sufficient gold and foreign exchange to neutralise the increasing outflow of hard currency from the country, West Germany became the first nation to receive an EPU bailout. To avoid the collapse of the newly established multilateral clearing regime, the credit line of the Federal Republic was even extended, and the OEEC allowed the German government to temporarily halt the implementation of import liberalisation and to terminate the issue of new import licences (Bührer

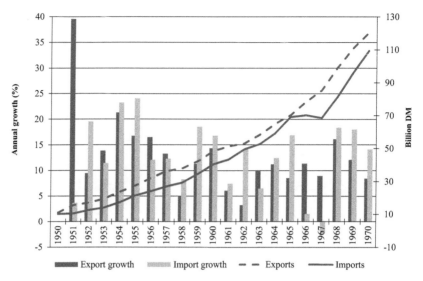

Figure 4.3 The growth of West German exports and imports in 1962 DM prices.

Sources: See Figure 4.1. Author's calculations.

1990, 159). Since these emergency measures remained in place until the end of 1951, the volume of imports could hardly grow in the course of that year. Import prices already began to plummet in the spring of 1951, and thus, by the end of the year, the West German trade deficit was eradicated and the Terms of Trade recovered to its earlier level (Hardach 1993, 93–4). This is why we do not observe any change between 1950 and 1951 in the annual average rates reported in Figure 4.1.

Monetary Protectionism and Price Competitiveness

Interpretations that emphasised the role of international institutions and the favourable demand conditions of the post-war era have received strong criticism in the recent literature. These factors, it is claimed, made conditions conducive to trade expansion, but they cannot explain specifically the competitiveness of West German exporters, whose world market share increased at the expense of their major rivals (see Delhaes-Guenther 2003). The surge of industrial exports and the growing surplus on the current account have been, instead, frequently explained as the results of favourable movements in unit labour costs and average export prices compared to those of international competitors (Carlin 1989; Giersch et al. 1992).

Economists at the time and economic historians often remarked on the unparalleled price stability that characterised West Germany in the post-war era. The central bank, it was argued, followed a restrictive course for much of the period, particularly during the 1950s, keeping the annual inflation rate 2.1 percentage points below the average rate for OEEC member states (Giersch et al. 1992, 68–71). Under fixed exchange rates, this made the Deutschmark increasingly undervalued, which increased the export surplus and, with that, the net inflow of foreign exchange. Once official reserves had become large enough to facilitate the return to convertibility, the Bundesbank raised interest rates even further to stem imported inflation. This attracted even more foreign exchange into the country, especially with the mounting troubles of the French franc and British sterling and with record deficits piling up in the United States (Ambrosius 1984, 289–92).

The evolution of monetary policy in West Germany will be discussed in Chapter 5. In this section, it suffices to stress that monetary protec-tionism, as the literature referred to the stemming of imported inflation by restricting the money supply rather than by revaluing the currency, could have only boosted West German exports, if it had been manifested either in relatively low export prices or in relatively low unit labour costs. The former would have driven competitors out of the market; the latter would have implied extraordinary profits, alluring domestic producers into external markets. The first scenario never materialised; the second did, but only for a short period. Relative to the main competitors, the unit values of manufacturing exports remained stable throughout the 1950s and 1960s. If anything, West German industrial exports were relatively expensive. Relative unit labour costs declined marginally between 1951 and 1958, but increased sharply thereafter. During the 1960s, labour input per unit of output was approximately 14 per cent more expensive in the Federal Republic than in the major competitor countries (Lindlar and Holtfrerich 1997).

In fact, the competitiveness of West German manufacturers improved temporarily in the early 1950s as the consequence rather than the cause of the export boom. Industrial reconstruction generated remarkably fast labour-productivity growth in export-oriented industries, includ-ing chemicals and investment goods, that increased their share in total manufacturing output, and thus made the industrial sector as a whole more competitive. This argument was strongly supported by Henker (1976), who applied constant-market-share analysis to determine the role of competitiveness in the surge of West German foreign trade. This approach isolates the structural components of export growth from fac-tors that influence competitive positions. The commodity structure and the geographic distribution of exports accounted for the sharp increase of the export surplus between 1959 and 1972. In addition, West Germany specialised in the production of highly income-elastic goods and her main markets were in Western Europe, where trade expansion outpaced the growth of world trade itself. In fact, the competitive component of export growth was negative in several years, most notably in transport vehicles and electrical engineering, two of the leading export industries of the period.

The exchange rate secured substantial price advantage for West German manufactures only in relation to the United States. The 20.6 percent devaluation of the Deutschmark in September 1949 made American products, on average, at least 10 percent more expensive relative to those of German competitors in heavy industry until 1953 (Lindlar 1997, 260). Not surprisingly, the total value of US exports to Western Europe declined by 2 per cent between 1953 and 1958, while German exports into the same region increased by 75 per cent (Hardach 1993, 102). However, this pattern was not specific to West Germany. Since all major European currencies were devalued against the dollar in the autumn of 1949, in regional comparison, the Deutschmark became even slightly overvalued (Schmieding 1989). Based on relative manufacturing prices and production costs, the West German export boom remains a puzzle.

Path Dependency and Endogenous Trade Blocs

One way to solve this puzzle has been to argue that exports surged simply as German industry was regaining the positions it had traditionally occupied in international, particularly European, markets. In 1952 and 1953, no fewer than four-fifths of all export articles were marketed with brands that were established before 1939 (Neebe 1989, 55). The leading export industries were the old locomotives of the German economy, iron and steel, machinery and vehicles, electrical and precision engineering, and chemicals. The production capacity of these industries increased substantially as a consequence of the armaments boom in the late 1930s and early 1940s. Freed from the defence burden after the war, they were destined for fast growth at the onset of the economic miracle (Ambrosius 1984; Kramer 1991). Between 1950 and 1959, while German exports of consumer goods climbed from 1.2 billion to 5.5 billion DM, exports of production goods jumped from 4 billion to 12 billion DM, and exports of investment goods from 3 billion to 22 billion DM (Neebe 1989, 54). As a result of the growing share of intra-industry trade within the EEC, the share of intermediate inputs and machinery in West German exports continued to increase during the 1960s (Abelshauser 1983).

These developments followed long-established patterns, manifested throughout the first half of the twentieth century despite recurrent crises and reconstruction phases. The anomalies of the interwar period and the war years even helped to conserve the production structure of the German economy in an anachronistic way: they increased the share of industrial output in national product and the importance of heavy industry within the former for much longer than in other developed countries (Abelshauser 2001). Final goods already made up two-thirds of German exports prior to World War I, and their share continued to increase during the interwar period, despite the minor setback under Nazi autarchy. The share of chemicals and machinery in manufacturing exports was already very large by international standards in 1912 and grew continuously at the expense of textiles. The most dynamic German industries, electrical engineering and transport vehicles, increased their exports eightfold between 1912 and 1937 (Höpfner 1993). These were the same industries that achieved the most remarkable export growth during the 1950s.

Abelshauser (2001) and Delhaes-Guenther (2003) explained this persistence by arguing that the production regime of German industry was institutionally path dependent. Their interpretation is derived from the theory of comparative institutional advantages that augments the standard Ricardian model with an institutional cost dimension. Institutions and the social framework of production constitute key determinants of export success but only in relation with the prevailing conditions in product markets. The demand structure of these markets must be compatible with the social framework of production in the exporter country for the latter to be successful in export-led growth. The German production regime, it has been argued, was marked by long-term cooperative relationships between employers and employees, between producers and customers and, most crucially, between different firms within the same industry. The building blocks of this architecture were established during the Second Industrial Revolution of the late nineteenth century. They included the dominance of craft-based flexible production with skilled labour, the high share of engineers in management, strong vertical integration and regional clusters, the instrumental role of banks in investment planning and financing, and the high service content of industrial quality products.

The interwar period and the years after World War II did not witness fundamental changes in this regard. The most innovative industries in Germany continued to have many small and medium-sized firms, which cooperated through complex networks in the entire production chain, generating substantial synergy effects. Competition was preserved among them not in price, but more typically in quality, design, delivery times, and innovative potential. According to Abelshaser (2001) and Delhaes-Guenther (2003), this regime has been particularly well suited to exporters specialising in differentiated quality products (DQPs), which are manufactured in complex production processes employing well-established technologies and highly skilled workers, and are flexibly tailored to customer needs, including post-sale services. The competitiveness of German industry in DQPs reflected very low institutional transaction costs, stemming from established networks among producers, customers, and financiers. Unfavourable external demand and severe capital shortage in the interwar period could not support any alternative regime based on capital-intensive production techniques and/or the application of cutting-edge technologies.

Furthermore, the expropriation of German patents by Anglo-American firms, in accord with the 1946 London Agreement, and the prohibition of nuclear power generation as well as aircraft manufacturing until 1955 effectively excluded West Germany from the high-tech industries of the time (Neebe 1989, 50–3). By contrast, based on their comparative institutional advantages, German exporters could capitalise on booming demand for engineering products in the period of post-war reconstruction and industrial modernisation in Western Europe. Buchheim (1990) and Milward (1987) argued accordingly that trade expansion following the Korea Boom, by and large, restored the continental trade relations that had broken down during the 1930s as a result of national autarchy and bilateralism. Rebuilding the intra-European division of labour was enormously beneficial for West Germany, in particular, given the long-established dominance of European markets in her external trade (Höpfner 1993, 197–8).

Dedinger (2006) arrived at similar conclusions using the trade-intensity indicator, which neutralises the impact that differences in the size of countries have on their respective trade shares, and thus highlights the effect of other factors, such as trade costs. The export intensity of Germany with a given country is computed as the share thereof in German exports divided by the share thereof in total world imports. Values greater than 1 signal stronger than average trade integration between the exporting and importing nations. Over the long run, Germany's export intensity with Europe has been on the rise. It was already around 1.3–1.4 prior to World War I and climbed to 1.5–1.6 before the Great Depression. Following the temporary setback caused by Nazi autarchy, it came close to 2 in the early 1950s, but dropped to 1.5 by the mid-1960s. Only after the completion of the EEC's customs union in 1968 did the export intensity of West Germany with Europe increase persistently and substantially above the interwar level (Dedinger 2006, 262–75).

These results demonstrate a great deal of inertia in trade patterns that proved resistant to exogenous shocks, such as the creation of discriminatory currency blocs in the 1930s and the economic imperialism of the early 1940s. The international institutions of the post-war era that aimed at promoting trade liberalisation and regional market integration could, therefore, influence continental trade relations only inasmuch as they were intended to restore Western Europe 'as a natural trading bloc' (Lindlar and Holtfrerich 1997, 232).

The potential caveat of this interpretation is that there may have been little to restore, meaning that market integration in Europe may have been enhanced, not reversed, during the war. The so-called 'new economic order' that Nazi Germany imposed on occupied and satellite states created a 'greater economic space' (*Großwirtschaftsraum*) around the Third Reich and a multilateral clearing system with its central clearinghouse in Berlin. The literature has devoted much attention to the exploitation of occupied lands for their natural resources, their labour, and their produce (Buchheim 1986; Eichholtz 1978, 1997; Overy 1997; Boldorf and Scherner 2012; Scherner 2012; Spoerer 2001, 2015; Custodis 2016). The immediate and long-term consequences of Nazi hegemony in Europe have been discussed most recently and comprehensively in the extensive collection edited by Scherner and White (2016). Many have argued that Germany exploited, in particular, smaller nations in her backwater in southeast Europe through bilateral trade agreements, and tied them increasingly to her economy during the war (Hirschman 1945; Volkmann 1975; Neal 1979; Ránki 1983; Riemenschneider 1987; Grenzebach 1988; Gross 2015; Asenova 2016).

Recent scholarship, however, has suggested that the wartime reorientation of Germany's external trade might have been a sheer myth. Ritschl (2001) studied the secret payments and foreign-exchange balances of the Third Reich, which survived in the archival records of the Ministry of Commerce. Within the clearing system, Germany secured the largest net resource transfers from Western Europe and especially from the future EEC. 'In spite of all ideological commitment to the contrary, and in spite of the eastbound thrust of the Nazi war effort, the German war economy was in fact westward oriented' (Ritschl 2001, 340). The apparent eastward reorientation of German foreign trade in the late 1930s was the result of a composition effect, as the contraction of external trade was due almost exclusively to disengagement from the Western powers. This was not the outcome of strategic decisions to achieve autarchy; it was simply the response to the scarcity of foreign exchange that forced Germany to default on her external debt. Imports from southeast Europe could not substitute for the loss of Western trade, which was, at least on the continent, swiftly restored under Nazi occupation in the early 1940s. Moreover, the much-advocated intensification of trade with the Balkans was economically unattractive: Germany had to pay 20 to 40 per cent above world market prices for essential raw-material imports from the region during the late 1930s (Abelshauser 1999, 519–20).

According to this logic, Nazi economic imperialism did not destroy the continental division of labour; it only deepened it further in the form of forced trade integration. Germany continued to supply the occupied regions of Western Europe with intermediate inputs and machinery, in exchange for finished products to be consumed by Hitler's all-dreaded armies. These trade links required no additional production capacity; they relied on the input–output web that tied the industries of the Ruhr, Belgium, Luxembourg, and Lorraine together since the late nineteenth century. Berger and Ritschl (1995b, 227) even saw in the continental economic system centred at Nazi Germany and in the clearing mechanism that mobilised it the nuclei of the main institutional pillars of the post-war European trade regime, the EEC and the EPU.

Deeper introspections into the history of occupied economies have shown that the German new order was a far cry from a well-integrated European market. The leaders of the Nazi economy, Göring and Speer, had little influence over German authorities in the occupied countries and thus the exploitation of their resources was far more limited than what would have been possible. In the East, the struggle for *Lebensraum* and racial purification reduced the labour force. In the West, insufficient deliveries of coal and intermediate inputs from Germany created recurrent production bottlenecks in the industries of occupied nations. As the system of bilateral clearing vis-à-vis Germany destroyed almost all trade between countries under Nazi occupation, they emerged from World War II economically isolated from rather than integrated with each other (Klemann and Kudryashov 2012, 368–70). Their international trade was reoriented towards an enlarged German empire that, following its collapse and disintegration in 1945, could neither provide them with the necessary capital goods to refuel their economies nor absorb their manufacturing exports.

The notion of continuity between wartime and post-war trade expansion found support among business historians, who argued that both Nazi economic imperialism and post-war trade integration in Europe served, above all, the interests of big business in Germany. German industry discovered in regional trade blocs another form of expansionism after the failed military option (Berghahn 1999). This interpretation grew out of earlier Marxist scholarship that defined market integration as a tool to achieve the internationalisation of capital and production and viewed the

EEC as the community of the large corporations (Galtung 1973). It also drew inspiration from the old concept of formal versus informal empire, first developed by Gallagher and Robinson (1953). German opinion-makers and business elites had long yearned for an extended economic space to satisfy the expansionary dynamic of German industry. After the colonial ambitions of the Kaiser had become unrealistic and his mighty armies defeated in war, calls for the informal economic domination of Europe grew louder during the interwar period. The quest for formal empire reappeared in the 1930s and for both economists and political leaders was strongly linked to trade interests. Particularly in southeast Europe, German 'soft power' paved the way for Nazi imperialism before the war (Gross 2015). However, while Hitler's *Drang nach Osten* was fuelled by pan-German ideologies about vital living space and racial superiority, the bulk of the business community remained focussed on Western trade expansion and preferred a more informal economic space around Germany that would be dominated by German-led cartels. After World War II, German industry had to succeed in an environment radically different from the one it had been trying to construct until 1945. This was achieved by reverting to the strategy of the interwar period, restoring trade with established European markets.

As with the reconstruction thesis, in general, many reject that the reintegration of West Germany into the international division of labour can be interpreted as another reconstruction process. The growth potential of the export industries after World War II, they argue, cannot be explained by re-convergence to pre-existing patterns because the trade structures of the interwar and post-war periods were fundamentally different owing to the growing dominance of intra-industry trade. This evolution enabled manufacturers in Western Europe to achieve scale economies through greater specialisation, which in turn allowed them to catch up with American labour-productivity levels. This is why the new post-war institutions were attributed such essential a role in the West German export miracle (see Paqué 1994). This debate is critically important for our understanding of the *Wirtschaftswunder* that, during the early 1950s, was undoubtedly export-driven. Whether and to what extent reconstruction dynamics suffice to explain the development of German exports during the golden age can be determined only with the careful analysis of detailed trade statistics.

4.2   The Geography of German Exports

For the purpose of this analysis, I constructed a dataset of country-shares in total German or West German exports (in current prices) in eight benchmark years. Data for 1950, 1955, 1960, 1965, and 1970 have been obtained from the annual foreign trade statistics.[1] The 1950 trade statistics also report comparable figures for 1936 (according to 1936 borders), which represents a good benchmark for the post-Depression years but is not yet strongly influenced by war preparations. To demonstrate how much regional patterns of trade were distorted by the impact of the Great Depression, I also collected data for 1928.[2]

At the country level, the data cannot be adjusted for the border changes that the post-war settlement in Europe and, within that, the partition of Germany invoked. The more substantial redrawing of maps overseas after decolonisation can be neutralised by adhering to the territorial units reported in the interwar trade statistics, which reflect colonial boundaries. Thus, my dataset includes regions such as the Arab Middle East that covers modern-day Jordan, Iraq, and the countries on the Arab Peninsula, or French, British, Portuguese, and Spanish West Africa, the Union of Rhodesia and the Nyasaland, French Indochina, or British Malaya. Following these adjustments, we are left with ninety-five countries or regions, for which one can construct by and large territorially consistent figures over time.

The confidential wartime trade statistics that I shall describe in detail later report data on both the commodity structure and the geographical distribution of German exports.[3] The nomenclature of product groups is perfectly compatible with the official peacetime statistics. By contrast, regional data are affected to a large but non-quantifiable extent by the border changes that took effect between 1938 and 1941. Until 1939, the statistics refer to the 1937 national borders. The wartime data pertain to the Greater German Empire (see Figure 4.4) that included Austria; the Sudetenland; the Protectorate of Bohemia and Moravia; the annexed territories of Luxembourg, Malmedy and Eupen, and Alsace-Lorraine; Posen; the eastern part of Upper Silesia; West Prussia; the city of Danzig; the Memel area; the district of Bialystok; and part of modern-day Slovenia. Nevertheless, this material constitutes the only source on actual wartime trade flows that allows for direct comparison with interwar and post-war patterns.

In order to provide a long-term perspective, we must also take account of pre-1914 trade structures. As explained in the previous section, the literature has frequently argued that during the post-war era German foreign trade converged to patterns established during the first age of

[1] Außenhandel, Part 1 (1950), 12–13; ibid. (1955), 34–6; ibid. (1961), 32–3; Fachserie G/ 1 (1965), 36–7; ibid. (1970), 42–3.
[2] StatDR, Vol. 366.2 (1929), 4–7.
[3] See footnote 5.

Figure 4.4 The expansion of the German Empire between 1937 and 1942.

Note: In the wartime trade statistics, the Protectorate of Bohemia and Moravia was treated as part of Germany, whereas the General Government of Poland was not.

Sources: US Holocaust Memorial Museum. Reproduction permitted by the US Holocaust Memorial Museum Office of General Counsel.

globalisation. Reconstructing 1913 trade data at country level according to interwar or post-war territorial boundaries is impossible given the substantial redrawing of maps in East Central Europe and the Middle East, but we can determine the share of the continents and major regions of Europe in German exports.[4] This requires only two adjustments to ensure comparability over time: (1) assuming that Austria within her post-1919 borders accounted for 25 per cent of German trade with the Austro-Hungarian Empire, which equals her approximate share in GDP (Maddison 2006, 426, 476); and (2) assigning Turkish possessions in the Middle East 30 per cent of German trade with the Ottoman Empire, based on the actual trade patterns of the interwar period.

The rest of this section begins with a general overview, followed by more in-depth analyses of both wartime and post-war trade patterns. World War I did not invoke significant changes in the geography of

---

[4] StatDR, Vol. 366.2 (1929), 4–7. Author's calculations.

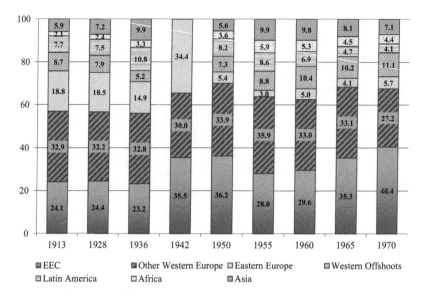

Figure 4.5 The geographical distribution of German/West German exports (%).

Sources: See beginning of Section 4.2 for references.

Notes: EEC refers to member states only, excluding their overseas possessions. Asia includes New Guinea and Polynesia. Western offshoots include the United States, Canada, Australia, and New Zeeland.

Germany's external trade, at least on the export side (Figure 4.5). The relative weight of exports to Europe remained exactly the same, and we cannot observe shifts between different parts of the continent either. The relative importance of specific countries undoubtedly changed, as the Balkans and Scandinavian economies absorbed the earlier trade shares of Britain and Russia. Still, this redistribution made little impact on the overall orientation of German exports. We do not need pre-1914 data to demonstrate the influence of long-established patterns on the evolution of Germany's external trade, since these patterns had survived World War I 'unwounded'. The volume of exports may have declined considerably between the early 1900s and the 1920s, but their regional composition remained remarkably resistant to wartime distortions.

Essentially the same can be argued about the impact of the Great Depression. Between 1928 and 1936, the share of Western Europe in German exports remained practically unchanged. The very minor shift away from the future EEC reflects economic stagnation during the mid-1930s in the Gold Bloc countries and strong growth in Scandinavia.

Outside of Europe, exports to the Western offshoots declined more rapidly than exports in total, but this resulted solely from diminished import demand in the United States. By contrast, Asia, Latin America, and Africa became relatively more important markets for German firms. Some of the major primary producing economies began to embark on import-substituting industrialisation, which, at its early stages, required the import of capital goods that Germany could provide. There was no general disengagement from Western markets; the share of exports to Eastern Europe even declined marginally, despite the political efforts to intensify economic cooperation with the Balkan countries.

World War II caused a much more significant diversion of German exports, as the Nazi state gradually lost access to its overseas markets. Trade with the British colonies and dominions was shut down in 1939. Albeit in small volumes, exports to the Americas and Asia, particularly Japan and her possessions, continued until 1941. After the United States had declared war on Germany, the African colonies of France, Italy, Spain, and Portugal remained the only accessible trade partners outside of Europe. Even these were lost in 1943, with the exception of Spanish West Africa, when the Allies conquered North Africa. German exports were reoriented also within continental Europe. The future member states of the EEC absorbed more of this trade than before the war. By contrast, the share of other Western European countries declined, due to the termination of exports to Britain and the annexation of Austria. However, contrary to the view advocated by Berger and Ritschl (1995b, 225), German exports became increasingly eastward oriented with the eastbound drive of the war effort, so much so that by 1942 Eastern Europe absorbed nearly as much, and from 1943 even slightly more, of German exports as the future EEC. This result is striking given the fact that economic activity along the Eastern Front was disrupted to a much greater extent than elsewhere on the continent.

The increasing eastward orientation of German exports during the war marks a clear break with the prevailing geography of both the interwar and post-war trade patterns. In 1950, Eastern Europe accounted for only 5 per cent of West German exports. By contrast, the weight of Western Europe remained considerably larger than what it had been during the interwar years. Cold War tensions and the establishment of COCOM in 1949 are mainly to blame for this seismic shift, as the aforementioned literature has already explained. Capital goods exports to Eastern Europe were redirected to Germany's major western trading partners, particularly the Netherlands and Scandinavia. Additionally, the contraction of trade with the Soviet bloc was just as much the consequence of the post-war territorial settlements that dismantled the eastern half of Hitler's empire as the staggering growth of German exports to Eastern Europe during the war had resulted from the eastward expansion of the Third Reich between 1938 and 1941.

Exports to the Americas and Africa recovered quickly after the war, but shifted away from Latin America, where import substitution from the late 1930s had built up substantial domestic industrial capacity. In the early 1950s, the share of exports to Asia remained below the inter-war benchmarks, primarily due to the communist takeover in China and sluggish import demand in Japan, where reconstruction efforts were just beginning to bear fruit. The geography of German exports that had evolved by the interwar period was, by and large, restored until 1955, except for the fact that the share of Eastern Europe hit an all-time low, which was largely offset by the increased weight of overseas markets.

Despite the establishment of the ECSC, the relative importance of its member states for West German exports compared with the rest of Western Europe was remarkably similar to what we can observe for the interwar period. In the second half of the 1950s, we do not find signifi-cant changes in regional trade patterns. Only after 1960 did the EEC absorb significantly larger proportions of West German exports, initially at the expense of both overseas markets and state-trading economies. After the European customs union was concluded in the late 1960s, the share of exports to other Western European nations also began to decline. Overall, the data suggest that the strong westward orientation of Germany's external trade after 1950 corresponded to interwar rather than wartime patterns. In the late 1950s, these restored patterns were largely conserved. It was only after the EEC had created a more discriminatory trading bloc that the share of continental Western Europe in German exports and imports was propelled to unprecedented heights. During the 1960s, the weight of Western industrialised nations in Germany's external trade also grew at the expense of less developed markets, which confirms the rising importance of intra-industry trade. The seemingly contrasting interpretations of the West German export boom introduced earlier are, in fact, complementary, once we recognise that the dynamics of trade expansion changed over time.

Trade Diversion in 'Fortress Europe'

Much has been written on the trade diversion caused by the building of currency blocs and the widespread application of discriminatory trade policies after the Great Depression (see among others Eichengreen and Irwin 1995; Kitson and Solomou 1995; and Ritschl and Wolf 2011). Influenced by the seminal scholarly study of European payment patterns by Howard Ellis (1941), historians have emphasised the importance of the bilateral trade agreements that Nazi Germany had signed with the countries of southeast Europe, commonly referred to as the Reichsmark bloc (Volkmann 1975; Neal 1979; Milward 1981; Gross 2015). The trade statistics offer very little support for these interpretations, especially on the export side. The geography of imports was shaken up relatively more strongly. The French and US shares in total German imports fell sharply between 1928 and 1936 because Germany was in short supply of the hard currency necessary to purchase goods from these markets. By contrast, countries that had concluded bilateral trade agreements with the Nazi state during the 1930s became increasingly dominant sources of imports.

However, these economies had already accounted for the bulk of German imports from Europe in the 1920s and recovered faster after the Great Depression than France and the United States. In other words, controlling for the standard gravity factors, economic size, and geographic vicinity to Germany, countries that conducted trade with the Third Reich through bilateral clearing in 1936 had supplied relatively large proportions of German imports already before the Depression. This concurs with the econometric results of Ritschl and Wolf (2011), who suggested that the currency blocs and bilateral trade networks of the 1930s were endogenous to pre-existing patterns of trade. Trade diversion in Europe before 1939 was not driven by Hitler's geo-political aspirations, except for the radically diminished share of German exports to Czechoslovakia, Poland, and the Soviet Union, countries alienated by the Führer's bellicose rhetoric.

This changed fundamentally during World War II as a consequence of the political reorganisation of continental Europe. Most existing accounts of Germany's wartime trade relations used scattered quantitative evidence. Until recently, scholars examined the foreign payments balances of the Third Reich, as the official trade statistics were not published after 1940. Clearing accounts demonstrate to what extent other nations were economically exploited by Nazi Germany. However, they do not provide an accurate picture of the structure and balance of German exports and imports, mainly because the payments balances incorporated a long list of items other than merchandise trade. Fortunately, the confidential trade statistics for the years 1941–4 survived in the archives.[5] They were compiled for internal use only; their publication and further distribution were strictly forbidden, and thus could not serve propaganda purposes.

---

[5] Außenhandel, *Ergänzungshefte 1941, 1942, 1943*; BArch R 3/1626a, 38–9. In the summer of 1944, aggregate trade statistics were made public at a government press conference and some extracts were published in Länderrat (1949), 390 ff.

The analysis of this material makes an important contribution to the historiography of the Nazi war economy.

The export statistics are believed to be trustable, but the analysis of import data is made difficult by several distortions and conceptual controversies. Direct deliveries to German troops, the SS, or civilian organisations and their members abroad did not account towards German imports, even if they had passed through German customs borders. Foreign supplies of both civilian goods and war material transported into the Reich were to be included in the import statistics, if not labelled *Wehrmacht* supplies, regardless of whether they were final or intermediary products destined for further processing within Germany.[6] In a recent study, Scherner (2012) documented numerous flaws in the official statistics, which the authorities were increasingly aware of. There is plenty of evidence that a large proportion of foreign goods actually consumed by German firms and households entered the country as *Wehrmacht* supplies. These included black-market purchases by the occupying forces that were transported to Germany. In addition, a vast share of foreign food and fuel transports to the German troops on the Eastern Front never passed through German customs borders. The re-estimation of German imports on the basis of payments transactions, the foreign purchases of the armed forces, and the accounts of the occupation authorities results in much larger numbers than the official statistics, especially from the occupied territories (Scherner 2012, Appendix, Table 5, 112–13).

These revised estimates, however, are difficult to make use of in the present framework. The purpose of Scherner's study was not to provide import data according to conventional definitions of international trade, but to reconstruct how Nazi Germany had used different financial means to extract resources from foreign lands. Imports were defined as goods produced abroad and purchased by Germany for consumption anywhere outside the country of origin and for any purpose. The Third Reich had three means to finance its imports: (1) revenue earned from exports, (2) clearing credits received from foreign countries, and (3) the occupation tributes. *Wehrmacht* supplies, in particular, were purchased through means (2) and (3), which, however, Germany never repaid to the countries it had occupied during the war. Therefore, these supplies are better classified as bounty, or war contributions, rather than as conventional imports. This logic follows the peculiar division of labour within 'Fortress Europe' in the context of total war. While the armies of Germany and her allies sustained the military effort, the labour force of

---

[6] Außenhandel, *Ergänzungsheft 1941*, 3.

the occupied lands, particularly in Western Europe, was employed predominantly on the home front.

Consequently, rising imports from the territories under Nazi occupation did not reflect the intensified use of production capacities in these
regions but rather the diversion of output from domestic to foreign
military consumption and the redirection of labour from armed service
to material production. By contrast, it was difficult to secure imports
from neutral states or nations allied with Germany, as their productive
potential and male labour force were used to equip and man their own
expanding armies. In particular, Germany had to export to her allies
in the East substantial and increasing volumes of intermediate inputs
and manufactures (mostly coal, metals, and machinery) to sustain their
military contribution and, at the same time, to secure the essential raw-
material imports, which before 1939 Germany had purchased overseas.
The redirection of German exports to east and southeast Europe demonstrates that Nazi Germany made genuine efforts to reorient its war
economy eastwards. Previous research has failed to provide evidence for
this diversion because it focussed on the net resource transfers that the
Third Reich had extracted from other countries, and did not discuss
actual trade volumes.

Table 4.1 reports wartime exports and imports according to country
of destination and of origin in current prices, listing all European states
that continued to trade with Germany in notable volumes at least until
1943. Small quantities of German exports went to Iceland, the temporarily occupied British Channel Islands, and North Africa, from where
some raw-material imports had also been obtained. However, they were
negligible from the perspective of the big picture. On an enlarged territorial basis, Germany saw her trade expand with all countries of continental Europe between 1936 and the early 1940s. However, the official trade
balance shifted differently depending on the relation of the particular
nation to the Nazi state. Italy became the largest export market, heavily dependent on German coal and capital goods to maintain her own
war production and on imported armaments to supply her ill-equipped
troops. Exports also increased rapidly to smaller allies in the East, which
played a significant role both during the invasion of Yugoslavia and the
campaign against the Soviet Union. Exports to Romania and Croatia
surged the most dramatically. They were the main suppliers of crude oil
and bauxite respectively: essential raw materials that Germany had to
keep importing at all cost. The statistics indicate that the Third Reich
became increasingly dependent on her satellites until 1943. In light of
the subsequent military defeats, it was more and more important to keep
them in the war and maintain their economic contribution to the Nazi

Table 4.1 *German trade with continental Europe during World War II in million RM (current prices)*

Countries	1936 Imports	1936 Exports	1940 Imports	1940 Exports	1941 Imports	1941 Exports	1942 Imports	1942 Exports	1943 Imports	1943 Exports	1944 Imports	1944 Exports
General Government[a]	57.9	53.0	91.4	238.6	87.2	312.3	224.3	468.3	257.7	558.7	196	371
Belgium	138.6	211.5	227.9	117.2	562.0	384.6	705.0	292.5	681.4	308.1	434	184
Bulgaria	57.6	47.6	176.8	162.2	137.4	260.4	286.1	289.1	292.8	367.4	368	499
Denmark	154.3	182.3	494.5	324.9	410.2	431.9	314.0	363.7	420.9	377.3	522	401
Finland	46.1	40.5	79.2	82.8	144.9	252.9	149.0	371.3	271.5	404.4	246	471
France	98.9	254.5	224.0	13.3	751.8	315.3	1,404.0	546.3	1,416.1	559.9	1,006	260
Greece	68.4	63.5	90.3	63.3	81.2	10.5	130.0	58.6	103.5	75.6	25	71
Italy	208.5	240.6	507.9	724.3	937.8	1,192.4	1,022.0	1,304.7	780.9	950.5	1,145	400
Albania and Montenegro	0.0	0.9	0.1	2.0	0.1	4.1	0.5	5.0	0.5	3.5	0	2
Croatia	—	—	—	—	35.0	54.8	74.7	175.0	104.2	319.4	69	841
Yugoslavia[b]	75.2	77.2	239.7	317.1	83.8	90.9	—	—	—	—	—	—
Netherlands	168.5	395.5	406.4	440.0	640.1	694.7	857.7	533.7	824.5	427.3	601	250
Norway	87.9	91.3	141.8	192.3	280.4	430.1	239.4	369.5	228.3	500.4	223	282
Portugal	21.7	29.8	4.3	3.9	33.7	31.0	120.8	48.6	120.3	52.7	39	45
Romania	92.3	103.6	427.1	350.1	346.6	430.5	428.7	716.1	323.4	994.9	286	773
Sweden	191.7	230.4	346.0	403.0	476.9	455.2	410.3	423.5	386.0	479.2	240	437
Switzerland	106.2	225.5	166.1	272.7	314.7	414.3	424.4	398.4	297.7	332.3	196	264
Serbia[a]					43.7	13.2	120.8	44.0	192.9	70.4	136	70
Slovakia[a]	111.9	86.3	199.7	216.0	214.6	257.9	282.2	306.7	265.4	321.0	227	273
Spain	97.7	69.3	20.0	23.2	146.1	56.6	165.7	118.6	219.7	191.6	115	184
Turkey	118.5	79.4	51.1	13.0	81.8	25.8	100.3	109.4	161.5	249.1	138	77
Hungary	93.4	83.0	207.3	298.3	351.2	349.9	540.9	430.8	615.3	672.0	595	636
USSR	149.2	182.3	545.2	349.4	325.5	271.7	482.7	156.6	243.6	182.7	—	—

[a] Figures for 1936 refer to Poland and Czechoslovakia.

[b] Figures for 1941 refer to the period until the German invasion in April.

Sources: For 1940, data are reported in *Statistisches Jahrbuch* 1941/42, 322. For 1941–3, see *Der Außenhandel Deutschlands: Ergänzungshefte 1941, 1942, 1943.* Data for 1944 has been collected from BArch R 3/1626a, 38–9. The author thanks Jonas Scherner for sharing these data.

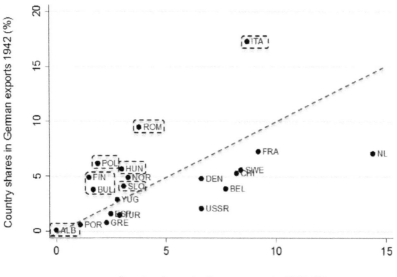

Figure 4.6 The reorientation of German exports within Europe, 1936–1942.

Sources: Table 4.1. Author's calculations.

Note: The diagram reports country shares in total German exports to Europe and only for countries that traded with Nazi Germany in 1942.

war effort. After the Allies had landed in Italy and the northern half of the country had fallen under German occupation, German exports shifted towards the Balkans even stronger than before.

Figure 4.6 compares country shares in total German exports to continental Europe between 1936 and 1942, when Nazi military expansionism reached its pinnacle. The diagram demonstrates clearly that German exports were reoriented towards the countries allied with the Third Reich and to the German administered General Government of Poland. Western economies lost their position as Germany's leading export markets. This was true for both neutrals, such as Sweden and Switzerland, and occupied states, such as France and the Netherlands. The eastward redirection of German exports transformed the trade deficits of the 1930s with southeast Europe into substantial trade surpluses by 1941; even in relation to Hungary and Slovakia, which were relatively most exposed to the danger of Nazi military occupation.

By contrast, enormous net imports were secured from most of the occupied territories, even without accounting for *Wehrmacht* supplies, and their exploitation through trade intensified during the war. This represents another break with the interwar years, when Germany maintained an export surplus with these countries. The largest imports arrived from France, Belgium, and the Netherlands, and from occupied Italy in 1944. However, in percentage terms, net imports from Serbia and the western regions of the USSR were just as significant. The capacity of Nazi Germany to exert pressure on neutral states diminished after Stalingrad. Until 1942, trade with Sweden, Switzerland, and Turkey was approximately in balance. From 1943, only large net exports could secure the economic cooperation of these countries with an evil regime that had less and less chance of winning the war. This finding is confirmed by recent studies of the German payments balances with European neutrals (see Golson 2014, 2016).

The General Government represents a unique case and offers insight into the working of the Nazi *Großwirtschaftsraum*. Its trade with Germany skyrocketed after 1940 and became vastly larger than interwar trade between the Polish state and the Third Reich. Even more strikingly, Germany maintained an enormous export surplus with perhaps the most brutally exploited region of wartime Europe. Two clarifications can solve this puzzle. First, as noted earlier, *Wehrmacht* supplies were not accounted for in official German imports. After 1939, Poland turned into a hell for underpaid Polish and forced Jewish labour, but it was a heaven for manufacturers with military contracts. As these supplies did not need to cross the German borders to reach the Eastern Front they were never recorded by customs officials. Second, the eastward reorientation of German exports was driven not only by the eastbound thrust of the Nazi war effort, but also by the eastward territorial expansion of the Reich. The annexation of Austria and the highly industrialised western regions of Czechoslovakia implied that their exports to Hungary, Poland, Romania, and Yugoslavia were now being accounted as German exports.

Furthermore, the exchange of merchandise between regions that had formerly constituted parts of the same country was suddenly reported as foreign trade. Transports of goods between Germany and Slovakia or between Germany and the General Government disguised, in large part, trade between parts of the former Czechoslovakia and Poland respectively. Similarly, the wartime division of labour in Western Europe was not based solely on the traditional input–output web that tied the industries of the Ruhr, Luxembourg, and Lorraine together, as Berger and Ritschl (1995b) argued. After 1940, these territories were annexed by Germany, meaning that trade with France, Belgium, and the Netherlands increased partly because their transactions with Luxembourg and Alsace-Lorraine now contributed to German exports and imports.

The Reconstruction of Peacetime Trade Patterns

Hitler's *Drang nach Osten* proved to be the major force of trade diversion within wartime Europe. With the demolition of the Nazi empire and the end to Germany's quest for world domination, the wartime division of labour became history; the legacy of 'Fortress Europe' was short-lived. Following the division of Europe, and within that Germany, trade with Eastern Europe virtually collapsed. Its share in West German exports continued to fall during the early 1950s, when Cold War tensions were exceptionally intense with the Korean War and the brutal suppression of the popular uprising in East Berlin in June 1953. The trade data confirm that the relations of the Federal Republic deteriorated with all state-trading countries, not just with a few important members of the Soviet bloc.

Table 4.2 reports the share of countries and country groups in German exports during the interwar period and in West German exports throughout the 1950s and the 1960s. Shortly after the war, German exports shifted towards western markets. As I noted in Chapter 1, the post-war occupation regime that incorporated the international control of the Ruhr under the aegis of the Inter-Allied Reparation Agency (IARA) entailed the forced export of coal, coke, scrap iron, and other materials well under world-market prices to reparations claimants, most notably France and the Benelux countries. The very same nations received the bulk of the industrial equipment dismantled in West Germany during the late 1940s, which further increased their dependence on West German machine-tool exports in the following years. Finally, just as the annexation of Alsace-Lorraine and Luxembourg had automatically led to the intensification of trade with France and Belgium during the war, the loss of these territories, which had been integrated into the German economy after 1940, generated the same result in the early post-war years. The extraordinarily high Dutch share in West German exports in 1950 can be explained additionally by the growth of German food imports from the Netherlands after the loss of traditional suppliers in Eastern Europe and in the East of Germany, in particular.

However, this unprecedented Western reorientation of German exports proved to be temporary. After the end of Allied occupation and the replacement of the IARA regime by the ECSC in 1952, the share of France and the Benelux nations in West German exports declined sharply and moved closer to the interwar benchmarks. The volume of exports to Western markets grew vigorously, but it was true in relation to all countries in the EPU, both the signatory states in Europe as well as their overseas possessions and members of their currency blocs. With the politically driven disengagement from the Soviet bloc, the relative weight of Europe for West German exporters fell below interwar levels. By contrast, exports to developing regions, especially in Africa and Asia, increased disproportionately. While the trade boom with the black continent reflected the general euphoria surrounding the development of colonial resources in post-war Europe, exports to the Far East were fuelled by the explosive growth of Japan, which gradually overtook India as Germany's most important trade partner in the region.

Although exports to the largest South American economies grew slower than exports to the rest of the globe, West German industry made successful inroads into markets that were dominated by US firms and that had become increasingly difficult to enter because of import substitution. German manufacturers swiftly recognised their unique potential in these markets. The global dollar shortage still limited their ability to purchase US imports, British competition was weak because of its long delivery times and inferior product quality, Germany was more penetrable for the products of the region than the United States, and finally German engineering companies were more flexible to customer preferences. In addition, moving into Latin America was strongly connected to both the dollar-saving principle and the embargo policy of COCOM. Buying raw materials in exchange for German capital goods reduced the net imports from the dollar zone while the similarity of the South American market to Eastern Europe helped German companies traditionally oriented towards *Mitteleuropa* survive. The biggest early deals, including the delivery of 700 trolley buses to Buenos Aires in 1952 by a consortium of major steel and machinery producers, were supported by the federal government in underwriting the loans exporters had to raise from banks to secure the necessary financing (Neebe 1999, 109–10).

The ruthless implementation of COCOM rules envisaged severe punishment for blacklisted Western firms found in breach of the embargo policy, which drastically reduced the share of communist countries in West German exports. Still, trade with Eastern Europe began to recover in the mid-1950s. In direct trade dealings with the East, 'business marched in front of the flag'. After deliberate efforts by industrialists, supported by the government, to restore trade relations with the USSR in 1952–3 (Rudolph 2004, 36–41), and especially after diplomatic relations between Bonn and Moscow resumed in September 1955, West German exports to the Soviet Union grew rapidly (Wörmann 1982, 19–29). By the late 1950s, the USSR had become the second largest market for West German iron and steel producers (Neebe 1999, 118–9). As the dominant Western trade partner of the Soviet Union, West Germany was poised to benefit from any future expansion of East–West trade. The key

Table 4.2 *Country shares in total German/West German exports (%)*

	1928	1936	1950	1955	1960	1965	1970
I. Europe	*75.1*	*70.8*	*75.4*	*66.9*	*67.6*	*72.4*	*73.3*
Belgium/Luxembourg	4.1	4.4	8.3	6.9	6.0	7.8	8.3
France	5.8	5.3	7.5	5.8	8.8	10.9	12.4
Italy	4.6	5.1	6.1	5.7	5.9	6.3	9.0
Netherlands	9.9	8.3	14.3	9.6	8.8	10.3	10.7
Austria	3.6	2.3	3.8	5.4	5.1	5.3	4.6
Denmark	3.6	3.8	4.3	3.5	3.4	3.3	2.3
Finland	1.8	1.1	0.9	1.2	1.7	1.6	1.2
Greece	0.5	1.3	1.7	1.0	0.8	1.0	0.6
Ireland	0.2	0.3	0.3	0.4	0.3	0.4	0.3
Norway	1.4	1.9	1.5	2.4	2.4	1.9	1.5
Portugal	0.4	0.6	0.5	1.0	0.9	0.9	0.8
Spain	1.8	1.4	0.9	1.5	0.8	2.2	1.7
Sweden	3.6	4.8	6.5	7.1	5.4	5.3	3.8
Switzerland	4.8	4.7	6.0	6.1	6.2	6.5	6.2
Turkey	0.6	1.7	2.9	2.0	1.0	0.6	0.6
United Kingdom	9.9	8.5	4.4	4.1	4.5	3.9	3.6
Bulgaria	0.3	1.0	0.2	0.1	0.3	0.3	0.2
Czechoslovakia	5.4	2.9	0.9	0.3	0.6	0.6	0.9
Hungary	1.3	1.7	1.6	0.6	0.5	0.4	0.4
Poland	4.2	1.6	0.4	0.5	0.6	0.5	0.5
Romania	1.4	2.2	0.3	0.2	0.3	0.6	0.6
USSR	4.8	3.8	0.0	0.4	1.6	0.8	1.2
Yugoslavia	1.0	1.6	1.9	0.9	1.1	0.8	1.9
Others	0.1	0.2	0.1	0.3	0.2	0.2	0.2
II. Western offshoots	*7.9*	*5.2*	*7.3*	*8.8*	*10.4*	*10.2*	*11.1*
United States	6.7	3.6	5.3	6.5	7.9	8.0	9.2
Canada	0.6	0.7	0.5	0.9	1.1	1.1	0.9
Australia and NZ	0.6	0.9	1.4	1.5	1.4	1.1	1.0
III. Africa	*2.4*	*3.3*	*3.6*	*5.9*	*5.3*	*4.5*	*4.4*
IV. Asia	*7.2*	*9.9*	*5.6*	*9.8*	*9.8*	*8.1*	*7.0*
China	1.0	1.8	0.2	0.4	0.8	0.4	0.5
Japan	1.5	1.4	0.4	0.7	1.1	1.1	1.6
India	1.4	2.0	0.9	2.3	1.7	1.5	0.5
Others	3.3	4.7	4.1	6.4	6.2	5.1	5.4
V. Latin America	*7.5*	*10.8*	*8.2*	*8.6*	*6.9*	*4.7*	*4.1*
Argentina	2.9	2.1	1.3	1.5	1.3	0.6	0.6
Brazil	1.6	2.8	1.8	1.2	1.1	0.5	0.9
Others	3.0	5.9	5.1	5.9	4.5	3.6	2.6

Note: Country shares are computed from trade data in current prices.
Sources: See the beginning of Section 4.2 for references.

to success in this market was to forge a coordinated response to the state monopoly of foreign trade in centrally planned economies that could act as a monopsony and were interested in large volume deals. German industry found a corporatist solution based on an umbrella organisation of business groups that negotiated trade deals with the Soviet partner in close cooperation with the relevant ministries and set general delivery times and payment methods to avoid competition among German firms. In addition, the Soviet economy was in grave need of Western machinery imports, partly still to rebuild certain sectors of the economy, partly to modernise factories dating back to the 1930s. Given the antagonism of the Anglo-Saxon powers, West Germany was a partner without alternatives (Spaulding 1999).

During the 1950s, the traditional patterns of German exports to Europe and the non-socialist world in general were largely restored. This trend changed after 1960, as the share of the EEC in West German exports increased continuously. After the establishment of the customs union in 1968, trade diversion within Europe reduced the relative importance of EFTA markets, even some of Germany's closest trade partners: Austria, Denmark, Sweden, or Switzerland. Exports to France surged most dramatically from the late 1950s, breaking with historical trends. Since the late nineteenth century, fierce political antagonism across the Rhine had imposed severe constraints on cross-border trade between the two neighbouring great powers, despite their complementary economic structures. The new alliance brokered between Paris and Bonn in the 1950s helped West German firms exploit a potential for export expansion that had long existed but had never been realised (Dedinger 2006, 573–4). Only after the establishment of the EEC could the other member states also increase their share in West German exports substantially, especially Italy during the late 1960s.

Figure 4.7 presents two scatter diagrams that plot country shares in West German exports in 1955 and 1970 respectively against the share of the same countries in German exports in 1936. In the mid-1950s, the diminished weight of state trading economies as well as Argentina and Brazil was offset predominantly by the increased importance of the Alpine and Scandinavian economies, but to a lesser extent also of developing regions. By contrast, in 1970 most nations outside the EEC carved out similar or significantly smaller shares from German exports than they had done in the interwar years, even long-established markets like Denmark or Sweden. Austria and Switzerland remained exceptions to this pattern. Austria was an integral part of the German economy for seven years following the Anschluss in 1938, while Switzerland was surrounded by the Axis powers and their occupied territories, and

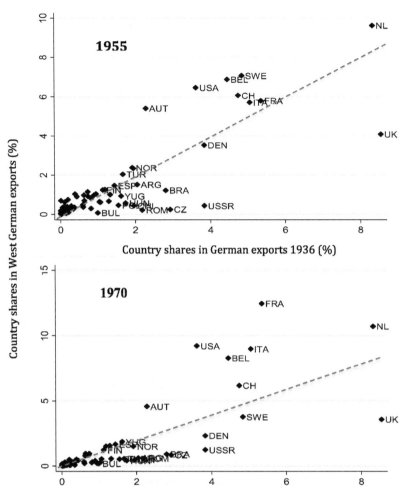

Figure 4.7 The diversion of West German exports after 1950.
Sources: See the beginning of Section 4.2 for references. Author's calculations.
Note: The country shares are not adjusted for border changes after 1945.

consequently had very limited access to alternative suppliers of industrial raw materials and intermediate inputs.

The most dramatic and lasting legacy of the war and the post-war settlement for West German foreign trade was the replacement of Britain by the United States as the primary market for Germany's most dynamic export industries, chemicals and high value-added

engineering products, automobiles, and electrical equipment in particular (Neebe 1989, 63). It is not surprising that the same industries were
at the forefront in adopting American mass-production methods from
the late 1950s onward and received the bulk of direct investment from
the United States (Kiesewetter 1992, 79–80). This geographic shift in
German exports was foremost the consequence of the staggering growth
of the American economy during the 1940s and the introduction of
trade policies that were much more liberal than what Washington had
pursued between the wars. The development of close cooperation with
US firms was also essential for German exporters that sought to enter
the Latin-American markets. Success in these emerging markets could
be guaranteed only by the services of export consultants and financiers in the United States who had both specialised knowledge of and
extensive networks within these regions. Not surprisingly, the Americas
were also the main destination for the burgeoning West German capital exports. Between 1945 and 1961, the export of capital in order to
establish production sites abroad was strictly forbidden, but from 1954,
thanks to the improving balance of payments, the federal government
allowed limited capital exports, provided that they were essential to
develop export opportunities (Schröter 1992, 88–91). By contrast, the
termination of trade with Britain in 1939 cast a long shadow. From
the late nineteenth century, the United Kingdom had been Germany's
leading export market and retained this position in the interwar period,
despite rising protectionism and preferential trade within the Sterling
Bloc following the Great Depression. After 1950, Britain could barely
make it into the top ten export markets of the Federal Republic and her
share in German exports continued to decline.

The critical importance of the US market for high-value-added
exports and technological cooperation explains, more than anything else,
the ambivalent attitude of West German industry towards the creation of
the EEC and especially the move towards an ever more inclusive form
of integration. German big business supported trade liberalisation, but
preferred to achieve this within the established frameworks of the OEEC
and GATT. The Treaty of Rome was viewed as the first step towards
the creation of a broader free-trade zone, and, crucially, which most
industrialists were convinced would finally be achieved. During the EEC
negotiations, their main concern was that the common tariffs would be
notably higher than the prevailing German rates and thus would make
imported raw materials more expensive. Therefore, the most consistent
campaigns of the industrial lobbyists focussed on tariff reductions and,
if possible, the quick expansion of 'the Six' into a larger trading bloc
(Rhenisch 1999, 254–6).

West German industry retained its formal support for the EEC only because the vanguard of its all-influential association, the Bundesverband der Deutschen Industrie (BDI), was still dominated by heavy industry (see Chapter 5). Already integrated within the ECSC and more competitive in the continent than worldwide, coal and iron exporters were more interested in European market integration than were most engineering and consumer industries. Furthermore, the giants in iron and steel were concerned about the future of the coal and steel community more than the further development of the integration process. History also played a key role. Within heavy industry, the ghost of Hjalmar Schacht was still present in the room: his concept of an extended economic space was still cherished (Rhenish 1999, 257). Finally, the BDI leadership, whose influence on policymaking in general will be discussed in Chapter 5, was adamant in supporting Adenauer against Erhard in his foreign policy agenda that placed greater weight on the Franco-German alliance than on international trade liberalisation.

4.3   The Commodity Structure of German Exports

The conclusions drawn from the regional trade statistics can be confirmed only if we can observe similar developments in the commodity structure of German exports. The restoration of pre-existing patterns of trade during the 1950s would not mean much if the same dynamics were not reflected in the commodity structure of West German exports. Similarly, we can consider the establishment of the EEC a structural break in the development of West German exports only if it fundamentally shifted their product composition away from established trends. We need to see significant changes in the areas of specialisation for German exporters. Otherwise, the EEC may have truly been a mechanism that, at most, deepened a natural trading bloc. The same argument can be made about wartime trade diversion, which we would expect to have distorted the structure of exports in accordance with the needs and productive capacity of the German war economy.

To confirm these hypotheses, I constructed a constant-price dataset on German/West German exports in sixty product categories for the same benchmark years referred to in the previous section. The dataset is reported in its entirety in Appendix 4, which includes detailed information on the statistical sources and computation methods for the aid of future research. Building consistent series required several adjustments. First, the product nomenclature of the foreign trade statistics was modified substantially between the 1920s and the 1930s, and to a lesser extent also after 1945. The industrial product groups, which numbered at least 148 from 1936 onwards, were aggregated into 56 categories and foodstuffs were classified into 4 groups. This catalogue aggregates several closely related products that alone would account for negligible shares in German exports. It also makes structural developments easier to describe; the official trade statistics disaggregate machinery into 12, chemicals into more than 20 sub-categories.

The total volume of German exports declined sharply between 1928 and 1936, but was maintained at close to peacetime levels during the early 1940s. From the post-war nadir of slightly more than 8 billion DM, exports grew rapidly, and by 1955 recovered to volumes unattained since the Great Depression. In the following decade, the rate of expansion fell back somewhat, but increased again during the late 1960s. By 1970, the volume of West German exports was five times as large as it had been in 1928. The sectoral aggregates confirm that, until the late 1950s, the total volume of industrial exports was in strong positive correlation with the share of finished goods. After the Great Depression, exports in this category contracted much faster than in raw materials and intermediates. The share of finished goods became even smaller during the war. This finding confirms the established view on the wartime division of labour within continental Europe: Germany supplied its allies and occupied territories with coal and intermediate inputs, particularly iron and steel, in exchange for finished goods, both civilian and military products.

The data do not justify, however, the argument that the outsourcing of war production was facilitated by machinery exports. The share of machine tools and steel constructions in German industrial exports had already been very low in 1936, but declined further after 1940. Shifts in the product composition of German foreign trade during the war were driven, in part, by border changes. The annexation of Moravia, Upper Silesia, Luxembourg, and Lorraine substantially enhanced the domestic reserves of hard coal and iron ore as well as production capacities in primary metals. While this increased the share of these goods in industrial exports, their producers also faced dramatically increased demand within the borders of an enlarged empire. In 1950, the share of intermediates in industrial exports remained at its wartime peak, while the share of finished goods increased slightly at the expense of raw materials. Cole, coke, and metals still accounted for a large proportion of German exports, which underlines the impact of the inter-Allied reparations regime. By 1955, the commodity structure of industrial exports had been restored to its peacetime norm, even though the share of intermediates was slightly smaller than what it had been in the interwar period. This shift reflected the diminished weight of chemical dyestuffs, which had traditionally constituted the largest item in German exports to the United Kingdom. After 1939, the British textile industry found alternative suppliers at home and abroad, and West Germany was unable to recapture her once dominant market position after 1945, hence the greatly diminished share of Britain in West German exports during the post-war era.

With the technology-driven switch away from coal to hydrocarbons, the share of raw materials in German industrial exports continued to decline in the late 1950s. After 1960, however, the share of finished goods also began to shrink, despite the continued expansion in the total volume of exports. This signals a structural break in the trend that had been manifested since the late nineteenth century. The increasing weight of intermediate inputs in West German exports reflects the intensification of intra-industry trade within the EEC, as input–output networks transcended national borders more than ever before. This phenomenon also marked a clear shift in regional specialisation patterns.

Figure 4.8 reports the composition of German/West German exports by eight major product groups, including foodstuffs. While the restoration of Germany's world market position in the 1950s confirmed long-established comparative advantages in quality engineering products, chemicals and textiles led the further surge of exports after 1960. Germany had always been a leading producer of chemical intermediaries, but the share of textiles in her exports had been in constant decline since the Second Industrial Revolution. The composition of exported chemicals also changed fundamentally. The once dominant role of dyestuffs, fertilisers, pesticides, and household chemicals was reassigned to synthetic materials, petrochemicals and other chemical intermediates, pharmaceuticals, and cosmetics. The EEC tariffs protected the new darlings of the German chemical industry from the competition of US firms that retained their technological leadership both in synthetic materials and petrochemicals. Similarly, Britain's self-imposed exclusion from 'the Six' eased the way of West German textile exports into France and the Benelux countries. In addition, the remarkable growth of synthetic materials enabled the German textile industry to establish its own, today well-respected, competitive positions in synthetic yarns and cloth, as well as in synthetic clothing. Finally, the enhanced application of synthetic materials in manufacturing also reduced the share of metals as well as paper and woodenware in West German industrial exports.

The legacy of 'Fortress Europe' for German exports was very short-lived. As Hitler's eastbound empire had been dismantled and Germany itself divided, the dependence of West Germany on food and raw-material imports increased substantially, relatively more than her thirst

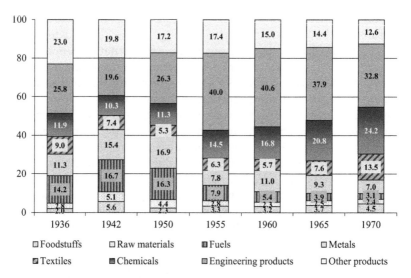

Figure 4.8 The share of major product groups in German/West German exports (%).
Sources and methods: See Appendix 4 for details.

for imported manufactures. The war and the post-war settlement not only increased the productive base of West German industry; they also made it much more export oriented. Therefore, it is difficult to establish a direct link between forced trade integration during World War II and the impact of trade diversion after the establishment of the EEC, especially as the relative weight of product groups within both intermediary and finished goods changed fundamentally between the 1940s and the 1960s. Within the Common Market, German manufacturers became successful even in industries in which they would not have been competitive, or at least not as competitive, without the protective tariff walls. Therefore, from a German perspective, the EEC cannot be interpreted as simply the institutionalisation of a natural trading bloc.

The strong correlation between interwar and post-war patterns in the commodity structure of German exports may be surprising at first, given the fact that the West German share in the production, and thereby export capacity, of the Third Reich varied strongly across different industries. Provincial data collected in the 1936 industrial census, already discussed in Chapter 3, can be used to calculate the share of West Germany in total German exports (sales) for each of the 56 industrial product groups in my dataset (Reichsamt 1939, 148–59) In several cases, where the industry classifications of the census did not correspond to the commodity structure of my dataset, I could only provide crude esti-mates. The figures are reported in Appendix 4, Table A4, under the head-ing 'West (%)'. The data provide important additional information about the development of German industrial exports. The West German share in the export of finished goods was relatively small. Consequently, raw materials and intermediates carved out larger slices from West German exports in 1950 than from German exports during the interwar period. Traditional export patterns could be restored only after West German firms had recovered the former export markets of their counterparts in East Germany, which had practically withdrawn from international trade outside the Soviet bloc. This was most critical in electrical and precision engineering, the glass and the pottery industries, paper processing and the printing industry, textiles, and the clothing industry, which all con-centrated strongly in Berlin and/or in Saxony until 1945.

Table 4.3 reports correlations between the commodity structure of West German industrial exports during the post-war period and that of German or West German industrial exports in 1936. The share of each product group in West German industrial exports in 1936 is computed as the product of its share in German industrial exports, derived from trade statistics, and the share of West Germany in the export of the relevant products, as computed from the industrial census. The comparison of the two sets of coefficients shows that restoring the pre-existing regional trade patters after 1950 depended on the reconstruction of the export structure that had prevailed before the war in Germany as a whole, not in her western half in particular. This finding is a novel addition to the historiography of the West German export miracle in the early post-war era, and provides an additional explanation for the rapid growth of the industries that, prior to 1945, were relatively underrepresented in the western half of Germany.

Finally, it is worth a brief examination, how the shifting commod-ity structure of industrial exports influenced the export orientation of different regions within the country. This investigation expands on the discussion in Chapter 2 on the regional dynamics of reconstruction growth. Figure 4.9 reports the share of each federal state in West German industrial exports during the 1950s and the 1960s. The large share of coal, coke, and metallurgical products in German exports in the early post-war years meant that North Rhine-Westphalia and, within that, the Rhine-Ruhr agglomeration, where heavy industry was still under inter-national control, dominated Germany's external trade.

In the following decade, especially until 1955, the composition of indus-trial exports according to region of origin became much more balanced.

Table 4.3 *Correlations explaining the commodity structure of West German industrial exports*

	1950	1955	1960	1965	1970
Germany 1936	0.881	0.901	0.885	0.831	0.720
West Germany 1936	0.914	0.809	0.796	0.742	0.612

Notes: All coefficients are significant at the 1 per cent level. Hard coal and transport vehicles are excluded from the dataset, as they would otherwise drive the results. The number of observations is 54.

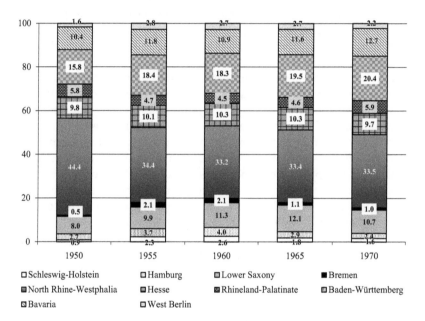

□ Schleswig-Holstein □ Hamburg □ Lower Saxony ■ Bremen
■ North Rhine-Westphalia ■ Hesse ■ Rhineland-Palatinate □ Baden-Württemberg
□ Bavaria □ West Berlin

Figure 4.9 The share of the federal states in West German exports (%). *Sources:* Außenhandel, Part 1 (1951), 37; ibid. (1956), 86; ibid.d (1961), 80; Fachserie G/1 (1966), 75; ibid. (1971), 81.

Shipbuilding was the most dynamic sector in the north, electrical engineering in West Berlin. Machine tools, electrical and precision engineering, and transport vehicles accounted for the growing share of Hesse, Baden-Württemberg, and Bavaria in West German exports. After 1960, only the south and the Rhineland-Palatinate could improve their relative positions, owing to their strength in chemicals, textiles, and the clothing industry. On the contrary, Schleswig-Holstein, Hamburg, and Bremen suffered from the crisis of shipbuilding in the face of mounting Japanese competition. Chemicals and textiles compensated for the declining share of heavy industry in the exports from North Rhine-Westphalia, while the strong performance of Volkswagen on foreign markets limited the impact of the falling exports of water vessels in Lower Saxony, at least until the recession of 1966–7.

4.4 The Export Boom and Industrial Expansion

The post-war export boom has featured prominently in the historiography of the West German economic miracle. Economic theory postulates that opening up to international trade leads to greater specialisation and to the more efficient utilisation of the factors of production. Growing exports promote investment at home, which, in turn, generates higher output and productivity. This makes the economy more competitive in external markets, leading to additional export growth (Lámfalussy 1963). Taking this argument one step further, increased international demand provides strong incentives for firms to reinvest their profits in new equipment and plant. The expansion of production capacities brings growing employment, which motivates trade unions to accept moderate wage gains. Wage moderation pushes profits upwards, inducing additional investment in fixed capital and, therefore, higher productivity and improved competitiveness (Eichengreen 1996). This interpretation of export-led growth follows the accelerator principle, according to which net investment is determined by profit expectations that, in turn, depend on the price of the complementary factors of production, mostly labour, and expected future product demand. Paqué (1988) considered this mechanism pivotal to the growth of labour productivity in West German industry during the 1960s, in particular, as it maintained high rates of net capital formation even in the face of severe labour scarcity, leading to the sharp increase in the capital-labour ratio documented in Chapter 3.

There is consensus in German historiography that industrial expansion during the post-war period was export-led. Exports, it has been argued, played a catalysing role in the economic miracle from the early 1950s. Soaring demand for capital goods in Western markets following the outbreak of the Korean War kick-started, or at least hastened, the recovery of the metallurgical and engineering industries, which subsequently became the main engines of growth (Weimer 1998, 94–5; Abelshauser 2004, 161). Economists interpreted the impact of the Korea Boom as a Keynesian stimulus in an industrial sector still hampered by mass unemployment and underutilised capacities without the crowding out effects normally associated with expansionary fiscal stimuli

(Giersch et al. 1992, 8–9). That the Korean War gave significant impetus to the growth of West German industry is debated (Temin 1997), but it certainly helped German big business in several ways: it (1) boosted exports in defence-related capital goods, where Germany had huge surplus capacity; (2) removed the still remaining restrictions on industrial production, such as shipbuilding and the establishment of a merchant fleet; (3) convinced the Western powers that the Federal Republic should be integrated into the Western alliance system; and finally (4) led to the EPU bailout (Neebe 1999).

After the occupation statutes were modified in March 1951, West Germany restored diplomatic relations with its international partners, and regained full national sovereignty in the following year, when Allied military occupation officially ended (Weimer 1998, 93–5). In addition, the 1952 London Agreement with the Allied powers reduced West German debt by 50 per cent and established a manageable payment schedule. Thus, in sharp contrast to the experience of the 1920s, the debt burden did not hinder the recovery of the German economy after World War II, especially as the permanent export surplus provided more than sufficient resources to meet the debt obligations (Abelshauser 1987, 27). Finally, the accession of West Germany to NATO in 1955 abolished the prohibition of munitions and aircraft production and opened the door for rearmament, promising gigantic contracts for the engineering industries. Roughly one-sixth of the labour-productivity gains achieved in manufacturing throughout the 1950s were the outcome of structural shifts that the literature has directly linked to export demand (Ambrosius 1984, 276).

In the 1960s, the establishment of the Common Market further cemented the export orientation of West German firms through the expansion of intra-industry trade. Moreover, since demand for quality engineering products in world markets was highly income-elastic, the period saw significant improvements in the Terms of Trade, providing further incentives for German manufacturers to specialise even more strongly on the production of high-value-added capital goods (Giersch et al. 1992, 164; Abelshauser 2004, 262). Increasing export demand induced structural shifts in favour of the most productive branches of industry and generated considerable efficiency gains from economies of scale. Finally, it has long been argued that soaring industrial exports created additional demand for capital goods at home, which were the prime export articles of the country in the first place (Michalski 1970).

To investigate how far in the post-war period the growth of output and productivity in West German industry can be characterised as export-led, I constructed values of export intensity for all branches of industry

Table 4.4 *Correlations testing for export-led growth in West German industry*

	Correlations of annual % increments in export intensity with			
	Growth of value-added (ln%)		Growth of labour productivity (ln%)	
	Coefficient	Sig. Level	Coefficient	Sig. Level
1951–5	0.653	0.000	0.510	0.000
1956–60	−0.324	0.041	−0.323	0.042
1961–70	0.147	0.293	−0.170	0.192

Note: The number of observations (branches of industry) is 32.

examined in Chapter 3. Export intensity is defined as the share of export revenue in total turnover, which are both reported in the official industry statistics.[7] Table 4.4 reports correlations between period-average growth rates of net industrial production and labour productivity on the one hand and the growth of export intensity on the other.[8] Since the intensity values are expressed in percentages and present a wide range across industries, the growth of intensity is measured by percentage-point increments instead of percentage growth rates. The usefulness of this approach can be understood through the following example. Doubling the rate of export intensity in a given industry is irrelevant for market expansion and hence for export-led growth if the initial rate of intensity is negligibly small.

The correlation coefficients confirm that the recovery of West German industry following the outbreak of the Korean War was strongly export-led. In addition, expansion into international markets also enhanced labour productivity. The relationship between the growth of export intensity and labour productivity turned negative in the late 1950s. In other words, by 1955, manufacturers had exhausted the scope for productivity gains that could be achieved through scale economies and increased specialisation. Thereafter, the growth of labour productivity was fastest in those industries that were prompted to rationalise by declining external demand, such as the mining sector, or increasing competition from foreign suppliers in the domestic market. In the early phase of post-war reconstruction, when the development of West

[7] IndBRD, Series 4, No. 9 (1955), 12–13; ibid., No. 14 (1957), 16–19; Fachserie D/1, Vol. 15 (1966), 20–24; ibid., Vol. 20 (1971), 22–3.
[8] Growth rates of output and labour productivity are computed from Tables 3.1 and 3.2 in Chapter 3.

German exports also followed a reconstruction dynamic, industrial recovery was fuelled, in large part, by external demand. However, contrary to the mainstream view in the literature, once the structure of West German exports began to part with long-established comparative advantages, the strong relationship between export intensity and industrial growth broke down.

This novel finding becomes less surprising if one investigates the actual trends in the growth of export intensity. For the industrial sector as a whole, the share of export revenue in total turnover jumped from 8.3 per cent to 13.4 per cent between 1950 and 1955, increased modestly until the mid-1960s, and then made another surge from 15.7 per cent to 19.3 per cent between 1965 and 1970. Since external demand for West German manufactures grew continuously throughout the post-war period, not least due to the increasingly under-valued currency and the gradually enhanced integration of European markets, the very uneven temporal distribution of the growth of export intensity must be explained by changing conditions in the domestic market. These changes, in turn, are directly linked to the role of economic policy in the West German growth miracle, which will be examined in the last chapter of this book.

5   Managing the Miracle: Economic Policy

Unravelling the mysteries of the German growth miracle cannot be complete without a critical discussion of the role that economic policy had played in the process. For contemporaries, this was a critical if not decisive role. Most observers at the time and numerous historians since saw the *Wirtschaftswunder* as the outcome of a political and ideological revolution that engineered a structural break in the institutional development of the West German economy and propelled its remarkable revival. This monograph began with an audit of the initial conditions for economic recovery after World War II. It has been demonstrated that German industry was endowed with ample resources for growth but the restrictive institutions and policies of Allied occupation stifled markets and subdued the forces of economic expansion. Thus, many have considered the subsequent liberalisation of markets and the lifting of administrative restrictions on private industry to be the catalysts of post-war recovery. In the traditional historiography, the key driver of the economic miracle was the Social Market Economy (SME), a uniquely German approach to economic policy that accepted neither unrestrained free-market capitalism nor the alternative of state management and central command.

In these interpretations, the *Wirtschaftswunder* began in the summer of 1948, when the currency reform and the abrupt removal of administrative prices and wages restored functioning markets in West Germany and revitalised a hitherto paralysed economy. In the same year, the Marshall Plan began to operate in the Western zones of occupation. Post-war scholarship not only claimed that American magnanimity lifted German society out of destitution; it also argued that it was above all foreign aid that transformed a fledgling recovery into sustained growth. As one such account summed it up, 'like all economic miracles, the German *Wirtschaftswunder* was the result of wise planning, hard work and well timed aid ... the German recovery would not have been accomplished alone' (Mayer 1969, 96). As the first two sections of this chapter will demonstrate, the historical evidence justifies neither this eulogy of the

173

Marshall Plan nor the tributes paid to the economic reforms of 1948 as propellers of change.

The recent literature has described a strongly corporatist West German economy that showed more continuity than discontinuity from the economic institutions of the Reich. The liberalisation of markets was incomplete: prices for necessities remained fixed, wage controls and rationing were retained for many years, capital markets were repressed, and there was extensive red tape over the financial sector at large until at least 1956. Markets were more competitive for sure than in the Nazi era, but the monopolistic structures that had long characterised the German economy, to a large extent, stayed in place. The evidence presented in the text that follows shall also make it clear that the preservation of direct controls and the special relationship between big industry and the state were not just relics of the past; they formed essential components of government policy and the political program of the ruling parties. Historical statistics suggest further that recovery had begun well before the currency reform and that it was not transformed into sustained growth until the early 1950s. As the previous chapters have shown, the most important limiting factors of industrial expansion in post-war Germany, namely the urban housing shortage and the structural disproportions caused by the redrawing of borders, persisted for many years after 1948. Foreign aid did little to improve these conditions, for it was not substantial enough and it was not focussed primarily on these critical bottlenecks.

The last two sections of the chapter discuss the role that fiscal and monetary policy instruments played in the West German growth miracle. I cannot aim to give a comprehensive overview of economic policy in the Federal Republic in the post-war era. This has been accomplished by a vast scholarship that the present chapter draws from and that is reviewed, in great part and detail, by the recently published monumental collective history of economic policy in Germany during the twentieth century commissioned by the Federal Ministry for Economic Affairs and Energy (Abelshauser et al. 2016). My objective with this final chapter is to discuss what role policy could play in a growth process that was ultimately driven by reconstruction dynamics. The investigation into the wartime origins of the German *Wirtschaftswunder* presented in the previous chapters helps us reassess the importance of economic policy in this context.

As I will demonstrate, fiscal policy never truly confirmed to the liberal blueprints. During the 1950s, it was strongly interventionist and made extensive use of direct controls as well as indirect subsidies that reflected the deep distrust policymakers had felt towards the ability of markets both to prevent supply shortages and to eliminate infrastructural bottlenecks. The instruments of state intervention remained in place long after they had lost their economic rationale, and as they were gradually removed in the 1960s they were replaced by universal demand management. State intervention in the economy did little to support growth. Public investment and government subsidies favoured predominantly declining sectors and industries that, in reality, had excess rather than insufficient capacity owing to the structural imbalances created by the division of Germany. Social policy rather than economic policy made the most critical contribution to the West German growth miracle through the leading role that the state assumed in rebuilding the urban housing stock and resettling the displaced populations trapped in rural areas after World War II.

At the same time, fiscal policy was chiefly responsible for the price stability that made West Germany the object of envy in the Western world and which earlier accounts as well as most international observers considered to be the achievement of the German Bundesbank. In reality, and most of the time, monetary policy played second fiddle. It managed the business cycle with more vigour and consequence than fiscal policy, but it was forced to act in response to the substantial, and often ill-timed, budgetary effects on aggregate demand. When the Bundesbank had to take the initiative, its response was inadequate because of the limited room for manoeuvre that central banks had in a world of fixed exchange rates.

5.1   1948 and the Social Market Economy

The meaning of the SME has never been precisely defined and it has evolved since the term was coined by Alfred Müller-Armack, academic advisor to and later the head of the policy department in the Ministry for the Economy. Like most of his contemporaries, Müller-Armack did not believe that laissez faire capitalism could facilitate the rebuilding of the war-shattered economy by simultaneously providing social security. Instead, he advocated a strong role for the state in guaranteeing the fairness of competition and the socially justifiable distribution of the gains from free enterprise. His vision combined liberal notions of freedom with the principles of solidarity and collective responsibility (Müller-Armack 1947). The SME has also been termed 'coordinated free-market economy', in which government regulation achieves the form of competition optimal for social progress (Koppstein and Lichbach 2005, 156). Initially, it was not seen as means to manage aggregate demand or to guarantee full employment. Nor was it a welfare-state program. The state was supposed to refrain from directly intervening in the market and from diverting the resources for growth to unproductive uses (Braun 1990, 177). The first federal minister for the economy and the leading political advocate of the SME, Ludwig Erhard, argued that prosperity and full employment could be best achieved with an economic policy that limited government intervention to the necessary minimum. Growth, in his view, was the best social welfare policy (Erhard 1957). Erhard deemed regulation effective only if it was market conform and, therefore, opposed, at least in principle, planning and the championing of monopolistic firms (Jäger 1988, 225).

The concept of the SME was strongly influenced by the political philosophy of 'Ordoliberalism', a German variant of social liberalism that distanced itself from both the nineteenth century laissez faire and the state-managed economy of totalitarianism. The term was coined only in 1950, but its origins can be found in the works of the Freiburg liberals Walter Eucken and Franz Böhm alongside Geneva economist Wilhelm Röpke. The word 'market economy' (*Marktwirtschaft*) was first used by Röpke but was not accepted until after the war (Spoerer 2007, 29). The most influential member of the Freiburg school and a vocal opposition of Nazism, Eucken conceived a similar term, the 'transit-economy' (*Verkehrswirtschaft*), as the antipode to the National Socialist command economy (*Zwangswirtschaft*) in his *Die Grundlagen der Nationalökonomie* (1940). The economic system he envisioned for the post-war order would constrain the power of individuals, companies, and associations within a legal framework that would guard private property, enforce private contracts, and guarantee free market entry and stable monetary conditions. In such an economy, the role of the state would be limited to providing a well-functioning competitive order (*Ordnung*), in which free enterprise could flourish without discretionary government interventions. Free and fair competition was fundamental to Ordoliberalism, which opposed collective ownership of the means of production and state management. At the same time, according to Eucken and his disciples, the market economy could achieve its theoretical potential only within a strong state that can effectively limit the undue concentration of market power and resist the influence of special interests in the formation of economic policy (Ambrosius 2001, 39–40). The theses of the Frankfurt school concur with the Olsonian interpretation of state capture inasmuch as the efficiency of free markets is limited by collusive special interests. The principle of market conformity was central to all the major works of Ordoliberalism, which implies that economic policy should operate with instruments that do not obstruct market exchange and do not undermine market incentives (Dürr 1996, 387).

The theories of Eucken influenced the post-war reforms that many considered to have set the stage for the *Wirtschaftswunder*. A member of the Academic Advisory Council at the Bizonal Economic Administration and later the Federal Ministry for the Economy, he left a formidable footprint on the policies of Erhard from 1948 onwards. Leonhard Miksch, student of Eucken, drafted the legislation that abolished price controls following the currency reform. However, the political establishment of post-war Germany was slow to adopt the SME and the philosophy of Ordoliberalism. Political life under Allied occupation was extremely limited. Economic policy was under the total control of the military governments: independent German initiatives could seldom gain ground. Initially, the Labour government in Britain advocated the nationalisation of the Ruhr industries and the introduction of a planned economy in Germany. The trade unions in the British occupation zone were supportive of these intentions. Only after the merger of the British and American zones and the escalation of tensions with the Soviet Union could free-market principles gain the upper hand. Even then, at first, the influence of Ordoliberalism was weak. In the first half of 1947, the Bizonal Economic Administration, controlled by the Social Democrats, sought to maintain administrative controls and the state management of industry. The economic program of the then opposition Christian union parties also owed more to Christian socialist views than to the liberal creed (Ambrosius 1977, 217–18).

The main circles of Christian socialism, especially the Frankfurt and Berlin schools, wished to replace free market competition with state coordination and a mixed economy achieved through the nationalisation of natural monopolies and strategic industries. The influence of conservative and liberal politicians was marginal. The Ahlen Program of February 1947 that remained the official doctrine of the union parties until 1948 was designed to be an electable alternative to democratic socialism and reflected the conviction that post-war economic revival required extensive state planning and oversight. It was the growing dissatisfaction with the bureaucratic controls of the military governments and the shifting priorities of American policy towards Germany that allowed liberal voices to gather momentum from the second half of 1947. The Christian socialist agenda was finally defeated with the reorganisation of the Economic Administration and the appointment of Erhard as its first director in early 1948, even though the union parties adopted the SME officially only in their 1949 election campaign (Ambrosius 1977, 219–25).

Although the Economic Administration under Erhard had been actively preparing liberal market reforms, the currency reform of June 1948 was imposed on West Germany by the occupying powers. It implemented the Colm–Dodge–Goldsmith Plan, which was officially presented to the US government in May 1946, and which differed substantially from the Homburg Plan that the Economic Administration published in March 1948 (Buchheim 2001, 158). The currency reform was introduced in four steps between June and October 1948. On 20 June, the Deutschmark replaced the Reichsmark and from the following day all wages, salaries, pensions, and other allowances were paid in the new currency with 1:1 conversion. In addition, every resident in the Western occupation zones received a quota of 40 DM in exchange for 40 RM, followed by an additional 20 DM in the course of August and September. Organisations, corporations, individual entrepreneurs, and the self-employed were given a start-up capital of 60 DM per employee (Weimer 1998, 41). The Conversion Law (*Umstellungsgesetz*) came into effect on 27 June. Reichsmark loans and sight deposits at commercial banks were exchanged into Deutschmark at the rate of 10:1. Public debt was not converted (Buchheim 2001, 159).

Finally, the Law on Blocked Accounts (*Festkontogesetz*), issued on 7 October, stipulated that 70 per cent of savings deposits would be not honoured in the new currency and an additional 10 per cent would be temporarily placed on blocked accounts. Consequently, the effective conversion rate for accounts above 600 RM was 100:6.5 rather than the official rate of 10:1 (Grosser 1990, 82). Since the reform did not directly affect prices, the purchasing power of cash holdings was reduced by more than 90 per cent. The reform acts also regulated the issuing of the new currency. The Bank deutscher Länder (BdL), established as a federal central bank on 1 March 1948, assumed the right of note issue. After the state central banks of the French zone also joined the BdL on 16 June, it became the first joint institution of the three Western zones, and with that the first manifestation of the still embryonic West German state (Abelshauser 1983, 49–50).

As savings deposits were converted only from October 1948, the money supply expanded gradually from only 4.4 billion DM by the end of June to 12 billion DM until December (Buchheim 2001, 160). To make money extremely scarce at the initial stages of the reform was the intention of the legislature, as it created strong incentives for firms to unload the goods they had been hoarding and to boost production, while it spurred employees to increase their work effort. The immediate effect on the market was staggering. On the morning of Monday, 21 June 1948, shop windows were filled with much-wanted consumer products, including goods that had been real scarcities since the final months of the war. The incentive for firms to clear their inventories was made even stronger by the fact that, with their accounts temporarily blocked, or worth only one-tenth of their original value, they had to rely almost exclusively on retained earnings in the new currency to finance their operations (Wolf

1993, 38). The drastic contraction of liquidity aimed to restore the equilibrium between the supply of available goods and effective demand. The currency reform alone could not introduce an efficient market economy; that required, in addition, the lifting of administrative restrictions and the liberalisation of prices and wages. However, it was only after the removal of the monetary overhang and with that the excess purchasing power that market prices for consumer goods could be reintroduced without the danger of runaway inflation (Klump 1989, 416).

Unlike the currency reform, the removal of administrative prices for most manufactured goods on 25 June 1948 (*Leitsätzegesetz*) and of rationing for the respective products five days later were entirely German initiatives and, in large part, the result of Erhard's audacity against the initial American objections (Spoerer and Streb 2013, 217). The Advisory Council to the Economic Administration had already recommended price liberalisation in its very first report published on 1 April 1948.

The currency reform will only serve its purpose, if it will be combined with a fundamental revision of the prevailing system of economic management. As an isolated technical move, it would be worthless, if not dangerous. Through the currency reform, effective demand will be reduced to such an extent that rationing and the command economy will lose their rationale … The Council unanimously finds the lifting of the price stop from 1936 necessary, for the then established and until today largely still prevalent price system does not reflect the current relative scarcities and is thus incongruent with the current economic situation.[1]

The reintroduction of market prices magnified the effects of the currency reform. The compensation deals of the shortage economy described in Chapter 1 were no longer necessary, that reduced transaction costs and raised the profitability of firms. This created strong incentives for manufacturers to run down their inventories of finished goods and to increase production through the improved utilisation of labour and productive capacity and by clearing the stockpiles of intermediary inputs accumulated prior to, and partly in preparation for, the currency reform. In order to alleviate the crippling raw-material shortages that had hampered economic recovery, the Joint Export–Import Agency (JEIA) allowed, from the spring of 1948, an increase in raw-material imports into the British and American zones, which doubled in the second quarter of the year and jumped another 40 per cent during the third quarter (Buchheim 1990, 61–2).

---

[1] Wissenschaftlicher Beirat, Gutachten vom 1.4.1948, paragraphs 2 and 11. In Wissenschaftlicher Beirat (1973), 1–3. Own translation from the German text.

The combined effect of the economic reforms over the summer of 1948 astonished contemporaries. According to the statistics of the military government, industrial production in the Bizonal Area increased from 47 per cent of the 1936 level in May 1948 to 75 per cent in November.[2] Between the second and third quarters, manufacturing output grew by 29 per cent, which appeared spectacular in comparison with the average quarterly growth rate of 5 per cent recorded in 1947.[3] In the second half of 1948, investment in fixed capital also began to increase, at an annual rate of 5.6 per cent. Investment activity picked up even though consumers had become net debtors after the currency reform. New investments were financed predominantly from higher profits, which signalled growing business confidence (Giersch, Paqué, and Schmieding 1992, 40). The currency reform in itself helped firms finance their expansion from retained earnings. The Conversion Law allowed companies to revalue assets that they could write off as part of their production costs, essentially ignoring general accounting rules. As a consequence, manufacturing firms faced an effective exchange rate of 10:8.4, which enhanced the relative value of their capital (Jákli 1990, 56–7).

The currency reform redistributed wealth from households to producers by sharply reducing the value of cash holdings and savings, while leaving the prices of real assets unaffected. Producers were relieved of 90 per cent of their debt obligations, whereas private investors, small deposit holders, and pensioners lost their hard-earned savings built up over many years. Although the Conversion Law foresaw some unspecified form of compensation for deposit holders, this took material form only in the Equalisation of Burdens Act (*Lastenausgleichgesetz*) of 1952 and, even thereafter, compensation for the inequities arising from the currency reform was only partial and was paid out over decades (Schröter 2000, 362). The myth, still shared by many today, that in June 1948 social inequality disappeared as every German started with the same 40 DM had little to do with reality (Kramer 1991, 137–8). Just two years after the currency reform, the richest percentile of the West German population earned 14.6 per cent of national income, while the population living below the median income received only 16 per cent (Leaman 1988, 29). Favouring private industry and the owners of productive capital at the expense of consumers and holders of financial assets by administrative means may have been effective in mobilising resources for growth, but it can hardly be justified as a manifestation of the SME.

---

[2] OMGUS, *Economic developments since the currency reform*, 3.
[3] *Wirtschaft und Statistik*, Vol. 1 (1949/50), cited in Ruhl (1982), Tables and Statistics, Document no. 25, 522, 523.

The drastic devaluation of their bank deposits and the reintroduction of wages with real purchasing power pushed labourers to work more, so that they could buy more consumer goods and gradually rebuild their savings. These incentives had a powerful impact on the labour market. Industrial workers spent, on average, three hours more on their jobs weekly in 1948 than they had done in the previous year. Total hours worked in mining and manufacturing increased by 13 per cent (Giersch et al. 1992, 39). According to a confidential report of the Economic Administration, firms in the iron and steel industry witnessed a sharp reduction in hours lost due to worker absenteeism, which averaged 16 per cent of contract hours between January and June 1948, fell to 10 per cent in July, and dropped below 10 per cent by December. Monthly output per worker in raw steel grew 10 per cent between June and July and an additional 10 per cent in the second half of the year.[4] Incentives for work increased further with an abrupt end to labour hoarding. Firms no longer competed for survival but for profits, and they could increase productivity by firing the least efficient workers (Kramer 1991, 138–46). The official unemployment rate climbed from 3.2 per cent to 5.3 per cent between June and December 1948 and reached 8.7 per cent by June 1949 (Klump 1989, 406).

In addition to the currency reform, tax reforms also raised the profitability of private firms and the income of shareholders. In order to reduce purchasing power, the Allied Control Authority drastically increased the levels of both income and corporate taxation in 1946 (Weimer 1998, 43–4). On 22 June 1948, the military government reduced the marginal rates of the income tax by one-third and replaced the progressive corporate tax with a flat rate. By contrast, it raised numerous local taxes. German experts recommended more ambitious general tax cuts, which were rejected, but the new tax code incorporated incentives for industrial investors.[5] The reforms of 1948 had a positive impact on the competitiveness of West German industry. From an admittedly low starting point, exports soared by 65 per cent in the third quarter of 1948 and by an additional 40 per cent in the fourth quarter (Buchheim 1990, 63). Besides the gradual reopening of European markets, export growth was fostered by the unified dollar exchange rate introduced for all foreign-trade transactions and by the merger of the export–import agencies of the Bizonal Area and the French occupation zone in August 1948 (Abelshauser 2004, 135).

---

[4] FSE, *Statistical quarterly report* (February 1949), 62–3.
[5] On Law No. 64 of the Military Government, see Federal Ministry for the Marshall Plan (1953), 118.

Contemporaries were astounded by the apparent acceleration of economic growth in the aftermath of the currency reform, but the careful re-examination of the quantitative evidence has lent support to more modest assessments. Abelshauser (1975) was among the first to emphasise that in the months preceding the reform, firms deliberately withheld their products from the market. Inventories were built up at such a pace that economic growth came to a halt and the supply of factories with intermediary products was sharply reduced. As these stockpiles did not appear in the national accounts, official statistics underestimated industrial production prior to the currency reform and, correspondingly, overstated the actual growth rates in the third quarter. In other words, the revival of economic activity over the summer of 1948 did not reflect the beginning of a more dynamic growth process; the economy simply returned to the growth path established already in 1947. According to the reports of the military government, industrial production in the Bizonal Area fell by 5 per cent between April and May 1948, before it surged almost 20 per cent between June and July. Labour productivity increased, too, but less spectacularly and more smoothly than output.[6] Production estimates corrected for the changes in inventories yield a considerably reduced growth rate of 14 per cent for the third quarter of 1948. This is still an impressive figure, but it is no longer exceptional in the context of the early years of post-war recovery (Kramer 1991, 138).

The economic reforms also had a more modest impact on the labour market than what unemployment statistics suggested. The spike in the overall unemployment rate from the summer of 1948 until early 1950 was primarily the outcome of population growth due to the continuing influx of expellees and refugees. As I have explained in Chapter 2, the urban housing shortage prevented industrial firms with surplus productive capacity from utilising these labour reserves. The number of unemployed in the Bizonal Area increased by half a million in the second half of 1948, but total employment grew from 14.2 million to 14.9 million in the same period (Görtemaker 2004, 157–8). The rate of joblessness was raised further by the fact that the unemployed had more incentive to register after the currency reform had increased the real purchasing power of their benefits (Buchheim 1988, 224).

Finally, the economic reforms did not restore the equilibrium between supply and effective demand overnight. Despite the sharp reduction of purchasing power, the growth of output could not keep pace with soaring consumer demand. During the first four months after the currency reform, the consumer price index increased at an annual rate of 33 per

---

[6] OMGUS, *Economic developments since the currency reform*, 6–12.

cent, while producer prices grew even faster, at an annual rate of 45 per cent. By the autumn, business confidence began to tumble, with manufacturers building up inventories and turning back to compensation deals (Giersch et al. 1992, 42). As supply became increasingly inelastic and firms expected even higher prices for the winter, they withheld goods from the market, which only enhanced excess demand, putting further pressure on prices (Buchheim 1988, 229). Even though inflation proved to be a temporary consequence of the economic reforms, it reduced real wages significantly, since wages remained fixed until November 1948. Outraged, and deeply suspicious towards price liberalisation, the unions called a national strike (Wolf 1993, 39). To bring the spiralling inflation under control, the BdL introduced draconian measures on 1 December. It raised reserve requirements from 10 to 15 per cent, increased the central bank rediscount rate, and ordered commercial banks to reduce their credit volume to the level of 31 October. This monetary contraction brought inflation to a halt, but it had the same effect on economic recovery. In the first quarter of 1949, the growth of industrial production slowed down and soon deflation rather than inflation caused headaches to central bankers (Giersch et al. 1992, 43–6).

The diverging growth trends of the Bizonal Area and the French zone in the second half of 1948 have been considered as evidence for the catalysing role of market reforms in economic recovery. The southwest of the country, where the reforms of the Erhard administration were not implemented, recorded relatively modest growth in industrial production after the currency reform. Here, the shortage economy survived a little longer and fixed prices reduced the profitability of firms relative to their competitors in the Bizonal Area (Buchheim 1988, 26–7). As a consequence, they could not harvest the fruits of the consumer boom in the second half of 1948, although they were also saved from the inflationary effects of price liberalisation (Ritschl 1985, 159). These arguments cannot be fully refuted, but the principal causes for the sluggish recovery of the French zone can be found in the relatively weaker initial conditions. Citizens of Baden and the Palatinate carried a significantly larger reparations burden than those living under British or American occupation. Whereas the military governments of the Bizonal Area worked on removing critical bottlenecks in the transport system throughout 1947, the French authorities requisitioned a tenth of current industrial output for reparations. In addition, the refusal of the French government to accept expellees and refugees into the occupation zone under its control meant that industrial recovery in the southwest was hampered by labour shortage to a much larger extent and from an earlier point in time than in the rest of the country. Therefore, firms could not raise production rapidly even after the currency reform had improved incentives for work (Abelshauser 1985, 216).

The economic reforms of 1948 did not invoke growth acceleration in the West German economy, in part because the recovery process was driven by reconstruction dynamics, but in part also because they did not represent a *tabula rasa* in economic policies either. Administrative prices were not removed for all goods and services, not even for the vast majority of them, and markets remained heavily regulated for years to come. Despite the fundamental principle of free-market prices in the SME, the government controlled the prices of nearly one-third of all consumer items throughout the 1950s, especially foodstuffs, housing, and public transport. For intermediary products and raw materials, including fuels, the share of regulated prices was even higher. Direct controls in the form of fixed prices, or price ceilings and thresholds, were typical for monopolies, such as the postal service, the railways, and public utilities, but also in housing. Indirect forms of intervention included subsidies, tax discounts or levies, and import controls. These tools were used to regulate producer prices in food processing (Zündorf 2006, 9–16). Although the rationing of coal was formally abolished in April 1950, fixed prices and subsidies in the coal industry remained cornerstones of government policy. Even Erhard, who championed free-market prices in most other regulated industries, was openly committed to the special relationship between coal and state and to protecting the special status of coal miners in the West German economy (Löffler 2002, 96–7).

Administrative prices seem contradictory to the principles of the SME, but they were an essential part of the political program of postwar German governments. Price stability was the maxim of economic policy and the relative scarcity of food as well as accommodation could have had significant inflationary effects under flexible prices. Price regulations enjoyed broad electoral support. Having experienced hyperinflation in the 1920s, the stability of basic consumer prices was one of the core demands that voters imposed on politicians. Stable and even falling prices for necessities were highly correlated with growing popularity of the governing parties. Finally, policymakers underestimated the capacity of the market to eliminate shortages in such necessities. The Ministry for Housing forecasted that the urban housing deficit would require twenty years to overcome. In reality, it took less than a decade, but state intervention in housing proved one of the most tenacious features of economic policy in West Germany. Rent control was eliminated only in the 1960s and even then only step-by-step. The government proposal from 1959 was enacted in 1961, but deregulation came into effect only in 1963 and thereafter was implemented gradually (Zündorf 2006, 133–50,

297–300). An essentially free market for housing was not achieved before the late 1960s (Fichtel 1980, 154–5).

That economic policy did not conform to the liberal vision was the consequence of three sets of factors: the persistence and undiminished power of corporatist institutions in industrial relations; the objections and frequent interventions of the Allied governments and of the organisations overseeing the Marshall Plan; and, finally, the influence of old-schooled government officials retained from the economic bureaucracy of the Nazi regime. Totalitarianism and foreign military occupation did not radically reshape the institutional foundations of the West German economy. Markets for both goods and factors of production had operated during the war and its immediate aftermath, even if to a limited extent and in a dysfunctional manner. Likewise, markets and economic agents remained regulated after 1948, even if regulation became less pervasive and more market conform than under Nazism or Allied occupation. An economic revolution did occur in post-war Germany, but it happened east of the Iron Curtain.

There was no Olsonian clean slate in industrial relations. Distributional coalitions had not become significantly weaker since the interwar period. This statement holds even if we acknowledge that the removal of the confessional – mainly Catholic – and socialist trade unions of the 1920s and their replacement with unified industry unions with the existence of national organisations for unions and enterprises made the coordination of industrial relations easier after 1945. The umbrella organisations for trade unions (Deutscher Gewerkschaftsbund, DGB) and for employers' associations (Bundesverband der Deutschen Industrie, BDI) were set up right after the proclamation of the West German constitution on 23 May 1949. In their quest to revive the German labour movement, the Allies had to work with union officials from the Weimar era. Even though OMGUS aimed at creating more encompassing unions independent of political parties and religious denominations, organisational efforts, initially, had to be confined to the local and, at most, the regional level.[7] The British military government, which ruled the industrial heartland of the Ruhr, was keen to support the militant unions in coal mining and the steel industry, which were sympathetic to its nationalisation plans (Giersch et al. 1992, 71–2). Thus, the major trade unions in West Germany regrouped unhindered. By 1950, the DGB had 5.5 million members, which represented a much higher rate of unionisation than what the country had hitherto ever seen. Unions did not become much more encompassing either. The umbrella organisations did not have the

---

[7] OMGUS, *Manpower, trade unions and working conditions*, No. 20, 3.

mandate to negotiate wage settlements: bargaining continued to take place between firms and industry trade unions at the local or state level (Paqué 1993, 9–12).

The notion of Eichengreen about a broadly based social contract secured by the state finds no support in the historical evidence. The legal framework for collective bargaining in West Germany was codified in the Collective Agreements Act of April 1949, which formally abolished the Allied wage controls and re-introduced autonomous wage bargaining between unions and employers associations without any form of government interference. Until the inauguration of the so-called 'Concerted Action' by the grand coalition in 1967, there was no explicit forum for tripartite wage settlements. Unions remained generally critical of free-market policies throughout the 1950s and made repeated complaints about the allegedly uncooperative behaviour of employers, whom they generally saw to have had the upper hand in the bargaining process. Finally, no extension was made to the welfare state before 1957 that could have served the purpose of buying off union support and thereby locking labour into collective agreements (Paqué 1995, 8–9, 12–19).

The founding program of the West German unions advocated state planning and labour representation at all levels of corporate decision making, much in the tradition of socialist trade unions from the 1920s. The Munich Program revived the industrial culture of the Weimar era and had little in common with Ordoliberal principles. Demands for co-determination invoked the first major industrial strikes of the post-war period in the course of 1946 and 1947 (Booth, Melling, and Dartmann 1997, 422). Despite the gradually improving economic conditions, labour militancy remained visible in the Ruhr until the early 1950s. Worker representation in the management and the board of overseers of mining enterprises and primary metals producers was finally achieved in the Co-Determination Act (*Mitbestimmungsgesetz*) of April 1951. Co-determination was certainly not the brainchild of liberal policymakers. It was pushed through the Bundestag by Adenauer against stiff opposition from his liberal coalition partners and, initially, even from Erhard. The political deadlock was resolved not through tripartite negotiations managed by the state but through American intervention. Concerned that industrial conflict would undermine the implementation of the Marshall Plan in the country, the Labour Division of the Economic Cooperation Agency threatened the German government with the termination of US aid until a satisfactory agreement over co-determination was reached with the unions (Booth et al. 1997, 431–3).

While the labour movement had to revive after the long years of Nazi dictatorship and foreign military occupation, the industrial and business elites in West Germany had survived these calamities remarkably intact. Despite their efforts to dismantle the industrial associations incriminated in the Nazi war crimes and to cleanse the management boards of large firms of former members of the Nazi Party, the Allies were forced to make concessions to employers' organisations in heavy industry in order to restart production and to remove critical bottlenecks in the transport and energy-supply networks. The barons of coal and iron retained their pre-eminent position in German big business and their special relationship with the state (Beghahn 1986). The BDI, in principle an umbrella organ-isation to represent four-fifths of West German industry, was still domi-nated by the Ruhr heavyweights and its leaders were largely independent in their actions from the membership (Rhenisch 1999, 256). The chair-man, Fritz Berg, was one of the closest advisors of Adenauer, commonly referred to as the chancellor's 'economic minister in everything but name' (Gillingham 1991). Political leaders were conscious of the undiminished power of coal and iron. The state secretary of the Economic Ministry in the late 1950s, Ludger Westrick, explained to a textile industrialist lobby-ing for subsidies that when the Ruhr protests, people can march not only into Bonn but possibly even into the offices of the government. Therefore, he responded to the plea of the manufacturer with the provocative ques-tion, 'Can the textile industry march?' (quoted in Löffler 2002, 91).

The influence of heavy industry over economic policy made it impos-sible to achieve the competitive market economy that liberal thinkers had envisioned. This failure was most clearly manifested in the inability, or unwillingness, of the government to effectively regulate firms with exces-sive market power. After the war, competition policy was determined by the occupying powers and was designed along the lines of American anti-trust legislation. This period saw the breakup of some of the most notori-ous industrial behemoths, notably IG Farben and the Herman Göring Works, and of the largest universal banks (Spoerer and Streb 2013, 251). However, de-concentration and de-cartelisation did not go much fur-ther. Before the establishment of the Bizonal Economic Administration, the Ruhr industries were under the direct control of the British mili-tary government, which envisioned their nationalisation rather than de-concentration. When the first de-cartelisation act for the British zone, Ordinance no. 78, was passed, iron and steel, the coal industry, and the Krupp concern specifically were exempted from the operation of the law. Law no. 75 issued for the Bizonal Area in 1947 stipulated that the ques-tion of eventual ownership and corporate structure would be determined by the future German federal government.[8]

---

[8] OMGUS, *Ownership and control of the Ruhr industries* (November 1948), 1–4.

During the 1950s, there was no consensus between the governing parties and even members of the cabinet on how to regulate competition. The Act Against the Limitation of Competition, or in its colloquial name the Cartel Act (*Kartellgesetz*), was passed in 1957 after many years of heated debate. However, the effective control of monopolistic organisations and the market power or large firms remained weak. The actual prohibition of cartels did not become law until 1998. The government tried to incorporate an explicit control of fusions into the 1957 act, but industrial lobbies successfully blocked this proposal. Effective control was achieved only in 1973, when the Bundestag passed an amendment to the original act. During the post-war golden age, the praxis of competition policy in West Germany had little in common with American blueprints or with the principles of the SME. It retained the corporatist character it had inherited from the Weimar era and was shaped with the active involvement of big industry, whose market power it was supposed to subdue (Neumann 2000, 44–5).

Before 1967, there was no political consensus over the SME as the economic constitution of the Federal Republic. The Social Democrats remained hostile to capitalism until the ratification of the Godesberg Program in November 1959. The unions supported regulated prices for consumer necessities, while business organisations forced the government to maintain industrial subsidies through an era of rapid productivity growth and soaring exports. In 1954, even the Constitutional Court ruled that the SME was one, but not the only, economic system consistent with the German constitution (Löffler 2002, 90). Most remarkably, the liberal agenda of Erhard found little sympathy even among the personnel of his Economic Ministry, at least in the founding years of the republic. Internal documents of the ministry demonstrate that in 1951–2 more than half of the overall staff had been employed in the central government apparatus, mostly in the Reich Economic Ministry, and by the state controlled chambers of commerce and industry (*Reichsgruppe*) before 1945. Among the heads and deputy heads of departments, the figure was even higher, close to 85 per cent (Löffler 2002, 98). Wartime experience educated ministerial bureaucrats and policymakers in the arts of state intervention and taught them how and when to use it effectively to help the industries they championed to expand and improve their competitiveness (Reich 1990, 302).

The policy department within the Economic Ministry harboured some of the most prominent experts on economic planning. The central figure among them was Günter Keiser, head of the Department for Planning and Statistics at the predecessor of the Economic Ministry, the bureau of the Bizonal Economic Administration. In his publications between

1943 and 1945, Keiser emphasised the incompatibility of full employment with the market economy and argued that the more expansionary fiscal policy of the Nazi state was instrumental in the restoration of full employment between 1933 and 1939. After 1949, he was named director of the policy department in the Economic Ministry. His deputy, Helmut Meinhold, presided over the departmental sub-division for long-term structural planning under the Economic Administration. He remained the most committed proponent of industrial planning until his removal from the ministry in 1951. He began his academic career a decade earlier at the Kiel Institute for the World Economy. From there, he was engaged at an institute created by Hans Frank in Cracow for 'labour management' in the East, and became personal advisor to Walter Emmerich, the president of the Economic Department of the General Government in occupied Poland. In Cracow, he worked in close collaboration with members of the planning apparatus in the civilian government and with SS officials, providing statistics and analysis for racial cleansing programs (Löffler 2002, 98–108). It is remarkable that experts with such a history were leading the departments of the Economic Administration and later the Economic Ministry that were supposed to lay the academic groundwork for the implementation of the SME.

The department of Keiser was instrumental in the Work Procurement Programme of February 1950 and in drafting the Investment Aid Act (*Investitionshilfegesetz*), perhaps the most controversial corporatist legislation from the early days of the economic miracle. The former cost 950 million DM and was effectively imposed upon the German government by Washington and the Organisation for European Economic Cooperation (OEEC) against vocal resistance from Erhard, who believed that the market would eventually absorb the growing army of unemployed (Lindlar 1997, 245). The Investment Aid Act was a unique policy instrument aimed at allocating resources to bottleneck industries for investments deemed essential for sustainable growth. It came into effect on 1 January 1952 and obliged manufacturers of consumer goods to raise funds in the value of 1 billion DM for the coal industry, electrical power, water supplies, iron and steel, and the Federal Railways over two years (Van Hook 2004, 228). Heralded as a great achievement of the SME, it was, in fact, incompatible with its free market principles; had little effect; and was largely, if not completely, unnecessary.

First, the state-coordinated capital transfer paid for only a minute fraction of the investments made in the targeted industries, merely a fourth of what corporate-tax deductions alone mobilised between 1952 and 1955 (Abelshauser 1987, 23–4). Second, as shown in previous chapters, coal mining as well as iron and steel had significant excess capacity in the early

1950s due, in part, to labour scarcity and, in part, to the structural disproportions in industrial production caused by the division of Germany. Expanding capacity was more urgent in the engineering and consumer industries that were relatively under-represented in West Germany before 1945. However, these industries received effective support from the economic reforms of 1948, which liberalised prices for their products but kept prices for their inputs fixed. These asymmetric price changes increased their profitability and, through that, their ability to finance investments from retained earnings. Poor profitability due to the maintenance of fixed prices for producer goods, not the lack of sufficient productive capacity, was the true reason for why the Ruhr heavyweights lobbied the federal government for subsidies (Kollmer 1995, 472–7). They were backed in their pursuit by the Marshall Plan administration and the planners in the Economic Ministry, who advocated an active investment policy in favour of the primary industries. Erhard tried to present the act as voluntary action from German industry supported only by limited administrative measures, but voluntary it was certainly not. Firms in the consumer industries provided investment aid through mandatory bond purchases. The Investment Aid Act continued in the tradition of German industrial policy from the 1930s that heavily favoured capital goods and that relied on bureaucratic means rather than free markets to allocate resources. Even though the policy department was reshuffled in 1952 after the appointment of Müller-Armack as its new director, by that time economic policy in the Federal Republic had been firmly detached from the principles of the SME (Löffler 2002, 106–9).

5.2   The Marshall Plan in Germany

The Marshall Plan, or in its official name the European Recovery Program (ERP), is to the present day considered by many as a major success story in the economic history of the twentieth century. As one of the most prominent scholars of the topic argued, 'not many foreign policies have earned the accolades won by the Marshall Plan. Its reputation has managed almost to transcend history and to become enshrined in the collective memory as wise government' (Maier 1991, 1–2). Contemporary public opinion saw in it the main catalyst of post-war recovery in Western Europe, saved by American magnanimity from destitution and communism. It was placed on centre stage in the early historiography of the German revival, since the years of the ERP corresponded to the phase of economic consolidation and the remarkably swift reintegration of the country into international trade. This convinced foreign observes that Western economic assistance had been essential to post-war reconstruction (see Price 1955 and Landes 1969 among others). The former US military governor in Germany, General Lucius Clay, wrote in the preface to one of the first monographs published outside of Germany on the history of the ERP in the Federal Republic that 'the rapid recovery of the German economy with Marshall Plan assistance was beyond the fondest hopes of those who had made it possible' (Mayer 1969, 1). The Advisory Council of the Economic Ministry concurred that 'the generous assistance of the Marshall Plan made it possible to revive economic activity in Germany' and argued that such speedy revival would have been unthinkable if based on domestic resources alone.[9]

The principal objective of the Marshall Plan was to lay the foundations of stable and self-sustaining economic growth in Western Europe. American aid, composed mainly of raw materials and capital goods, supported industrial expansion, which was the pre-condition to overcoming the dollar shortage in European economies and their one-sided dependence on the United States. At the same time, policymakers in Washington recognised that rebuilding the continent was unfeasible without unleashing Germany's colossal industrial potential. Only the restoration of the pre-existing European division of labour, in which Germany exported predominantly machine tools and industrial intermediates, could restrain the overwhelming wave of dollar imports. American assistance in the Federal Republic did not serve the purpose of revitalising the vanquished German economy per se; its central aim was to secure the resources indispensable for the ambitious reconstruction and modernisation programs of neighbouring nations (Berger and Ritschl 1995a, 474–5). To reflect on the main contributions of the ERP, this section is organised into three parts, which focus on the functions of dollar aid as means of import financing, as a source of investment in West German industry, and as facilitator of economic cooperation and integration in Western Europe.

The Marshall Plan in Numbers

Western aid was instrumental in German economic recovery practically from the end of hostilities. Starting in the early months of peace, the US Department of Defence sent food, seeds, chemical fertilisers, medical supplies, and fuel into the Western zones of occupation. Between 1946 and 1950, American military aid in the value of 1.6 billion dollars was distributed through GARIOA (Government and Relief in Occupied

---

[9] Wissenschaftlicher Beirat, Gutachten vom 26.2.1950, paragraph 15. In Wissenschaftlicher Beirat (1973), 68–9. Author's translation from the German text.

Areas), created to facilitate effective government in the occupied territories. Together with the British contribution, the Allied governments injected 2.4 billion dollars of aid into the paralysed West German economy. Initially, this assistance was available only to the Bizonal Area. The former French occupation zone could benefit from GARIOA only after the establishment of the Federal Republic. In the euphoria sparked by the announcement of the Marshall Plan by the US Secretary of State in June 1947, the German public and experts of the Economic Administration anticipated deliveries of yet significantly larger amounts. Since, however, in the Economic Cooperation Act, the US Congress made only about half of the originally proposed sum available to the ERP, of the 13.9 billion dollars granted to the participating nations and the European Payments Union (EPU) between 1948 and 1952, West Germany received only 1.4 billion dollars.[10]

Contrary to the initial expectations, the Western zones of occupation were, to use the expression of one prominent scholar, rather the 'stepchildren' of the Marshall Plan. While Austria, France, and the Netherlands received 36, 22, and 45 dollars per capita respectively during the second year of the ERP, the allotments to Germany, even with GARIOA assistance included, reached just over 12 dollars (Abelshauser 1989, 96). Between 1 July 1948 and 30 June 1949, the net aggregate value of Marshall Aid amounted to 24 per cent of national income in Austria, 11 per cent in the Netherlands, and 6.5 per cent in France, but only 2.9 per cent in West Germany (Milward 1987, 96).

In addition, aid deliveries were far behind schedule during the critical months after the currency reform. Until the end of 1948, little more than a quarter of the 361 million dollars worth of scheduled imports, reached Germany. When the first substantial raw-material contingents became available in early 1949, it required arduous efforts from government agencies to find willing importers. Domestic firms had to pay the Deutschmark counterpart of the dollar bill for imported goods, and ERP prices were usually set higher than world market prices (Abelshauser 1989, 97–8). It is indisputable that the Marshall Plan constituted a qualitative departure from the assistance of the Allied military governments as it provided foodstuffs of significantly greater nutritional value and industrial raw materials in increasing proportions, but this shift was gradual. Finally, US aid to West Germany, whether furnished under GARIOA or the ERP, did not include actual aid. Dollar allocations were designated as grants, conditional aid, or loans, but even 'grants' involved a claim on

---

[10] Federal Ministry for the Marshall Plan (1953), 19, 178.

the recipient, which, according to the bilateral agreement between the two countries, the Federal Republic had to repay to the United States.[11]

That being said, foreign aid proved to be vital for economic recovery in the immediate post-war years, when the modest export revenues did not suffice to finance even imports essential to satisfy basic needs. According to official statistics, even in 1948, two-thirds of total imports into the Western zones of occupation were still paid for by GARIOA and the ERP, and the share of Marshall Plan imports remained close to one-half until late 1949.[12] External assistance, therefore, contributed to securing the sustainability of the fledgling recovery, especially on the field of public nutrition, as agricultural production covered little more than half of domestic demand. Annual exports amounted to 165 million and 536 million dollars in 1947 and 1948, while the value of food imports alone reached 600 million and 942 million dollars over the two years respectively (Borchardt and Buchheim 1987, 319). When we take the dismal living conditions of the early post-war years outlined in Chapter 1 into consideration, it becomes clear that Western aid deliveries saved German society from the menace of starvation.

The bulk of Allied assistance arrived in West Germany during the initial phase of recovery, before the ERP began to operate. Abelshauser (1975, 1983), among others, argued that external financing made only a relatively insignificant contribution to restoring appropriate conditions for economic growth in Germany prior to and during the currency reform. Indeed, the majority of ERP allocations were made between 1949 and 1951, but they constituted only part of the total value of foreign aid. As shown in Table 5.1, the sum of external economic assistance was the largest in 1948. As an additional source of income, when measured as a percentage of GDP, foreign aid was even more important in 1946 and 1947, when the British contribution and private donations were still substantial.

Initially industrial raw materials represented only a small proportion of Marshall Plan deliveries; agricultural aid still dominated the first year of the ERP. Yet, the share of these imports in the total input consumption of certain consumer industries, struggling to keep pace with booming demand following the currency reform, was not insignificant. In their seminal study, Borchardt and Buchheim (1987) presented an illustrative example with the case of textile manufacturing. During the five months between November 1948 and March 1949, almost two-fifths of the raw cotton imports into West Germany were financed by foreign aid,

---

[11] Ibid., 22.
[12] Federal Ministry for the Marshall Plan (1951), 29.

Table 5.1 *Foreign aid in the Western occupation zones and the Federal Republic (million US dollars)*

	1945/46	1947	1948	1949	1950	1951	1952	1945–52
Military aid	195	—	—	—	—	—	—	195
GARIOA	75	237	788	503	18	—	—	1620
ERP			142	420	418	320	114	1413
Total US aid	270	237	930	923	436	320	114	3230
British contribution	264	363	90	32	1	—	—	750
Private charity	40	130	130	70	—	—	—	370
Total foreign aid	**574**	**730**	**1150**	**1025**	**437**	**320**	**114**	**4350**

Sources: Federal Ministry for the Marshall Plan (1953), 23–4; Berger and Ritschl (1995a), 479; Buchheim (1990), 76.

enabling firms to expand production rapidly without the need to hoard immense stocks of raw materials to secure the constant availability of inputs. Enhanced production and the swift depletion of inventories led to the sharp fall in the price of cotton cloth, which played an important role in bringing inflation down and thereby in consolidating the achievements of the economic reforms of 1948. The cotton industry was, however, the exception rather than an illustrative example, for raw cotton was the single largest item in Marshall Plan imports and accounted for more than one-third of all the industrial merchandise delivered.[13]

Initially, the composition of Marshall Aid resembled that of GARIOA, which was dominated by basic foodstuffs. By stimulating the imports of raw materials and food, US aid helped several branches of West German industry to mobilise their surplus capacity. It was precisely the aim of the ERP to increase the level of industrial output and international trade among the war-shattered nations of Western Europe, since all that was considered vital to secure sustainable economic growth on the continent. In this context, it achieved unequivocal success. The target figures of West German industrial production and export for 1952–3 were fulfilled a year in advance and the Federal Republic achieved, for the first time since World War II, a minor surplus on her balance of trade (Hardach 1991).

At last, we have to turn to the components of Marshall Aid that cannot be precisely quantified. Both contemporary public opinion and economic experts attributed great importance to the ERP Program of Technical Assistance. The motivation behind organising study trips for European,

[13] Idem (1953), 156.

among them West German, entrepreneurs and engineers to the United States was to promulgate modern technical know-how and American corporate philosophy and, in this way, to stimulate productivity growth in European industry. The establishment of trade relations and cooperation deals with American firms also attracted foreign direct investment (FDI) to West Germany, and hence promoted technology transfer (see Berghahn 1986). Apart from the actual aid and the technical assistance programs, the psychological effect of the Marshall Plan also provided a stimulus to industrial expansion, even if this boost proved temporary. Since initial expectations counted on a tremendous transatlantic resource-transfer, manufacturers quickly mobilised their inventories and disposable liquid assets, generating an overheated consumer boom in the second half of 1948.

ERP Assets as Sources of Investment for West German Industry

In the longer term, even if significantly contributing to the recovery of specific industries, foreign aid alone did not sustain this recovery beyond the months following the currency reform. Hence German economic historians in recent decades shifted focus onto another feature of the ERP, namely the use of the so-called counterpart funds to finance investment projects.

Importers of ERP goods were required to pay the counterpart of the dollar imports in their national currency into central government funds, which could be mobilised for investment in infrastructure or enhanced industrial capacity. The counterpart funds in Germany, held on an account of the BdL, functioned as a revolving capital fund and were administered by the Reconstruction Loan Corporation (*Kreditanstalt für Wiederaufbau*, KfW). According to directives of the Economic Administration and later of the Economic Ministry, the KfW extended loans, either directly or through commercial banks, for investment in bottleneck industries with the aim of simultaneously addressing the problems of capital shortage and the misallocation of resources. During the first two years of the Marshall Plan, ERP assets financed 6.4 and 8.6 per cent of gross investment in physical capital. Over the period 1949–52, the corresponding figure, on average, was 5.5 per cent and the aggregate sum of credits granted exceeded 1.5 billion dollars (Knapp 1990, 47).

Since access to the counterpart funds commonly required contributions from the own resources of the debtor, the volume of investments thus mobilised surpassed the KfW lines of credit (Knapp 1990, 49–50). The effect of ERP assets was enhanced further by the accumulation of similar counterparts under GARIOA. Between 1949 and 1952, one-tenth

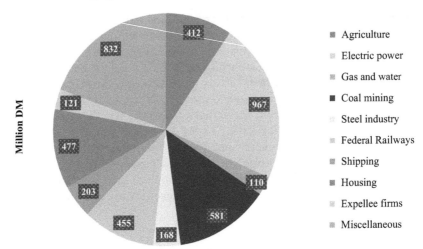

Figure 5.1 Investment programs financed by ERP assets by sector between 1949 and 1952.
Sources: Federal Ministry for the Marshall Plan (1953), 29.

of net investment in physical capital was financed by foreign aid, a non-trivial proportion even by international standards (Hardach 1991, 97). Investments supported by the counterpart funds were critical in overcoming capacity shortages in electricity generation, in particular, which was allocated almost 1 billion DM. However, the statistical evidence indicates that the ERP assets were not focussed primarily on the most pressing infrastructural bottlenecks. As shown in Figure 5.1, housing reconstruction received little more than one-tenth of the total investment aid, and one-third of these allocations was spent on housing for coal miners.[14] In total, some 125,000 dwellings were built by means of the counterpart funds. This may seem like a large figure, but it amounted to less than the wartime destruction of residential housing in the city of Cologne alone and less than half thereof in Hamburg (see Kästner 1949, 369). The distribution of loans across sectors was even more lopsided in West Berlin, which received about 10 per cent of the funding earmarked for Germany. Of the total allocations amounting to 568 million DM, only 64 million was spent on housing reconstruction, even though the city was still in ruins. By contrast, industry received loans amounting to 347 million DM, even though the sharp reduction in the resident population and thus the labour force after the war implied that even existing productive

---

[14] Ibid., 29–33.

capacity laid, in large part, idle. Of the nearly 5 billion DM available for reconstruction loans in the Federal Republic, only 200 million DM were allocated to the shipping industry, despite the fact that the size of the merchant fleet was reduced to a mere 5.5 per cent of its pre-war gross tonnage, while the railways, whose capacity had been restored to pre-war levels by 1947, received more than twice this sum.[15]

At the same time, the Ruhr industries, especially coal mining and (after the outbreak of the Korean War) iron and steel, were lavishly furnished with KfW loans, despite their enormous excess capacity and ability to increase exports without additional investment. Between April 1949 and September 1950, the counterpart funds of ERP and GARIOA together provided 625 million DM to coal mining, which accounted for 44 per cent of total investment in the industry.[16] Just like the Investment Aid Act, ERP assets benefited enterprises that had been penalised by the asymmetric and incomplete price reforms of 1948. Rather than addressing the most important infrastructural bottlenecks, the counterpart funds were applied to compensate heavy industry for the losses it suffered from the socially justified price regulations that liberal economic policy had left in place after the currency reform (Abelshauser 1989, 109).

This, from the perspective of the SME, perverted use of public resources not only enhanced surplus capacity in the primary industries. By doing so, it turned coal mining and the railways into black holes for government subsidies, once these enhanced capacities became redundant when manufacturers began to shift to cheaper imported inputs and other modes of transportation. This was precisely against the recommendations of the Advisory Council, which repeatedly argued in it reports for the need to reintroduce the free-market allocation of investment resources and thus replace the temporary 'command-economy regulations'.[17] In addition, state funding for investment in the energy sector delayed the revival of capital markets. While the high yields offered by electricity bonds crowded out other corporate securities, the frequent failure of energy firms to pay their investors due to poor profitability had a detrimental effect on investor confidence. Thus, the market capitalisation of West German industry remained very low (Borchardt and Buchheim 1987, 335–40).

The overall impact of Marshall Aid as a propeller of growth is difficult to judge. On the one hand, the counterpart funds played an instrumental role in financing investment in the primary industries. On the other

[15] Ibid., 30, 140–1.
[16] Federal Ministry for the Marshall Plan (1951), 49.
[17] See Wissenschaftliches Beirat, Gutachten 27.2.1949, paragraph 5, and Idem, Stellungnahme vom 29. April 1951, in Wissenschaftliches Beirat (1973), 30, 121–4.

hand, their assets were not focussed on the most critical bottlenecks that limited economic recovery in West Germany. The problem of bottlenecks is quintessential to the assessment of the role that foreign aid played in rebuilding the German economy. As long as the urban housing shortage was not eliminated, it made little use to expand productive capacity in urban industry further, as enhanced capacity could not be matched with increased employment. In addition, due to the structural disproportions in industrial production caused by the division of Germany in 1945, productive capacity in the capital goods industries was already surplus to domestic demand. Hence, the growth of these industries in the early phase of the economic miracle depended strongly on the return of West German firms to international markets.

Rebuilding the European Division of Labour

Accordingly, it has been argued that the role of US aid in reviving international trade within Western Europe was much more important for the German growth miracle than the direct financial assistance that the Federal Republic received (Milward 1991, 452). This role of the Marshall Plan adds a European dimension to post-war recovery in West Germany, inasmuch as the resources that German industry could provide were vital for the implementation of the reconstruction and development plans of neighbouring countries.

After the end of World War II, the United States dominated the world economy. This transformation was reflected in the critical dollar shortage caused by the lopsided dependence of European countries on American imports (Buchheim 1990, 99). The temporary absence of German capital goods from continental markets was a prime reason for the large European deficit in transatlantic trade. From the 1880s until World War II, the United States, the United Kingdom, and Germany had accounted for approximately 60 per cent of international trade in manufactured goods in roughly equal proportions. Their dominance was even more striking in the export of machine tools. Since, after the war, Britain had little spare production capacity, only American suppliers could substitute for German machinery exports. Therefore, reintegrating West Germany into the international division of labour presented the only viable solution to securing the foundations of sustainable economic growth in Europe (Milward 1991, 453-4).

One of the major aims of the European Cooperation Act was the reconstruction of pre-existing trade relations between European states, which Washington considered to be the fist step towards the creation of a global economic system free of trade barriers. At the convention of the OEEC on 16 April 1948, the member states unanimously committed to an international payments system and to the abolition of barriers to trade and capital flows among the participating nations. Since rebuilding a sound multilateral economic order put a heavy financial burden on European states possessing scanty gold- and foreign-currency reserves, in the transitional period, economic cooperation in Europe hinged on external support. This was the role of the Marshall Plan, which provided the means to finance imports indispensable for economic reconstruction (Buchheim 1990, 100–2). However, Marshall aid did not take the form of financial transfers, and the delivery of real commodities did not boost the exchange of goods and services between continental economies. On the contrary, they generally reinforced the dependence of OEEC member states on the United States. To find a way out of this imbroglio required new path-breaking institutional solutions.

The task of restoring intra-European trade was assigned to the European Payments Agreement (EPA), also termed the 'little' or 'European' Marshall Plan (Abelshauser 1984). The principal objective of the agreement was to finance the current-account deficits of countries that had a trade deficit with other OEEC members. Accordingly, countries in surplus, Belgium/Luxembourg, Italy, Sweden, Turkey, the United Kingdom, and West Germany, were required to deliver commodities to countries in deficit within the limited value of their ERP drawing rights. Since these exports did not alter the initial ERP allotments to OEEC members, the Marshall aid offered to surplus countries was effectively reduced by the net value of the drawing rights transferred to trading partners, who consequently received additional support on top of the actual ERP aid. Given the enormous demand for German capital goods on European markets, the Federal Republic became the largest net creditor after Belgium/Luxembourg already from the second ERP year (see Figure 5.2). Since subsidised exports to neighbouring countries absorbed 63 per cent of the Marshall aid offered to West Germany, the actual value of aid received did not even suffice to cover the cost of the federal government assistance to West Berlin (Wexler 1990, 144–53).

Based on the adjusted values of external aid, the main winners of the Marshall Plan were those countries that, after the years of Nazi ransacking, entered into the post-war era of economic recovery with ambitious industrialisation programs. Enhancing their industrial potential required massive investments, which were to be financed principally from the ERP counterpart funds. Consequently, it shall come as no surprise that, besides Switzerland and Sweden, these countries imposed the greatest demand for capital goods on the world market. Machine tools, vehicles, iron, steel, and other metallurgical products accounted for more than

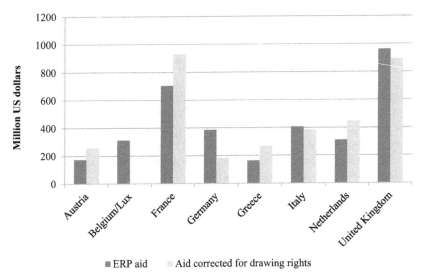

Figure 5.2 The value of ERP aid to the main recipient countries in the fiscal year 1949–1950.
Sources: Abelshauser (1984), 220.

one-fifth of all imports in Belgium, France, Holland, Norway, Portugal, and Sweden during the period of the Marshall Plan (Milward 1987, 101).

Small countries with high per capita income were the most dynamic and attractive markets for German manufacturers. Unable to specialise on a wide range of capital goods, they imported intermediate inputs in growing proportions. Especially after the launching of the EPA, these imports came increasingly from West Germany. Even if these trade patterns were not new, ERP aid accelerated the restoration of the European division of labour in a period when, as Chapter 4 has shown, the growth of West German industry was, to a substantial extent, export driven. Although the Federal Republic received a far smaller value of per capita aid than most other OEEC members, the Marshall Plan did support economic recovery in West Germany. By promoting trade and monetary stability in Europe, it gave a significant boost to German industrial exports and thus enabled the full-scale utilisation of available production capacities in the main export industries. Following this logic, one can argue that at least part of the assistance given to the countries that imported German products should also be counted as additional external support to the West German economy, to the extent that these imports were financed by dollar aid.

In addition, the countries that received the highest per capita ERP aid beside Austria, namely France and the Netherlands, had made the largest reparation claims against the Western zones of occupation. The eventual withdrawal, or moderation, of these demands can also be explained by the long-awaited advent of US aid, which offered compensation to nations formerly occupied by Germany. Thus, the West German state was far from being the 'stepchild' of the Marshall Plan. On the contrary, it may have been the main beneficiary of the ERP, since the restoration of the continental division of labour and the effective rollback of protectionism served, above all, the interests of German industry. This view becomes even more compelling if we recognise that Marshall Aid was indispensible in persuading the enemies of the Third Reich to re-establish economic cooperation with the nascent West German state. The Federal Ministry for the Marshall Plan already stressed in its interim reports that perhaps the most significant benefits that the Federal Republic had drawn from the ERP were political rather than directly economic.

The Marshall Plan has offered the first possibilities of taking up international relations again, of explaining the German conceptions and ideas as to common European interests, and of cooperating in their effective realization. The German members of the former Bizonal Delegation, and of the representation of the French Occupation Zone, with the OEEC in Paris were the first to be granted diplomatic status. October 31, 1949, the day on which the Federal Minister for the Marshall Plan ... took his seat for the first time in the OEEC Council of Ministers, can be considered the date of Germany's return to the European community ... The first international agreement concluded by the Federal Republic was the Agreement with the United States concerning the implementation of the Marshall Plan ... on December 15, 1949.[18]

The Marshall Plan, indeed, helped West Germany find its place in the post-war world order. However, this claim must not be overstretched. As I noted in Chapter 4, the effective end to military occupation in 1951, the haircut on the Federal Republic's international debt in 1953, its accession to NATO in 1955, and the formation of the ECSC owed more to security concern arising from the intensification of the Cold War in Europe and the beginning of the Korean War than to economic cooperation within the OEEC. Until 1951, output ceilings and prohibitions were still in place for strategic goods, most notably in shipbuilding. The ban on the construction of large ocean-going vessels implied that Germany could not begin rebuilding its merchant fleet before 1952. The production of military hardware and of all types of aerospace was forbidden until after the NATO accession (see Section 4.4). ERP aid

---

[18] Federal Ministry for the Marshall Plan (1951), 21.

202 Managing the Miracle: Economic Policy

did not increase the freedom of the federal government in domestic policy formation either. Not only were interventions of the Marshall Plan administration instrumental behind the Work Procurement Programme of 1950 and the Co-Determination Act of 1951; the targeted use of ERP assets in investment financing represented a clear departure from the free-market principles of Erhard and his allies. Favouring the energy sector, heavy industry, and the railways in the allocation of the counterpart funds helped conserve the fixed-price regime in basic industries for longer than would have been possible otherwise. This, in turn, cemented the special status of coal and iron and the corporatist organisations they dominated in policymaking, which maintained industrial subsidies and the excessive market power of the Ruhr giants in the West German economy.

Most importantly, despite her membership in the OEEC, the Federal Republic remained an occupied country. This implied, on the one hand, that the federal government could operate only under the auspices of the military governments, and could not pursue an independent foreign policy, even international economic policy. On the other hand, military occupation entailed the stationing of vast numbers of foreign troops and non-combatant military personnel on German soil. Since the Federal Republic did not have armed forces of its own until 1955, and the building up of potent national defences took many years even after the start of rearmament, the presence of the US Army remained a factor in West German economic life throughout the 1950s. The expenditures of the occupying forces made a critical contribution to the survival of numerous German firms and offered work for hundreds of thousands in the early post-war years. In November 1945, the US military employed 168,000 Germans, by 1951 almost a quarter million. At this time, only five industries in the country had a more sizeable workforce, but in the southern regions of Germany, where the American troops were stationed, they were the largest employer. The construction of buildings to cater for and accommodate the armed forces, the officers' families, and the supporting personnel cost 6 billion DM between 1950 and 1960, more than the sum of all investment loans financed by the counterpart funds. Although the direct occupation costs, which between 1951 and 1955 amounted to 14 billion DM, had to be borne by the West German government, the bulk of this expenditure funded purchases of goods and services provided by German companies and individuals. In addition, the US government pumped massive resources into the maintenance of its forces in Germany. Between 1945 and 1960, these transfers totalled 15.4 billion DM, which almost tripled the value of ERP aid to the Federal Republic (Browder 1993, 601–6).

5.3   Fiscal Policy: From Contraction to Expansion

The burden of the occupation costs and the BdL charter that prevented the central bank system from financing government debt placed fiscal policy within very narrow constraints in the early years of national sovereignty. The West German state had very limited capacity to stimulate economic recovery. Total public spending at the federal, state, and local levels increased from 14.4 billion DM in 1948 to 35.4 billion DM in 1951, in current prices and excluding West Berlin, but occupation costs, rising from 2.7 billion DM to 7.4 billion DM, accounted for a vast proportion of these expenditures. If one includes all spending on the direct consequences of the war, such as reconstruction costs and compensations for victims, then the figures jump to 4.1 billion and 8.7 billion respectively. Not surprisingly, until 1951, the federal government was running deficits. The record deficit in 1951 amounted to 6.2 per cent of total expenditure. In the following year, it turned into a 3.3 percent surplus. Regional governments were already in surplus in 1951, but their excess revenue tripled in 1952, which further enhanced the scale of fiscal contraction.[19] Figure 5.3 demonstrates that the total government surplus continued to grow relative to GDP until 1956, so that the overall effect of fiscal policy on aggregate demand remained negative. Even though the surplus increased mainly due to soaring government revenue, the share of public spending in GDP declined as well.

In the early 1950s, the federal government relied predominantly on indirect incentives to stimulate investment and exports in private industry. Between 1949 and 1953, retained earnings financed between 50 and 60 per cent of gross investment in fixed capital. Even with the assistance of the counterpart funds, firms had very limited access to long-term bank financing, and the reactivation of capital markets could not begin before the establishment of the required regulatory framework in 1952 (Kramer 1991, 200–1; Kleßmann 1997, 24). Increasing the profitability of private industry was, thus, key to boosting investment. Paragraph 7 of the Incomes Tax Act (*EStG*), introduced in 1949, allowed firms to write off half of their investments from their corporate income tax base up to the value of 100,000 DM (Abelshauser 1983, 74). Investments to replace or restore plant and equipment destroyed during the war as well as investments in residential construction and shipbuilding could be written off entirely (Paqué 1989, 475). In total, deductions allowed by the law provided 14.8 billion DM for private-sector investment between

---

[19] StatBRD, Vol. 59 (1957), 38–47.

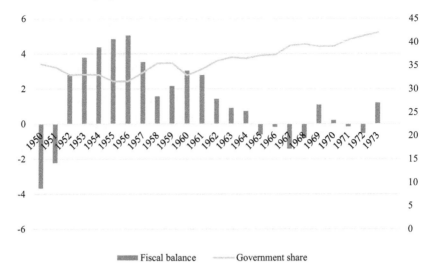

Figure 5.3 The overall fiscal surplus and total government spending as a share of GNP (%).

Note: Both series represent aggregate figures for all levels of state expenditure, including federal, regional, and local government.

Sources: Sachverständigenrat (1965), Table 65, 176–77; idem (1991), Table 22 and Table 33, 350, 366–7. Author's calculations.

1950 and 1956, three times the total value of loans financed by ERP assets until 1952 (Jákli 1990, 61).

Paragraph 7 of the *EStG* had the greatest effect in shipbuilding. Until 1954, the industry received 2.8 billion DM in corporate-tax deductions in addition to the 906 million DM worth of loans from the counterpart funds, while investments funded from normal profits amounted to only 750 million DM (Kramer 1991, 203). Between 1951, when the ban on the construction of large oceangoing vessels was lifted, and 1954, when these provisions of the *EStG* expired, the state subsidised the building of 587 ships. Direct and indirect subsidies covered half of the construction costs (Jákli 1990, 63–4). With continued public support, the West German merchant fleet could expand more than tenfold in gross tonnage over the 1950s, which eliminated one of the most important bottlenecks in industrial exports (Henning 1993, 223).

Exports were critical to the revival of German industry in the absence of positive fiscal stimuli to domestic demand. The Export Promotion Act provided incentives through corporate-tax deductions between 1951 and 1955, while international shipping, and from 1955 the armament industry, received additional export subsidies. Until 1957, the federal government helped commercial banks extend short-term loans to exporters at highly favourable rates, and in 1952 established a public corporation, the *Ausfuhrkredit AG*, to further support export financing (Ambrosius 1984, 283). The *Hermes* credit insurance program offered state guarantee for the repayment of loans that German firms provided to foreign clients, which were instrumental in the expansion of West German exports to developing markets (Braun 1990, 249). Despite the commitment of the Federal Republic to international trade liberalisation within the framework of General Agreement in Tariffs and Trade (GATT) and the OEEC, West German policy towards economic cooperation in Europe remained, in fact, strongly mercantilist. The overall tariff rate for imports declined sharply throughout the 1950s, but the structure of tariffs reflected the desire for import substitution as much as export promotion. Low tariffs were imposed on raw materials and intermediary inputs indispensable for the leading export industries, while considerably higher tariffs were levied on imports that hurt the least competitive sectors of the domestic economy, farming and the textile industry in particular (Giersch et al. 1992, 107–9). Moreover, until 1961, West German firms were allowed to export capital only in exceptional cases, when the proposed investments abroad were deemed essential for the promotion of German exports (Ambrosius 1990, 15–16).

The main limitation of indirect incentives was that their effectiveness depended on the profitability of firms. Industries making modest profits or even losses lacked the motives to expand into foreign markets and had limited scope to finance investments from tax deductions. To stimulate investment in industries, where product prices remained fixed after the currency reform and thus profitability was weak, the government had to provide direct subsidies, especially after the lines of credit furnished by the Investment Aid Act and the counterpart funds had expired. Agriculture was the first sector to be directly subsidised by the state. Since prices for foodstuffs plummeted in international markets after the end of the Korea Boom, prices for farm products in West Germany went above world market prices. From 1952 onward, fixed prices, together with stringent import restrictions, amounted to subsidising agriculture. West German farmers were never fully exposed to foreign competition, even before the introduction of the Common Agricultural Policy (CAP) at the European level (Zündorf 2006, 150–1). The Agricultural Subsidies Act, in its colloquial name the 'Green Plan', of 1956 increased the value of allowances and price subsidies to farmers fourfold between 1955 and 1957 (Jákli 1990, 35–6). Besides agriculture itself, federal and regional governments offered direct subsidies to structurally underdeveloped regions from the

early 1950s, when state support was essential to bring industrial investment into areas endowed with surplus labour (Owen Smith 1994, 77).
However, public funds available for regional development programs continued to increase even after rural unemployment had been eliminated.
From 1959, the focus of regional policy was on infrastructure building
and urban development in medium-sized towns with large rural hinter-
lands. By the late 1960s, nearly half of all regional subsidies went to West
Berlin alone, in an attempt to stem outmigration from and the depopula-
tion of the former capital (Jákli 1990, 211–12, 223).

After agriculture, coal mining became another black hole for government subsidies. With increased global supply and declining prices for
crude oil, Western economies began to shift away from coal in the mid-
1950s. This development turned dramatic after 1958. Within just two
years, the share of coal in West German fuel consumption fell from 70
per cent to 56 per cent, while the share of oil and oil derivatives increased
from 17.5 per cent to 24 per cent. The crisis of coal continued throughout the 1960s, and by 1970 hydrocarbons accounted for 60 per cent
of total energy use.[20] At odds with Ordoliberal philosophy, the federal
government introduced massive subsidies to keep Ruhr coal competitive
and to protect the jobs of miners in the all-powerful unions. Between
1958 and 1967, these subsidies totalled 16.7 billion DM and increased
from 855 million to 3.3 billion annually (Jákli 1990, 109–13). The shift
from coal to petroleum was closely connected to the motorisation of
transport, which ended the century-old dominance of the railways in
Western Europe. In 1949, two-thirds of all goods transported over long
distance within the Federal Republic were carried on the rails. By 1960,
this share had fallen to 54 per cent, and declined even faster during the
1960s. Despite generous state subsidies and the introduction of levies
on crude oil and trucks with the objective of making rail transport more
competitive, the cumulative losses of the Federal Railways cost taxpayers
7.2 billion DM until 1965 (Braun 1990, 196; Henning 1993, 147–8).

While immense resources were allocated to fading but politically influential sectors, investments critical for future growth and structural development were often neglected. The inadequate road network was recognised by private industry as the most important infrastructural bottleneck
to economic expansion from the mid-1950s, but the funds mobilised by
the Transport Finance Act of 1955 sufficed for the construction of only
600 kilometres of highways over seven years (Südbeck 1993, 174–5).
Even more critical was the neglect of education and industrial innovation, which the literature has described as perhaps the most significant

---

[20] Author's calculations. Data from Sachverständigenrat (1991), Table 77, 426.

failure of government policy in the 1950s and the early 1960s. The rapidly expanding West German economy could mobilise vast reserves of human capital first by reintegrating the rural unemployed in the urban production process and later by relying on skilled manpower fleeing East Germany. Education did not appear to be a limiting factor of industrial expansion, especially general forms of education that did not focus on skills directly applicable to manufacturing tasks. As a result, regional governments made limited efforts to expand the public school system and the facilities for higher learning. The share of public expenditure on formal education in GDP increased from 2.4 per cent in 1950 to 3 per cent in 1962 but remained considerably lower than in other advanced Western countries in the same period (Abelshauser 1983, 99).

Low levels of investment in human capital may not have limited the growth of West German industry at the time, but they had dire consequences for future growth and industrial innovation. In the 1950s, the Federal Republic not only maintained a deficit in its trade with the outside world in licences and patents; this deficit grew continuously over the period. German firms lagged behind international market leaders especially in high tech and thus did not make notable contributions to the development of semiconductors, computers, or nuclear research (Stokes 1991). The roots of German underperformance in industrial research and development (R&D) go back to the early post-war years. The London Agreement of July 1946 gave the signatory states unrestrained access to German patents and commercial brands. The establishment of the Federal Patent Office in 1949 suspended this practice, but German efforts in subsequent years focussed predominantly on the repatriation of patents formerly owned by German firms (Neebe 2004, 248). New research and development was limited not least by the loss of talent as a consequence of the Holocaust and the resettlement of thousands of leading German scientists and technical experts to the United States under US Army special operations. Brain drain did not cease with the regaining of national sovereignty and the recovery of living standards in the 1950s. Between 1949 and 1966, no fewer than 1,800 natural scientists and 4,200 engineers and technicians left the Federal Republic. Nuclear innovation was further hampered by the prohibition of any research activity focussed on military technologies (Neebe 1989, 51).

Defence and defence-related R&D received very little state support even after the NATO accession in 1955. The newly appointed minister for nuclear affairs, Franz Josef Strauß, viewed his post merely as a jumping board to a stellar political career. His successor, Siegfried Balke, went as far as to question the very rational for the ministry. On his appointment as minister of defence, Strauß was unable to persuade the Economic Ministry to back his proposal to build a German aircraft industry, which was considered to be an unnecessary luxury. The project was received with even less enthusiasm by the Chamber of Industry and Commerce, as the leading engineering firms showed little interest in rearmament. Industrialists of the time did not fully comprehend the potential of technological spill-overs from military R&D and feared that a resurgence of West German weapons exports would tarnish the Made in Germany label on world markets. Remarkably, even Krupp, once the greatest profiteer from global warfare, distanced itself from armaments manufacturing. The management board, even though it included several members who were as well trained in gunnery as in commerce, found the defence market too risky and unpredictable (Radkau 1993, 133–4).

Big business and liberal policymakers concurred that scientific research was economically inefficient as its potential returns were incalculable and it would have diverted substantial resources from productive investment. Public expenditure on education and science did not increase significantly even in the second half of the 1950s. By contrast, the share of direct subsidies in the federal budget climbed from an average of 1.4 per cent over the period 1950–5 to an average of 5.7 per cent over the following five years (Jákli 1990, 35). These figures did not even include the tremendous burden of state spending on the railways and on social housing. Even though, according to the system of government, social housing was considered part of social and not economic policy, it made a more powerful and to the rebuilding of the German economy more critical contribution than any other form of fiscal stimulus. It engineered a stunning rush in residential construction and provided affordable housing for the displaced millions willing to resettle into the industrial heartlands of the country. The physical impact of the social housing programs was unmistakeable. In their first year in 1949, more dwellings were built on West German territory than in the previous four years combined (Hafner 1994, 176). From 1950 to 1952, when social housing accounted for 70 per cent of all newly built homes, the volume of new construction nearly doubled. From 1954, more than half a million dwellings were added to the existing stock almost every year until the end of the golden age, as shown in Figure 5.4. Although private financing mobilised by the banking system and capital markets became increasingly accessible to home buyers and developers, social housing remained predominant throughout the 1950s, and its share never dropped below 30 per cent until the early 1970s. Between 1950 and 1970, almost 5 million dwellings were built with state support amounting to almost tenfold the sum of investment loans furnished by the ERP counterpart funds (Krummacher 1988, 453–7).

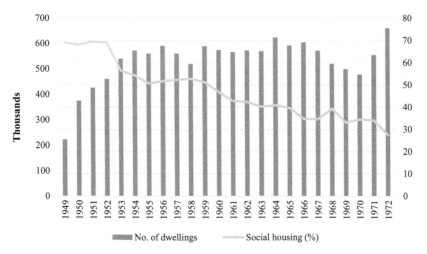

Figure 5.4 Total housing construction and the share of social housing in the Federal Republic.
Source: Hafner (1994), 186, 361–2.

The legal framework for post-war policy on social housing was laid out in Law No. 18 of the Allied Control Authority in 1946, which introduced full public control over the allocation of rental housing with rents fixed at their 1935 level and a general moratorium on evictions. The First Housing Construction Act of 1950 specified the exact forms of government support differentiated between three types of rental housing: social housing for poor working class families with administratively set rents, housing subsidised through tax concessions for the developer in exchange for favourable rents, and free-market housing that could count only on the tax deductions allowed under paragraph 7 of *EStG* (Buchheit 1984, 134–5). Even though the Second Housing Construction Act of 1956 sought to shift focus from publicly subsidised rental housing to supporting privately owned family homes, the praxis of housing policy was still dominated by large-scale projects for urban working-class housing. This was a clear case of failure of liberal policy in the face of stiff opposition from the industrial trade unions and the Social Democrats in the federal and state legislations. Publicly subsidised rents remained in place even after the partial liberalisation of the rental market in 1963, which was implemented only in counties where the estimated housing deficit was less than 3 per cent (Schulz 2009). Social housing was not only one of the most activist instruments of public policy in post-war Germany, it also created legacies that persist even today, especially in the excess supply of affordable urban housing and the still comparatively low rate of homeownership (Voigtländer 2009).

Social housing and the linking thereof to industrial policy were themselves legacies of the past, in particular of the Nazi economic vision for the post-war order (see Hafner 1994, 64) and of the use of targeted housing provisions to foster industrial development during the armaments boom, as in the construction of the industrial complex around the Herman Göring Works in the area of Wolfsburg, Braunschweig, and Salzgitter (Walz 1978). The broad support of German industry for housing programs reflected long-term continuity: the tradition of building homes for workers by manufacturers and other entrepreneurs reached back to pre-industrial times. Spatial development experts already emphasised at the time the importance of housing for the successful reintegration of expellees into the labour market. Home building had to be subsidised where jobs were available, and jobs had to be created where the expellees had found temporary accommodation (Granicky and Müller 1950, 9). Social housing was the key to achieving the former, while the regional development subsidies of the federal government and the subsidised loans extended by state governments to expellee firms played an important role in the latter. According to surveys of the state statistical offices in 1949, most expellee firms were active in handcrafts and employed predominantly other expellees. Therefore, they contributed significantly to the growth of rural handcrafts and to the reemployment of the temporarily displaced. In Schleswig-Holstein, expellee and refugee firms accounted for 12.5 per cent of all enterprises and for 23.5 per cent of total employment in handcrafts (Kornrumpf 1950b, 98–100).

The significance of social housing for the rebuilding of the urban economy is underlined by the fact that economic concerns were prioritised over social policy goals from the start. While lawmakers wished social housing to be available mainly for poor families, in practice, subsidies were used above all to provide lodgings for skilled workers in coal mining and in the primary industries. The wage ceiling for families determining eligibility for social or subsidised rents was set so high that housing allocation actually favoured families with average incomes and the required skills for urban industry over the poor. Rules regulating the maximum size of living space in social housing were 'loosely interpreted' (Krummacher 1988, 444–50). The generosity of the social housing programs extended not only to the quantity but also the quality of affordable housing. Between 1952 and 1967, the average size of dwellings allocated at subsidised rents increased from 48 to 75 metres squared, that of all types of housing from 55 to 82 metres squared (Hafner 1994, 448). The share of social housing in total residential construction and the total number of dwellings built with public subsidies did fall considerably between the 1950s and the 1960s. But, owing to rising construction costs and substantial improvements in the quality of housing, the federal and regional governments spent three times as much on social housing between 1960 and 1970 as in the preceding decade, when the urban housing stock had to be rebuilt (Krummacher 1988, 452–7). Thus, social housing policy made an important, if not the largest, contribution to the increasingly expansionary impact of fiscal policy and the absorption of the budgetary surplus during the 1960s.

5.4 Monetary Policy: From Expansion to Contraction

According to the constitution of the German Bundesbank, enacted on 26 July 1957, the principal objectives of monetary policy, as in the charter of the BdL, were the stability of domestic prices and the maintaining of dollar parity of the Deutschmark. Official statistics painted a glorious record for the central bank in the years of the economic miracle. Between 1950 and 1958, inflation averaged 2.6 per cent annually, modest by international comparison, while the exchange rate remained unchanged from September 1949 until April 1961 (Glastetter, Högemann, and Marquardt 1991, 81–2). Accordingly, economic historians often attributed a role of paramount importance to the independent Bundesbank and its predecessor in sustaining price stability in an age of rapid economic growth. Adherents of the structural-break hypothesis posited that the truly miraculous achievement of the German miracle was the conservation of low inflation in a revitalised economy geared for expansion.

However, this eulogy of the federal bank of issue is exaggerative and, at least in part, erroneous. Until the mid-1950s, there was no need for monetary policy in keeping inflation at bay. High unemployment contained wages and household consumption; prices for many consumer goods, especially textiles, declined after the end of the Korea Boom, and the improvement of the Terms of Trade removed the danger of imported inflation (Leaman 1988, 132–3). As a result, monetary policy was rather expansionary. While cumulative GDP growth between 1950 and 1954 amounted to 61.8 per cent, the volume of money in circulation, including bank notes and sight deposits, increased by 73.3 per cent, the total money supply with fixed-term and saving deposits by almost 150 per cent. While the central bank rediscount rate fell from 6 per cent in October 1950 to 3 per cent by May 1954, the value of commercial bank loans grew from 21.8 billion DM to 61.5 billion DM.[21] Urban reconstruction and the

[21] BdL (1955), 4, 57, 226.

resurgence of German industry went along with low rates of inflation but also cheap money: the BdL actively supported post-war recovery.

The prevention of runaway inflation was the achievement of fiscal policy. Between 1952 and 1956, under finance minister Fritz Schäffer, the large federal budget surpluses were consistently deposited in the central bank for the purpose of eventual rearmament. The vast war chest that by 1956 amounted to 7.8 billion DM became known to the German public as the *Juliusturm*, reminiscent of the tower of the ancient Spandau Fortress, which treasured an ocean of gold before 1914 to fund the mobilisation of Kaiser Wilhelm's all-dreaded armies (Weimer 1998, 121). By withdrawing money from circulation, the government tamed the expansion of macroeconomic liquidity (Braun 1990, 179). In addition, as the size of the federal budget surplus almost perfectly corresponded to the surplus of the current account over the same period, restrictive fiscal policy contained inflationary pressures arising from the net inflow of foreign currency as a result of surging exports. Consequently, monetary policy gained considerable room for manoeuvre. Not having to embark on contractionary measures even during the boom of 1955, it made a substantial contribution to the staggering rate of GDP growth in that year.

After the economy had reached full employment, both domestic and international developments drastically altered the conditions under which the central bank was to fulfil its obligations. The continuing improvement of the Terms of Trade, buoyant investment in industry, and the generous tax reductions granted by the federal government in 1955 further increased the competitiveness of German manufacturers, resulting in a scamper of industrial exports and a massive inflow of foreign exchange. The cumulative surplus of the current account exceeded 20 billion DM between 1956 and 1959, while the gold and foreign exchange reserves of the Bundesbank more than doubled (Weimer 1998, 146). Furthermore, owing to the commencement of remilitarisation in 1955 and the acceleration of the armament race following the 'Sputnik-shock' in 1957, the share of defence expenditure in federal spending rocketed from 10 per cent in 1956 to 32 per cent by 1964. To fund the rebuilding of the armed forces, the surging farm subsidies, and above all the social welfare programs at the core of the union parties' election campaign in 1957, the government released the billions it had accumulated in central bank deposits, despite the opposition of finance minister Schäffer (Leaman 1988, 85). As the previous section explained, the subsidies to the Ruhr introduced in response to the coal crisis put further pressure on state finances. Figure 5.3 demonstrates that, even though the overall fiscal surplus returned to 3 per cent of GDP by 1960, regional development subsidies and the growing expenditures on social housing made fiscal policy more and more expansionary in the early 1960s.

The pension reform of 1957 had particularly severe repercussions for fiscal sustainability, as it increased the value of retirement allowances by 60 to 75 per cent with one stroke. In addition, pensions were linked to real wages and the increased costs were to be covered from the superannuation tax paid by the currently employed. In the late 1950s, a few tax increases still sufficed to finance the new dynamic pensions, but they became the key factor behind public overspending in subsequent decades, when demographic shifts began to reduce the active/ inactive ratio (Giersch et al. 1992, 81–2). Due to fiscal expansion and the stubbornly increasing inflow of foreign exchange, money in circulation was growing at an even greater speed than before, which raised the risk of inflation. Finally, the return to full employment ended the era of wage moderation in German industry, with wages increasing significantly faster than labour productivity between 1956 and 1966. As the result of accelerating real-wage growth, private consumption increased at higher rates than during the early 1950s, especially for durables, such as automobiles and electrical household appliances (Grosser 1990, 89– 90; Carlin 1996, 467). To bring inflation under control, the Bundesbank changed course over the fall of 1959 and introduced a set of restrictive measures. Together with the minimum reserve ratio, it raised the central bank rediscount rate by 2.25 percentage points, and began to curb the money supply through open market operations (Berger 1997, 66–7).

However, higher short-term market rates of interest made the Federal Republic even more attractive for foreign investors, especially with the recessionary climate on American stock markets. The inflow of hot money added a monumental 8 billion DM to official reserves in the course a single fiscal year (Sommariva and Tullio 1987, 233–9). Monetary policy entered into a vicious circle. In order to stabilise domestic prices, contractionary measures became inevitable. Since German central bankers were much more effective in the implementation of such policies than their European counterparts, the domestic rate of inflation continued to lag behind the inflation rates of neighbouring countries. Under the fixed parities of the Bretton Woods system, the Deutschmark appeared to be increasingly undervalued, propelling industrial exports into overdrive and further enhancing the current-account surplus. The mass inflow of foreign exchange added to the inflationary pressures, which, in turn, pushed monetary policy towards even more restrictive measures, even though higher rates of interest only accelerated the inflow of capital (Ambrosius 1984, 292). When a new wave of speculation emerged in 1960, anticipating a Deutschmark revaluation, the Bundesbank was unable to hold the exchange rate even with aggressive open market operations. This episode finally convinced the federal government that the stability of domestic prices in the long run was impossible to guarantee without revaluation. Following the proposal of Erhard, on 4 March 1961, the Deutschmark was revalued against the US dollar by 4.6 per cent (Wagner-Braun 2002, 342).

The way in which external economic equilibrium was restored reveals that the government mistakenly overestimated the effectiveness of monetary policy in taming inflation under fixed exchange rates following the return to full convertibility in 1958. The cabinet rejected proposals, including from the Advisory Council at the Economic Ministry, to either complement monetary contraction with restrictive fiscal policy instruments or to revalue the Deutschmark, until the very last moment, although revaluation would clearly have done no harm to export growth (Berger 1997, 42). First, the promotion of capital exports, which until 1961 were practically forbidden, would have made the financing of investment essential for the further expansion of exports easier and, therefore, would have improved the competitive position of West German firms in foreign markets. Second, it would have made imported industrial raw materials cheaper, which would have turned the Terms of Trade even more in favour of the Federal Republic. Third, the effective rollback of inflation would have resulted in relatively smaller domestic production costs on the one hand, and the faster increase of real wages and thereby of domestic demand on the other. Finally, an optimal exchange rate, by strengthening import competition in several branches of manufacturing, textiles in particular, would have accelerated the process of structural change, and through that productivity growth, in West German industry (Ambrosius 1984, 294).

The intention of the federal government to tackle imported inflation through trade liberalisation instead of revaluation was economically ill advised. In theory, neither the price level nor the current-account balance depends on the level of trade protection, since cheap imports stimulate exports by reducing the price of raw materials and intermediates, and, therefore, their effect on the balance of trade and on net inflows of foreign exchange is difficult to assess (Giersch et al. 1992, 108). The main reason for the ineffectiveness of monetary policy was the Bretton Woods system itself. Under fixed parities, the abstention from currency revaluations on both sides of the Atlantic resulted in a liquidity gap that prevented a faster removal of barriers to trade and international capital flows and, therefore, acted to slow down economic growth in Europe. Milton Freedman argued already in a 1950 memorandum for flexible exchange rates, even though at that time the undervaluation of the dollar, and the overvaluation of the Deutschmark threatened the fledgling post-war revival.[22] A decade later, West German resistance to amend the exchange rate resulted in a similar effect. While the Federal Republic was exporting real products in increasing value, it imported, in growing proportion, foreign-currency reserves in exchange. In order to contain imported inflation, this capital inflow could not be used to fund domestic investment, leading to growing capital exports and reduced rates of economic growth over the course of the 1960s.

The task of the Bundesbank to maintain internal price stability and the external equilibrium was made difficult especially during the 1950s, when fiscal policy was predominantly pro-cyclical. Erhard and his circle did not believe in the active management of aggregate demand, as it did not concur with the liberal view on the self-equilibrating power of free markets. Political pressures and the corporatist nature of economic policy would have also made the consistent pursuit of an anti-cyclical fiscal policy unfeasible. As shown in Table 5.2, the fiscal stimulus of the federal government had the opposite sign in each year until 1954 to what would have been recommended based on the business cycle, and the contribution of federal spending to the overheating of the economy in both election years of 1957 and 1961 was largely discretionary.

Berger (1997) used official national accounts data to compute the fiscal stimulus as the change in the size of net federal spending in a given year compared to the previous year as the percentage of GDP in the previous year. An increase in the deficit, or reduction in the surplus, constitutes an expansionary and thus positive effect; a reduction of the deficit, or expansion of the surplus, gives a contractionary and thus negative impulse. The distinction between automatic and discretionary components of the stimulus relates to the fact that certain items in public spending and revenue are automatically affected by cyclical movements in the economy. These instruments, commonly labelled 'automatic stabilisers', include among others taxes on personal and corporate income, or unemployment benefits. Expenditure on public services or on direct subsidies depend on discretionary choice by the government (Berger 1997, 138). That the automatic component takes a different sign in a few years from the recommended stimulus can be explained by statutory changes pertaining to the automatic stabilisers in these years.

Even though the Advisory Council devoted one of its most extensive reports to explaining the importance of managing the business cycle and

---

[22] Milton Friedman (1950), Flexible exchange rates as a solution to the German exchange crisis, cited in Hetzel (2007), 12.

Table 5.2 *Fiscal stimuli of the federal government and monetary policy in the 1950s*

	Budgetary stimulus (% of GDP)[a]			Recommended stimulus (+/–)	Central bank discount rate (%)[b]
	Aggregate	Discretionary	Automatic		
1951	–1.14	–1.13	–0.02	+	6.00
1952	–1.11	–1.13	–0.03	+	5.25
1953	–0.33	–0.39	0.06	+	3.75
1954	–0.42	–0.89	0.47	+	3.25
1955	–1.44	–0.85	–0.59	–	3.25
1956	–0.38	–0.36	–0.02	–	4.75
1957	1.25	1.01	0.25	o	4.375
1958	1.20	0.79	0.41	+	3.25
1959	–0.1	0.28	–0.28	o	3.00
1960	–0.57	–0.24	–0.33	–	4.45
1961	1.11	0.89	0.22	–	3.25

[a] Federal government only.
[b] Average rate over the year.
Sources: Berger (1997), Table 11, 137; *Deutsche Bundesbank Zinsstatistik*, available at www.bundesbank.de

to describing in great detail the instruments at the disposal of both fiscal and monetary policy in 1955, its proposals were not integrated into government policy for another decade.[23] This was not always the intention of policymakers. Between 1955 and 1957, the economic and finance ministries, together with the opposition and the unions, advocated measures to cool down the economy. But, the coalition of Andenauer and Berg, the all-powerful chairman of the BDI, successfully maintained a relatively expansionary course, so that the BdL was forced to take the initiative towards restrictive measures (Zündorf 2006, 251).

The first step in the direction of greater policy coordination in achieving macroeconomic stability was the establishment of the Council of Economic Experts (*Sachverständigenrat*) in 1963. The council did not have a direct role in policy drafting but was given a strong mandate to make recommendations for both fiscal and monetary policy based on its assessment of macroeconomic developments. Its independent voice and high academic standard lent considerable influence to its reports and placed macroeconomic issues at the heart of public discourse in the Federal Republic (Giersch et al. 1992, 139). Already in its second

[23] Wissenschaftlicher Beirat, Gutachten vom 3. Juni 1956 und 8. Juli 1956. In Wissenschaftlicher Beirat (1973), 291–320.

annual report published in November 1965, the Sachverständigenrat argued for the need of a 'concerted action' between the major macroeconomic actors, the federal government, the Bundesbank, and the social partners, both trade unions and employers' organisations, to mount a coordinated response to the overheating of the economy and to avoid an inflationary outcome.[24] Even though Erhard continued to reject demand management, by this time, he was the last man standing to defend Ordoliberalism. As the economy came to standstill in 1966, even his closest disciple and former advisor Müller Armack accepted the Keynesian doctrine of academic experts (Görtemaker 2004, 432–3). Erhard, who had succeeded Adenauer as chancellor in 1963, was defeated by the first recession in post-war Germany. It ended the political hegemony of the Christian union parties and, with the departure of its emblematic figure, the era of liberal economic policy in the Federal Republic. The newly appointed economic minister, the Social Democrat Karl Shiller, convened the first Concerted Action in February 1967 (Schröter 2000, 381). It became the symbol of the new consensus politics of the grand coalition and was codified in the Stability and Growth Act, the Magna Charta of Keynesian economic policy in West Germany, on 8 June 1967 (Braun 1990, 183).

The Stability and Growth Act gave a new definition of the SME and ushered in a new era of economic policy. It compelled the actors of both fiscal and monetary policy to safeguard the main macroeconomic goals set out by the Sachverständigenrat. Commonly referred to as the 'magical quadrangle' (*magischer Viereck*), these included the stability of domestic prices, the external equilibrium, a stable and sufficient rate of economic growth, and high levels of employment.[25] Even though the implementation of the act soon revealed the ineffectiveness of global demand management and the Concerted Action practically collapsed after the walkout of the trade unions in 1970, the course of economic policy had changed fundamentally and for good. Deficit spending became the key instrument in fighting the recession and monetary policy was temporarily relieved, as public spending became strongly anti-cyclical. However, as the share of government expenditure in GDP increased sharply with the introduction of the progressive welfare reform programs following the election victory of the Social Democrats in 1969, the fiscal surplus once again turned into deficit during the boom of the early 1970s (see Figure 5.3). Welfare spending increased from 118.6 billion DM in 1970 to 171.7 billion DM in 1972, while public expenditure on education and research

---

[24] See Sachverständigenrat (1966), paragraphs 187–208.
[25] For a detailed exposition, see Glastetter (1993), 60–88.

climbed from 28 billion DM to more than 40 billion DM (Leaman 1988, 189; Roeper and Weimer 1997, 181). Facing an increasingly expansionary fiscal policy and the mounting pressure of capital inflows amidst the weakening of the dollar, the efforts of the Bundesbank to maintain both domestic price stability and the exchange rate remained futile, even after the Deutschmark revaluations of 1969 and 1971 (see Giersch et al. 1992, 152–80). The Sachverständigenrat gave the title *Bravery to stabilise* to its annual report for 1973/4, but its cautiously optimistic outlook was tarnished by the geopolitical calamities that demolished the Bretton Woods system and ended the post-war golden age of economic growth.

Conclusions

World War II represents a milestone in the history of modern Europe and was a watershed in the history of Germany. It brought physical destruction on a scale that few could have imagined and few imagined could be overcome in their lifetime. Beyond sheer material damage, the amok run of Nazism left devastating legacies in the displacement of people, disillusionment in ideals and ideologies that had inspired nations, the disintegration of countries and societies that had bound them together, the distrust in institutions that post-war reconstruction had to rely on, and disbelief shared by millions who survived the carnage that such a revival was even feasible. That a Germany economically more dynamic and more prosperous than ever could emerge from such desolate conditions astonished contemporaries at home and abroad alike. The impression that the West German economy had hit Ground Zero and had to rebuild as a phoenix rising from ashes instilled the notion of an economic miracle in post-war historiography and public discourse.

Based on a new consensus of moderation concerning the impact of the war and its aftermath on the fundaments of German economic power, economic historians have since fundamentally revised this view of post-war recovery. While German cities were laid to ruins, productive capacity, especially in manufacturing, witnessed a period of expansion rather than decline. West German industry was endowed with more plentiful and more modern equipment after the war than it had possessed ever before 1939. The dire living conditions of the early post-war years held back reconstruction, without doubt, but the supply of labour did not limit the economic resurgence of Germany. Ethnic Germans driven out of East and Central Europe by the Soviet military advance and by political vengeance in countries liberated from the Nazi yoke, together with those fleeing communism from East Germany, vastly outnumbered the West German casualties of war. Critical bottlenecks in the transport and energy-supply systems and the restrictive institutions of Allied occupation, which initially threatened to dismantle large parts of German industry and purge large parts of the German business elite, thwarted

219

economic recovery. But, they were soon overcome thanks to the efforts of the Western military governments and the radical shift in their policies towards the former nemesis in the backdrop of mounting Cold War tensions. Industrial dismantling, de-concentration, and de-Nazification were ephemeral features of post-war economic life. The reforms of 1948 restored efficient markets and the incentives for work, while the Marshall Plan removed most of the remaining input–output bottlenecks in industrial production and reintegrated the West German economy into the European division of labour.

The present monograph drew extensively from the contributions of recent scholarship, but challenged this revisionist view on the limited extent and persistence of wartime destruction and post-war dislocation. Despite enhanced endowments of both productive capital and labour, industrial production lagged behind pre-war levels until the early 1950s because the West German economy remained dislocated for considerably longer than conventionally argued. The wartime destruction of large and medium-sized cities and the inadequate reconstruction efforts of the early post-war years made urban housing extremely scarce. While urban industry could not tap into the labour reserves of the countryside, the growth of rural industry and handcrafts was limited by the shortage of capital. Producers in the rural economy had to substitute labour for capital in order to increase output in response to booming demand, which acted to depress labour productivity in manufacturing. These conditions, in turn, laid the foundations for the growth miracle of the early 1950s that was driven by the improved allocation of productive forces.

The ability to grow into existing capacities implied that industrial production could increase with little additional investment in physical capital. At the same time, the vast reservoirs of labour initially displaced in the countryside but gradually reintegrated into the urban economy allowed West German governments to achieve high growth with relatively low investment in human capital. As long as manufacturing firms could raise output through the improved utilisation of existing capacities and could expand sales at home and abroad with established product lines, they had little incentive for product and process innovation. In high-tech industries, the position of West German companies was also weakened by the loss of technical expertise as a consequence of the Holocaust and the emigration of leading scientists both before and after the war and by the restrictive measures of the Allied military governments that remained in place until the early 1950s.

An additional factor behind the persistence of post-war dislocation in the West German economy was the division of Germany itself. Due to the high degree of regional specialisation, the carving up of the former empire created structural disproportions in industrial production. Whereas most of the primary industries of the Reich had concentrated in the West of Germany, engineering and consumer goods were relatively underrepresented within West German manufacturing. To the extent that East–West trade after 1945 fell short of internal trade between the respective regions before and during World War II and as long as external trade did not alleviate the resulting input–output bottlenecks, industrial recovery depended on rebalancing the disproportionate production structure that the redrawing of maps in the centre of Europe had left behind. The coal industry and steel-based capital goods had to capture foreign markets in order to exploit their production capacities, which were vastly enhanced during the war, while engineering and light manufacturing could expand thanks to increased market potential at home.

World War II dislocated the West German economy in more ways than one. As long as these effects persisted, the pre-war levels of industrial efficiency could not be surpassed. Millions of displaced workers had to be reintegrated into the urban production process, and new capacities had to be built up both in the overpopulated rural areas and in industries that had been relatively underrepresented within West German manufacturing. Consequently, industrial recovery was driven by the extended use of capital and labour, rather than productivity growth. In fact, the opportunity to grow on the basis of existing capacities and the need to meet the demand of a war-shattered population for manufactures that had already been on the market before 1939 thwarted technological progress and product innovation. Labour productivity was limited further by the scarcity of skilled manpower due to the tremendous wartime casualties among young and middle-aged men and the disruptions vocational training had suffered during the hostilities. The resulting backlog in productivity growth created further scope for improvement in industrial efficiency through the adoption of more capital-intensive technologies in the late 1950s and the 1960s, when labour-supply constraints became increasingly harder to overcome. Technological modernisation and the end to mass immigration from East Germany following the construction of the Berlin Wall demanded increased investment in highly skilled labour, both engineers and technicians. Therefore, growth rates of industrial labour productivity and Total Factor Productivity remained remarkably high by international standards until the end of the golden age. The post-war phase of extraordinary growth lasted until the early 1970s. The growth of national income slowed down considerably from the late 1950s, but this was mostly the reflection of first stagnating and then declining labour input and the diminishing pace of structural change. Labour productivity continued to increase at remarkably high rates, while productivity growth within industry even accelerated between the 1950s and the 1960s.

The persistence of structural disproportions in West German industry and the significance thereof for subsequent growth highlights an important link between the internal dynamics of post-war reconstruction and its external determinants. In particular, to the extent that West Germany had surplus capacity in the primary industries and capital goods, its reintegration into international markets was critical for her post-war revival. In the early phase of the economic miracle, industrial expansion and the rise of labour productivity in manufacturing were strongly export led. In this period, until the mid-1950s, the surge of West German exports also exhibited a reconstruction pattern. During the war, Nazi Germany reorganised intra-European trade in order to maximise its war production and to maintain its war effort. The German economy became more eastward oriented with the eastward expansion of the Third Reich and the eastbound thrust of the Nazi war effort. Hitler's *Drang nach Osten* was the major force of trade diversion in wartime Europe, but the legacy of 'Fortress Europe' was short lived: the early 1950s, by and large, restored the trade patterns of the interwar era. The post-war settlement and the new international order did not fundamentally re-shape Germany's external trade, except in relation with Eastern Europe. The geography and the commodity structure of West German exports began to deviate from long-established patterns only after the European Economic Community launched an exclusive form of market integration in Western Europe. Contrary to the dominant view in the literature, the growth of West German industry from the late 1950s was no longer export-driven. This shift in the dynamics of industrial development reflected, in large part, a radical reorientation of fiscal policy in the Federal Republic, which, together with buoyant real-wage growth, provided a powerful stimulus to domestic demand during the 1960s.

The role of economic policy is arguably the most intensely debated aspect of the West German growth miracle and the one on which the predominant view in the literature has shifted the most. Contemporaries located the origins of the *Wirtschaftswunder* in the currency reform of 1948 and the introduction of a liberal economic system based on market prices, stronger competition aimed at the dismantling of monopolistic structures, and a general restraint from government intervention. The Social Market Economy has retained some weight in more recent accounts, not least thanks to the Olsonian interpretation of post-war growth, which stressed that the break-up of distributive coalitions and monopolistic corporate networks enabled markets to better allocate scarce resources. However, recent scholarship has described a strongly corporatist West German economy that showed more continuity than discontinuity from the economic institutions of the German Reich. The liberalisation of markets was incomplete, price controls remained pervasive, the monopolistic organisations that had long characterised the German economy, to a large extent, stayed in place. In direct contradiction with the principles of Freiburg liberalism, corporatist industrial relations and the special relationship between big industry and the state were not just relics of the past; they formed essential components of government policy and the political program of the ruling parties. A broadly based social contract that some advocated as the propeller of post-war growth in Europe was not anchored in legislation in West Germany until 1967, and even thereafter broke down, in practice, within a few years.

The historical evidence has also confirmed that economic recovery had begun well before the currency reform and that it was not transformed into sustained growth until the early 1950s. The most important limiting factors of industrial expansion in post-war Germany persisted for many years after 1948. Foreign aid did little to improve these conditions, for it was not substantial enough and did not focus primarily on the most critical bottlenecks. Economic policy remained strongly interventionist throughout the post-war period, but state intervention provided, in general, limited support for growth. Public investment and government subsidies favoured predominantly declining sectors and industries that, in reality, had excess rather than insufficient capacity due to the structural disproportions created by the division of Germany. Resources were misallocated, in large part, because of the misconception shared by contemporaries that wartime destruction had significantly diminished the productive arsenal of German industry. By the time the German Institute of Economic Research revealed the scale of wartime accumulation in physical capital and the limited impact of both strategic bombing and post-war dismantling on industrial assets, heavy industry was lobbying for state support no longer to expand but in order to survive in the face of adverse shifts in the structure of demand and increasing competition from low-cost producers abroad. By contrast, until the mid-1960s, the Federal Republic invested very modestly in education and scientific research by international comparison and, consequently, was lagging behind in industrial innovation, particularly in frontier technologies. The most significant contribution of public policy to the West German growth miracle was the leading role that the state assumed in rebuilding the urban housing stock and in resettling the displaced populations trapped in rural areas after World War II into the industrial heartlands of the country.

Displacement was the defining characteristic of the post-war crisis and public policy in the Federal Republic was driven predominantly by the need to respond to the challenges it had presented. Without the influx of millions of expellees and refugees into West Germany during and after the war, there would not have been much of a housing shortage after 1950, at least not at the national level. There would have been no mass unemployment, and the provision of post-war society with basic consumer goods could have been achieved with limited effort after the rebuilding of the transport infrastructure and the lifting of restrictions on international trade. The resettlement of these displaced millions into urban areas and their integration into the urban economy may have been critical for the economic miracle, but for contemporaries it represented, above all, a political imperative, for it was vital to avoid the explosion of social conflict in rural communities and through that the reinvigoration of political extremism in Germany. At the same time, without the presence of the expellees and refugees, West German industry could not have surged so spectacularly in the course of the 1950s, as manufacturing firms would have been competing with other sectors of the economy for scarce labour, and they would have required larger investments in both new technologies and in human capital. Rural communities would have attracted much less of investment and thus could not have shared the fruits of reconstruction growth as much as they did.

The human misery that displacement embodied also reminds us that there was a heavy price to pay for the economic miracle of the post-war era. Germans who survived the carnage until 1945 and lived to witness the *Wirtschaftswunder* soon enjoyed a level of prosperity unprecedented in their nation's history, but not everyone survived. Riches could not make up for the loss of loved ones and could do little to alleviate the pain of millions haunted by the oppressions of war, soldiers wearing the scars suffered in battle and women scarred by the humiliation of abuse at the hands of the enemy and often of their husbands returning from the torments of frontline service. West German industry emerged from the abyss of defeat with vastly enhanced productive capacity, but its wartime expansion was carried through at the expense of other sectors of the economy, including small-scale manufacturing and handcrafts, whose resources were systematically diverted to support the aims of war production from 1939 onwards. The war machinery of the Third Reich was funded to a large extent by the brutal exploitation of occupied lands and by the effective expropriation of small savers, whose loans extended to the Nazi government during the war were never fully honoured. For some, the wiping out of savings by the currency reform without compensation and the blatantly discriminatory post-war reforms were the end, or even the pinnacle, of totalitarian war financing that had requisitioned the painfully accumulated resources of German society to manage the

Conclusions225

self-inflicted crisis of a reckless German state (Benz 1991). After 1948, the supposedly liberal market economy of Erhard kept public spending to a minimum, while the federal government and the institutions it funded continued to pour resources, both domestic and foreign, into the very industries that had benefited from the command economy of Göring and Speer.

Finally, a balanced assessment of the West German growth miracle cannot overlook the fact that post-war Germany was more than just the Federal Republic. The West German economy was saved from the fate of deindustrialisation that until at least 1946 was very much on the cards. However, the magnanimity, or better judgment, of the Western Allies, if anything, only enhanced the crippling reparations burden imposed upon Germans who lived under Soviet occupation. Their mass exodus in the late 1940s and throughout the 1950s, which initially went hand in hand with the outmigration of manufacturing firms, contributed to the expansion of West German industry, but it was detrimental for social and economic progress east of the Elbe. The staggering growth of the West German economy and its dramatic divergence from its cold-war counterpart during the early post-war era were not engineered by the Social Market Economy or by the new institutions of a new international order. They were primarily the economic consequences of the war.

Appendices

Appendix 1: Estimating Industrial Turnover in Urban and Rural Counties for 1938

Total turnover for 1938 is estimated from data on tax returns. In principle the main caveat of this approach would be that different sectors of the economy paid different tax rates and some industries were exempted. As a result of structural differences, counties, therefore, could have faced different average tax rates. However, the 1935 and 1950 tax records demonstrate that both the regional and industrial structure of tax revenue and total turnover remained very similar throughout the period. Thus, the average tax rate of a representative region in 1938 differed from its post-war equivalent mainly because of the increase in tax rates that came into force in 1946. This was proportionally the same in all sectors: tax rates were raised universally by one half.[1]

In 1950, the turnover tax was collected mainly from industry and handcrafts (60.7 per cent), and commerce (28.2 per cent), which had concentrated largely in the same areas. Consequently, average tax rates did not differ much across federal states, except in Hamburg and Bremen, where the high proportion of wholesale trade and manufacturing located in the duty-free ports depressed the ratio of tax revenue to total turnover. Structural differences within industry could, in theory, impose challenges, but the average tax rates on turnover were very similar across industries, with the exception of power utilities, flourmills, and bakeries. The range was somewhat wider in commerce, but tax revenue concentrated in a few branches with similar tax rates for both wholesale and retail trade.[2] Thus, minor structural shifts within particular regions did not have a significant effect on average tax rates.

The 1950 tax records report both tax revenue and actual turnover for federal states and for sectors of the economy.[3] Based on these aggregates,

[1] StatBRD, Vol. 112 (1955), 15.
[2] Ibid., 23–30.
[3] Ibid., 39, 159.

Table A1.1 *Estimated average tax rates on total turnover in the federal states (%)*

Federal states	Urban counties		Rural counties	
	1950	1938	1950	1938
Schleswig-Holstein	1.87	1.24	2.00	1.33
Hamburg	1.43	0.95	—	—
Bremen	1.32	0.88	—	—
Lower Saxony	1.89	1.26	2.04	1.36
North Rhine Westphalia	1.84	1.23	2.01	1.34
Hesse	1.76	1.17	2.01	1.34
Rhineland-Palatinate	1.92	1.28	2.07	1.38
Baden-Württemberg	1.99	1.33	2.26	1.50
Bavaria	2.06	1.37	2.19	1.46
West Germany	1.82	1.21	2.06	1.37

I determined the difference in average tax rates between urban and rural counties within each federal state, as listed in Table A1.1. The average rates for 1938 are then estimated by accounting for the overall rate of increase in the official tax rates.

Total turnover for 1938 in a given county is computed as tax revenue divided by the corresponding estimated tax rate. All figures are converted into 1950 DM. Even if not a perfect proxy for national income, total turnover represents an aggregate for most sectors of the economy. Thus, of all the available composite price indexes, the GNP deflator is the most appropriate. Ritschl and Spoerer (1997, 51–2) constructed a deflator with 1913 as the base year. Their deflators for 1938 and 1950 were 128.09 and 204.82 respectively, which yield a conversion rate of 1.60 DM in 1950 to 1 RM in 1938. In 1956 and 1961, the GNP deflator with 1950 as the base level reached 123.35 and 144.16 respectively (Sachverständigenrat 1965, 172).

The reader may question the validity of computations that assume away inter-sectoral shifts in economic activity between 1938 and 1950. It was precisely one of the most important consequences of post-war dislocation that it temporarily halted, or more precisely reversed, the broad structural shifts that had occurred in the German economy during the early 1940s. Hence, the percentage share of the major sectors in total employment did not change significantly between 1938 and 1950. In June 1938, workers in industry, handcrafts, and construction made up 54.8 per cent of all wage earners. Those employed in transportation and trade as well as in public and private services accounted for 18.3 and 19.7 per cent respectively. The corresponding figures for June 1950 are 54.4, 18.2, and 19.1 per cent (Mertens 1964, 24).

Appendix 2: Estimating the Capital Stock of West German Industry, 1938–1950

The DIW published estimates of gross capital stock, both buildings and machinery, in forty-one industries for all years between 1950 and 1968 and of the corresponding levels of gross investment in 1962 prices going back to 1924 (Baumgart and Krengel 1970, 48–82; for estimates on other sectors of the economy, see Kirner 1968, and Görzig and Kirner 1976). The investment series are adjusted for wartime damage, post-war dismantling, and territorial changes. The source reports capital stock only for the period after 1950. The perpetual-inventory method used by the authors in their estimation requires investment series to be sufficiently long to cover the average working life of fixed capital in a given industry under the assumption of non-linearity for capital retirement.

A non-linear retirement function cannot be used to derive capital-stock estimates for earlier years by backward projection, since this would require comparable investment data from prior to 1924, which are not available. Therefore, I assumed the rate of capital retirement to be constant over time, meaning that at zero gross investment the capital stock would shrink at a constant rate. The retirement rate is computed as the reciprocal of the average working life of fixed assets in a given industry. This procedure, even if not precisely correct, enables us to determine the gross value of the capital stock for any given year based on existing investment data and the capital-stock of subsequent years. Baumgart and Krengel (1970, 49) provide industry-specific estimates for the average working life of machine tools. With these data, we can compute industry-specific rates of capital retirement. The gross capital stock (K) of industry i in year t is determined by the following formula.

$$K_i^t = K_i^{t+1} - I_i^t + A_i^t \qquad (A2.1)$$

I_i stands for investment in fixed capital and A_i for capital retirement in industry i. A_i is, in turn, the product of the industry-specific retirement rate (a_i) and the capital stock of industry in a given year.

$$K_i^t = K_i^{t+1} - I_i^t + a_i K_i^t \qquad (A2.2)$$

Equation (A2.2) can be rewritten to express the capital stock at the start of year t with variables that have already been calculated in a sequential procedure starting from 1950 and projecting backwards to 1938.

$$K_i^t = \frac{K_i^{t+1} - I_i^t}{1 - a_i} \tag{A2.3}$$

While adjusting their investment series for the impact of wartime destruction and post-war dismantling, Baumgart and Krengel (1970) distributed the estimated losses evenly over all potentially affected investment years. Therefore, their data do not precisely account for the timing of the damage that occurred to fixed capital during the mid-1940s. Albeit perfectly suitable for the purpose of determining capital-stock levels for the post-1950 period, these estimates are inappropriate, if we wish project these levels backward in time. First, investment levels have to be readjusted to exclude the evenly distributed effects of war damage and post-war dismantling. Second, based on estimates published in an earlier study by the DIW (Krengel 1958, 95, 104), we can determine (1) the size of these effects as a proportion of the capital stock in 1950 and (2) the timing of the losses. Third, lower retirement rates are assumed for the period 1945–9. At very modest capacity utilisation, industrial machinery was not run down as fast as normally, and, with little market incentive to increase production, firms employed a large part of their workforce to carry out essential repairs.

$$K_i^t = \frac{K_i^{t+1} - I_i^t}{1 - a_i} + DAM_i \tag{A2.4}$$

Following these adjustments, I used the extended formula (A2.4), where $DAM_i t$ is capital lost in industry i in year t due to either war damage or post-war dismantling, and I denotes actual gross investment unadjusted for these effects. Aircraft manufacturing is excluded from the dataset for the reason explained in the main text of Chapter 3. The estimates are reported in Tables A2.1 and A2.2 for machinery and structures respectively. For the latter, I have assumed an identical rate of capital retirement of 2 per cent annually for all industries and periods, since the number of years buildings are expected to last without major renovation is unlikely to be strongly affected by the type and intensity of industrial activity carried out in them.

Table A2.1 *Estimates of gross capital stock in West German industry at the start of each year: Machinery and equipment (million 1962 DM)*

	1950	1949	1948	1947	1946	1945	1944	1943	1942	1941	1940	1939	1938
Hard coal	7,450	7,316	7,376	7,531	7,702	8,182	8,504	8,287	7,720	7,134	6,551	6,057	5,709
Brown coal and lignite	1,121	1,047	1,022	1,027	1,036	1,104	1,179	1,164	1,103	1,042	982	933	903
Iron ore	172	161	158	159	161	171	173	165	154	143	133	125	121
Rock and potassium salt	659	642	634	641	648	692	739	741	717	688	660	630	600
Crude oil and natural gas	614	583	573	583	590	631	656	638	600	556	511	473	451
Other mining	79	70	63	61	59	62	66	66	63	61	59	57	56
Construction materials	1,728	1,671	1,663	1,695	1,744	1,876	1,979	1,973	1,883	1,767	1,634	1,518	1,467
Iron making	4,194	4,222	4,365	4,607	5,030	5,624	5,692	5,364	4,879	4,410	3,977	3,625	3,373
Iron and steel foundries	1,123	1,119	1,143	1,179	1,229	1,323	1,358	1,293	1,192	1,095	1,004	927	874
Rolling mills	544	543	559	586	643	714	723	683	623	565	512	468	437
Non-ferrous metals	1,970	1,993	2,040	2,115	2,234	2,415	2,467	2,360	2,197	2,035	1,881	1,741	1,576
Chemical industry	10,405	10,492	10,734	11,120	11,700	12,652	12,828	12,091	11,026	9,965	8,965	8,084	7,472
Fuel industry	1,670	1,674	1,694	1,729	1,767	1,870	1,904	1,801	1,652	1,504	1,377	1,273	1,205
Rubber and asbestos	732	698	685	683	686	721	742	704	655	607	563	528	502
Timber industry	473	366	305	278	259	263	296	308	312	315	315	316	319
Paper and pulp	981	933	918	928	942	1,002	1,067	1,075	1,061	1,042	1,015	984	940
Steel constructions	479	456	453	464	482	519	530	503	465	433	403	378	355
Machine tools	3,760	3,613	3,606	3,761	4,092	4,537	4,531	4,248	3,894	3,619	3,383	3,191	3,049
Transport vehicles	2,123	2,077	2,105	2,190	2,324	2,534	2,540	2,367	2,145	1,973	1,824	1,703	1,600
Shipbuilding	617	613	623	651	707	783	773	714	641	581	527	480	445
Electrical engineering	2,252	2,097	2,045	2,098	2,281	2,559	2,570	2,411	2,205	2,041	1,895	1,782	1,717
Optical and precision engineering	353	345	353	374	414	465	467	435	394	374	341	312	286
Fabricated metal products	1,201	1,143	1,134	1,172	1,245	1,371	1,413	1,359	1,278	1,207	1,142	1,089	1,039
Pottery industry	197	177	163	161	162	176	195	195	189	184	179	170	162

(continued)

231

Table A2.1 (continued)

	1950	1949	1948	1947	1946	1945	1944	1943	1942	1941	1940	1939	1938
Glass industry	237	213	203	201	202	218	233	233	225	221	214	206	201
Woodworking	491	397	328	301	295	326	362	369	368	369	366	360	354
Entertainment products	54	52	52	52	51	52	59	62	63	64	65	66	67
Paper and board	202	179	164	158	157	169	184	189	191	189	185	180	180
Printing and publishing	593	539	519	525	541	592	648	670	682	688	688	682	678
Plastic products	117	107	103	102	105	111	114	107	99	93	87	83	80
Leather making	203	189	179	179	178	192	209	210	204	202	198	191	181
Leather processing	67	60	57	57	57	61	68	69	67	66	64	62	59
Footwear industry	269	254	247	253	257	278	297	290	277	267	257	250	244
Textile industry	3,476	3,237	3,146	3,188	3,272	3,529	3,748	3,776	3,748	3,691	3,617	3,525	3,446
Clothing industry	220	176	155	149	146	159	172	172	170	170	172	176	184
Flouring mills	802	756	735	730	735	779	819	811	795	783	771	762	761
Oil pressing and margarine	480	473	467	474	483	514	534	517	501	482	468	457	448
Sugar industry	465	431	411	413	420	447	465	450	435	421	412	407	398
Brewing and malting	1,334	1,281	1,262	1,282	1,319	1,423	1,531	1,561	1,557	1,542	1,517	1,477	1,454
Other food and tobacco	3,386	2,921	2,624	2,546	2,530	2,711	2,915	2,932	2,902	2,885	2,876	2,878	2,886
Total Industry	57,293	55,316	55,069	56,402	58,886	63,804	65,750	63,360	59,333	55,473	51,792	48,610	46,280

Table A2.2 Estimates of gross capital stock in West German industry at the start of each year: Structures (million 1962 DM)

	1950	1949	1948	1947	1946	1945	1944	1943	1942	1941	1940	1939	1938
Hard coal	3,711	3,662	3,654	3,678	3,706	4,015	4,365	4,320	4,110	3,875	3,633	3,420	3,258
Brown coal and lignite	485	460	446	442	441	481	534	531	508	483	456	433	417
Iron ore	153	151	150	151	151	165	175	170	159	147	136	128	122
Rock and potassium salt	421	417	416	417	420	458	507	516	510	502	493	483	473
Crude oil and natural gas	245	236	229	227	226	245	268	264	251	235	219	205	195
Other mining	27	23	20	20	21	23	26	25	25	24	23	22	21
Construction materials	941	886	843	840	843	924	1,023	1,029	998	956	909	867	844
Iron making	1,812	1,755	1,728	1,758	1,795	1,980	2,130	2,080	1,970	1,854	1,742	1,649	1,577
Iron and steel foundries	644	627	619	624	633	689	745	729	691	651	612	578	551
Rolling mills	363	356	354	358	366	400	430	418	395	371	347	327	312
Non-ferrous metals	825	820	819	837	857	936	1,004	979	925	866	808	754	692
Chemical industry	6,018	5,970	5,960	6,055	6,167	6,716	7,151	6,875	6,381	5,848	5,321	4,850	4,497
Fuel industry	668	651	634	635	640	694	748	724	679	631	587	550	524
Rubber and asbestos	354	331	310	305	304	327	356	346	325	303	281	263	248
Timber industry	304	242	193	179	170	185	222	232	233	234	234	235	235
Paper and pulp	399	362	338	336	337	370	416	423	419	412	402	392	378
Steel constructions	342	321	308	307	306	332	358	346	323	301	279	260	242
Machine tools	3,203	3,097	3,037	3,089	3,159	3,462	3,697	3,589	3,393	3,222	3,066	2,934	2,829
Transport vehicles	1,708	1,658	1,638	1,663	1,691	1,843	1,953	1,868	1,733	1,614	1,503	1,408	1,324
Shipbuilding	732	735	742	761	779	852	885	825	741	664	590	524	472
Electrical engineering	1,732	1,623	1,546	1,552	1,578	1,742	1,852	1,763	1,619	1,490	1,367	1,266	1,195
Optical and precision engineering	328	318	316	324	332	365	389	374	350	325	301	280	262
Fabricated metal products	992	940	909	913	922	1,010	1,102	1,089	1,049	1,010	971	937	904
Pottery industry	198	184	170	166	167	185	210	213	211	208	205	201	197

(continued)

233

Table A2.2 (continued)

	1950	1949	1948	1947	1946	1945	1944	1943	1942	1941	1940	1939	1938
Glass industry	248	232	223	224	225	245	273	276	272	269	263	257	252
Woodworking	486	418	361	344	341	381	438	448	446	442	435	427	418
Entertainment products	150	149	149	150	153	166	187	194	196	199	201	203	205
Paper and board	127	111	98	93	90	98	112	115	114	112	109	106	104
Printing and publishing	732	695	676	681	687	754	848	873	882	885	888	886	885
Plastic products	82	72	68	67	66	73	81	77	72	67	63	60	57
Leather making	157	144	134	132	130	141	161	165	164	163	162	160	156
Leather processing	90	85	80	80	82	90	101	102	101	101	99	96	94
Footwear industry	165	149	139	140	137	149	168	167	162	156	151	147	143
Textile industry	2,199	1,993	1,871	1,865	1,884	2,082	2,336	2,387	2,384	2,371	2,350	2,323	2,300
Clothing industry	318	287	267	264	261	290	324	328	325	323	322	323	327
Flouring mills	380	362	352	352	354	390	431	433	427	420	413	407	405
Oil pressing and margarine	360	358	354	357	362	392	429	428	422	412	404	396	390
Sugar industry	236	222	213	213	215	236	260	256	249	242	235	230	224
Brewing and malting	1,019	997	986	995	1,010	1,106	1,228	1,251	1,244	1,230	1,211	1,182	1,161
Other food and tobacco	2,066	1,888	1,751	1,729	1,728	1,905	2,140	2,178	2,166	2,156	2,145	2,139	2,135
Total Industry	35,420	33,989	33,100	33,322	33,736	36,899	40,061	39,406	37,623	35,775	33,939	32,311	31,026

Appendix 3: Computing Labour Hours for West German Industry, 1938–1950

Between 1950 and 1970, labour input can be measured directly from the annual industry statistics that report total hours worked by the manual workforce.[4] From 1960 onward, these statistics include the Saarland and West Berlin. An official publication reports 1960 levels for both territorial definitions, allowing for the necessary adjustments to be made on the index numbers presented in Chapter 3 (Statistisches Bundesamt 1973, 48–9). For earlier years, comparisons are made based on official employment data adjusted for changes in average weekly hours worked, using a number of different sources. Employment statistics have been obtained from the non-agricultural workplace censuses of 17 May 1939 and of 13 September 1950.[5] Using the provincial records of the 1939 census, we can construct aggregate figures for West Germany, excluding the Saarland and Berlin, that correspond to the post-war industry classification.

The Federal Ministry for Labour published territorially adjusted employment estimates for 1938 (Bundesministerium für Arbeit 1952, 12–23) derived from annual data reported in the workbook statistics (*Arbeitsbucherhebung*).[6] In theory, one could construct the 1938 benchmark using this primary source. However, the level of disaggregation does not suffice to match the post-war industry classification, especially in primary metals and the metal working industries. In addition, the provincial labour bureau districts (*Landesamtbezirke*) did not correspond to the actual provincial or state boundaries within the Reich. In particular, Nordmark and Mitteldeutschland contained vast territories falling under both West and East German jurisdiction after 1945. Both had relatively large weights in industrial employment: including the port cities of Hamburg, Kiel and Lübeck in the former, and the emerging industrial cluster around Braunschweig, Salzgitter, and Wolfsburg in the latter. Without data for local labour bureau districts, we cannot accurately adjust the figures for post-war territory. It is also not entirely clear how industrial employment was defined in the workbook statistics, and whether or not it corresponds to the definitions used in the industry statistics.

The alternative approach followed here estimates employment in 1938 based on data from the 1939 census adjusted for employment growth

---

[4] IndBRD, Series 4, No. 9 (1955), 9; ibid, No. 14 (1957), 14; Fachserie D/1, Vol. 15 (1966), 12–13; Fachserie D/1, Vol. 20 (1971), 6–7, 14–15.
[5] StatDR, vol. 568.8–14 (1942–4); StatBRD, Vol. 45.2 (1952), 4–18.
[6] Reichsministerium für Arbeit, No. 2993, 19–21.

Table A3.1 *Levels of employment in West German industry between 1938 and 1950 (thousands)*

	Census data		Estimate		Industry statistics	
	May 1939	Sept. 1950	1938	1950	1948	1950
Mining	*443.8*	*557.4*	*438.1*	*557.5*	*534.3*	*572.8*
Coal mining	392.4	503.2	388.5	504.4	486.2	517.4
Metallic ores	37.1	30.1	34.2	29.4	25.3	29.6
Salt mining	9.8	15.1	9.8	14.7	15.5	16.7
Crude oil and natural gas	4.5	9.0	3.9	9.0	7.3	9.0
Production goods	*1,203.5*	*1,189.3*	*1,132.0*	*1,133.9*	*859.0*	*1,099.8*
Fuel industry	19.1	16.2	17.9	16.0	17.9	20.3
Iron and steel	474.4	335.5	436.3	320.9	248.2	332.6
Non-ferrous metals	77.2	73.7	71.0	69.3	49.7	69.6
Construction materials	256.0	260.2	247.3	238.9	155.4	194.5
Chemical industry	192.9	272.2	180.9	262.8	223.1	281.3
Rubber and asbestos	43.8	58.7	41.5	55.6	45.7	58.4
Timber industry	90.8	111.0	87.7	109.0	85.0	87.7
Paper and pulp	49.3	61.8	49.4	59.9	34.0	55.3
Investment goods	*1,404.0*	*1,558.9*	*1,279.0*	*1,490.4*	*1201.3*	*1,432.6*
Steel constructions	97.4	131.1	84.7	125.9	118.9	118.1
Machine tools	382.8	485.3	339.9	469.6	380.7	450.4
Transport vehicles	144.8	190.3	130.4	181.8	146.3	190.7
Shipbuilding	91.5	47.6	79.5	44.9	35.8	44.0
Electrical engineering	165.9	276.9	150.8	263.8	214.5	252.6
Optical and precision engineering	78.9	85.3	74.8	82.0	70.6	77.7
Fabricated metal products	442.8	342.3	419.0	322.3	234.5	299.0
Consumer goods	*1,288.0*	*1,505.9*	*1,240.9*	*1,447.9*	*935.1*	*1,326.3*
China and earthenware	48.3	59.4	49.0	57.3	42.9	56.2
Glass industry	28.3	49.8	28.3	47.7	30.5	43.5
Entertainment instruments	26.4	38.9	25.4	35.6	26.8	30.1
Woodworking	144.9	183.3	139.4	174.2	160.5	167.2
Paper and board	67.9	63.3	64.7	59.8	32.8	56.3
Printing and publishing	93.6	125.8	89.8	122.4	62.8	104.7
Plastic products	16.2	31.4	14.6	29.6	15.5	21.3
Leather industry	68.4	65.2	65.7	63.0	49.3	54.2
Footwear industry	89.8	90.1	81.7	86.5	72.1	81.7
Textile industry	508.4	582.6	500.4	566.6	299.8	527.7
Clothing industry	195.8	216.0	182.0	205.0	142.0	183.5
Food and tobacco	*431.8*	*457.0*	*431.8*	*416.2*	*253.4*	*336.9*
Food and beverages	294.8	368.4	294.8	339.1	217.4	269.2
Tobacco manufactures	137.0	88.6	137.0	77.4	36.1	67.7
Total industry	**4,766.4**	**5,178.8**	**4,521.9**	**4,964.8**	**3796.2**	**4,768.4**

at the industry level within Germany as a whole between 1938 (annual average) and May 1939. Index numbers for monthly industrial output are taken from the statistical yearbook.[7] The post-war industry statistics report employment both for the end of September and averaged over the year.[8] The ratio of these levels for each industry is used to adjust the census data in order to estimate annual average levels of employment for 1950. This later adjustment is necessary because we cannot use the annual estimates from industry statistics directly, for they are not perfectly consistent with the census data. Inconsistency arises from differences (1) in the mechanism of reporting by industrial establishments and (2) in the way the two sources distinguish between industry plants and handcraft workshops. Thus, to be methodologically consistent, census data in 1939 must be compared with census data in 1950.

Industrial employment for West Germany in 1948 is determined by aggregating the average of monthly employment levels in the Bizonal Area and in the French occupation zone.[9] Conceptually, these figures are consistent with the annual industry statistics published from 1950 onward. Table A3.1 reports levels of employment by industry. To account for the growth of labour input between 1938, 1948, and 1950, the rate of employment expansion is adjusted for changes in average working hours. Several sources are used in combination that report average weekly hours for manual labour at the industry level.[10] The only critical simplifying assumption is that there were no significant differences in the length of the workweek within individual industries between the different parts of Germany in the year 1938.

Appendix 4: The Commodity Structure of German Exports, 1928–1970

This appendix reports a constant-price dataset of pre-war German and post-war West German exports (Table A4.1). Values for 1950 and 1955 are drawn directly from the official trade statistics.[11] For 1960, 1965, and 1970, they were computed by linking several constant-price datasets that

[7] *Statistisches Jahrbuch* 1939/40, 382–3.
[8] IndBRD, Series 4, No. 9 (1955), 5–6.
[9] Control Commission for Germany (UK), *Monthly Statistical Bulletins*, different volumes (1948–9); Commandement en Chef Francais en Allemagne, *Bulletin Statistique*, No. 7 (Oct. 1948), No. 9 (April 1949).
[10] For 1939, see Hachtmann (1989), 51; Länderrat (1949), 469–71; and *Statistisches Jahrbuch* 1939/40, 384–85. For 1948 and 1950, see Schudlich (1987), 158–67; and *Statistisches Jahrbuch* 1951, 412–18.
[11] Außenhandel, Part 1 (1951), 7–11; ibid. (1956), 19–21.

Table A4.1 *The commodity structure of German/West German exports in million 1950 DM*

Product groups	West (%)	1928	1936	1942	1950	1955	1960	1965	1970
I. Foodstuffs		1,196.9	279.1	647.2	195.7	709.6	1,235.2	2,172.3	4,850.8
Live animals		34.2	1.2	29.3	21.8	45.2	38.5	75.4	221.9
Animal products		38.4	21.5	44.3	25.9	137.4	211.6	356.9	1,053.7
Crops (raw and processed)		1,015.6	153.5	444.1	70.1	338.7	666.1	1,139.3	2,828.4
Beverages		108.7	103.0	129.5	77.8	188.3	319.0	600.6	746.8
II. Industrial raw materials	76.9	2,695.3	1,898.0	2,169.7	1,218.1	1,309.5	1,830.9	2,191.2	3,457.6
Wool and furs	65.4	577.1	53.8	46.4	95.7	129.9	247.7	285.3	381.6
Cocoon, textile plants and rag	75.4	136.7	25.0	127.7	55.7	177.5	284.1	686.8	1 512.7
Stump-wood, timber and cellulose	71.7	115.1	116.8	107.1	82.0	54.6	91.9	87.5	121.3
Animal and vegetable fats	66.8	50.5	11.2	40.2	4.9	5.5	4.1	4.2	32.4
Hard coal	80.0	1,164.5	1,474.1	1,519.7	799.2	660.3	897.9	677.8	809.9
Brown coal and briquette	90.5	77.6	36.4	51.4	51.5	53.9	44.4	39.5	32.5
Crude oil	100.0	7.1	0.5	10.5	0.7	0.0	0.1	15.4	13.4
Metallic ores	5.5	287.7	22.7	109.9	12.6	67.0	54.2	108.5	121.3
Rock and potassium salt	45.9	138.6	80.3	119.6	47.1	21.6	29.7	27.2	35.9
Other minerals	87.4	111.3	67.1	33.0	57.7	95.5	117.4	188.8	276.0
Other raw materials and waste	64.1	29.1	10.0	4.3	11.0	43.7	59.3	70.0	120.6
II. Intermediary goods	72.8	7,280.9	5,257.2	4,597.4	3,474.1	7,059.6	13,305.3	21,085.9	41,649.3
Textiles (yarn)	56.8	368.5	292.9	163.7	103.6	230.3	491.8	1,082.6	5,731.4
Textiles (cloth)	58.3	998.3	544.5	433.3	277.1	823.0	1,086.5	2,042.4	3,851.5
Cured leather and furs	85.1	640.3	269.2	148.3	24.1	165.5	232.6	335.6	470.2
Rubber (raw and processed)	77.5	90.0	79.3	73.1	54.0	190.7	338.2	473.1	797.3
Cement, other building materials	78.1	171.9	137.5	105.3	123.6	190.7	253.0	349.6	571.2
Paper and pulp	46.5	451.6	387.3	355.4	61.6	87.7	151.9	235.6	731.5
Plywood	87.6	19.7	13.5	19.6	7.0	42.3	86.0	111.8	176.4
Iron and ferrous alloys	87.9	186.8	108.9	300.1	341.8	214.2	656.7	840.9	1,047.5
Non-ferrous metals	83.9	232.3	18.1	138.7	194.3	184.0	335.8	351.1	466.6
Coke	95.1	517.0	417.9	251.0	474.1	655.7	634.2	568.1	603.3
Petrochemicals	86.3	45.1	39.8	100.2	39.8	325.8	553.8	983.8	1,825.6
Chemical fertilisers and pesticides	74.4	299.2	186.0	89.3	177.1	461.6	692.0	732.3	801.5
Glass	55.6	53.3	48.5	59.6	17.6	74.9	171.8	273.5	569.1

Technical oils, grease and wax	77.2	43.5	37.8	42.2	25.1	151.9	182.2	291.6	539.6
Glue and gelatine	85.6	36.2	14.6	5.2	7.3	50.5	102.0	173.2	170.0
Dye-stuffs	74.4	789.9	545.9	275.9	254.6	381.1	622.9	997.5	1,938.2
Explosives, ammunition and matches	28.6	20.3	29.7	62.4	5.2	28.5	47.2	42.9	52.8
Synthetic materials	74.4	35.2	45.9	47.8	22.5	283.5	953.3	2,540.7	6,739.1
Other chemical intermediaries	78.8	640.1	522.6	414.2	340.1	1,068.3	2,117.6	4,012.5	8,124.1
Iron and steel products	66.1	1,268.6	1,198.1	1,215.5	773.0	1,059.0	2,994.2	3,693.0	5,004.9
Non-ferrous metal products	82.6	227.8	245.4	129.4	111.3	214.2	331.4	585.3	968.0
Other intermediary goods	59.4	145.3	73.8	167.5	39.4	176.2	270.1	369.0	469.7
III. Finished goods		10,375.6	6,444.2	4,134.6	3,510.3	12,262.8	22,797.1	33,435.0	57,717.4
Clothing, hosiery and napery	25.3	556.6	411.5	254.2	64.2	287.6	670.5	1,356.5	4,958.4
Leather products (incl. footwear)	77.2	213.2	101.3	85.4	15.2	140.4	175.9	292.2	521.1
Stationary products	54.0	317.3	269.4	212.3	18.5	63.9	119.0	247.8	607.5
Printed products	43.1	85.2	111.4	115.9	23.9	135.4	361.7	622.0	1,189.7
Woodenware (incl. furniture)	69.9	56.7	29.3	18.3	32.9	76.9	168.4	312.9	728.7
Pottery (incl. China-ware)	39.1	212.2	169.7	90.7	61.6	201.7	267.1	324.7	408.1
Glass products	53.2	127.9	88.6	60.9	33.8	144.2	173.1	184.6	277.6
Fabricated metal products	82.2	2,454.6	1,072.9	624.3	823.5	1,514.3	2,199.5	2,851.1	4,617.6
Steel constructions	85.3	620.5	371.1	175.4	206.6	576.5	1,011.2	1,327.5	1,913.7
Machine tools	56.3	2,149.3	1,429.6	827.5	969.9	2,977.2	4,811.1	6,825.8	10,286.3
Water vessels	75.9	345.1	444.3	391.7	14.3	465.0	1,344.7	1,112.3	1,108.0
Transport vehicles	78.9	41.4	186.5	195.0	404.6	1,761.0	4,038.3	6,971.7	11,472.2
Other vehicles	71.1	180.1	128.7	89.3	71.7	207.1	216.4	269.9	390.5
Electrical equipment	40.3	769.5	698.5	467.6	308.1	1,805.0	3,277.2	4,408.1	7,982.7
Watches	95.8	163.4	112.2	12.4	56.5	172.3	196.7	192.9	278.3
Optical and precision instruments	47.9	324.5	208.3	109.5	175.1	570.4	990.9	1,295.8	1,877.8
Musical instruments	66.2	276.6	84.0	38.1	28.2	68.7	76.3	89.5	94.2
Toys and decorations	51.5	348.3	155.6	23.3	37.5	126.0	114.5	143.9	191.4
Celluloid and plastic products	74.8	198.7	74.7	31.1	17.4	118.0	246.2	507.5	1,712.2
Photochemical products	74.4	96.2	65.7	65.3	11.0	77.8	131.1	211.9	446.5
Pharmaceuticals and cosmetics	74.4	279.9	144.5	131.6	93.3	364.6	939.3	1,776.6	3,390.9
Other chemical products	75.4	231.9	43.5	74.0	28.9	306.3	843.7	1,420.5	2,866.2
Other finished goods	78.5	326.5	43.0	40.7	13.7	102.5	424.5	789.2	397.7
IV. All commodities	65.8	20,351.8	13,599.4	10,901.7	8,202.5	20,631.9	37,933.2	56,712.1	102,824.3

used different benchmarks.[12] I converted the values for 1928, 1936, and 1942 into 1950 DM based on the ratio of export weights reported in the pre-war, wartime, and post-war trade statistics.[13] For water vessels, the sources report numbers instead of gross tonnage.

From 1936 onward, the official trade statistics report data for almost 200 product types, which catalogued into 60 product groups. This re-aggregation makes the statistics for 1928 compatible with the data for later years and groups closely related products, which alone would have accounted for very small fractions of German exports. The conversion of all export values into 1950 DM was made based on all product types reported in the official sources, in order to account for differences in unit values between the aggregated products.

The West German share in German industrial exports in 1936 was computed on the basis of provincial data reported in the 1936 industry census (Reichsamt 1939, 148–59). The census only reports data on mining and manufacturing. I assumed that West Germany had exactly the same share in the export of non-food agricultural raw materials, such as wool and furs, cocoon and textile plant, as well as animal and vegetable fats, from Germany as a whole as in the exports of the sub-industries that processed these materials. This approach can be justified on the ground that material-intensive industries tend to locate to their domestic raw-material deposits, if those are domestically produced. In addition, I assumed equal shares for West Germany in the export of all chemical products. This assumption can be justified by the fact that the German chemical industry was dominated by giant firms operating in concentrated locations, such as Bayer in Leverkusen or BASF in Ludwigshafen. The West German share in the miscellaneous product groups of raw materials, intermediaries, and finished goods was estimated based on census data reported for the sub-industries that did not correspond to any of the re-aggregated product groups in the dataset.

[12] Außenhandel, Part 1 (1961), 19–21; Fachserie G/ 1 (1966), 19–21; ibid. (1970), 21–3.
[13] StatDR, Vol. 383.1 (1930), 10–13; Außenhandel. *Ergänzungsheft 1942*, 8–12; Außenhandel, Part 1 (1951), 7–11.

Bibliography

Archival Sources

Bundesarchiv, Berlin-Lichterfelde

BArch R 3/1626a Hunscha, Kurt. *Die wirtschaftlichen und finanziellen Beziehungen Deutschlands zu den von ihm besetzten Ländern Kontinentaleuropas 1940–1944.* Confidential statistical report, used as evidence at the International Military Tribunal in Nuremberg.

BArch R 3102/3309. *Gesamtabsatz und beschäftigte Personen in der deutschen Industrie 1936, gegliedert nach deutschen Ländern und Provinzen.*

BArch R 3102/5922. *Produktions-Aufwand und Ertrag 1936.*

LSE Library Archives

Fachstelle Stahl und Eisen der Verwaltung für Wirtschaft des Vereinigten Wirtschaftsgebiets (FSE). *Statistical quarterly report October to December 1948 and yearly summary 1948.* Confidential (February 1949), 43/1940.

Office of the Military Governor for Germany, US Zone (OMGUS). *Ownership and control of the Ruhr industries.* Special report of the military governor (November 1948), 43/1480.

Economic developments since the currency reform. Special report of the military governor (November 1948), 43/1481.

Three years of reparations: Progress of reparations from Germany in the form of capital industrial equipment. Special report of the military governor (November 1948), 43/1482.

Economic data on Potsdam Germany. Special report of the military governor (September 1947), 43/1483.

Reichsministerium für Arbeit. *Die Ergebnisse der Arbeitsbucherhebung vom 25. Juni 1938*, No. 2993 [Classified], 43/710.

Statistisches Reichsamt. Der Außenhandel Deutschlands. Sondernachweis (Außenhandel). *Ergänzungs-heft 1941: Der deutsche Außenhandel nach Ländern*, No. 55 [Classified], 43/ HA 201.

Außenhandel. *Ergänzungsheft 1942: Der deutsche Außenhandel nach Ländern*, No. 64 [Classified].

Außenhandel. *Ergänzungsheft 1943: Der deutsche Außenhandel nach Ländern*, No. 330 [Classified].

Verwaltung für Wirtschaft des Vereinigten Wirtschaftsgebiets, Amt für Stahl und Eisen (ASE). *Statistical annual report 1947.* Confidential (February 1948), 43/1940.

Staatsbibliothek zu Berlin

OMGUS. *Reparations (cumulative review): Report of the military governor,* September 1945–June 1948, No. 48, 10 Per 138/6–48.

Food and agriculture: Monthly report of military governor, US zone, 20 September 1945, No. 2 (Confidential), Zsn 125123–2/32.

Food and agriculture: Monthly report of the military governor, US zone, 20 April 1946, No. 9, Zsn 125123–9/32.

Food and agriculture (cumulative review): Monthly report of military governor, 1 March 1946–28 February 1947, No. 20, Zsn 125123–20/32.

Food and agriculture (cumulative review): Report of military governor, March 1947–February 1948, No. 32, Zsn 125123/32.

Public health and medical affairs (cumulative review): Report of the military governor, US zone, 20 May 1946, No. 10, Zsn 124144/10.

Public health and medical affairs (cumulative review): Report of the military governor, US zone, 1 May 1946–31 March 1947, No. 22, Zsn 124144/22.

Manpower, trade unions and working conditions: Monthly report of the military governor, 8 May 1945–28 February 1947, No. 20, Zsn 125159/20.

Manpower, trade unions and working conditions (cumulative review): Report of the military governor, March 1947–February 1948, No. 32, Zsn 125159/32.

Industry, including coal (cumulative review): Report of the military governor, 1 July 1946–30 June 1947, No. 24, Zsn 125165–24/31.

Industry, including coal: Monthly report of the military governor, US zone, 20 July 1946, No. 12, Zsn 125165–12/31.

Transportation: Monthly report of the military governor, US zone, 20 September 1945, No. 2 (Restricted), Zsn 1251166–2/31.

Transportation (cumulative review): Monthly report of the military governor, US zone, 20 September 1946, No. 14, Zsn 1251166–14/31.

Transportation (cumulative review): Report of the military governor, 1 September 1946–31 August 1947, No. 26, Zsn 1251166–26/31.

Official Publications

Bank deutscher Länder (BdL). 1955. *Statistisches Handbuch der Bank deutscher Länder 1948–1954.* Frankfurt: Druck- und Verlagshaus Frankfurt a. M.

Bundesministerium für Arbeit. 1955. *Die Arbeiter und Angestellten nach Beruf und Alter sowie die Lehrlingshaltung in der Bundesrepublik Deutschland am 31. Dezember 1950: Ergebnisse einer Sondererhebung der Arbeitsämter.*

1952. *Die beschäftigten Arbeiter, Angestellten und Beamten in der Bundesrepublik Deutschland 1938 und 1951.*

1951. *Arbeits- und Sozialstatistische Mitteilungen,* 2 (1).

Bundesministerium für Arbeit und Sozialordnung. 1972. *Hauptergebnisse der Arbeits- und Sozialstatistik 1971.*

1966. *Hauptergebnisse der Arbeits- und Sozialstatistik 1965.*

Bundesministerium für Vertriebene. 1954. *Dokumentation der Vertreibung der Deutschen aus Ost-Mitteleuropa.* Wolfenbüttel: Rock & Co. Vol. 1: Die Vertreibung der deutschen Bevölkerung aus den Gebieten östlich der Oder-Neisse.

Commandement en Chef Française en Allemagne. *Bulletin Statistique*, No. 7 (October 1948) and No. 9 (April 1949).

Control Commission for Germany (British Element). *Monthly statistical bulletins of the Control Commission for Germany*, different volumes.

Federal Ministry for the Marshall Plan/Bundesministerium für den Marshallplan. 1953. *Recovery under the Marshall Plan, 1948–1952: Twelfth, and final report of the German Federal Government on the progress of the Marshall Plan.* Bonn and Lüdenscheid: Carl v. d. Linnepe.

1951. *Fifth and sixth report of the German Federal Government on the progress of the Marshall Plan.*

Kultusministerkonferenz: Ständige Konferenz der Kultusminister der Länder in der Bundesrepublik Deutschland. 1969. *Der Ausbau der Ingenieurschulen 1958 bis 1968.* Dokumentation, Nr. 28.

Länderrat des Amerikanischen Besatzungsgebiets (Länderrat). 1949. *Statistisches Handbuch von Deutschland, 1928–1944.* Munich: F. Ehrenwirth.

OMGUS, Ministerial Collecting Center, Economic Division, APO 742. 1946. *Statistical handbook of Germany.* Part I: Population and employment; Part III.A: Industry and handicraft: general.

Reichsamt für Wehrwirtschaftliche Planung (Reichsamt). 1939. *Die Deutsche Industrie: Gesamtergebnisse der amtlichen Produktionsstatistik.* Berlin: Verlag für Sozialpolitik, Wirtschaft und Statistik.

Sachverständigenrat für Begutachtung der Gesamtwirtschaftlichen Entwicklung (Sachverständigenrat). 1965. *Jahresgutachten 1964/65: Stabiles, Geld stetiges Wachstum.* Stuttgart and Mainz: Kohlhammer.

1968. *Jahresgutachten 1967/68: Stabilität im Wachstum.* Stuttgart and Mainz: Kohlhammer.

1991. *Jahresgutachten 1990/91: Auf dem Wege zur wirtschaftlichen Einheit Deutschlands.* Stuttgart: Metzler-Poeschel. Statistischer Anhang.

Statistisches Bundesamt. 2000. *50 Jahre Wohnen in Deutschland.* Stuttgart: Metzler-Poeschel.

1973. *Lange Reihen zur Wirtschaftsentwicklung.* Stuttgart and Mainz: W. Kohlhammer.

1958. *Die deutschen Vertreibungsverluste: Bevölkerungsbilanzen für die deutschen Vertreibungsgebiete 1939/50.* Stuttgart: W. Kohlhammer.

Der Außenhandel der Bundesrepublik Deutschland (Außenhandel), Part 1, Zusammenfassende Übersichten. *Jahresheft*, different volumes.

Fachserie A. 1967. VZ 1961, Vol. 6. Bevölkerung und Kultur. *Volks- und Berufszählung vom 6. Juni 1961: Vertriebene und Deutsche aus der SBZ, Verteilung und Struktur.*

Fachserie A/1. 1961. Bevölkerung und Kultur. Gebiet und Bevölkerung. *Bevölkerungsstand und -entwicklung: 1960.*

Fachserie A/4. 1966. Bevölkerung und Kultur. Vertriebene und Flüchtlinge. *Bevölkerungs-, kultur- und wirtschaftsstatistische Ergebnisse 1954 bis 1966.*

Fachserie C. 1965. Unternehmen und Arbeitsstätten. Einzelveröffentlichungen. *Arbeitsstättenzählung vom 6. Juni 1961: Nichtlandwirtschaftliche Arbeitsstätten (örtliche Einheiten) und Beschäftigte in den Ländern und deren Verwaltungsbezirken.*

Fachserie D/1. 1966. Industrie und Handwerk. Beschäftigung und Umsatz, Brennstoff- und Energie-versorgung. *Jahreszahlen der Industrieberichterstattung 1960–1965.*

Fachserie D/1. 1971. Industrie und Handwerk. Betriebe und Unternehmen der Industrie. *Beschäftigung und Umsatz, Brennstoff- und Energieversorgung 1970.*

Fachserie D/4. 1964. Industrie und Handwerk. Sonderbeiträge zur Industrie-statistik. *Regionale Verteilung der Industriebetriebe nach Industriegruppen: Betriebe und Beschäftigte in den kreisfreien Städten und Landkreisen in September 1962.*

Fachserie E. 1961. Bauwirtschaft, Bautätigkeit, Wohnungen. *Gebäudezählung vom 6. Juni 1961,* Vol. 3: *Hauptergebnisse nach Kreisen.*

Fachserie G/1. Außenhandel. Zusammenfassende Übersichten. *Jahresheft,* different volumes.

Fachserie L/7. 1963. Finanzen und Steuern. Umsatzsteuer. *Ergebnisse der Umsatzsteuerstatistik 1961.*

Industrie der Bundesrepublik Deutschland (IndBRD), Part 1. Beschäftigung und Umsatz, Brennstoff- und Energieversorgung. *Ergebnisse der monatlichen Industrieberichterstattung,* different volumes.

IndBRD, Series 4. 1956. Sonderveröffentlichungen, No. 8. *Neuberechnung des Index der industriellen Nettoproduktion.*

IndBRD, Series 4. 1955. Sonderveröffentlichungen, No. 9. *Beschäftigung und Umsatz, Brennstoff- und Energieversorgung in den Jahren 1950 bis 1954: Jahreszahlen der Industrieberichterstattung.*

IndBRD, Series 4. 1957. Sonderveröffentlichungen, No. 14. *Beschäftigung und Umsatz, Brennstoff- und Energieversorgung in den Jahren 1952 bis 1956: Jahreszahlen der Industrieberichterstattung.*

IndBRD, Series 4. 1957. Sonderveröffentlichungen, No. 16. *Die regionale Verteilung der Industriebetriebe: Betriebe und Beschäftigte der Industrie in den kreisfreien Städte und Landkreisen 1950 bis 1956.*

Statistik der Bundesrepublik Deutschland (StatBRD), Vol. 34. 1955. *Einführung in die methodischen und systematischen Grundlagen der Volks- und Berufszählung vom 13.9.1950.*

StatBRD, Vol. 35.3. 1953. *Die Bevölkerung der Bundesrepublik Deutschland nach der Zählung vom 13.9.1950: Die Bevölkerung nach dem Wohnort am 1.9.1939.*

StatBRD, Vol. 35.9. 1956. *Die Bevölkerung der Bundesrepublik Deutschland nach der Zählung vom 13.9.1950: Textheft.*

StatBRD, Vol. 38.2. 1955. *Gebäude- und Wohnungszählung in der Bundesrepublik Deutschland vom 13.9.1950: Hauptergebnisse nach Kreisen.*

StatBRD, Vol. 39. 1955. *Der Bestand an Gebäuden in der Bundesrepublik Deutschland nach der Zählung vom 13.9.1950.*

StatBRD, Vol. 40. 1955. *Der Bestand an Wohnungen und Unterkünften außerhalb von Wohnungen in der Bundesrepublik Deutschland nach der Zählung vom 13.9.1950.*

StatBRD, Vol. 41. 1955. *Die Bewohner in Wohnungen und Unterkünften außerhalb von Wohnungen in der Bundesrepublik Deutschland nach der Zählung vom 13.9.1950.*

StatBRD, Vol. 45.2. 1952. *Die nichtlandwirtschaftlichen Arbeitsstätten in der Bundesrepublik Deutschland nach der Zählung vom 13.9.1950: Die nichtlandwirtschaftlichen Arbeitsstätten (örtliche Einheiten) und die darin beschäftigten Personen.*

StatBRD, Vol. 46.1–7. 1953. *Die nichtlandwirtschaftlichen Arbeitsstätten in den Ländern und deren Verwaltungsbezirken nach der Zählung vom 13.9.1950.*

StatBRD, Vol. 47.1. 1956. *Die nichtlandwirtschaftlichen Arbeitsstätten in der Bundesrepublik Deutschland nach der Zählung vom 13.9.1950: Textband mit Kartenwerk, Textband.*

StatBRD, Vol. 59. 1957. *Die öffentliche Finanzwirtschaft in den Rechnungsjahren 1948 bis 1954.*

StatBRD, Vol. 90. 1954. *Die Verdienste der Arbeiter in der Gewerblichen Wirtschaft im November 1951: Ergebnisse der Gehalts- und Lohnstrukturerhebung 1951/52.*

StatBRD, Vol. 112. 1955. *Die Umsätze der Umsatzsteuerpflichtigen und deren Besteuerung.*

StatBRD, Vol. 114. 1955. *Die Vertriebenen und Flüchtlinge in der Bundesrepublik Deutschland in der Jahren 1946 bis 1953.*

StatBRD, Vol. 201.1. 1957. *Wohnungsstatistik 1956/57: Wohnungen und Wohnparteien nach der allgemeinen Erhebung vom 25.9.1956.*

StatBRD, Vol. 203.2. 1958. *Handwerkszählung vom 25.9.1956: Betriebe und Beschäftigte in den kreisfreien Städten und Landkreisen.*

StatBRD, Vol. 211. 1958. *Der Eingliederungsstand von Vertriebenen und Sowjetzonenflüchtlingen.*

StatBRD, Vol. 212. 1958. *Die Umsätze der Umsatzsteuerpflichtigen und deren Besteuerung 1956.*

StatBRD, Vol. 246.1. 1960. *Gehalts- und Lohnstrukturerhebung 1957: Verdienste der Arbeiter in der Industrie im Oktober 1957.*

Statistisches Jahrbuch für die Bundesrepublik Deutschland, different volumes.

Statistisches Reichsamt. Statistik des Deutschen Reichs (StatDR), Vol. 366.2. 1929. *Der Auswärtige Handel Deutschlands im Jahre 1928 verglichen mit den Jahren 1926 und 1927: Spezialhandel nach Erdteilen und Ländern und Anteil der einzelnen Länder.*

StatDR, Vol. 383.1. 1930. *Der Auswärtige Handel Deutschlands im Jahre 1929: Spezialhandel einschließlich der Reparations-Sachlieferungen.*

StatDR, Vol. 550. 1941. *Amtliches Gemeindeverzeichnis für das Deutsche Reich auf Grund der Volkszählung 1939.*

StatDR, Vol. 568.8–14. 1942–4. *Volks-, Berufs- und Betriebszählung vom 17. Mai 1939: Nichtlandwirtschaftliche Arbeitsstättenzählung: Die nichtlandwirtschaftlichen Arbeitsstätten in den Reichsteilen und Verwaltungsbezirken.*

StatDR, Einzelschriften, No. 39. 1941. *Die Steuerleistung der Finanzamtsbezirke in den Rechnungsjahren 1926 bis 1938.*

Statistisches Jahrbuch für das Deutsche Reich, different volumes.

The United States Strategic Bombing Survey (USSBS). 1945. *Over-all report: European war.* Washington, DC: US Government Printing Office.

USSBS, Overall Economic Effects Division (OEED). 1945. *The effects of strategic bombing on the German war economy.* Washington, DC: Government Printing Office.

Wissenschaftlicher Beirat beim Bundesministerium für Wirtschaft (Wissenschaftlicher Beirat). 1973. *Sammelband der Gutachten von 1948 bis 1972.* Göttingen: Schwartz & Co.

Secondary Literature

Abelshauser, Werner. 2004. *Deutsche Wirtschaftsgeschichte seit 1945.* Munich: C. H. Beck.

2001. Umbruch und Persistenz: Das deutsche Produktionsregime in historischer Perspektive. *Geschichte und Gesellschaft* 27 (4): 503–23.

1999. Kriegswirtschaft und Wirtschaftswunder: Deutschlands wirtschaftliche Mobilisierung für den Zweiten Weltkrieg und die Folgen für die Nachkriegszeit. *Vierteljahreshefte für Zeitgeschichte* 47 (4): 503–38.

1989. Hilfe und Selbsthilfe: zur Funktion des Marshallplans beim westdeutschen Wiederaufbau. *Vierteljahrshefte für Zeitgeschichte* 37 (1): 85–113.

1987. *Die langen fünfziger Jahre: Wirtschaft und Gesellschaft in der Bundesrepublik Deutschland 1949–1966.* Düsseldorf: Schwann.

1985. Schopenhauers Gesetz und die Währungsreform: Drei Anmerkungen zu einem methodischen Problem. *Vierteljahrshefte für Zeitgeschichte* 33 (2): 214–18.

1984. Der Kleine Marshallplan: Handelsintegration durch inneneuropäische Wirtschaftshilfe 1948–1950. In *Wirtschaftliche und politische Integration in Europa im 19. und 20. Jahrhundert,* ed. Helmut Berding, 212–24. Geschichte und Gesellschaft, Sonderheft 10. Göttingen: Vandenhoeck & Ruprecht.

1983. *Wirtschaftsgeschichte der Bundesrepublik Deutschland 1945–1980.* Frankfurt: Suhrkamp.

1977. Die Rekonstruktion der Westdeutschen Wirtschaft und die Rolle der Besatzungspolitik. In *Politische und Ökonomische Stabilisierung Westdeutschlands,* ed. Claus Scharf and Hans-Jürgen Schröder, 1–17. Wiesbaden: Steiner.

1975. *Wirtschaft in Westdeutschland 1945–1948: Rekonstruktion und Wachstumsbedingungen in der amerikanischen und britischen Zone.* Stuttgart: Deutsche Verlagsanstalt.

Abelshauser, Werner, Stefan Fisch, Dirk Hoffmann, Carl Ludwig Holtfrerich, and Albrecht Ritschl, eds. 2016. *Wirtschaftspolitik in Deutschland 1917–1990.* Abschlussberichts der Unabhängigen Geschichts-kommission zur Aufarbeitung der Geschichte des Bundeswirtschaftsministeriums (BMWi) und seiner Vorgängerinstitutionen. IV vols. Oldenburg: De Gruyter.

Abramovitz, Moses. 1994. Catch-up and convergence in the postwar growth boom and after. In *Convergence and productivity: Cross-national studies and historical evidence,* ed. William J. Baumol, Richard R. Nelson, and Edward N. Wolff, 86–125. Oxford: Oxford University Press.

1986. Catching up, forging ahead and falling behind. *Journal of Economic History* 46 (2): 385–406.

Ambrosius, Gerold. 2001. *Staat und Wirtschaftsordnung: Eine Einführung in Theorie und Geschichte.* Grundzüge der modernen Wirtschaftsgeschichte. Stuttgart: Steiner.

2000. Von Kriegswirtschaft zu Kriegswirtschaft, 1914–1945. In *Deutsche Wirtschafts-geschichte: Ein Jahrtausend im Überblick,* ed. Michael North, 282–350. Munich: C. H. Beck.

1996. Der Beitrag der Vertriebenen und Flüchtlinge zum Wachstum der westdeutschen Wirtschaft nach dem Zweiten Weltkrieg. *Jahrbuch für Wirtschaftsgeschichte* 37 (2): 39–71.

1993. Wirtschaftlicher Strukturwandlung und Technikentwicklung. In *Modernisierung im Wieder-aufbau: Die westdeutsche Gesellschaft der 50er Jahre,* ed. Axel Schieldt and Arnold Sywottek, 107–28. Bonn: J. H. W. Dietz.

1990. *Staat und Wirtschaft im 20. Jahrhundert.* Enzyklopädie Deutscher Geschichte, Vol. 7. Munich: Oldenburg.

1984. Europäische Integration und wirtschaftlicher Entwicklung der Bundesrepublik Deutschland in den Fünfziger Jahren. In *Wirtschaftliche und politische Integration in Europa im 19. und 20. Jahrhundert,* ed. Helmut Berding, Geschichte und Gesellschaft, Sonderheft 10, 271–94. Göttingen: Vandenhoeck & Ruprecht.

1977. *Die Durchsetzung der Sozialen Marktwirtschaft in Westdeutschland, 1945–1949.* Studien zur Zeitgeschichte, Band 10. Stuttgart: Westdeutsche Verlags-Anstalt.

Ambrosius, Gerold, and Hartmut Kaeble. 1992. Gesellschaftliche und wirtschaftliche Folgen des Booms der 1950er und 1960er Jahre. In *Der Boom 1948–1973: Gesellschaftliche und wirtschaft-liche Folgen in der BRD und Europa,* ed. Hartmut Kaeble, 7–32. Opladen: Westdeutscher Verlag.

Arndt, Klaus Dieter. 1955. *Wohnungsversorgung und Mietenniveau in der Bundesrepublik.* DIW Sonderhefte, No. 35. Berlin: Duncker & Humblot.

Asenova, Vera. 2016. German economic exploitation of Bulgaria, 1932–44: Short-term policies and long-term institutional effects. In *Paying for Hitler's war: The consequences of Nazi hegemony for Europe,* ed. Jonas Scherner and Eugene N. White, 366–89. Cambridge: Cambridge University Press.

Baar, Lothar, Rainer Karlsch, and Werner Matschke. 1995. Kriegsfolgen und Kriegslasten Deutschlands: Zerstörungen, Demontagen und Reparationen. In *Enquete-Kommission Aufarbeitung von Geschichte und Folgen der SED-Diktatur in Deutschland: Machtstrukturen und Entscheidungsmechanismen im SED-Staat und die Frage der Verantwortung,* ed. Deutscher Bundestag, Vol. II.2: *Macht, Entscheidung, Verantwortung,* 868–988. Frankfurt: Suhrkamp Nomos.

Barro, Robert J. 1991. Economic growth in a cross section of countries. *Quarterly Journal of Economics* 106 (2): 407–44.

Barro, Robert J., and Xavier Sala-i-Martin. 1995. *Economic growth.* New York: McGraw-Hill.

1992. Convergence. *Journal of Political Economy* 100 (2): 223–51.

Bauer, Thomas, and Klaus F. Zimmermann. 1996. Gastarbeiter und Wirtschaft-sentwicklung in Nachkriegsdeutschland. *Jahrbuch für Wirtschaftsgeschichte* 37 (2): 73–108.

Bauer, Wilhelm. 1947. Die Kriegsschäden am deutschen Volkskörper. In *Die deutsche Wirtschaft zwei Jahre nach dem Zusammenbruch: Tatsachen und Probleme,* ed. Ferdinand Friedensburg, 14–36. Berlin: Albert Nauck & Co.

Baumgart, Egon. 1972. Produktionsvolumen und -potenzial, Produktionsfaktoren der Industrie im Gebiet der Bundesrepublik Deutschland: Ergebnisse für die Zeit von 1959 bis 1970 mit Ausblick auf 1971/72. *Vierteljahreshefte zur Wirtschaftsforschung* 41 (1–2): 61–78.

Baumgart, Egon, and Rolf Krengel. 1970. *Die industrielle Vermögensrechnung des DIW: Ergebnisse einer Neuberechnung.* DIW Beiträge Zur Strukturforschung No. 10. Berlin: Duncker & Humblot.

Baumgart, Egon, Rolf Krengel, and Werner Moritz. 1960. *Die Finanzierung der industriellen Expansion in der Bundesrepublik während der Jahre des Wiederaufbaus.* Berlin: Duncker & Humblot.

Baumol, William J. 1986. Productivity growth, convergence, and welfare: What the long-run data show. *American Economic Review* 76 (5): 1072–85.

Becker, Erich. 1951. Beschäftigte und Arbeitslose 1950 und 1951: Für die Städte über 20.000 Einwohner im Kalenderjahr 1950 und am 30. Juni 1951. *Statistisches Jahrbuch deutscher Gemeinden* 39 (1): 68–85.

Beer, Matthias. 2000. … die gleichen Erinnerungen und eine ähnliche Lebensauffassung: Zur Eingliederung der Siebenbürger Sachsen in der Bundesrepublik Deutschland. *Zeitschrift für Siebenbürgische Landeskunde* 23 (2): 218–28.

Bengtsson, Erik. 2015. Wage restraint in Scandinavia: During the postwar period or the neoliberal age? *European Review of Economic History* 19 (4): 359–81.

Benz, Wolfgang. 1991. *Zwischen Hitler und Adenauer: Studien zur deutschen Nachkriegsgesellschaft.* Frankfurt: Fischer.

Berger, Helge. 1997. *Konjunkturpolitik im Wirtschaftswunder: Handlungsspielräume und Verhaltensmuster von Bundesbank und Regierung in den 1950er Jahren.* Tübingen: Mohr Siebeck.

Berger, Helge, and Albrecht O. Ritschl. 1995a. Die Rekonstruktion der Arbeitsteilung in Europa: Eine neue Sicht des Marshallplans in Deutschland 1947–1951. *Vierteljahrshefte für Zeitgeschichte* 45 (3): 473–520.

1995b. Germany and the political economy of the Marshall Plan, 1947–52: A re-revisionist view. In *Europe's post-war recovery,* ed. Barry Eichengreen, 199–245. Cambridge: Cambridge University Press.

Berghahn, Volker R. 1999. Introduction: German big business and the quest for a European economic empire in the twentieth century. In *Quest for Economic Empire: European Strategies of German Big Business in the Twentieth Century,* ed. Volker R. Berghahn, 1–33. Providence and Oxford: Berghahn Books.

1986. *The Americanisation of West German industry, 1945–1973.* Leamington Spa: Berg.

Bignon, Vincent. 2009. Cigarette money and black market prices around the 1948 German miracle. EconomiX Working Papers, 2009–2. University of Paris West – Nanterre la Défense.

Boelcke, Willi A. 1993. Die Finanzpolitik des Dritten Reiches: Eine Darstellung. In *Deutschland 1933–1945: Neue Studien zur nationalsozialistischen Herrschaft,* ed. Karl D. Bracher, Manfred Funke, and Hans-Adolf Jacobsen, 95–117, Schriftenreihe Band 314. Bonn: Bundeszentrale für Politische Bildung.

1975. Probleme der Finanzierung von Militärausgaben. In *Wirtschaft und Rüstung am Vorabend des Zweiten Weltkriegs,* ed. Friedrich Forstmeier and Hans E. Volkmann, 14–38. Düsseldorf: Droste.

Boldorf, Michael, and Jonas Scherner. 2012. France's occupation cost and the war in the East: The contribution to the German war economy, 1940–4. *Journal of Contemporary History* 47 (2): 291–316.

Boltho, Andrea. 2001. Reconstruction after two world wars: Why a difference. *Journal of European Economic History* 30 (2): 429–58.

1982. *The European economy: Growth and crisis.* Oxford: Oxford University Press.

Booth, Alan, Joseph Melling, and Christoph Dartmann. 1997. Institutions and economic growth: The politics of productivity in West Germany, Sweden, and the United Kingdom, 1945–1955. *Journal of Economic History* 57 (2): 426–44.

Borchardt, Knut. 1991. *Perspectives on modern German economic history and policy.* Cambridge: Cambridge University Press.

Borchardt, Knut, and Christoph Buchheim. 1987. Die Wirkung der Marshallplan-Hilfe in Schlüsselbranchen der deutschen Wirtschaft. *Vierteljahrshefte für Zeitgeschichte* 35 (3): 317–47.

Bornemann, Fritz Otto, and Hans-Otto Linnhoff. 1958. *Die seit der Währungsreform begebenen Industrie-Anleihen.* Berlin: Duncker & Humblot.

Bosworth, Barry, and Susan M. Collins. 2003. The empirics of growth: An update. *Brookings Papers on Economic Activity* 34 (2): 113–206

Brakman, Steven, Harry Garretsen, and Marc Schramm. 2004. The strategic bombing of German cities during World War II and its impact on city growth. *Journal of Economic Geography* 4 (2): 201–18.

Braun, Hans-Joachim. 1990. *The German economy in the twentieth century.* London: Routledge.

Braun, Sebastian, and Toman O. Mahmoud. 2014. The employment effects of immigration: Evidence from the mass arrival of German expellees in postwar Germany. *Journal of Economic History* 74 (1): 69–108.

Broadberry, Steven N. 1997. Anglo-German productivity differences, 1870–1990. *European Review of Economic History* 1 (2): 247–67.

1996. Convergence: What the historical record shows. In *Quantitative aspects of post-war European economic growth*, ed. Bart van Ark and N. F. R. Crafts, 327–46. Cambridge: Cambridge University Press.

Browder, Dewey A. 1993. The GI dollar and the Wirtschaftswunder. *Journal of European Economic History* 22 (3): 601–11.

Buchheim, Christoph. 2001. Währungsreformen in Deutschland im 20. Jahrhundert: Ein Vergleich. *Vierteljahrschrift für Sozial- und Wirtschaftsgeschichte* 88 (2): 145–65.

1993. Marshall Plan and currency reform. In *American policy and the reconstruction of West Germany, 1945–1955*, ed. Jeffry M. Diefendorf, 69–83. Cambridge: Cambridge University Press.

1991. Die Notwendigkeit einer durchgreifenden Wirtschaftsreform zur Ankurbelung des west-deutschen Wirtschaftswachstums in den 1940er Jahren. In *Ordnungspolitische Weichen-stellungen nach dem Zweiten Weltkrieg*, ed. Dietmar Petzina, 55–66. Berlin: Duncker & Humblot.

1990. *Die Wiedereingliederung Westdeutschlands in der Weltwirtschaft, 1945–1958.* Munich: Oldenburg.

1989. Die Währungsreform in Westdeutschland im Jahre 1948: Einige ökonomische Aspekte. In *Währungsreform und Soziale Marktwirtschaft: Erfahrungen und Perspektiven nach 40 Jahren*, ed. Wolfram Fischer, 391–402. Berlin: Duncker & Humblot.

1988. Die Währungsreform 1948 in Westdeutschland. *Vierteljahreshefte für Zeitgeschichte* 36 (2): 189–231.

1986. Die besetzten Länder im Dienste der deutschen Kriegswirtschaft während des Zweiten Weltkriegs: Ein Bericht der Forschungsstelle für Wehrwirtschaft. *Vierteljahreshefte für Zeitgeschichte* 34 (1): 117–45.

Buchheit, Ronald. 1984. *Soziale Wohnungspolitik? Sozialstaat und Wohnungsversorgung in der Bundesrepublik*. Darmstadt: Verlag für wissenschaftliche Publikationen.

Budrass, Lutz, Jonas Scherner, and Jochen Streb. 2010. Fixed-price contracts, learning, and outsourcing: Explaining the continuous growth of output and labour productivity in the German aircraft industry during the Second World War. *Economic History Review* 63 (1): 107–36.

Bührer, Werner. 1997. *Westdeutschland in der OEEC: Eingliederung, Krise, Bewährung 1947–1961*. Munich: Oldenburg.

1990. Erzwungene oder freiwillige Liberalisierung? Die USA, die OEEC und die westdeutsche Außenhandelspolitik 1949–1952. In *Vom Marshallplan zur EWG: Die Eingliederung der Bundesrepublik in die westliche Welt*, ed. Ludolf Herbst, Werner Bührer, and Hanno Sowade, 139–62. Quellen und Darstellungen zur Zeitgeschichte, No. 30. Munich: Oldenburg.

1986. *Ruhrstahl und Europa: Die Wirtschaftsvereinigung Eisen- und Stahlindustrie und die Anfänge der europäischen Integration 1945–1952*. Munich: Oldenburg.

Buxbaum, Richard M. 2013. From Paris to London: The legal history of European reparation claims, 1946–1953. *Berkeley Journal of International Law* 31 (2): 323–47.

Carlin, Wendy. 1996. West German growth and institutions, 1945–90. In *Economic growth in Europe since 1945*, ed. N. F. R. Crafts and Gianni Toniolo, 455–97. Cambridge: Cambridge University Press.

1989. Economic reconstruction in Western Germany, 1945–55: The displacement of a 'vegetative control'. In *Reconstruction in post-war Germany: British occupation policy and the western zones, 1945–55*, ed. Ian D. Turner, 37–65. Oxford and New York: Berg.

Cass, David. 1965. Optimum growth in an aggregate model of capital accumulation. *Review of Economic Studies* 32 (3): 233–40.

Churchill, Winston. 1948. *The Second World War*. Vol. 1: *The gathering storm*. London: Cassel.

Crafts, N. F. R. 2009. Solow and growth accounting: A perspective from quantitative economic history. *History of Political Economy* 41 (Suppl. 1): 200–20.

1995. The golden age of economic growth in Western Europe, 1950–1973. *Economic History Review* 48 (3): 429–47.

Crafts, N. F. R., and Gianni Toniolo. 2010. Aggregate growth, 1950–2005. In *The Cambridge economic history of modern Europe*, Vol. 2: *1870 to the present*, ed. Stephen N. Broadberry and Kevin H. O'Rourke, 296–332. Cambridge: Cambridge University Press.

1996. Postwar growth: An overview. In *Economic growth in Europe since 1945*, ed. N. F. R. Crafts and Gianni Toniolo, 1–37. Cambridge: Cambridge University Press.

Custodis, Johann. 2016. Employing the enemy: The economic exploitation of POW and foreign labor from occupied territories by Nazi Germany. In *Paying for Hitler's war: The consequences of Nazi hegemony for Europe*, ed. Jonas Scherner and Eugene N. White, 67–100. Cambridge: Cambridge University Press.

Dedinger, Beatrice. 2006. Trade, history and geography: The geographical structure of trade in Germany since the late 19th century. *Journal of European Economic History* 35 (3): 551–79.

Delhaes-Guenther, Linda von. 2003. *Erfolgsfaktoren des westdeutschen Exports in den 1950er und 1960er Jahren*. Untersuchungen zur Wirtschafts-, Sozial- und Technikgeschichte, No. 22. Dortmund: Gesellschaft für westfälische Wirtschaftsgeschichte.

Denison, Edward F. 1967. *Why growth rates differ: Postwar experience in nine western countries*. Washington, DC: Brookings Institution.

Dezséri, Kálmán. 2000. Introducing currency convertibility in Western Europe in the 1950s. *Journal of European Economic History* 29 (1): 131–171.

Dowrick, Steve, and Duc-Tho Nguyen. 1989. OECD comparative economic growth 1950–85: Catch-up and convergence. *American Economic Review* 79 (5): 1010–30.

Dumke, Rolf H. 1990. Reassessing the Wirtschaftswunder: Reconstruction and postwar growth in West Germany in an international context. *Oxford Bulletin of Economics and Statistics* 52 (2): 451–91.

Dürr, Ernst. 1996. Die Soziale Marktwirtschaft: Ausgangsbedingungen, Programm, Realisierung. In *Wirtschaftsordnung und Wirtschaftspolitik in Deutschland, 1933 bis 1993*, ed. Jürgen Schneider and Wolfgang Harbrecht, 383–96. Stuttgart: Steiner.

Eichengreen, Barry. 2007. *The European economy since 1945: Coordinated capitalism and beyond*. Princeton, NJ: Princeton University Press.

1996. Institutions and economic growth: Europe after World War II. In *Economic growth in Europe since 1945*, ed. N. F. R. Crafts and Gianni Toniolo, 38–66. Cambridge: Cambridge University Press.

1995. The European Payments Union: An efficient mechanism for rebuilding Europe's trade. In *Europe's post-war recovery*, ed. Barry Eichengreen, 169–95. Cambridge: Cambridge University Press.

Eichengreen, Barry, and Douglas A. Irwin. 1995. Trade blocs, currency blocs, and the reorientation of world trade in the 1930s. *Journal of International Economics* 38 (1): 1–24.

Eichengreen, Barry, and Torben Iversen. 1999. Institutions and economic performance: Evidence from the labour market. *Oxford Review of Economic Policy* 15 (4): 121–38.

Eichengreen, Barry, and Albrecht O. Ritschl. 2009. Understanding West German economic growth in the 1950s. *Cliometrica* 3 (3): 191–219.

Eicher, Friedrich. 1952. Berufliche und soziale Gliederung der Bevölkerung: Ergebnisse der Berufs-zählung vom 13. September 1950. *Statistisches Jahrbuch deutscher Gemeinden* 40 (1): 57–74.

Eichholz, Dietrich. 1999. *Geschichte der deutschen Kriegswirtschaft 1939–1945*. Vol. 3: 1943–1945, Part 2: *Agonie und Katastrophe 1945*. Munich: K. G. Saur.

1997. Institutionen und Praxis der Wirtschaftpolitik im NS-besetzten Europa. In *Die "Neuordnung" Europas: NS-Wirtschaftspolitik in den besetzten Gebieten*, ed. Richard J. Overy, Richard Otto, and Johannes Houwink ten Cate, 29–62. Berlin: Metropol.

1978. Kriegswirtschaftliche Resultate der Okkupationspolitik des faschistischen deutschen Imperialismus 1939–1944. *Militärgeschichte* 17 (2): 133–51.

Eisendrath, Ernst. 1950. *Anlagevermögen und Dekapitalisation der deutschen Industrie*. DIW Sonderhefte, No. 8. Berlin: Duncker & Humblot.

Ellis, Howard S. 1941. *Exchange control in Central Europe*. Cambridge, MA: Harvard University Press.

Erhard, Ludwig. 1962. *Deutsche Wirtschaftspolitik: der Weg der Sozialen Marktwirtschaft*. Düsseldorf: Econ-Knapp.

1957. *Wohlstand für alle*. Düsseldorf: Econ Verlag.

Erker, Paul. 1988. Revolution des Dorfes: Ländliche Bevölkerung zwischen Flüchtlingszustrom und landwirtschaftlichem Strukturwandel. In *Von Stalingrad zur Währungsreform: zur Sozialgeschichte des Umbruchs in Deutschland*, ed. Martin Broszat, 367–425. Munich: Oldenburg.

Eucken, Walter. 1940. *Die Grundlagen der Nationalökonomie*. Jena: Fischer.

Federau, Fritz. 1953. Der Interzonenhandel Deutschlands von 1946 bis Mitte 1953. *Vierteljahrshefte zur Wirtschaftsforschung* 22 (4): 385–410.

Feinstein, Charles. 1999. Structural change in the developed countries during the twentieth century. *Oxford Review of Economic Policy* 15 (4): 35–55.

Fichtel, Lorenz. 1980. *Wohnungspolitik in der sozialen Marktwirtschaft: Darstellung und Analyse des Systems der Wohnungspolitik in der Bundesrepublik Deutschland*. Augsburg: Heuser.

Fischer, Fritz. 1979. *Bündnis der Eliten: zur Kontinuität der Machtstrukturen in Deutschland 1871–1945*. Düsseldorf: Droste.

1969. *Krieg der Illusionen: die deutsche Politik von 1911 bis 1914*. Düsseldorf: Droste.

Fischer, Wolfram. 1968. *Deutsche Wirtschaftspolitik 1918–1945*. 3rd rev. ed. Opladen: Leske.

Fishback, Price, and Joseph A. Cullen. 2013. Second World War spending and local economic activity in US counties, 1939–58. *Economic History Review* 66 (4): 975–92.

Friedrich, Jörg. 2002. *Der Brand: Deutschland im Bombenkrieg*. Berlin: Propyläen.

Gabriel, Horst. 1950. Trümmerreumung und –verwertung 1945–49. *Statistisches Jahrbuch deutscher Gemeinden* 38 (2): 433–50.

Gallagher, John, and Ronald Robinson. 1953. The imperialism of free trade. *Economic History Review* 6 (1): 1–15.

Galtung, Johan. 1973. *Kapitalistische Großmacht Europa oder die Gemeinschaft der Konzerne: A superpower in the making*. Hamburg: Rowohlt.

Gehrig, Gerhard. 1961. Eine Zeitreihe für den Zachkapitalbestand und die Investitionen. In *Bestimmungsfaktoren der deutschen Produktion*, ed. Gerhard Gehrig, 7–60. Ifo-Studien, No. 7. Munich: IFO.

Giersch, Herbert, Kal-Heinz Paqué, and Holger Schmieding. 1993. Openness, wage restraint and macroeconomic stability: West Germany's road to prosperity, 1948–1959. In *Postwar economic reconstruction and lessons for the East today*, ed. Rudiger Dornbusch, Wilhem Nolling, and Richard Layard, 1–27. Cambridge, MA and London: MIT Press.

1992. *The fading miracle: Four decades of market economy in Germany.* Cambridge: Cambridge University Press.

Gillingham, John. 1995. The European Coal and Steel Community. In *Europe's post-war recovery*, ed. Barry Eichengreen, 151–68. Cambridge: Cambridge University Press.

1991. *Coal, steel and the rebirth of Europe, 1945–1955: The Germans and French from Ruhr conflict to European Community.* Cambridge: Cambridge University Press.

Gimbel, John. 1976. *The origins of the Marshall Plan.* Stanford, CA: California University Press.

1968. *The American occupation of Germany: Politics and military, 1945–1949.* Stanford, CA: Stanford University Press.

Glastetter, Werner, Günter Högemann, and Ralf Marquardt. 1991. *Die wirtschaftliche Entwicklung in der BRD 1950–1989.* New York and Frankfurt: Campus.

Gleitze, Bruno. 1956. *Ostdeutsche Wirtschaft: Industrielle Standorte und volkswirtschaftliche Kapazitäten des ungeteilten Deutschland.* Berlin: Duncker & Humblot.

Golson, Eric. 2016. Sweden as an occupied country? Swedish-belligerent trade during World War II. In *Paying for Hitler's war: The consequences of Nazi hegemony for Europe*, ed. Jonas Scherner and Eugene N. White, 266–95. Cambridge: Cambridge University Press.

2014. Swiss trade with the Allied and Axis powers during the Second World War. *Jahrbuch für Wirtschaftsgeschichte* 55 (2): 71–98.

2012. Did Swedish ball bearings keep the Second World War going? Re-evaluating neutral Sweden's role. *Scandinavian Economic History Review* 60 (2): 165–82.

Görtemaker, Manfred. 2004. *Geschichte der Bundesrepublik Deutschland: von Gründung bis zur Gegenwart.* Licensed edition. Frankfurt: Fischler Taschenbuch Verlag.

Görzig, Bernd. 1972. *Die Entwicklung des Wachstumspotenzials in den Wirtschaftsbereichen der Bundesrepublik Deutschland.* DIW Beiträge zur Strukturforschung, No. 18. Berlin: Duncker & Humblot.

Görzig, Bernd, and Wolfgang Kirner. 1976. *Anlageinvestitionen und Anlagevermögen in den Wirtschaftsbereichen der Bundesrepublik Deutschland: Ergebnisse einer Neuberechnung.* DIW Beiträge zur Strukturforschung, No. 41. Berlin: Duncker & Humblot.

Granicky, Günter, and Georg Müller. 1950. Die Flüchtlinge in Westdeutschland. In *Das deutsche Flüchtlingsproblem.* Sonderheft der Zeitschrift für Raumforschung, 4–10. Bielefeld: Eilers.

Grenzebach, William S. 1988. *Germany's informal empire in East Central Europe: German economic policy toward Yugoslavia and Rumania, 1933–1939.* Stuttgart: Steiner.

Gross, Stephen G. 2015. *Export empire: German soft power in Southeastern Europe, 1890–1945.* Cambridge: Cambridge University Press.

Grosser, Dieter. 1990. *Soziale Marktwirtschaft: Geschichte, Konzept, Leistung.* 2nd ed. Stuttgart: Kohlhammer.

Gruchmann, Lothar. 1991. *Totaler Krieg: vom Blitzkrieg zur bedingungslosen Kapitulation.* Munich: DTV.

Grüner, Gustav. 1989. Berufsausbildung in Fachschulen. In *Handbuch der deutschen Bildungsgeschichte.* Vol. V: *Die Weimarer Republik und die national-sozialistische Diktatur,* ed. Dieter Langewiesche and Christa Berg, 299–306. Berufsbildung. Munich: C. H. Beck.

Hachtmann, Rüdiger. 1989. *Industriearbeit im Dritten Reich: Untersuchungen zu den Lohn- und Arbeitsbedingungen in Deutschland 1933–1945.* Kritische Studien zur Geschichtswissenschaft, 82. Göttingen: Vandenhoeck & Ruprecht.

Hafner, Thomas. 1994. *Sozialer Wohnungsbau in Westdeutschland, 1945–1970: Mit einer Betrachtung des Zeitraums 1848–1945 und ausgewählten Beispielen aus Baden-Württemberg.* Stuttgart: Städtebauliches Institute Universität Stuttgart.

Hall, Robert I., and Charles I. Jones. 1999. Why do some countries produce so much more output per worker than others? *Quarterly Journal of Economics* 114 (1): 83–116.

Hansmeyer, Carl-Heinrich, and Rolf Caesar. 1976. Kriegswirstchaft und Inflation, 1936–1948. In *Währung und Wirtschaft in Deutschland 1876–1975,* ed. Deutsche Bundesbank, 115–55. Frankfurt: Knapp.

Hardach, Gerd. 1993. Die Rückkehr zum Weltmarkt, 1948–1958. In *Modernisierung im Wiederaufbau: Die westdeutsche Gesellschaft der 50er Jahre,* ed. Axel Schieldt and Arnold Sywottek, 80–104. Bonn: J. H. W. Dietz.

   1991. Transnationale Wirtschaftspolitik: der Marshall-Plan in Deutschland 1947–1952. In *Ordnungs-politische Weichenstellungen nach dem Zweiten Weltkrieg,* ed. Dietmar Petzina, 67–100. Berlin: Duncker & Humblot.

Harris, Sir Arthur. 1947. *Bomber offensive.* London: Collins.

Hatton, Timothy J., and George R. Boyer. 2005. Unemployment and the UK labour market before, during and after the golden age. *European Review of Economic History* 9 (1): 35–60.

Hefele, Peter. 1998. *Die Verlagerung von Industrie- und Dienstleistungsunternehmen aus der SBZ/DDR nach Westdeutschland unter besonderer Berücksichtigung Bayerns 1945–1961.* Stuttgart: Steiner.

Heidemeyer, Herbert. 1994. *Flucht und Zuwanderung aus der SBZ/DDR, 1945/1949–1961: Die Flüchtlingspolitik der Bundesrepublik Deutschland bis zum Bau der Berliner Mauer.* Düsseldorf: Droste.

Henker, Klaus. 1976. *Wettbewerbsrelationen im Außenhandel westlicher Industrieländer 1959 bis 1973: Zur empirischen Bestimmung von Wettbewerbs- und Struktureinflüssen im Internationalen Handel mit Industrieerzeugnissen unter besonderer Berücksichtigung der Bundesrepublik Deutschland.* DIW Beiträge zur Strukturforschung, No. 39. Berlin: Duncker & Humblot.

Henning, Friedrich-Wilhelm. 1993. *Wirtschafts- und Sozialgeschichte.* Vol. 3: *Das Industrialisierte Deutschland 1914 bis 1992,* 8th rev. ed. Paderborn and Munich: Ferdinand Schöningh.

Hertfelder, Thomas. 2007. Modell Deutschland: Erfolgsgeschichte oder Illusion? [Introduction]. In *Modell Deutschland: Erfolgsgeschichte oder Illusion?,* ed. Thomas Hertfelder and Andreas Rödder, 9–27. Göttingen: Vandenhoeck & Ruprecht.

Hetzel, Robert L. 2007. The contributions of Milton Friedman to economics. *Federal Reserve Bank of Richmond Economic Quarterly* 93 (1): 1–30.

Hilger, Susanne. 2004. *'Amerikanisierung' deutscher Unternehmen: Wettbewerb sstrategien und Unternehmenspolitik bei Henkel, Siemens und Daimler-Benz.* Vierteljahrschrift für Sozial- und Wirtschaftsgeschichte, Beiheft 173. Stuttgart: Steiner.

Hirschman, Albert O. 1945. *National power and the structure of foreign trade.* Berkeley: California University Press.

Hockers, Hans-Günther. 1986. Integration der Gesellschaft: Gründungskrise und Sozialpolitik in der frühen Bundesrepublik. *Zeitschrift für Sozialreform* 32 (1): 21–41.

Hoffmann, Ernst. 1962. *Zur Geschichte der Berufsausbildung in Deutschland.* Bielefeld: Bertelsmann.

Höpfner, Berndt. 1993. *Der deutsche Außenhandel 1900–1945: Änderungen in der Waren- und Regional-struktur.* Frankfurt: Lang.

Jäger, Hans. 1988. *Geschichte der Wirtschaftsordnung in Deutschland.* Frankfurt: Suhrkamp.

Jahn, Eberhard. 1950. Das DP-Problem in Deutschland. In *Das deutsche Flüchtlingsproblem.* Sonderheft der Zeitschrift für Raumforschung, 101–15. Bielefeld: Eilers.

Jákli, Zoltán. 1990. *Vom Marshallplan zum Kohlepfennig: Grundrisse der Subventionspolitik in der Bundesrepublik Deutschland 1948–1982.* Opladen: Westdeutscher Verlag.

Jánossy, Ferenc. 1969. The end of the economic miracle: Appearance and reality in economic development. New York: ISAP. Translation of the German edition (1966), *Das Ende der Wirtschaftswunder: Erscheinung und Wesen der wirtschaftlichen Entwicklung.* Frankfurt: Neue Kritik.

Jorgenson, Dale W., Frank M. Gollop, and Barbara Fraumeni. 1987. *Productivity and U.S. economic growth.* Amsterdam: North-Holland.

Kaldor, Nicholas. 1966. *Causes of the slow rate of economic growth of the United Kingdom: An inaugural lecture.* Cambridge: Cambridge University Press.

1946. The German war economy. *Review of Economic Studies* 13 (1): 33–52.

Karlsch, Rainer. 1993. *Allein bezahlt? Die Reparationsleistungen der SBZ/DDR 1945.* Berlin: Links.

Kästner, Friedrich. 1949. Kriegsschäden: Trümmermengen, Wohnungsverluste, Grundsteuerausfall und Vermögenssteuerausfall. *Statistisches Jahrbuch deutscher Gemeinden* 37 (2): 361–91.

Keyser, Erich, ed. 1952. *Deutsches Städtebuch. Handbuch städtischer Geschichte.* Im Auftrage der Arbeitsgemeinschaft der historischen Kommissionen und mit Unterstützung des Deutschen Städtetages, des Deutschen Städtebundes und des Deutschen Gemeindetages. Stuttgart: Kohlhammer. Vol. 3: *Nordwest Deutschland,* Part 1: *Niedersachsen und Bremen.*

1956. *Deutsches Städtebuch. Handbuch städtischer Geschichte,* Vol. 3: *Nordwest Deutschland,* Part 2: *Westfälisches Städtebuch.*

1964. *Deutsches Städtebuch. Handbuch städtischer Geschichte.* Vol. 4: *Südwest Deutschland,* Part 3: *Rheinland-Pfalz und Saarland.*

1971. *Deutsches Städtebuch. Handbuch städtischer Geschichte.* Vol. 5: Bayrisches Städtebuch.

Kiesewetter, Hubert. 1992. Amerikanische Unternehmen in der Bundesrepublik Deutschland, 1950–1974. In *Der Boom 1948–1973: Gesellschaftliche und wirtschaftliche Folgen in der BRD und in Europa*, ed. Hartmut Kaeble, 63–81. Opladen: Westdeutscher Verlag.

Kindleberger, Charles P. 1967. *Europe's postwar growth: The role of labor supply.* Cambridge, MA: Harvard University Press.

1949. Germany and the economic recovery of Europe. *Proceedings of the Academy of Political Science* 23 (3): 68–81.

Kirner, Wolfgang. 1968. *Zeitreihen für das Anlagevermögen der Wirtschaftsbereiche in der Bundesrepublik Deutschland.* DIW Beiträge zur Strukturforschung, No. 5. Berlin: Duncker & Humblot.

Kitson, Michael and Solomos Solomou. 1995. Bilateralism in the interwar world economy. *Bulletin of Economic Research* 47 (3): 197–219.

Klein, Burton H. 1959. *Germany's economic preparations for war.* Cambridge, MA: Harvard University Press.

Klein, Lawrence R. 1961. A model of Japanese economic growth. *Econometrica* 29 (3): 277–92.

Klemann, Hein A. M., and Sergei Kudryashov. 2012. *Occupied economies: an economic history of Nazi-occupied Europe, 1939–1945.* London: Berg.

Klemm, Bernd, and Günther J. Trittel. 1987. Vor dem 'Wirtschaftswunder': Durchbruch zum Wachstum oder Lähmungskrise. *Vierteljahrshefte für Zeitgeschichte* 35 (4): 571–624.

Kleßmann, Cristoph. 1997. *Zwei Staaten, eine Nation. Deutsche Geschichte 1955–1970.* 2nd rev. ed. Schriftenreihe Band 343. Bonn: Bundeszentrale für politische Bildung.

1982. *Doppelte Staatsgründung: Deutsche Geschichte, 1945–1955.* Göttingen: Vandenhoeck & Ruprecht.

Klump, Rainer. 1989. Die Währungsreform von 1948: Ihre Bedeutung wachstumstheoretischer und ordnungspolitischer Sicht. In *Währungsreform und Soziale Marktwirtschaft: Erfahrungen und Perspektiven nach 40 Jahren*, ed. Wolfram Fischer, 403–22. Berlin: Duncker & Humblot.

1985. *Wirtschaftsgeschichte der Bundesrepublik Deutschland. Zur Kritik neuer wirtschaftshistorischen Interpretationen aus ordnungspolitischer Sicht.* Stuttgart: Steiner.

Knapp, Manfred. 1990. Deutschland und der Marshallplan: Zum Verhältnis zwischen politischer und ökonomischer Stabilisierung in der amerikanischen Deutschlandpolitik nach 1945. In *Marshallplan und westdeutscher Wiederaufstieg. Positionen-Kontroversen*, ed. Hans-Jürgen Schröder, 35–59. Stuttgart: Steiner.

Kollmer, Gert. 1995. Die Wirtschaftspolitik Erhards als Fessel des wirtschaftlichen Aufschwungs? Kritische Forderungen der südwestdeutschen Wirtschaft. *Vierteljahrschrift für Sozial- und Wirtschaftsgeschichte* 82 (3): 458–77.

Koppstein, Jeffrey, and Mark I. Lichbach. 2005. *Comparative politics: Interests, identities, and institutions in a changing global order.* Cambridge: Cambridge University Press

Kornai, János. 1980. *The economics of shortage.* Amsterdam: North-Holland.

Kornrumpf, Martin. 1950a. Das Vertriebenenproblem im Spiegel der Bevölkerungsstatistik. Die Flüchtlinge in Westdeutschland. In *Das deutsche*

Flüchtlingsproblem. Sonderheft der Zeitschrift für Raumforschung, 36–41. Bielefeld: Eilers.

1950b. Eingliederung der Vertriebenen in die gewerbliche Wirtschaft. In *Das deutsche Flüchtlingsproblem.* Sonderheft der Zeitschrift für Raumforschung, 94–101. Bielefeld: Eilers.

Kramer, Alan. 1991. *The West German economy, 1945–1955.* Oxford and New York: Berg.

Krause, Michael. 1997. *Flucht vor dem Bombenkrieg: Umquartierungen im Zweiten Weltkrieg und die Wiedereingliederung der Evakuierten in Deutschland 1943– 1963.* Düsseldorf: Droste.

Krengel, Rolf. 1962. *Arbeitszeit und Produktivität: Untersuchungsergebnisse wissenschaftlicher Forschungsinstitute.* Volkswirtschaftliche Untersuchungen. Berlin: Duncker & Humblot.

1960. Zur Entwicklung der Brutto-Anlage-Investitionen und des Brutto-Anlagevermögens der westdeutschen Industrie bis 1958/59 und 1969/70. *Vierteljahreshefte zur Wirtschaftsforschung* 29 (1): 61–88.

1958. *Anlagevermögen, Produktion und Beschäftigung der Industrie im Gebiet der Bundesrepublik von 1924 bis 1956.* Berlin: Duncker & Humblot.

Krengel, Rolf, Egon Baumgart, Arthur Boneß, Rainer Pischner, and Käthe Droege. 1973. Produktionsvolumen und -potential, Produktionsfaktoren der Industrie im Gebiet der Bundesrepublik Deutschland einschließlich Saarland und Berlin (West). Working paper. DIW Statistische Kennziffern, No. 14, 1961–72.

Krummacher, Michael. 1988. Sozialer Wohnungsbau in der Bundesrepublik in den fünfziger und sechziger Jahren. In *Massenwohnung und Eigenheim: Wohnungsbau und Wohnen in der Großstadt seit dem Ersten Weltkrieg,* ed. Axel Schieldt and Arnold Sywottek, 440–60. Frankfurt and New York: Campus.

Lámfalussy, Alexander. 1963. *The United Kingdom and the Six: An essay on economic growth in Western Europe.* London: Macmillan.

Landes, David. 1969. *The unbounded Prometheus: Technological change and industrial development in Western Europe from 1750 to the present.* Cambridge: Cambridge University Press.

Leaman, Jeremy. 1988. *The political economy of West Germany, 1945–1989: An introduction.* London: Macmillan.

Lehmann, Alex. 2000a. *Der Marshall-Plan und das neue Deutschland: Die Folgen amerikanischer Besatzungspolitik in den Westzonen.* Münster, Munich, and Berlin: Waxmann.

Lehmann, Hans G. 2000b. *Deutschland-Chronik 1945 bis 2000.* Schriftenreihe Band, No. 366. Bonn: Bundeszentrale für politische Bildung.

Levin, Alan J. 1992. *The strategic bombing of Germany, 1940–1945.* Westport, CT: Praeger.

Liefmann-Keil, Elisabeth. 1964. Erwerbstätigkeit, Ausbildung und wirtschaftliches Wachstum. In *Struktur-wandlungen einer wachsenden Wirtschaft,* ed. Fritz Neumark, 378–440. Schriften des Vereins für Sozialpolitik, Gesellschaft für Wirtschafts- und Sozialwissenschaften, No. 30.1. Berlin: Duncker & Humblot.

Lindlar, Ludger. 1997. *Das missverstandene Wirtschaftswunder: Westdeutschland und die west-europäische Nachkriegsprosperität.* Tübingen: Mohr Siebeck.

Lindlar, Ludger, and Carl-Ludwig Holtfrerich. 1997. Geography, exchange rates and trade structures: Germany's export performance in the 1950s. *European Review of Economic History* 1 (2): 217–46.

Löffler, Bernhard. 2002. *Soziale Marktwirtschaft und administrative Praxis: Das Bundeswirtschafts-ministerium unter Ludwig Erhard.* Vierteljahrschrift für Sozial- und Wirtschaftsgeschichte Beiheft 162. Stuttgart: Steiner.

Lutz, Friedrich A. 1949. The German currency reform and the revival of the German economy. *Economica* 16 (62): 122–42.

MacIsaac, David. 1976. *Strategic bombing in World War Two: The story of the United States Strategic Bombing Survey.* New York: Garland.

Maddison, Angus. 2006. *The world economy.* Vol. II: *Historical Statistics.* Paris: OECD.

1996. Macroeconomic accounts for European countries. In *Quantitative aspects of post-war European economic growth*, ed. Bart van Ark and N. F. R. Crafts, 27–83. Cambridge: Cambridge University Press.

1991. *Dynamic forces in capitalist development.* Oxford: Oxford University Press.

Maier, Charles S. 1991. Issue then is Germany and with it future of Europe. In *The Marshall Plan and Germany: West German development within the framework of the European Recovery Program*, ed. Charles S. Maier, 1–39. Oxford: Berg.

1981. The two postwar eras and the conditions for stability in twentieth-century Western Europe. *American Historical Review* 86 (2): 327–52.

Mandel, Ernest. 1969. *Die deutsche Wirtschaftskrise: Lehren der Rezession 1966/67.* Frankfurt: Europäische Verlagsanstalt.

Mankiw, N. Gregory, David Romer, and David N. Weil. 1992. A contribution to the empirics of economic growth. *Quarterly Journal of Economics* 107 (2): 407–37.

Manz, Matthias. 1985. *Stagnation und Aufschwung in der französischen Besatzungszone von 1945 bis 1948.* Dissertation, Mannheim, 1968. Ostfildern: Scripta Mercaturae

Markmann, Heinz. 1964. Wandlungen der industriellen Lohnstruktur in Westdeutschland zwischen 1949 und 1961. In *Strukturwandlungen einer wachsenden Wirtschaft*, ed. Fritz Neumark, 441–54. Schriften des Vereins für Sozialpolitik, Gesellschaft für Wirtschafts- und Sozialwissenschaften, No. 30.1. Berlin: Duncker & Humblot.

Matschke, Werner. 1988. *Die industrielle Entwicklung in der Sowjetischen Besatzungszone Deutschland (SBZ) von 1945 bis 1948.* Berlin: Arno Spitz.

Mausbach, Wilfried. 2004. Restructuring and support: Beginnings of American economic policy in occupied Germany. In *The United States and Germany in the era of the Cold War, 1945–1990*, ed. Detlef Junker, Vol. 1, 278–86. Cambridge: German Historical Institute and Cambridge University Press.

Mayer, Herbert C. 1969. *German recovery and the Marshall Plan 1948–1952.* Bonn, Brussels, and New York: Edition Atlantic Forum.

Menderhausen, Horst. 1949. Prices, money and the distribution of goods in postwar Germany. *American Economic Review* 39 (3): 646–72.

Meinecke, Friedrich. 1946. *Die deutsche Katastrophe: Betrachtung und Erinnerungen.* Wiesbaden: Eberhard Brockhaus.

Mertens, Dieter. 1964. *Die Wandlungen der industriellen Branchenstruktur in der Bundesrepublik Deutschland 1950 bis 1960: Ein Beitrag zur Analyse der Ursachen und Wirkungen differenzierten Wachstum*. DIW Sonderhefte, No. 68. Berlin: Duncker & Humblot.

Mierzejewski, Alfred C. 1988. *The collapse of the German war economy: Air power and the German national railway*. London: Macmillan.

Michalski, Wolfgang. 1970. *Export und Wirtschaftswachstum: Schlussfolgerungen aus der Nachkriegszeit in der Bundesrepublik Deutschland*. Hamburg: Verlag Weltarchiv.

Milward, Alan S. 1992. *The European rescue of the nation-state*. Assisted by George Brennan and Federico Romero. Berkeley and Los Angeles: University of California Press.

1991. The Marshall Plan and German foreign trade. In *The Marshall Plan and Germany: West German development within the framework of the European Recovery Program*, ed. Charles S. Maier, 452–87. Oxford: Berg.

1987. *Reconstruction in Western Europe, 1945–1951*. London: Meutheun & Co.

1981. The Reichsmark Bloc and the international economy. In *The 'Führer state': myth and reality: Studies on the structure and politics of the Third Reich*, ed. G. Hirschfeld and L. Kettenacker, 377–413. Stuttgart: Klett-Cotta.

1977. Arbeitspolitik und Produktivität in der deutschen Kriegswirtschaft unter vergleichendem Aspekt. In *Kriegswirtschaft und Rüstung 1939–1945*, ed. Friedrich Forstmeier and Hans-Erich Volkmann, 73–91. Düsseldorf: Droste.

1975. Der Einfluß ökonomischer und nich-ökonomischer Faktoren auf die Strategie des Blitzkriegs. In *Wirtschaft und Rüstung am Vorabend des Zweiten Weltkriegs*, ed. Friedrich Forstmeier and Hans E. Volkmann, 189–201. Düsseldorf: Droste.

1965. *The German economy at war*. London: University of London, Athlone Press.

Mokyr, Joel. 1990. *The lever of riches: Technological creativity and economic progress*. Oxford: Oxford University Press.

Müller, Rolf-Dieter. 1993. Grundzüge der deutschen Kriegswirtschaft, 1939–1945. In *Deutschland 1933–1945: Neue Studien zur nationalsozialistischen Herrschaft*, ed. Karl Dietrich Bracher, Manfred Funke, and Hans-Adolf Jacobsen, 357–76. Schriftenreihe Band, No. 314. Bonn: Bundeszentrale für politische Bildung.

Müller-Armack, Alfred. 1947. *Wirtschaftslenkung und Marktwirtschaft*. Hamburg: Verlag für Wirtschaft und Sozialpolitik.

Murrell, Peter. 1983. The comparative structure of the growth of West German and British manufacturing industries. In *The political economy of growth*, ed. Dennis C. Mueller, 109–31. New Haven, CT: Yale University Press.

Neal, Larry. 1979. The economics and finance of bilateral clearing agreements: Germany, 1934–8. *Economic History Review*, Second Series, 23 (2): 391–404.

Neebe, Reinhard. 2004. *Weichenstellungen für die Globalisierung: Europa und Amerika in der Ära Erhard, 1944–1963*. Cologne: Böhlau.

1999. German big business and the return to the world market after World War II. In *Quest for economic empire: European strategies of German big business in the twentieth century*, ed. Volker R. Berghahn, 95–121. Providence and Oxford: Berghahn Books.

1989. Technologietransfer und Außenhandel in den Anfangsjahren der Bundesrepublik Deutschland. *Vierteljahrschrift für Sozial- und Wirtschaftsgeschichte* 76 (1): 49–75.

Nelson, Richard R., and Gavin Wright. 1992. The rise and fall of American technological leadership: The postwar era in historical perspective. *Journal of Economic Literature* 30 (4): 1931–64.

Neuborg, Torsten. 1989. *Wirtschaftsgeschichte: Deutschland im 20. Jahrhundert.* Darmstadt: Winkler.

Neumann, Manfred. 2000. *Wettbewerbspolitik: Geschichte, Theorie und Praxis.* Wiesbaden: Gabler.

Nicholls, Anthony J. 1994. *Freedom with responsibility: The social market economy in Germany 1918–1963.* Oxford: Clarendon.

Niederschlag, Robert. 1947. Die Kriegsschäden. In *Die deutsche Wirtschaft zwei Jahre nach dem Zusammen-bruch: Tatsachen und Probleme*, ed. Ferdinand Friedensburg, 37–48. Berlin: Albert Nauck & Co.

Nishida, Satoshi. 2007. *Der Wiederaufbau der japanischen Wirtschaft nach dem Zweiten Weltkrieg: Die amerikanische Japanpolitik und die ökonomischen Nachkriegsreformen in Japan 1942–1952.* Vierteljahrschrift für Sozial- und Wirtschaftsgeschichte, Beiheft 193. Stuttgart: Steiner.

Olson, Mancur. 1983. The political economy of comparative growth rates. In *The political economy of growth*, ed. Dennis C. Mueller, 7–52. New Haven, CT: Yale University Press.

1982. *The rise and decline of nations: Economic growth, stagflation, and social rigidities.* New Haven, CT: Yale University Press.

O'Mahony, Mary. 1999. *Britain's relative productivity performance: International comparisons.* London: National Institute of Economic and Social Research.

1996. Measures of fixed capital stocks in the post-war period: A five-country studys. In *Quantitative aspects of post-war European economic growth*, ed. Bart van Ark and N. F. R. Crafts, 165–214. Cambridge: Cambridge University Press.

Ott, Erich. 1990. Die Bedeutung des Marshall-Plans für die Nachkriegsentwicklung in Westdeutschland. In *Marshallplan und westdeutscher Wiederaufstieg. Positionen – Kontroversen*, ed. Hans-Jürgen Schröder, 60–78. Stuttgart: Steiner.

Overy, Richard J. 1997. The economy of the German 'New Order'. In *Die "Neuordnung" Europas: NS-Wirtschaftspolitik in den besetzten Gebieten*, ed. Richard J. Overy, Richard Otto, and Johannes Houwink ten Cate, 11–28. Berlin: Metropol.

1994. *War and economy in the Third Reich.* Oxford: Clarendon.

Owen Smith, Eric. 1994. *The German economy.* London and New York: Routledge.

Paqué, Karl-Heinz. 1995. *How cooperative was the spirit? A note on the 'Eichengreen-view' of Europe after World War II.* Kiel Working Papers, No. 701. Kiel: Kiel Institute for the World Economy.

1994. *The causes of post-war slumps and miracles: An evaluation of Olsonian views on German economic performance in the 1920s and the 1950s.* CEPR Discussion Papers, No. 981.

1993. *How clean was the slate? Some notes on the Olsonian view of the postwar German economic miracle.* Kiel Working Papers, No. 588. Kiel: Kiel Institute for the World Economy.

1989. Unterbeschäftigung in der Sozialen Marktwirtschaft: Der bundesdeutsche Arbeitsmarkt 1949-54 und 1982-87 im Vergleich. In *Währungsreform und Soziale Marktwirtschaft: Erfahrungen und Perspektiven nach 40 Jahren,* ed. Wofram Fischer, 471–88. Berlin: Duncker & Humblot.

1988. *The mixed blessing of labour shortage: German overemployment in the 1960s.* Kiel Working Papers, No. 332. Kiel: Kiel Institute for the World Economy.

1987. *Labour surplus and capital shortage: German unemployment in the first decade after the currency reform.* Kiel Working Papers, No. 290. Kiel: Kiel Institute for the World Economy.

Pätzold, Günter. 1989. Handwerkliche, industrielle und schulische Berufserziehung. In *Handbuch der deutschen Bildungsgeschichte.* Vol. V: *Die Weimarer Republik und die nationalsozialistische Diktatur,* ed. Dieter Langewiesche and Christa Berg, 259–87. Berufsbildung. Munich: C. H. Beck.

Petzina, Dietmar. Vierjahresplan und Rüstugspolitik. In *Wirtschaft und Rüstung am Vorabend des Zweiten Weltkriegs,* ed. Friedrich Forstmeier and Hans E. Volkmann, 65 80. Düsseldorf: Droste.

Plumpe, Werner. 1999. Die Reparationsleistungen Westdeutschlands nach dem Zweiten Weltkrieg. In *Die Wirtschaft im geteilten vereinten Deutschland,* ed. Karl Eckart and Jörg Roesler, 31–46. Berlin: Duncker & Humblot.

Pohl, Manfred. 1983. Die Entwicklung des privaten Bankwesens nach 1945: Die Kreditgenossenschaften nach 1945. In *Deutsche Bankengeschichte,* ed. Institut für Bankhistorische Forschung, Vol. 3: Vom Ersten Weltkrieg bis zur Gegenwart, 207–78. Frankfurt: Knapp.

Price, Harry B. 1955. *The Marshall Plan and its meaning.* Ithaca, NY: Cornell University Press.

Radkau, Joachim. 1993. "Wirtschaftswunder" ohne technologische Innovation? Technische Modernität in den 50-er Jahren. In *Modernisierung im Wiederaufbau: Die westdeutsche Gesellschaft der 50er Jahre,* ed. Axel Schieldt and Arnold Sywottek, 129–54. Bonn: J. H. W. Dietz.

Ránki, György. 1993. *The economics of the Second World War.* Vienna: Böhlau.

1983. *Economy and foreign policy: The struggle of the Great Powers for hegemony in the Danube valley, 1919–1939.* New York: Columbia University Press.

Reich, Simon, 1990. *Fruits of Fascism: Postwar prosperity in historical perspective.* Ithaca, NY: Cornell University Press.

Reichling, Gerhard. 1989. *Die deutschen Vertriebenen in Zahlen.* Bonn: Kulturstiftung der deutschen Vertriebenen. Vol. 2: *40 Jahre Eingliederung in der Bundesrepublik Deutschland.*

1986. *Die deutschen Vertriebenen in Zahlen.* Bonn: Kulturstiftung der deutschen Vertriebenen. Vol. 1: *Umsiedler, Verschleppte, Vertriebene, Aussiedler 1940–1985.*

Rhenisch, Thomas. 1999. *Europäische Integration und industrielles Interesse: Die deutsche Industrie und die Gründung der Europäischen Wirtschaftsgemeinschaft.* Vierteljahrschrift für Sozial- und Wirtschafts-geschichte, Beiheft 152. Stuttgart: Steiner.

Riemenschneider, Michael. 1987. *Die deutsche Wirtschaftspolitik gegenüber Ungarn 1933–1944: Ein Beitrag zur Interdependenz von Wirtschaft und Politik unter dem Nationalsozialismus.* Frankfurt: Lang.

Ristuccia, Cristiano Andrea, and Adam Tooze. 2013. Machine tools and mass production in the armaments boom: Germany and the United States, 1929–44. *Economic History Review* 66 (4): 953–974.

Ritschl, Albrecht O. 2005. Der späte Fluch des Dritten Reichs: Pfadabhängigkeiten in der Entstehung der Bundesdeutschen Wirtschaftsordnung. *Perspektiven der Wirtschaftspolitik* 6 (2): 151–70.

2001. Nazi economic imperialism and the exploitation of the small: Evidence from Germany's secret foreign balances. *Economic History Review* 54 (2): 324–45.

1993. Wirtschaftspolitik im Dritten Reich. In *Deutschland 1933–1945: Neue Studien zur nationalsozialistischen Herrschaft,* ed. Karl D. Bracher, Manfred Funke, and Hans-Adolf Jacobsen, 118–34. Schriftenreihe Band 314. Bonn: Bundeszentrale für Politische Bildung.

1985. Die Währungsreform von 1948 und der Wiederaufstieg der westdeutschen Industrie. *Vierteljahrshefte für Zeitgeschichte* 33 (1): 136–65.

Ritschl, Albrecht O., and Mark Spoerer. 1997. Das Bruttosozialprodukt in Deutschland nach den amtlichen Volkseinkommens- und Sozialproduktstatistiken 1901–1995. *Jahrbuch für Wirtschaftsgeschichte,* 38 (2): 27–54.

Ritschl, Albrecht O., and Tamás Vonyó. 2014. The roots of economic failure: What explains East Germany's falling behind between 1945 and 1950? *European Review of Economic History* 18 (2): 166–84.

Ritschl, Albrecht O., and Nikolaus Wolf. 2011. Endogeneity of currency areas and trade blocs: Evidence from the interwar period. *Kyklos* 64 (2): 291–312.

Roeper, Hans, and Wolfram Weimer. 1997. *Die D-Mark: Eine Wirtschaftsgeschichte.* Frankfurt: Sicietäts Verlag.

Rohrbach, Justus. 1955. *Im Schatten des Hungers: Dokumnetarisches zur Ernährungspolitik und Ernährungswirtschaft in den Jahren 1945–1949.* Hamburg and Berlin: Parey.

Roseman, Mark. 1989. The uncontrolled economy: Ruhr coal production, 1945–48. In *Reconstruction in post-war Germany: British occupation policy and the western zones, 1945–55,* ed. Ian D. Turner, 93–124. Oxford and New York: Berg.

Roskamp, Karl W. 1965. *Capital formation in West Germany.* Detroit: Wayne State University Press.

Rotschild, Kurt W. 1964. Langfristige Verschiebungen der Warenstruktur im Welthandel. In *Strukturwandlungen einer wachsenden Wirtschaft,* ed. Fritz Neumark, 349–63. Berlin: Duncker & Humblot.

Rudolph, Karsten. 2004. *Wirtschaftsdiplomatie im Kalten Krieg: Die Ostpolitik der westdeutschen Großindustrie 1945–1991.* Frankfurt and New York: Campus.

Ruhl, Klaus-Jörg, ed. 1982. *Neubeginn und Restauration: Dokumente zur Vorgeschichte der Bundesrepublik Deutschland 1945–1949.* Munich: DTV.

Scherner, Jonas. 2013. Armament in the depth or armament in the breadth? German investments pattern and rearmament during the Nazi period. *Economic History Review* 66 (2): 497–517.

2012. Der deutsche Importboom während des Zweiten Weltkriegs: Neue Ergebnisse zur Struktur der Ausbeutung des besetzten Europas auf der Grundlage einer Neuschätzung der deutschen Handelsbilanz. *Historische Zeitschrift* 294 (1), 79–113.

2010. Nazi Germany's preparation for war: Evidence from revised industrial investment series. *European Review of Economic History* 14 (3): 433–68.

Scherner, Jonas, and Eugene N. White, eds. 2016. *Paying for Hitler's war: The consequences of Nazi hegemony for Europe*. Cambridge: Cambridge University Press.

Scherner, Jonas, and Jochen Streb. 2014. Supplier networks in the German aircraft industry during World War II and their long-term effects on West Germany's automobile industry during the 'Wirtschaftswunder'. *Business History* 56 (6): 996–1020.

Schmidt, Christoph M. 1996. German economic growth after the demise of socialism: The potential contribution of East-West migration. *Jahrbuch für Wirtschaftsgeschichte* 37 (2): 109–26.

Schmieding, Holger. 1989. Strategien zum Abbau von Handelshemmnissen: O rdnungspolitische Lehren des bundesdeutschen Liberalisierungsprozesses 1949–1957 für die Gegenwart. In *Währungsreform und Soziale Marktwirtschaft: Erfahrungen und Perspektiven nach 40 Jahren*, cd. Wofram Fischer, 253–68. Berlin: Duncker & Humblot.

Schröter, Harm. 2000. Von der Teilung zur Wiedervereinigung, 1945–2000. In *Deutsche Wirtschafts-geschichte: Ein Jahrtausend im Überblick*, ed. Michael North, 351–420. Munich: C. H. Beck.

1992. Außenwirtschaft in Boom: Direktinvestitionen bundesdeutscher Unternehmen im Ausland 1950–1970. In *Der Boom 1948–1973: gesellschaftliche und wirtschaftliche Folgen in der BRD und in Europa*, ed. Hartmut Kaeble, 82–106. Opladen: Westdeutscher Verlag.

Schudlich, Edwin. 1987. *Die Abkehr vom Normalarbeitstag: Entwicklung der Arbeitszeiten in der Industrie der Bundesrepublik seit 1945*. Frankfurt: Campus.

Schulz, Günther. 2009. Regulierung und Deregulierung im Wohnungswesen. *Vierteljahrschrift für Sozial- und Wirtschaftsgeschichte* 96 (4): 471–5.

1994. *Wiederaufbau in Deutschland: Die Wohnungspolitik in den Westzonen und der Bundesrepublik von 1945 bis 1957*. Düsseldorf: Droste.

Schwartz, Thomas. 1991. European integration and the special relationship: Implementing the Marshall Plan in the Federal Republic. In *The Marshall Plan and Germany: West German development within the framework of the European Recovery Program*, ed. Charles S. Maier, 171–215. Oxford: Berg.

Schwarzer, Oskar. 1995. Der Lebensstandard in der SBZ/DDR 1945–1989. *Jahrbuch für Wirtschaftsgeschichte* 36 (2): 119–146.

Settel, Arthur. 1947. *The deutsche Wirtschaft seit Potsdam: Ein Arbeitsbericht der Wirtschaftsabteilung der Amerikanischen Militärregierung*. The German translation edited by Wilhelm Cornides. Oberursel/ Taunus: Europa Archiv.

Seume, Franz, 1947. Industrie. In *Die deutsche Wirtschaft zwei Jahre nach dem Zusammenbruch: Tatsachen und Probleme*, ed. Ferdinand Friedensburg, 104–43. Berlin: Albert Nauck & Co.

Sleifer, Jaap. 2006. *Planning ahead and falling behind: The East German economy in comparison with West Germany, 1936–2002*. Berlin: Akademie Verlag.

Sloniger, Jerry. 1980. *The VW story*. Cambridge: Patrick Stephens.

Solow, Robert M. 1957. Technical change and the aggregate production function. *Review of Economics and Statistics* 39 (3): 312–20.

    1956. A contribution to the theory of economic growth. *Quarterly Journal of Economics* 70 (1): 65–94.

Sommariva, Andrea, and Giuseppe Tullio. 1987. *German macroeconomic history, 1880–1979*. London: Macmillan.

Spaulding, Robert M. 1999. 'Reconquering our old position': West German Osthandel strategies of the 1950s. In *Quest for economic empire: European strategies of German big business in the twentieth century*, ed. Volker R. Berghahn, 123–43. Providence and Oxford: Berghahn Books.

    1997. *Osthandel and Ostpolitik: German foreign trade policies in Eastern Europe from Bismarck to Adenauer*. Providence and Oxford: Berghahn Books.

Spoerer, Mark. 2015. Forced labour in Nazi-occupied Europe, 1939–1945. In *Economies under occupation: The hegemony of Nazi Germany and Imperial Japan in World War II*, ed. Marcel Boldorf and Tetsuji Okazaki, 73–85. London: Routledge.

    2007. Wohlstand für alle? Soziale Marktwirtschaft. In *Modell Deutschland: Erfolgsgeschichte oder Illusion?*, ed. Thomas Hertfelder und Andreas Rödder, 28–43. Göttingen: Vandenhoeck & Ruprecht.

    2001. *Zwangsarbeit unter dem Hakenkreuz: Ausländische Zivilarbeiter, Kriegsgefangene und Häftlinge im Dritten Reich und im besetzten Europa 1939–1945*. Stuttgart and Munich: DVA.

Spoerer, Mark, and Jochen Streb. 2013. *Neue deutsche Wirtschaftsgeschichte des 20. Jahrhunderts*. Munich: Oldenburg.

Steinberg, Heinz-Günter. 1991. *Die Bevölkerungsentwicklung in Deutschland im Zweiten Weltkrieg mit einem Überblick über die Entwicklung von 1945 bis 1990*. Bonn: Kulturstiftung der deutschen Vertriebenen.

Steinert, Johannes-Dieter. 1995. Die große Flucht und die Jahre danach. Flüchtlinge und Vertriebene in den vier Besatzungszonen. In *Ende des Dritten Reiches, Ende des Zweiten Weltkriegs: Eine perspektivische Rückschau*, ed. Hans Erich Volkmann, 557–80. Munich and Zurich: Piper.

Stokes, Raymond G. 1991. Technology and the West German Wirtschaftswunder. *Technology and Culture* 32 (1): 1–22.

Südbeck, Thomas. 1993. Motorisierung, Verkehrsentwicklung und Verkehrspolitik in Westdeutschland in den 50-er Jahren. In *Modernisierung im Wiederaufbau: Die westdeutsche Gesellschaft der 50er Jahre*, ed. Axel Schieldt and Arnold Sywottek, 170–87. Bonn: J. H. W. Dietz.

Temin, Peter. 2002. The golden age of European economic growth reconsidered. *European Review of Economic History* 6 (1): 3–22.

    1997. The 'Koreaboom' in West Germany: Fact or fiction? In *Selected cliometric studies on German economic history*, eds. John Komlos and Scott Eddie, 351–67. Stuttgart: Steiner.

Tenorth, Elmar H. 1993. Bildung und Wissenschaft im Dritten Reich. In *Deutschland 1933–1945: Neue Studien zur nationalsozialistischen Herrschaft*, ed. Karl D. Bracher, Manfred Funke, and Hans-Adolf Jacobsen, 240–55, Schriftenreihe Band 314. Bonn: Bundeszentrale für Politische Bildung.

Timmer, Marcel P., Robert Inklaar, Mary O'Mahony, and Bart van Ark. 2010. *Economic growth in Europe: A comparative industry perspective.* Cambridge: Cambridge University Press.

Tinbergen, Jan. 1942. Zur Theorie der Langfristigen Wirtschaftsentwicklung. *Weltwirtschaftliches Archiv* 55 (1): 511–49.

Tolliday, Steven. 1995. Enterprise and the state in the West German Wirtschaftswunder: Volkswagen and the automobile industry, 1939–1962. *Business History Review* 69 (3): 273–350.

Toniolo, Gianni. 1998. Europe's golden age, 1950–1973: Speculations from a long-run perspective. *Economic History Review* 51 (2): 252–67.

Tooze, Adam. 2006. *The wages of destruction: The making and breaking of the Nazi economy.* London: Allen Lane.

——— 2005. No room for miracles: German industrial output in World War II reassessed. *Geschichte und Gesellschaft* 31 (3): 439–64.

Turner, Ian. 1985. Das Volkswagenwerk: Ein deutsches Unternehmen unter britischen Kontrolle. In *Britische Deutschland- und Besatzungspolitik, 1945–1949,* ed. Josef Foschepoth and Rolf Steininger, 281–300. Paderborn: Schöning.

Van Ark, Bart. 1996. Sectoral growth accounting and structural change in postwar Europe. In *Quantitative aspects of post-war European economic growth,* ed. Bart van Ark and N. F. R. Crafts, 84–164. Cambridge: Cambridge University Press.

Van Hook, James C. 2004. *Rebuilding Germany: The creation of the Social Market Economy, 1945–1957.* Cambridge: Cambridge University Press.

Vogelgsang, Tobias. 2016. *Cognitive artefacts: Remaking economies, 1917–1947.* Dissertation, London School of Economics and Political Science.

Voigtländer, Michael. 2009. Why is the German homeownership rate so low? *Housing Studies* 24 (3): 355–72.

Volkmann, Hans E., ed. 1984. *Wirtschaft im Dritten Reich: Eine Bibliographie.* Vol. 2: *1939–1945.* Munich: Bernard & Grafe.

——— 1975. Außenhandel und Aufrüstung in Deutschland 1933 bis 1939. In *Wirtschaft und Rüstung am Vorabend des Zweiten Weltkriegs,* ed. Friedrich Forstmeier and Hans E. Volkmann, 81–131. Düsseldorf: Droste.

Vonyó, Tamás. 2017. War and Socialism: Why Eastern Europe fell behind between 1950 and 1989. *Economic History Review* 70 (1): 248–74.

——— 2012. The bombing of Germany: the economic geography of war-induced dislocation in West German industry. *European Review of Economic History* 16 (1): 97–118.

——— 2008. Post-war reconstruction and the golden age of economic growth. *European Review of Economic History,* 12 (2): 221–41.

Wagenführ, Rolf. 1954. *Die deutsche Industrie im Kriege, 1939–1945.* Berlin: Duncker & Humblot.

Wagner-Braun, Margarete. 2002. Die Aufwertung der D-Mark im Jahre 1961: eine kritische Stellungnahme zum Währungssystem von Bretton Woods. In *Weltwirtschaft und Wirtschaftsordnung,* ed. Rainer Gömmel and Markus A. Denzel, 339–63. Stuttgart: Steiner.

Wallerstein, Michael. 1990. Centralized bargaining and wage restraint. *American Journal of Political Science* 34 (4): 982–1004.

Wallich, Henry C. 1955. *The mainsprings of the German revival.* New Haven, CT: Yale University Press.

Walz, Manfred. 1978. *Wohnungsbau- und Industrieansiedlungspolitik in Deutschland 1933–39: Dargestellt am Aufbau des Industriekomplexes Wolfsburg-Braunschweig-Salzgitter.* Frankfurt: Campus.

Wehler, Hans-Ulrich. 1975. *Modernisierungstheorie und Geschichte.* Göttingen: Vandenhoeck & Ruprecht.

———. 1973. *Das Deutsche Kaiserreich 1871–1918.* Deutsche Geschichte, Vol. 9. Göttingen: Vandenhoeck & Ruprecht, 1973.

Weimer, Wolfram. 1998. *Deutsche Wirtschaftsgeschichte.* Hamburg: Hoffman und Campe.

Wellhöner, Volker. 1996. *"Wirtschaftswunder", Weltmarkt, westdeutscher Fordismus: Der Fall Volkswagen.* Münster: Westfälisches Dampfboot.

Wexler, Imanuel. 1990. *The Marshall Plan revisited: The European Recovery Program in economic perspective.* London: Greenwood Press.

Wildt, Michael. 1993. Privater Konsum in Westdeutschland in den 50-er Jahren. In *Modernisierung im Wiederaufbau: Die westdeutsche Gesellschaft der 50er Jahre,* ed. Axel Schieldt and Arnold Sywottek, 275–89. Bonn: J. H. W. Dietz.

Willenbacher, Barbara. 1988. Zerrüttung und Bewährung der Nachkriegsfamilie. In *Von Stalingrad zur Währungsreform: Zur Sozialgeschichte des Umbruchs in Deutschland,* ed. Martin Broszat, 595–618. Munich: Oldenburg.

Winkel, Harold. 1974. *Die Wirtschaft im geteilten Deutschland 1945–1970.* Wiesbaden: Franz Steiner.

Wolf, Holger C. 1995. Post-war Germany in the European context: Domestic and external determinants of growth. In *Europe's post-war recovery,* ed. Barry Eichengreen, 323–52. Cambridge: Cambridge University Press.

———. 1993. The lucky miracle: Germany 1945–1951. In *Postwar economic reconstruction and lessons for the East today,* ed. Rudiger Dornbusch, Wilhem Nolling, and Richard Layard, 29–54. Cambridge, MA and London: MIT Press.

Wolff, Edward N. 1991. Capital formation and productivity convergence over the long term. *American Economic Review* 81 (3): 565–79.

Wörmann, Claudia. 1982. *Der Osthandel der Bundesrepublik Deutschland: Politische Rahmenbedingungen und ökonomische Bedeutung.* Frankfurt and New York: Campus.

Zank, Wolfgang. 1987. *Wirtschaft und Arbeit in Ostdeutschland 1945–1949: Probleme des Wiederaufbaus in der Sowjetischen Besatzungszone Deutschlands.* Studien zur Zeitgeschichte, No. 31. Munich: Oldenbourg.

Zilbert, Edward R. 1981. *Albert Speer and the Nazi ministry of arms: Economic institutions and industrial production in the German war economy.* London: Associated University Presses.

Zündorf, Irmgard. 2006. *Der Preis der Marktwirtschaft: Staatliche Preispolitik und Lebensstandard in Westdeutschland 1948 bis 1963.* Vierteljahrschrift für Sozial- und Wirtschaftsgeschichte, Beiheft 186. Stuttgart: Steiner.

Index

Foreign phrases, except names of institutions, are in Italics. Page numbers in Italics refer to words in tables or figures.

For EU product safety concerns, contact us at Calle de José Abascal, 56–1°,
28003 Madrid, Spain or eugpsr@cambridge.org.

www.ingramcontent.com/pod-product-compliance
Ingram Content Group UK Ltd.
Pitfield, Milton Keynes, MK11 3LW, UK
UKHW012157180425
457623UK00018B/240